CLASH OF IDENTITIES

Clash of Identities

*Explorations in Israeli
and Palestinian Societies*

BARUCH KIMMERLING

Columbia University Press   New York

Columbia University Press
Publishers Since 1893
New York   Chichester, West Sussex
Copyright © 2008 Columbia University Press
All rights reserved

Library of Congress Cataloging-in-Publication Data
Kimmerling, Baruch.
Clash of identities : explorations in Israeli and Palestinian societies /
Baruch Kimmerling.
p. cm.
Includes bibliographical references and index.
ISBN 978-0-231-14328-8 (alk. paper)
ISBN 978-0-231-51249-7 (e-book)
1. Group identity—Palestine. 2. Palestinian Arabs—Ethnic identity.
3. Militarism—Social aspects—Israel. 4. National security—Social aspects—Israel.
5. Israel—Politics and government—Psychological aspects. I. title.
HN660.A8K53   2008
305.80095694—dc22   2007039907

Columbia University Press books are printed
on permanent and durable acid-free paper.

Printed in the United States of America
Designed by Audrey Smith

c 10 9 8 7 6 5 4 3 2 1

To my friend Joel S. Migdal

CONTENTS

PREFACE

I arrived at the Department of Sociology of the Hebrew University of Jerusalem as a freshman in 1962, ten years after I immigrated to Israel with my parents and a younger brother from Transylvania, Rumania. Before immigrating, my small family escaped Nazi headhunters by hiding and wandering in the Carpathian Mountains. Later, we endured the oppressive communist regime in Rumania. My parents' lengthy "absorption process" into what was then a very poor state brutalized them, but they never complained and never regretted coming to Israel. In spite of their difficulties, they sent both of their children to university and positioned them in the country's upper-middle class. My brother Adam and I gave meaning to their lives.

The Hebrew University was founded in 1925 as part of the Zionist nation-building program. During the 1960s, it was the only university in Israel, making its sociology department the only one in the country. It was established and headed by Martin Buber in the mid-1940s. Buber was a highly charismatic figure who developed an almost personal sociology, a mixture of philosophy, history, Jewish mysticism, and moral attitudes based on metaphysical dialogues. His most prominent young student was Shmuel N. Eisenstadt. According to Eisenstadt, Buber gave him his "basic intellectual perspective," but in time, he diverged intellectually with his mentor. It appears that Eisenstadt was determined to nurture research on Israeli society, but "the breaking point between Buber and Eisenstadt was due to the latter's opposition to scholarly academic work which was removed from the empirical reality of the so-called *Yishuv* [the pre-state Jewish polity in Palestine and in Israel]." In an attempt to present a more integrated and practical option, Eisenstadt developed a new tradition of empirical research that was not customary at the time in the Hebrew University, abandoning work on the philosophical questions that occupied Buber and concentrating instead on the burning issues in Israeli society at that time. Even during his training, Eisenstadt felt a certain discomfort with Buber's strong emphasis on the German historical tradition. Despite his love of history, he told Buber that he wanted to learn "real sociology" and was interested in "more sociology" in his studies. In response, Buber gave him new reading assignments that represented the breadth of sociological writing at that time. Through this independent study, Eisenstadt continued to go beyond the heritage of his teacher and study American sociology, which was new for him, in-depth. Due to Martin Buber's reading assignments, Eisenstadt was exposed to the philosophy of Talcott Parsons, who was the leading representative of American sociology at that time.[1]

After a post-doctoral year at the London School of Economics, Eisenstadt was recalled to Jerusalem to reorganize the sociology program at Jerusalem. Soon, he not only completed this assignment, but became recognized as one of the world's most able and creative sociologists, especially following the publication of his book *The Political System of Empires* (1963), which was ranked with works by the founding fathers of modern sociology, such as Max Weber. Eisenstadt's formidable memory, the breadth and depth of his knowledge, and his extraordinary ability to integrate various subjects made him an excellent but very demanding teacher. His international fame also contributed to the reputation of the young department, which was reinforced by the interest of Western sociology in its almost unique topics of research—the kibbutz and other communal settlements and the role of the family within them, youth movements and the techniques of modernization and de- and re-socialization of Jewish immigrants from underdeveloped countries. Eisenstadt built a relatively strong and highly centralized department around his dominant personality and specific research and teaching agenda. The Jerusalemian School of Sociology, as it liked sometimes to regard itself, was not only overtly dominated by the structural-functionalist paradigm, but also served the Zionist ideology by mixing ideological presuppositions and terminologies with sociological ones, defining what a sociological *problemstellung* was and was not and deciding which research topics were taught and which terminology employed.

This was the department I encountered in 1962. Its strengths were apparent immediately, but it took me almost two decades to discover its limitations. Retrospectively, these strengths and limitations were an inevitable part of that glorious period of building a new nation and a sociology—and later an anthropology—that was part of it. The department as a whole—most of the lecturers were just doctoral students—aspired enthusiastically to take part in this enterprise.

In addition to all this, I found sociology itself to be an extremely exciting ontological tool. I was like person "born again" into a new religion. It seemed that everything in the human world was interlinked, explainable, and had a purpose, or if not, was a kind of mutation that the self-regulatory homeostatic order would fix sooner or later.

After graduating with my bachelor's degree, I spent some years working mainly as a research assistant with a comparative modernization research team. In 1968, I was placed in charge of collecting materials on Uganda, the Ivory Coast, and Ghana. At first, African issues didn't interest me too much, but this was the job that the department offered me, and soon I found the questions of development and social change intriguing. As a bonus, I was permitted to use the collected material for my masters thesis and later for my doctoral dissertation. Within about eighteen months, I completed my thesis and had published two papers in prestigious journals, being already aware of the "publish or perish" rules of the game in academia. Following this, I prepared to continue on this path and to put together a doctoral thesis. It is perhaps relevant to mention here that before I graduated with my first degree, I had not considered an academic career; I saw myself as a writer and journalist. The gradual change in my personal identity and calling came as I discovered the brave new world of scientific research, its intellectual challenges, and potential for creativity.

The Jewish-Arab conflict drew my attention as I became politically aware during high school, but at that time, it was impossible to obtain any information or interpretation other than the official one. The only information available to me then that deviated from the hegemonic view was found in the fringe and selective publication *Haolam Hazeh*, a weekly edited by Uri Avnery, who had also written several books on the subject. My interest in the conflict considerably increased following the 1967 war and its consequences, but I did not yet see it in sociological terms. Within the department, issues concerning the Arabs of Israel were conceptually excluded from the syllabi of the Israeli Society courses and hardly mentioned in textbooks. The wars and the conflicts underlying them were also excluded from the sociology curriculum. To the extent that courses on these subjects existed, they were almost always the responsibility of classical Arabist historians of the sort that Edward Said might call Orientalists.

In the middle of working on my doctoral dissertation on comparative agricultural modernization in sub-Saharan African states, I made what was probably the most important decision of my life. I made an appointment with Eisenstadt and implored him to switch my dissertation subject to a sociological analysis of the Jewish-Arab conflict. Eisenstadt unequivocally and promptly refused, arguing that the conflict was a political and not a sociological theme. I know that later Eisenstadt regretted his verdict about the non-sociological nature of research on the conflict and probably also his refusal to tutor me on the subject. But at the time, his refusal created an almost impossible dilemma for me: to give up and complete my initial project, or to find another tutor within the department—a senior staff member willing to advise me on this taboo subject, knowing that it was incompatible with Eisenstadt's decisive opinion about what was and was not sociology.

It was not easy to find a mentor for my problematic thesis in that small and homogenous department, especially because everybody knew that Eisenstadt rejected the theme. The other central person at the department, Joseph Ben-David, was openly hostile to my efforts to develop the sociology of the Jewish-Arab conflict at the department. This was still the formative period of Israel's sociology and anthropology, and there had only been a handful of doctorates awarded; thus, every dissertation that received approval was considered the beginning of a new field of expertise and teaching in Israeli sociology. After a frustrating period of attempting to get a tutor, a young member of the department, Moshe Lissak, who had just received his tenure, agreed to be my mentor. A decade later, he became my fiercest academic rival during the great but futile debate around the so-called new historians and critical sociologists. The dissertation was submitted in late 1974 and approved by my committee in the spring of 1975.

My undeclared rupture from Eisenstadt potentially jeopardized my career, but the break was never total. It was apparently the first time that a graduate student had challenged his authority, but later I came to understand that he appreciated my rebellious personality, and his professional integrity toward me was spotless. He followed my professional development from a distance and with some suspicion, offering the salt of criticism but also some encouragement. In the academic year of 1978, he helped me to participate in a seminar in Cambridge, Massachusetts, led by Samuel P. Huntington, called the Joint (Harvard-MIT) Seminar on Political Development. During that year, I was provided with full office space and facilities at MIT's Center for International Studies.

The year in Cambridge was probably the most exciting and intellectually inspiring period of my professional life. The team's members were among the brightest young social scientists of the period: I met Theda Skocpol, Susan Berger, Jorge Dominguez, Ian Lustick, and Joel Migdal, who later became my close friend and research collaborator. The Harvard-MIT complex, with its courses, talks, conferences, libraries, and faculty clubs, offered me a unique opportunity to encounter a restless and intense intellectual environment that influenced my entire intellectual and professional orientation, and I was included in it only on the basis of being Shmuel N. Eisenstadt's student.

A few years after completing my belated post-doctoral year at MIT, I secured a publisher for my dissertation. For many years, I had tried to publish it without success; my senior colleagues at the Hebrew University explained to me, with a strain of pity, that because everybody who lived then in Israel knew precisely what happened, my work was not yet publishable, but perhaps would be in a hundred years or so. Others kindly advised me to find more interesting topics for research. However, I persisted, and finally found a publisher in the Institute of International Studies of the University of California at Berkeley. The book appeared in 1983 under the title *Zionism and Territory: The Socio-Territorial Dimensions of Zionist Politics*. Being a "dry" and nonjudgmental professional text, it did not draw public attention and achieved limited circulation, but became well known and widely quoted by a small circle of experts.

The subject was less focused on Zionist ideology than it was on the different techniques of land acquisition employed from the first wave of modern Jewish immigration to Palestine until the late 1960s and their relationship to other political doctrines. In the earlier stages of my research, I was shocked to discover that a major "purification" of the land of its Arab Palestinian inhabitants—the term "ethnic cleansing" was unknown during that period—was done during the 1948 war by Jewish military and paramilitary forces. During this research, relying solely on Israeli sources, I found that about 350 Arab villages were "abandoned" and their 3.25 million dunums of rural land confiscated; over time, the land became the property of the Israeli state or the Jewish National Fund.[2] I also found that Moshe Dayan, then the minister of agriculture, disclosed that about 700,000 Arabs who "left" the territories of the Jewish state had owned four million dunums of land.

I also found out that from 1882 to 1948, all of the Jewish companies and private individuals in Palestine, including the Jewish National Fund, an organ of the World Zionist Organization, had succeeded in buying only about 7 percent of the total land in British Palestine. All of the rest was taken by sword and nationalized during the 1948 war and after. Today, only about 7 percent of Israeli land is privately owned, about half of it by Israeli Arabs. Israel is the only democracy in the world that nationalized almost all of its land and prohibited even the leasing of most agricultural lands to non-Jews, a situation made possible by a complex framework of legal arrangements.

My book compared the internal structure of the Israeli polity with those of other immigrant settler societies, such as those in North and South America, Australia, New Zealand, Algeria, and white South Africa, and emphasized the similarities and differences in internal structure. Reversing the model of Frederic Jackson Turner's frontier thesis, the book explored the question of how the amount of available "free land," conceptualized as different degrees of "frontierity," was now considered a central variable that could determine many elements of a regime, including its ideology and political and economic practices. I found these characteristics to be instrumental in constructing at least a partial explanation for the highly centralized and collectivistic Israeli state system created during the first two decades of Israel's existence. The system owed its existence mainly to the monopoly that political institutions had over the land and its distribution to various societal segments. My next book, *Zionism and Economy* (1983), explored similar questions, but concentrated on the economic policies of Labor Zionism.

Later, I was engaged in a series of studies, empirical and theoretical, both on my own and with some colleagues—Dan Horowitz, Victor Azarya, and Moshe Lissak. I studied the impact of the military and wars on Israeli society. The major outcome of this series of studies was *The Interrupted System: Israeli Civilians in War and Routine Times* (1985), an analytical and empirical examination of the direct and indirect impact of wars on Israeli civilian society. It also produced several additional comprehensive papers, including "Patterns of Militarism in Israel," which appears as Chapter Six of the present volume.

Comparing the three works can be said to show the developments and changes in my professional approach. *The Interrupted System*, which presents and summarizes a series of quantitative and empirical research studies conducted during and after the 1973 war, asks how individuals, as well as the civilian society as a whole, functioned in two different situations: during a protracted but highly routinized conflict and during active warfare. The foremost conclusion was that collectivity absorbed both phases into its routine institutional and value systems, thus minimizing the emotional cost of the conflict and the wars. This book perhaps represents the last remains of my functional education at the sociology department at Hebrew University.

During the 1990s, I revisited and revised my own and others' research in this field, reaching additional and varying conclusions. Adopting a less institutional and more culture-oriented and critical approach, I reinterpreted past findings with the support of new evidence. This led me to characterize the Israeli state as a special, but not unique, type of militaristic society. I found civilian militarism to be not only a basic cultural code, but also an organizational principle around which large segments of Israeli society are ordered. This type of militarism—compared, for example, with the classic praetorian type—is much more subtle and mainly a consequence of the intrusion of "military-mindedness" into civilian institutions and cultures. This led me to analyze the peace process from both sides in terms of the militaristic culture and the power game, in the 1997 paper "The Power-Oriented Settlement Bargaining between Israelis and Palestinians." In an additional paper, "Jurisdiction in an Immigrant-Settler Society: The Jewish and Democratic State," I analyzed the internal contradictions within the Israeli regime.

In the articles mentioned and others that followed, I raised doubts and concerns about the ability of the mainstream Israeli social sciences and historiography to free themselves of Zionist ideologies, the nation-building mindset, and their degree of Jewish ethnocentrism when dealing conceptually and theoretically with "the other" and "the conflict," within the social and conceptual boundaries of "Israeli society," however defined (see "Ideology, Sociology and Nation Building," *American Sociological Review* 1992, and "Academic Historians Caught in the Cross-Fire: The Case of Israeli-Jewish Historiography," *History and Memory*, 1995). As long as my criticism of the conceptualization and research of Israeli society remained an internal controversy, matters remained calm. However, when I published it in the flagship journal of the American Sociological Association, a furor erupted. My Ph.D. mentor and later colleague, who previously prized my work, suddenly discovered its "anti-Zionist" nature and recruited many colleagues, including persons in the media, writers, and intellectuals, to debunk my intentions and scholarship. Many other colleagues, however, supported my position and Eisenstadt himself remained quiet during the controversy. The entire debate was a part of a larger political, cultural, and very bitter argument about the past and roots of Israeli society and its interpretation, research, and teaching, as Laurence J. Silberstein examined and summarized in *The Postzionism Debates: Knowledge and Power in Israeli Culture* (1999), though he wrongly equated post-Zionism with postmodernism. In his book *The Changing Agenda of Israeli Sociology* (1995), Uri Ram referred to my work, together with Gershon Shafir's book *Land, Labour and the Origins of the Israeli-Palestinian Conflict* (1980) as opening a new paradigm in Israeli sociology—"the colonization paradigm." For a while, my promotion process was slowed down, but not for long, as the Hebrew University proved its commitment to academic freedom and research. Retrospectively, the case can be seen in Thomas Khun's terms of paradigmatic and intergenerational conflict.

The next major step in advancing my work was to formulate a more coherent and developed sociohistorical conceptual framework of "the conflict," or, more appropriately, the whole spectrum of Jewish-Arab relations. This important step was rooted in my conclusion, mainly following Simmel and Coser, that a conflict—any conflict—is an integral social system, and to be fully analyzed and understood, information about all of the parties involved must be included. In other words, a more accurate picture of the "Jewish side" of the relationship must include the "Arab side" and "Palestinian side," analyzed with the same tools (see Chapter Eleven).

As mentioned above, the Arabs of Palestine were not previously incorporated into analysis or research on the Israeli state and society, conceptually or theoretically. Moreover, despite the abundance of monographs on Palestinian society, no comprehensive social or sociohistorical research on this collectivity existed. Thus, together with Joel Migdal, I undertook an extensive research study on the Palestinian society-building process from a sociohistorical perspective, both in terms of institution and identity formation. The initial version of the study—*Palestinians: The Making of a People* (1993)—comprised a case study of a stateless society divided into various internal segments and facing many hostile external and internal forces, among them Ottomans, Egyptians, Zionist colonization, colonial powers, the world market, and Arab and Islamic societies, states, and cultures. The book was founded on the basic assumptions of a refined world-system approach. Later, we developed our study into a more comprehensive volume, *The Palestinian People: A History* (2002).

Another aspect of my professional pursuits has been the study and development of my basic field of expertise, the sociology of politics. I developed a Hebrew-language textbook for the Israeli Open University, *Between State and Society: The Sociology of Politics* (1995), and served as guest editor of a special issue of *Current Sociology* that surveyed the state of the art of political sociology across much of the world.

In my book *The Rise and Decline of Israeliness*, I analyzed the changes that have occurred within the Israeli state and its collective identity in the past five decades. A summary of the revised Jewish social history in Palestine and Israel from 1882 to the present was published, in its entirety, in Hebrew, in a volume entitled *Immigrants, Settlers, and Natives* (2003).

Apart from my professional activities, I have functioned as a "public sociologist," deeply involved in Israeli public discourse both intellectually and politically, mainly as a regular freelance writer for the past three decades for various sections of the Hebrew daily *Ha'aretz,* from its literary and cultural supplements to its op-ed page. A polemical book I wrote in Hebrew, entitled *The End of Ashkenazi Hegemony,* made the bestseller list. Another book, *Politicide: Ariel Sharon's War against the Palestinians* (2001), was published in seven languages.

The present volume contains twelve essays and an epilogue on the Israeli and Palestinian societies and the interrelations among them. Although they have been published over a twenty-year period, they are unified by the common puzzles they tackle—sometimes explicitly and sometimes implicitly—of Jewish, Israeli, and Palestinian collective identities, as well as the clashes, tensions, and complementarities among them. From the start of my research in these topics, I preferred to approach the issues from the conceptual framework of collective identities instead of theories of nationalism, despite the vast quantity of literature in the latter field and its more central place in historical, philosophical, and social science discourse. Thus, although the essays examine Palestinian and Israeli nationalisms as well as theories about the construction of nationalism and nation states, they go beyond these questions to explore ethnic and religious identity in the context of nationalism. The book is by no means a historical account of Arab-Jewish relations, but a conceptual treatment of them from an interactional approach, based on a large body of historical facts and events. To provide the reader with a background of the analysis, the book contains a detailed linear chronology.

Rereading my earliest essays, I was amazed that though the local and global social world has changed dramatically over two decades, and social theories and terminologies have been forgotten and replaced by others, our basic social facts and problematics, as a set of interrelated problems, remains the same or has changed very little. That is why, apart from the wish to preserve the authenticity of the essays, I decided not to update, upgrade, or make any substantial changes except minor stylistic ones. I also avoided presenting the chapters in a clear chronological order; instead, I tried to build a loose thematic order, from more general to more specific, and to produce some hidden dialogue among the diverse essays while leaving it to readers to decipher these dialogues. From this point of view, each essay or chapter stands independently, but taken together, they form a coherent volume in which it is hoped that the whole is more than the sum of its parts.

1. See Gad Yair and Noa Apeloig, "Israel and the Exile of Intellectual Caliber: Local Position and the Absence of Sociological Theory," *Sociology* 40, no. 1 (2006).

2. The *dunum* is the most common measure of land area in the Middle East. 4.5 dunums equals approximately one acre.

CLASH OF IDENTITIES

A Model for Analyzing Reciprocal Relations Between the Jewish and Arab Communities in Mandatory Palestine*

This essay presents an interactional model for analyzing the effects of the reciprocal influences between two collectivities on the processes of crystallization and the building of society and identity within them—the first being the Jewish settlers in the territory referred to as the Land of Israel, and the second being the local Arab population. The time period considered begins with the first wave of Jewish immigration in the 1880s and concludes with the social, political, and military collapse of the latter collectivity in 1947. This essay deals with the past, but is not a historical study because it does not investigate the development of events by discovering previously unknown facts, though it may make such discoveries. Rather, it is a case-study analysis of the meeting of two collectivities that developed a wide variety of interrelations, beginning with cooperation and exchange in several areas and ending in total conflict that resulted in the social and political

* From Baruch Kimmerling "A Model for Analysis of Reciprocal Relations Between the Jewish and Arab Communities in Mandatory Palestine," *Plural Societies* 14, no. 3/4 (1983): 45–68.

destruction of one of them, but did not end the mutual relations between them that persist to this day. The axiom of this study is that a wide range of mutual relations led to certain processes—or prevented certain others—within each of the two collectivities, influencing the directions of their formations and crystallizations; and conversely, the particular characteristics of each of the two collectivities shaped the patterns of the mutual relations between them.

The emphasis on the interactions between the two collectivities should not lead to the error of determinism. It is possible to analyze and understand the phenomena and processes that took place within the two collectivities independently of each other without having to systematically analyze their mutual relations,[1] and it would be a mistake to see the complex of developments within the two collectivities as an exclusive result of the relations between them. Yet there is no doubt that analyzing the two societies from such a perspective will add significantly to understanding their developments. The study is also not a comparative examination of two case studies, though at first glance it may appear to be the case, as we have not made a primary assumption that the two are independent. On the contrary, we have assumed interdependence, and thus, this is a single case study, despite the use of comparative methods.

The Framework of Interaction

From the time of Jewish settlement to 1947, the two collectivities under discussion acted under a common political framework: in the beginning, Ottoman rule, and afterward, British rule, a situation that left its mark on their mutual interrelations, mainly by determining the limits of the basic rules of the game that developed between the two collectivities. The primary function of this ruling third side in the interaction was to regulate interaction, preventing rapid and drastic changes in the power relations between the two sides. This function was expressed in the political and military protection given to the Jewish community—protection that prevented its physical, political, and social destruction—and in defending the Arab collectivity from rapid changes in the balance of power between it and the Jewish side by limiting Jewish immigration and accumulation of territorial resources.[2]

The two sides were involved in continuous bargaining with the third side in at least three spheres: bargaining over changes in the basic rules of the game, mentioned above, such that the third side became a means for each side to advance its ultimate goals; bargaining over the granting of recognition and legitimization to institutions and organizations that were to become the center—in the sense of Shils[3] and Eisenstadt[4]—of each of the two collectivities, or over institutions and organizations that are the privilege of a sovereign society; and bargaining within the framework of the existing rules of the game over changing or maintaining power relations between the Jewish and Arab collectivities. The bargaining took place on the level of general policy, centering mostly on the issue of Jewish immigration quotas and licenses for the transfer of lands from Arab to Jewish ethno-national ownership, and on the level of competition over specific resources, such as jobs, public office, subsidies, and other government appropriations, that the third side was distributing or redistributing.

Patterns and Spheres of Interaction

Most of the encounters between any two such partners can be divided into two types: concrete interactions and model interactions. The concrete interactions were the systems of exchange and competition, cooperation, and conflict between the two sides in different spheres, on the levels of individuals fulfilling social roles, groups or social strata operating within each of the collectivities, and elites directing the policy of the entire collectivity. The model interaction, positive or negative, derives from each side's attitude toward the existence of the other side, regarding its image, its perception of the other's essence, and its activities. Thus, for different parts of the collectivity, the other side becomes a positive or negative reference group, either in its entirety or in differential spheres of action. As a result of its becoming a reference group, the other collectivity may or may not become a partial or complete model to be imitated or rejected. Complete or partial imitation of a perceived model is not to be interpreted as adoption of a positive attitude toward that model or a nonconfrontational attitude toward it.

When a group of immigrants moves into any territory already populated by a local population or a population that previously settled there with the aim of establishing a permanent collectivity,[5] both sides must clarify for themselves, implicitly or explicitly, the answers to a series of questions on the relations between them. These answers are not necessarily final answers; they are partially, mostly, or totally liable to change. The answers that the partners give themselves may depend on the answers—and especially the behavior that follows from the answers—that the other partner gives himself. The basic relations between the two sides are a two-dimensional complex.

The first is their position in relation to each other in the different spheres of activity. In its pure form, this dimension can be mainly of three sorts. First, the immigrants can be absorbed within the local population in a manner independent of the concrete relations, such as ruler to subject. This is usually the case when a system of exchange in one or more areas exists, such as exchange in the economic and social realms. The existence of this situation does not imply that there are symmetrical, equal, or sympathetic relations between the participants. In our schema, presented below, such relations are marked with a +. Second, immigrants may move alongside the native population. This situation entails desire for segregation of the partners in one or more areas, such as housing, education, and friendship groups, and for preventing exchange in those areas. In the schema, this situation is marked with a o. Third, the immigrants can be opposed to the local native population in one or more areas, such as in competition for housing or jobs. This is a situation of competition and conflict, over either scarce material resources, such as territory, or symbolic contents. This situation is marked with a −.[6]

The second dimension that determines the nature of the basic relations between the two partners is the sphere of interaction. The decision to locate the position of the immigration in a certain sphere is not necessarily transitive to another sphere. In at least the first stage of contact, it appears that great importance is given mostly to four spheres: economy, politics, culture, and primary relations.

Theoretically, there are eighty-one different profiles of answers that each segment can give or attempt to attain in its relations with the other segment. At the same time, the profiles may be the result of the total interaction between the two social systems. The profiles can be presented schematically as follows.

At a given point in time, three profiles can be active simultaneously. The immigrant population can aim at profile (+,−,−,o), and in opposition to

Table 1.1

Economic	Cultural Religious	Political	Primary Relations
+	+	+	+
0	0	0	0

this, the local population at (o,–,o,–). If we see the local population and the immigrants as a single system, the result or output of the system may be (o,–,–,–). Moreover, there may be disagreement or conflict within each segment over the answers that should be given to the questions of its relations with the other segment. So empirically, eighty-one different profiles will not be found; there is not complete independence among the approaches a partner holds in the various spheres. The answers that each of the partners give and the systemic result depend on the characteristics of each of the partners and on particular and changing conditions—political, economic, and even physical—for each of the participants in the interaction.

The Interaction in the Economic Sphere

The concrete interaction in the economic sphere was characterized by an unfree[7] flow of Jewish capital to different sectors of the Arab population in exchange for land assets,[8] labor, and merchandise—mainly agricultural products—from the Arab population. These exchanges were neatly interwoven with two basic processes of transformation in the local Arab economy and society. First, Arab villages partially transitioned from autarchic subsistence economies at the village level to monetary economies raising cash crops, mainly citrus groves, but also any agricultural produce needed by the new urban population, Jewish and Arab. Complementing this process was the urbanization of Arab society, especially the crystallization of three distinct urban strata: the *a'yan,* urban notables who were sometimes great landowners; professionals, mainly lawyers, a few doctors, and the educated class, not always with the same background as the *a'yan;* and the *shabab,* or urban *lumpenproletariat,* which in the context of traditional Arab society was not bound by traditional obligations and thus was more open than the other strata to social mobilization (in the sense of Deutsch).[9] The presence of Jewish capital did not cause these processes, but the movement of capital certainly accelerated them. Two kinds of struggle within Arab society can be distinguished within this sphere: whether to maintain economic exchange with the Jewish collectivity at all, and who should profit from the exchange—sheiks or *fellahin,* sheiks or *a'yan,* small landowners or great landowners, Muslims or Christians, and so on. Sometimes use was made of a conflict of the first sort to solve a problem of the second sort.

The significance of economic exchange with the Jews was relatively marginal for the total Arab collectivity, but for the Jewish society, the very

existence of the exchange was central, though it aroused internal conflict and controversy. The purchase of lands was a necessary condition to
constructing the community. Jewish agriculture, and to a small degree,
crafts, could not meet all of the needs of the collectivity until the later
stages of development. The Jewish labor market was also insufficient to
supply the required laborers. However, as is well known, there was bitter
conflict within the Jewish sector over this issue, over both the determination of the nature and content of the collectivity and the power relations
among its right-wing, urban and rural bourgeois, and social-nationalist
components. Analysis of the spheres of concrete economic interaction
(and spheres lacking interaction) between the two collectivities appears to
prove that the economic sphere had very far-ranging influences because
of the creation of the Jewish collectivity and the directions in which it
developed. When the Arab political leadership tried to stop the economic
interaction as part of the conflict waged against the Jewish collectivity, the
Jewish collectivity had already reached a stage where it could withstand
the segregation. Not only was the damage done to it marginal, but it made
considerable profits from the cessation of interaction.[10]

In the sphere of model economic interaction, the attitudes of the two sides
were very ambivalent. The economic models according to which they operated were a priori fundamentally different. Yet it was in this sphere that a reduction of general models to methods of operating and technological items
could be made with relative ease. Economic models are more easily adopted
in processes of acculturation than are norms, values, and ideologies.

In the beginning of the wave of immigration, the Jewish sector could
relate to the economy and technology of the *fellah* as a positive reference
model due to certain romantic and populist elements in the Zionist movement, but even this approval was selective. Afterward, mostly due to the
influence of the second and third waves of immigration, this positive attitude was replaced by a negative one; in other words, the Arab economy and
technology were perceived as a counter-model for imitation.[11]

It is very difficult to determine whether the entire model of Jewish economic activity served the Arab system as a reference model or not, as it
depends on how the model was perceived and defined. When the Jewish
model was perceived as a modern economy, then it served, in its entirety, as
a model for imitation—that is, not just selected items from it were chosen.
However, when it was perceived as a fragment or agent of a political model—a communist or capitalist economy—or as fitted to the specific needs of

the Jewish collective, then the model was related to negatively. As a result of the Arabs' constant contact with the economics and technology of Jewish immigrants, there was a process of adopting innovations, mostly material. Joseph Klausner and Moussa Smilansky[12]claim that the standard of living and degree of advancement of the Arab villages was a direct function of their contacts with the Jews. The opposed view on this issue[13] holds that the Jews generated artificial needs for the Arab population and created demand for consumer items that did not raise the standard of living, but instead inflated demand. Meanwhile, mainly during the early period of settlement, there was a parallel process of Jews learning technology from the Arabs, especially in agriculture, citrus growing, and construction. In the last area, there were even attempts to capture the so-called Oriental style of building. Finally, as pointed out above, in spite of attempts to stop the supply of Arab workers, particularly unskilled workers (in both communities, there was demand for more skilled workers than were available) by means of ideological claims of the need for exclusively Jewish labor, there was still a shared labor market for the two communities, though the market was not perfect. One of the interesting results of this situation was that, despite the egalitarian ideology that prevailed in the Jewish community, wide gaps between the incomes of skilled and unskilled workers were created throughout the entire period. During the 1930s, Palestine had one of the highest ratios of incomes of skilled to unskilled workers among developing countries: the earnings of a skilled laborer in Palestine were almost twice those of his unskilled counterpart. Even the Histadrut, the Jewish labor union, did not fight for equality of income, despite the ideological demands for it.[14]

Interaction in the Cultural Sphere

Some of the examples cited above from the economic sphere can also serve as examples of concrete interaction in the cultural sphere. Jewish adoption of Arab dress and behavior, mainly Bedouin, in the early period of settlement,[15] and the adoption of technology, Western dress, and Western behavioral norms, which some of the Arab leadership blamed the Jews for spreading, were results of concrete interaction in the cultural sphere. Rafiq Jabor[16] complains that "the Zionists greatly influenced life in Palestine . . . customs which the Arabs never knew before have penetrated the country. Vulgarity has spread through the country. The ways of dressing have changed. Before the Jews came we never saw young girls with décolletage, or wearing dresses which don't cover their bodies from head to toe." It appears that both sides' adoptions of technological items took place in a manner very reminiscent of the patterns of adoption of parts of the Spanish culture by the eastern Pueblo peoples, in that they "accept[ed] from the Spanish certain traits and trait complexes which remained peripheral to their major cultural interests and also to resist traits which would have altered the main orientations of their culture."[17]

The model interaction in the cultural sphere can be analyzed on three levels—first, as a meeting between two great traditions, the Muslim and the Jewish. This meeting took place only at the peripheries of the two traditions, and the Arabs gave it much more prominence than did the Jews, but it made a great impression. On this level, apparently, neither side deliberately attempted to exert influence on the other; that is, the Muslims did not try to convert Jews to Islam, and certainly, the Jews did not try to convert Muslims, which seems to have served the Arab leaderships' aim of mobilizing support from the Arab collectivity to characterize the conflict as a religious one.[18] Second, the interaction was an encounter between fragments of a Western culture and a traditional society that was beginning to experience the disintegration of its traditional fabric, and which was in an even earlier stage of development and change. At this level, as on the third level, the Jewish collectivity saw itself not only as the passive representation of a model worthy of imitation, but at times, as engaged in a social and cultural mission, sometimes used to partially justify immigration in the first place. The conflict between the two collectivities was sometimes explained in terms of social and cultural gaps, and its conclusion perceived as the bridging of those gaps. Third, as the left wing from socialism to Marxism, parts of which were oriented towards active missionary activity, became more and more evident in the Jewish community, the diverse ideological and political factions within the Jewish community initiated attempts to transfer to the opposite side specific social and cultural models. More than once, the Arab side could not differentiate among the three levels, and tended to see the Jewish community as representing a unified and dangerous counter-model of Jews, Westerners, and communists, or of different variations of possible combinations, that threatened traditional society and culture, which was represented as healthy and pure. In the context of this study, the two sides agreed that on the level of a meeting between two great traditions, the immigration would take place alongside the local population, whereas on the other two levels, the attitude of the Jews was that immigration should take place into the local population.

The local native population usually took Jewish attitudes and actions as a threat, effectively placing its own tradition opposite the model of the immigrants. The ambivalence in the sphere of model cultural interaction, mostly on the part of the Arab community, was much greater in the cultural sphere than in the economic sphere. In general, the Jewish collectivity was perceived as representing Western culture, or one segment of it. Different strata of the educated populace, including graduates of European colleges, related to this culture and accepted the Jews, as well as the British administration, as its representatives. But it was impossible not to notice the conflicts of interest between the two collectivities, and that the Jews represented what they considered to be a more advanced culture only sharpened such awareness of these conflicts of interest.[19]

Of course, the Jews were not the only model of Western culture with which the Middle Eastern traditions came into contact that could be selectively imitated and incorporated into a syncretic culture. The colonial administrations and the cultures they represented served as models for imitation or rejection throughout the Middle East and in all other colonial or developing areas during that period. The model influence of the Jewish community in the cultural sphere should not be exaggerated, but rather seen as only a small and selective part of a wider European influence. It is even conceivable that because of the political conflict between the two communities, Western culture came to be considered a counter-model for sections of the local Arab population to a far greater degree than would have been the case otherwise. As Jewish culture was perceived as part of European culture, the entire package was rejected.

Interaction in the Political Sphere

The conflict between the two communities stood out in the political sphere more than in any other sphere, even when as an integral part of its tactics for conflict management, the Jewish side would deny the very existence of any confrontation, or would make light of its importance or magnitude. When the processes of Jewish immigration to Eretz Israel are considered from a political point of view, usually immigration is positioned opposite the local population, implicitly or explicitly. Clearly, the ultimate goals of both collectivities—the gaining of exclusive political control over all of the territory within the political boundaries of the British Mandate—were incompatible.[20] The immediate aim of Zionist policy was to accumulate political power, by means of the accumulation of land and population resources,[21] which would alter the political status quo. The immediate aim of the Arab community was at least to maintain the status quo, which was generally perceived as beneficial to them.

However, maintaining or disrupting the status quo to favor one side or the other amounted to more than the mere accumulation of territorial resources. The Arab and Jewish communities were also engaged in a nation-building race that revealed an asymmetry between the two sides. The central problem on the Jewish side was to accumulate the resources mentioned above, though there were also internal struggles over the nature of the collectivity's identity. On the Arab side, the main problems included creating both a specific identity for the collectivity and effective organizational tools that could cut across traditional structures and particular loyalties, as well as mobilize the periphery for coordinated social and political activity, whether to forward the conflict with the Jewish immigrants or to meet the needs of a political collectivity on its way to sovereignty, as was the situation in areas with Arab populations in the region. In short, on the Arab side, the problem was to crystallize a political center that could operate authoritatively even though it lacked sovereignty.[22] From this point of view, the Jewish side possessed an a priori advantage, not only in that the particularistic loyalties within its midst did not prevent effective political action, but also in that its political center, which was undergoing the process of crystallization, had more to distribute than did the embryonic Arab center. This was due both to the capital that streamed in from the outside as well as to the fact that the Jews could fix the criteria of eligibility for immigration permits. In contrast, the Arab organizations that were the potential nucleus around which the center would crystallize had but small independent means, and the apparatus to mobilize the resources and their redistribution was even smaller. On the level of concrete interaction, that the two collectivities were in opposed positions should have hastened the crystallization of their collective identities and organizations, just as it would be expected to increase the internal solidarity of each partner.[23] Moshe Ma'oz claims, implicitly or explicitly, that "the Arab-Palestinian sense of identity . . . grew and expanded during the Mandate era, due to its conflict with and imitation of the national Jewish movement."[24] In the area of administration, especially the creation of voluntary organizations parallel to those of the Jews that would counter the lack of political sovereignty, the accepted thesis, voiced by Yehoshua Porath, is that "toward the end of World War I a drastic shift in the direction of political activity became apparent, brought about by the challenge posed to the Palestinian-Arab public by Zionism. It was perceived as a severe danger and led to the *acceleration* [my emphasis] of a process which under normal circumstances would have developed more gradually."[25]

However, in both areas, the positive influences of Arab contact with the Jewish side should not be overstated, and comparisons should also be made with other Arab collectivities that did not face the challenge that Zionism posed for the Palestinian Arabs. An alternative hypothesis can be advanced, claiming that at such an embryonic stage of the development of both the collective identity and the organizational apparatus for the political activity of a given collectivity, conflict with another group that can handle the challenge with relative ease may have a destructive effect on the entity's crystallization. This hypothesis is consistent with a more general hypothesis that external conflict increases internal solidarity if and when at least the following two necessary conditions are fulfilled at the outset: there is a high degree of a priori consensus within the collectivity[26] and the collectivity is more or less capable of handling the conflict. It appears that the Jewish side fulfilled both necessary conditions, but the Arab side was more problematic. Even so, the claims of Ma'oz and Porath do not essentially contradict and the hypothesis put forward here. It is possible that the Jewish settler-immigrant society influenced the creation of the Palestinian Arab collectivity's identity, and at some point hastened the processes of building its institutions, but also harmed the collectivity's potential for final crystallization and the degree of effectiveness of their operations. A clear example of this can be found in the attempt, originating in a tactical move, to define the territory of Palestine as Southern Syria (Suriya al-Janubiya), which had far-reaching implications to inhibit and obscure the Arab-Palestinian collective identity. This attempt occurred after the local elite had been made aware that Syria and Iraq, and probably other areas, had been promised independent governments, whereas Palestine was not covered by this policy because of the British commitment to Zionism. To circumvent the problem, the first congress of the Muslim-Christian Association (al-Jam'iya al-Islamiya al-Masihiya),[27] which took place in February 1919 in Jerusalem, decided that "our-area, Southern Syria or Palestine, will not be cut off from the independent Syrian Arab government,"[28] even though the Third Palestinian Congress, which convened in Haifa in December 1920, had already discarded the idea of Southern Syria and demanded that the British "set up a native government which would be responsible to a representative council, to be chosen from the Arab population which had lived in Palestine until the beginning of the war, as had been done in Iraq and Trans-Jordan."[29] Echoes of the Southern Syrian identity still reverberate within the local Arab population. This identity and the identity of indigenous Palestinian were not mutually exclusive; however, the former seems to have slowed the process of crystallizing the collectivity's identity and its social and physical borders.

An additional illustration of the hypothesis is found in the riots that broke out in 1928 over the issue of rights over the Western Wall. Porath analyzes how, with the help of Muslim religious symbols, the Arab community could overcome its internal divisions to such an extent that it could be mobilized to actively oppose the Jews ("since secular nationalist slogans still did not reach their hearts").[30] The phenomenon of the center mobilizing the periphery for activities previously unknown to them with the aid of traditional symbols and organizations is well known, especially in developing countries. In this case, the use of Muslim religious symbols signifies a redefinition of the Arab collectivity. Christian elements, which had been a significant part of the collectivity, were excluded from it. The price of mobilizing the periphery for the struggle against the Jews was the fragmentation of the collectivity.

Excluding Christianity was a constant problem for the Arab leadership. The Christians, who were usually better educated and more progressive than the Muslims, were one of the most active elements in the national reawakening and the Arab-Palestinian national crystallization. However, when mobilization of the periphery was necessary, it was also necessary to use Muslim symbols. There was an attempt to transform the annual festivities of the Prophet Musa (Moses) from popular and religious to national. Some of the symbols were explicitly directed against Christianity as a religion.[31]

The most extreme illustration is the Arab revolt of 1936–39. On the surface, it may appear that the revolt was the most impressive demonstration that the Arabs in the country were conscious of their collective identity, as a large part of the periphery mobilized for armed conflict with the immigrant Jewish society and the British colonial government; by then, the British Mandate was perceived as acting in the interests of the Jewish society. Yet the revolt, as characterized by Tom Bodwen,[32] "was in essence made up of an integral set of smaller wars resulting in main from lack of a single, binding, political objective. . . . It was a racial, religious, colonial, class, familial and peasant struggle intermingled." In 1936, before the outbreak of the Arab rebellion, the Jewish economy bought 3,657,000 Palestinian pounds of goods and services from the Arab sector, about 11 percent of the sum of the Jewish economy's gross domestic product of 33.5 million pounds. The Jewish economy sold 1,108,000 pounds in goods and services to the non-Jewish sector, which included the Mandatory Government, constituting about 3 percent of the total domestic product of Palestine. In the same period, the Jewish economy imported about another 26 percent of its resources from the outside, and exported 8.3 percent of its goods and services.[33] It seems that Arabs depended on the Jewish economy more than did the Jews on the Arab economy. Most of the flow of capital into the Arab economy came from the Jewish economy. In 1936, before the rebellion, the Jews bought between 33 and 40 percent of Arab agricultural produce,[34] agriculture being the main sector of the Arab economy. It is not surprising that in the wake of the rebellion, the Arab economy collapsed as the Jewish economy flourished.

Yet the main weakness of the revolt was not its many often-contradictory motives, but rather some of its far-reaching results: The central leadership lost control over what was happening at the beginning of the armed revolt, which had been preceded by a general strike.[35] As a result, instead of strengthening the center in terms of political authority, symbol creation, and order, the revolt weakened it. Most of the mobilization of the periphery to participate in the collectivity by means of revolt was based on particularistic loyalties, mainly kinship.[36]

Although mobilization of the periphery based on particularistic loyalties is often a useful and functional tool—industrialization in Japan was carried out in this manner—when the particularistic loyalties are in competition, sometimes to the point of active conflict, it is a symptom of social disintegration. That control of the conflict was in the hands of an organization yet not fully developed in effect contributed to social disintegration, rather than to crystallization, integration, and strengthening of the collective consciousness. Today there is almost full agreement that the collapse of Palestinian Arab society in the period of the revolt was a prelude to its military, economic, social, and moral defeat in 1947. Arab societies that had not faced the Jewish challenge were more successful in stabilizing their collective identities, except in Lebanon, where problems of a different nature developed. Thus, the concrete conflictual interaction in the political sphere affected the Palestinian Arab community in an unforeseen way.

In contrast, the conflictual interaction contributed to a process of crystallization and strengthened the political center of the Jewish society, as most of its elements were mobilized for participation in waging the conflict, and were subjected to its authority despite its lack of sovereignty.[37] The very existence of a conflictual situation strengthened the position of predominance in the system of one element of the political scene—the left—in return for its assuming an active role in the conflict. The escalation of the conflict hastened the processes of segregation, mainly in the economic sphere, forcing the Jewish settlement not only to be autarchic, but gradually to become a more fully autarchic society even before it attained full political sovereignty.

Two main questions about model interaction in the political sphere can be raised. First, to what degree did the patterns of political activity of each collectivity serve as a model for the other? Second, to what degree did the developing organizational apparatus of each side serve as an example for imitation or rejection by the opposing side? In theory, the framework of British colonial rule greatly restricted freedom of political action and dictated the rules of the game. In practice, however, the two sides had wide margins in which to work, both inside and outside the British framework. Thus, the crystallization of patterns of action and organization specific to each side—that is, appropriate to its social system, political culture, and particular goals—was possible.

On the Jewish side, every act that was part of the process of nation building, especially the purchase of land, the founding of settlements, and the very act of immigration, was not only a political act, but one directed against the Arab Palestinian community, which is how the Arab side perceived them, considering even the Purim carnival that used to be held in Tel Aviv as a demonstration of power. The Arab side potentially had direct control only over the transfer of lands from Arab to Jewish ownership, but due to the weakness of the political center and its inability to efficiently oversee members of the collectivity, even this was not fully exploited.

During this period, in all spheres other than that of land, the Arabs were forced either to use the British government to prevent or slow down the processes of Jewish nation building, or to resort to violent behavior, which was illegal and dealt with accordingly by the British. As a result of their contradictory aims and their diverse objectives, even if we forget momentarily their different political cultures, it was almost impossible for either side to be a model for the other in the sphere of patterns of political activity. Despite this, there were several areas in which Jewish political activities were at least a partial model, which some in the Arab community tried to copy. The attempt to convert economic power into political power, mainly through establishing the Arab National Fund (Sanduk-al-Uma al-Arabiya), almost completely copied the Jewish National Fund's methods of operation. The Arab National Fund was set up in 1931 with the support of the Supreme Muslim Council, and reestablished at the initiative of the Istiqlal Party in 1943. However, its success was only symbolic, as by 1946 it had raised only 150 pounds sterling and transferred to the *waqf,* the Islamic religious endowments, only about 15,000 *dunums* of land. By the beginning of the 1930s, the leadership of both sides were considering the idea that the solution to the conflict lay in the use of force.[38] An organized Jewish defense in the form of a semi-underground militia that came to be called the Haganah had existed for some time, though it was neither very active nor very efficient,[39] and its existence, structure, and activities were well known to the Arab side. The Arab community did not copy the Haganah's modes of operation, but the desire to establish armed forces that would operate deliberately rather than sporadically and by chance and was certainly influenced by the Jewish paramilitary organization. Arab paramilitary organizations were characterized by their regional nature, among other things, even though their members were drawn "from a class which until then had taken no part in nationalist political activity—villagers who for various reasons had left their villages and moved to the cities . . . [these] organization(s) provided them with the framework they so badly needed and with Muslim identity symbols with which they were familiar."[40]

From the Arab point of view, the most problematic issue in the area of model interaction was the Arab social and political system's copying, partial or complete, of the central tool of Jewish political action, the Jewish Agency, and its methods of operation. On one hand, the Jewish Agency, whose authority was defined in the fourth chapter of the Mandate, was seen as a very efficient tool and worthy of imitation, as the Arab Executive Council was engaged in a constant battle to be recognized as a representative body for the entire Arab community in Palestine.[41] On the other hand, the Jewish Agency's structure and modes of operation did not fit the political and social structure of the Arab system. The Arab leadership rejected the British offer in 1923, repeated with minor changes in 1937, to establish an Arab agency with a status completely analogous to that of the Jewish Agency, because the Arabs interpreted the offer as granting to the Jewish minority a status equal to that of the Arab majority, and as Arab agreement to establishing a political body on the basis of parity with the Jews, rather than fulfillment of the Arab demand for independent rule.[42] Thus the model problem was not how to copy a specific institution, such as the Jewish Agency or the National Council, but how to crystallize an effective political center, similar to the Jewish center, which would act with authority even when lacking sovereignty or an institution of self-government like those of the neighboring Arab countries.

Two bodies, the Supreme Muslim Council and the Arab Executive, competed for the position of political center, and both had intrinsic difficulties in fulfilling the task. The Executive not only lacked resources, but also, except for a short period, had difficulty compromising with the various sectors of Arab Palestinian society. Even the Supreme Muslim Council, which competed with the Executive, was unable to crystallize organizational tools and create symbols that could generate collective consciousness and activities that would cut across the internal fragmentation of Arab Palestinian society. The Supreme Muslim Council had resources to distribute—the rights to use *waqf* lands, offices, and budgetary allocations—but Haj Amin al-Hussayni's goal, paraphrasing David Ben-Gurion's saying that his goal was to turn "a class into a nation," was to turn "a family into a nation." Desire to achieve this goal forced a difficult dilemma on him. On one hand, to become a national leader for whom national interests came before particularistic loyalties, he had to allocate resources to traditional enemies, something he did in fact try to do from time to time, as in the appointment of al-Hatib al-Tamini as Mufti of Hebron. On the other hand, allocating resources to elements outside of his immediate bases of support threatened his standing within his own camp.

Several resourceful Jewish political leaders tried to exploit the situation of two organizations vying for leadership by pouring capital into the treasuries of both the Muslim Council and the Executive. The method succeeded best in the Agriculturist Party (1924–27), which was founded by rural sheiks in opposition to the urban elite, and which had massive Jewish support. The most serious problem of the Supreme Muslim Council, and the reason for its inability to lead all the Arabs of Palestine, was the fact that in essence it was a religious organization, thus excluding the most active element of the Arab national movement, the Christians.[43]

The most interesting attempt to introduce modern political activity into the Palestinian Arab community began in 1932 with the founding of the Istiqlal (Liberty) party. Istiqlal did not necessarily choose its leaders from the traditional leadership, but from among educated professionals who in many cases had received Western educations. The party solicited members on the basis of personal membership, as opposed to the ascriptivism that prevailed in the rest of the Arab social and political organizations; the latter drew members from either the educated class or the urban proletariat, which had broken away from traditional and familial obligations. Istiqlal also adopted a pan-Arab ideology, raising anew the idea that Palestine was "a natural and integral part of Syria" immediately after it was founded.[44] At the same time, it considered Jerusalem to be its headquarters, and one of its aims was to "raise the economic, social and political standards of the Palestinian Arabs."[45]

The second and relatively late modern political crystallization was the League of National Liberation, the Jqzbat al-Tahrur al-Vatani, which was basically a communist-nationalist party, though it did not publicly declare itself as such.[46] It began as a group of Christian intellectuals, mainly from the north and most of whom had belonged to the Palestinian Communist Party (PCP). This party is a most interesting phenomenon in the study of the development of the Jewish and Arab political systems: In practice, it was the only political framework within which Jews and Arabs worked together regularly over a long period of time, mainly between 1927 and 1944.

Primary Relations

There were many potential points of meeting between Jews and Arabs: Arabs and Jews lived in mixed cities, though mostly not in mixed neighborhoods; Arab workers, sometimes with their families, lived within or on the outskirts of some of the settlements; and both were subject to the framework of British colonial rule. There were sporadic attempts at joint enterprises, stressing mutual interests, but these were not significant in scope or weight. It is difficult to measure their scope statistically, but it appears that primary relations existed between Jews and Arabs mostly on the levels of individuals and families. Patterns of continuous friendship were not uncommon, some of them withstanding the pressures of the escalating political conflict between the two communities. Despite this, the relations between the two communities were very similarly exclusionary to relations between two castes. The main expression of the situation was and remains the almost total absence of intermarriage between the two communities.

While the Jewish immigration was not usually demographically balanced and there was a shortage of women, the Arab sector could not supply this demand, mainly because of the severe restrictions placed on girls and women in traditional Muslim society. In the few mixed marriages that did take place, it was several Jewish women who married Arab men.[47] But the barriers were not only in one direction: the Jewish society, even the nontraditional elements in it, fiercely denounced mixed marriage. This prevented the generation of an ethnic stratum of a new and mixed people, as has happened in Latin America. Using the concept of social distance, we can conclude that on the concrete plane, relations of friendship, mainly on the personal or familial level, were common enough; there was a tendency toward ecological separation in the sense that there were two completely difference social systems in operation; and there was almost total separation in the sphere of intermarriage. Neither side offered a model to which the other could relate positively in the sphere of model interaction of primary relations, and the primordial differences between the two populations perpetuated the social distances between them, increased the xenophobic tendencies that already existed on both sides, and remained an additional dimension of the conflict that grew and became more explicit, in addition to the dimension of cultural gaps.

The Connections Between the Spheres of Interaction

Three types of interrelated basic questions arise from the model presented here. The first type concerns the nature of possible changes in the kind of interaction in each sphere. The second concerns the kinds of linkages between the spheres. The third is related to the output of the system as a whole, as different answers can be given to questions about the interactions in the various spheres by the two partners. The three types of questions can also be broken down into a number of smaller questions. It appears that there are two basic types of interaction in each of the economic, cultural, religious, political, and primary-relations spheres: intensification of one of the modes of interaction (that is +, -, or o) within a particular sphere and transition from one mode of interaction to another (e.g., from "minus" to "plus" in the cultural-religious sphere, interpreted as transition from Kulturkampf to cooperation to the point of mutual or one-sided assimilation and the creation of a syncretic culture). For the second type of change, the following questions can be raised. Are such changes possible? If so, in which spheres can they occur and in which are they impossible? Keeping the sphere constant, is the transition from "plus" to "minus" easier or more frequent than the opposite transition? Is the transition from "zero" to "plus" or "minus"—and the other way around—more frequent than from "minus" to "plus"—or the other way around—directly?[48]

The linkages between the spheres raise further questions. Does the form of interaction in a given sphere, or changes in it, cause changes in the interaction in another sphere? Is spillover possible from sphere to sphere that affects the kind of interaction, or has any influence whatsoever on its intensity? If so, from which spheres can there be spillover? Can one of the modes of interaction (+,-, and o) be much more predominant than one or both of the other modes? Can the very existence of conflictual interaction in a certain area lead to identical interaction in the other spheres? Are certain combinations of a specific sphere of interaction with a specific mode of interaction more influential than others? Conflict in the sphere of the economy determines whether there will also be conflict in the other spheres, but exchange in the sphere of the economy does not influence what mode of interaction exists in the remaining spheres—just as hostile relations in the political sphere do not necessarily lead to conflict in the economic sphere.

The problem of linkages among the different spheres of interaction can also be put differently; we can ask to what degree there exist tendencies within the system to balance the modes of interaction among the different spheres, either by maintaining the same mode of interaction in all of them or by canceling the differentiation between the institutionalized areas. The question assumes that to relate to a partner differently in the various spheres—for example, to have economic cooperation together with political conflict—is to maintain an unbalanced situation, and that the system will aim to balance it. If this tendency exists, then out of the eighty-one possible profiles, the system will trend toward only three: cooperation, segregation, or conflict in each of the spheres.

The hypothesis above was that each of the partners in the interaction—the native population and the immigrants—try to answer, implicitly or explicitly, the question of what its relations with the opposite side should be like, in each of the spheres and perhaps generally. It was also assumed that these answers are not final, that they may be influenced by the answers given by the opposing side and sometimes by the actions of a third side, and that the output of the entire system is not necessarily identical to that of one or even both of the partners in the interaction. Here, some additional questions can be raised. What determines each side's answers to the problems arising from the very existence of the other side? How are one side's answers influenced by the answers given by the other? Is it relevant to suggest a hypothesis of symmetric aspirations—that is, if one side unambiguously tends to give a certain answer in a specific area, does the opposing side, over time, give the same answer? How do the changing power relations between the sides fit in? Is the choice of a certain answer[49] in effect an attempt to improve the power relations or the bargaining position of one side at the expense of the other side, even if the choice is to cooperate? Does a dominant strategy exist, that is, what game theory defines "a course of action which leads to the most preferred outcome regardless of what else may happen or what others may do?"[50] In the case before us, is it worthwhile for one of the sides to choose a strategy of cooperation in the economic sphere regardless of the answer that the other side chooses?

Of course, answers given about concrete interaction must be distinguished from those about model interaction, and all of the above questions must be asked about the mutual influences of concrete and model interactions. On the basis of one case study, it is impossible to give valid general answers concerning relations between immigrants and local native populations; generalizing would require a comparative study of different patterns of junction and types of societies, which was not an immediate goal of the conceptual framework within which this analysis was carried out. Still, partial answers at least can be given about the case of meetings between Jews and Arabs in the area defined as Eretz Israel by the Jews and Filastin by the Arabs, when the interaction is examined over a period of time. The period of time is an additional variable assuming that for whatever reasons, changes are taking place, whether in the strategy adopted by each of the sides or in the outputs of the system.

As a starting point for the analysis, an arbitrary model designates the modal profile of interactions between Jews and Arabs. The mode refers to the total amount of time in which a particular interaction was maintained by one side or another in a given sphere.

Table 1.2 presents a schematic summary of our hypotheses about the strategies adopted by each of the sides. The presentation is limited in not expressing the strength and scope of the interaction, which accounted for some of the most striking changes that took place. However, this limitation does not lessen the utility of using this interactional model. If the schematic representation reflects the normal (modal) situation of interaction between the Jews and the local Arabs up to 1947, then several conclusions follow.

Table 1.2

	Economic	Cultural	Political	Primary relations
Jewish strategy				
Concrete interaction	+	o	o	o
Model interaction	-	-	o	o
Arab strategy				
Concrete interaction	-	-	-	o
Model interaction	+	-	o	o
Output of the system				
Concrete interaction	+	-	-	o

The differentiation between the spheres, in the choice of a strategy for concrete interaction, the choice of the opposing side as a model (+) or a counter-model (–), or the choice of a strategy of not relating to the other side (o), is valid mainly on the Jewish side and as the output of the system, but the differentiation tends to be cancelled when there the strategy of conflict in the political sphere intensifies, usually on Arab initiative, as occurred in the period 1936–39. In general, as part of its management of the conflict, the Jewish system tended to choose a strategy of segregation in the political sphere while trying to insist that there was no conflict because of the asymmetry of the power relations. However, when the conflict in the political sphere intensified from the Arab side, there was a tendency to move toward a strategy of conflict in other areas, or at least to deepen segregation, especially those of culture and primary relations. Moreover, Arab intensification of conflict forced the Jewish side to adopt a strategy of conflict in the political sphere that it had wanted to avoid, moving the general output of the system toward segregation or conflict on the level of concrete interaction. From this it can be concluded that the political sphere to some degree predominated over the others.

It may be that the combination of a strategy of intensive conflict in the political sphere predominates; thus, if a certain side adopts this strategy, then the output of the entire system, whatever the strategy of the other side, is either conflict or some blend of conflict and segregation. In general, the strategy of conflict or segregation in any sphere is apparently stronger than cooperative strategy in that it determines the output of the system in some sphere. Also, it appears that the tendency to spill over from sphere to sphere is greater under intensive conflict than under cooperation.

It seems that most of the Jewish success from the time of the beginning of the Zionist settlement until the mid-1930s was both in dictating partial cooperation to the system in the economic sphere, despite the emerging Arab center's pressure and choosing conflict, and in preventing spillover of tendencies toward conflict from the political sphere (and others) to the economic sphere. This success resulted mainly from the Arab center's inability to control its members efficiently, but also from the hope, based on premises drawn from the theory of materialism popular in the Jewish sector, that partial cooperation in the economic sphere would create vested interests in leading or powerful strata of the Arab community, preventing the intensification of conflict in the political sphere as long as demographic power relations did not favor the Jews and at least some of the processes of Jewish nation-building that depended on economic exchange with the Arab community. However, either these interests were not strong enough, or else the spillover from the economic to the political sphere did not take place. In the political sphere the dominant Jewish strategy was exclusion and segregation, despite the aggressive nature of the dominant strategy and the output of the entire system. For the Jews, it was worthwhile to present a cooperative strategy in the political sphere because it moderated the total output of the system.

In the concrete interaction in the cultural sphere, there were also a number of changes during the period. At the beginning of the settlement, there was a tendency to adopt selectively cultural items—such as behavior, language, and buildings—from the Arabs, resulting from Jewish willingness for partial model interaction. With the arrival of British rule, this tendency weakened to the point of indifference. The other side, however, was not indifferent, and it tended to exploit cultural and religious differences to mobilize the periphery for the conflict against the Jews.[51] There was a tendency to obscure the differentiation between the political and cultural spheres, especially in the area of religion. What characterized the interaction on the level of primary relations was the shared tendency toward separation in sensitive areas, such as living quarters and marriage, not necessarily connected to political relations between the two communities. Cultural and primordial differences were an part of the social structures of the two communities, and had as much effect as the conflicting political interests. Although from time to time there were changes in the strategies of interaction—mainly, the Arab strategies during the period of intensification of political conflict—it seems that there were no rapid or drastic changes in the system's output, and so not only is there justification for presenting a model profile for the partners' interaction, but the profile even maintains relative stability throughout the period studied.

Another dimension of the relations between the two partners is the model interaction, referring to the degree of explicit or implicit willingness to imitate patterns of behavior, fully or partially, or to reject them as diabolical examples. The patterns of behavior referred to here are chosen from the repertoire of the behaviors of the other partner to the interaction. In other words, model interaction measures the degree to which the partner served, in a given sphere, as a model (+) or a counter-model (–) for imitation, or the collectivity's indifference to the presence of the other side. Here the strategy of each collectivity is identical to that of the entire system because each collectivity has complete control, independent of the other side, over its imitation or rejection of a model. The schema clearly shows that there is differentiation between the spheres and no constant relation between the concrete and the model interaction in a given sphere, except for the sphere of primary relations.

On the other hand, there is considerable correlation in three of the four spheres between the ways in which the collectivities related to each other. In the political sphere and that of primary relations, each collectivity was indifferent to the model that the other presented. In the cultural sphere, there was usually a negative and hostile approach to the partner's model, or more accurately, to the model as the other side perceived it. But in the economic sphere, while the Jewish side tended to reject the example of an undeveloped economy that the Arab system presented, the Arab side tended usually to accept, sometimes partially or with the restrictions imposed by its structure, the Jewish example. When intensification of the conflictual interaction in the political sphere was registered, there was not necessarily rejection, or more intense rejection, of the Jewish model. In the political and economic spheres, the approach of "to beat the Jews their methods must be imitated" was likely to be followed. Here there are hints of influence, but perhaps in a direction opposite to that expected.

It is very difficult to decide what the image of the Jewish society in the country would have been had Israel Zangwill's famous saying about the return "of a people without a land to a land without a people" corresponded to the real situation. Similarly, it is difficult to know exactly what the sociopolitical character of the Arab society in the country would have been without the Jewish immigrants, and without the geopolitics that the Mandate's framework dictated as a result of its ambiguous commitment to Zionism. Posing these hypothetical questions has no utility anyway. As a temporary conclusion, we can say that it is quite surprising how marginal the mutual influences between the two collectivities were, despite the vigorous interaction between them. The contacts and disputes were usually more catalytic for, though they sometimes slowed down, processes that occurred within each of the systems. However, for the Arab side, the appearance and growth of the Jewish system had a more extreme final result, and the Arabs' perception of Zionism as standing in a zero-sum position to their national aims became, to a large degree, a self-fulfilling prophecy.

CHAPTER TWO

Collective Identity as Agency and Structuration of Society

The Israeli Example*

WITH DAHLIA MOORE

The Problem

Filling the gap that lies between the individual, replete with a free will that appears in different degrees of unpredictable social conduct, and the whole or systematically structured society is one of the major puzzles in sociology and the social sciences. The problem is how to conceptualize and theorize the existence of the individual to match the concepts that we have of institutions, societies, and cultures. After all, it is the individual that provides our hard data, while institutions, cultures, and societies are theoretical constructs or metaphysical entities.

* From Baruch Kimmerling and Dahlia Moore, "Collective Identity as Agency, and Structuration of Society: Tested by the Israeli Case," *International Review of Sociology* 7, no. 1 (1997): 25–50. The authors would like to acknowledge the generous financial support of the Eshkol Institute for Social, Political, and Economic Research, and its director Michael Shalev. The research was carried out with the assistance of the Louis Guttman Institute of Applied Research and managed by Hanna Levinson and Majid al-Haj. The authors would also like to thank Ezra Kopelowitz for his substantial contribution.

The Empty Agent

The first substantial efforts to fill this gap were the Parsonian and Mertonian generalized actor theories and the fragmented role-player framework.[1] Both theories, however, eliminated the possibility of choice and the existence of alternative social action. Action outside of an acceptable margin was automatically categorized as deviant, and even when roles appeared to conflict, all of the alternatives for conflict resolution were built into the system. The result was an over-socialized image of individuals who were objectified as good or bad products of the system.

After four decades of extensive criticism of structuralism, functionalism, and their various derivatives, the weaknesses of the theories are well known. However, this has not produced convincing alternative theories on the macro- or middle-range levels that can deal with basic problems, such as locating the individual as an actor in social processes, as was suggested by philosophers such as Husserl and Wittgenstein. One of the most ambitious and promising attempts to retheorize the role of the individual in social processes is Anthony Giddens' structuration theory.[2] At the core of the theory are individuals, known as agents—apparently, agents of the social system—who do not create systems or cultures per se, but "produce or transform them, remaking what is already made in the continuity of *praxis*."[3] Agents are autonomous, knowledgeable, and skillful, though never fully aware of their action. Agents' actions are always bound by historical-situational contexts, compounded by given power structures that are not of the agents' choosing. However, agents are never fully culturally preprogrammed; they have a wide range of knowledge about their world and can explain rationally the reasons and motives for their action.[4]

Every action involving agents combines three major dimensions that can be thought of as a loop: unacknowledged conditions of action, which are anchored in sets of rules and resources (e.g., the capitalistic regime or widespread use of money rather than barter); the action itself—including verbal behavior—during which agents and their counterparts in social interaction monitor and rationalize their actions and motivations; and the unintended consequences of the action, which may or may not change the initial conditions on the micro or macro level.[5] The continuous feedback generated by the movement around the loop is the process of structuration, to use the Giddensian neologism. To the degree that the flow is regular and uniform—institutionalization, in non-Giddensian terminology—the praxis is reproduced or alternatively shaped into new practices. Thus, "structure is both a medium and outcome of the reproduction of practices,"[6] an approach that brings the entire theory dangerously close to tautology.[7] However, Giddens does not give deterministic or historical priority to any particular form of either production of new practices or reproduction of old conducts; correspondingly, no universalistic needs are implicitly or explicitly assumed, for either collectivities or actors.[8] Giddens has contributed enormously to the understanding of the mechanics of production and reproduction of cultures and collectivities on various levels, and provides partial insight into the link between the individual and the social system. However, the term "agent" remains devoid of any significant social content and is no less metaphysical than any other traditional structuralist or poststructuralist term. Agent and agency must be everything or nothing. We aim to merge two different approaches and levels of analysis, and then to test our proposal empirically. The theoretical approach that we use to complement that of Giddens is the collective identity approach at different levels of the social order. Our empirical test consists of a case study comparing the Israeli Jewish population to the Israeli Arab population.

Social Agents as Carriers of Social Identity

Every valid collective identity—that is, one that is held by substantial numbers of a real or imaginary collectivity and defines the boundaries and rules within this collectivity—must also be a personal identity. In other words, many people sharing a common identity, implying a degree of loyalty and active or passive membership in a collectivity, confirm that a specified identity is indeed collective. The identities are an integral part of the social construction, transformation, and dismantling of collectivities on diverse levels. We assume that every social actor, or agent,[9] has a relatively limited repertoire of personal or collective social identities (SIs), constructed by the individual's desire for membership in a specific collectivity and culture. However, like Giddens' agent in the loop structure, almost every chosen identity simultaneously determines the relevant collectivity for the individual at a given time and place, also constituting, in an aggregate with other individuals, the collectivity itself. Thus, even identities that possess different meanings[10] are the common denominator and societal space of the collectivity in its Giddensian meaning, lending a patterned consistency to the construction of societal boundaries.

Some SIs are mutually exclusive, such as male and female. Some are clustered, such as White Anglo-Saxon Protestant. Others are hierarchically ordered by their generalizability across situations. However, most SIs compete for preferential status within a particular person, and as such, they are a part of an ongoing sociopolitical struggle in every collectivity, including struggles over alternative SIs and the content of them.

Consciously or unconsciously, certain SIs can be prioritized over alternative SIs. In addition, an agent's identity can be changed by shifting an SI, or emphasizing one over the other, depending on place, time, and the nature of the participant in the social interaction. Our central theoretical assertions in this paper are that SIs are implanted into agents by the agents' very membership in a collectivity and the traits constructed by a specific culture, leading the agents toward specific social conducts, and that the agent's flexibility of choices within certain margins of an SI is a major mechanism of the structuration process, or the process of continuous production and reproduction of a social order. By social order we mean the forming of institutions and organizations that include the shaping of their cultural meanings,[11] or the fusion between institutional structure and the accepted rules of the game.

Many social theorists deal with different aspects of SIs, but none have placed them in the larger context of structuration or any other forms of the production and reproduction of social order. Some focus on SIs as an expression of social categorization and group relationships.[12] Others deal with the relative importance of diverse components of an SI.[13] Still others focus, theoretically and empirically, on the behavioral aspects of an SI, such as voting behavior or partisan support.[14] We examine several strategic SIs that, when adopted by an agent from the larger repertoire, determine large parts of the social order as carried, produced, and reproduced by that agent. We demonstrate how strategic SIs work within the context of the sociopolitical processes of contemporary Israeli society, and show the existence, within this society, of competing sociopolitical orders.

SI theories offer sociopsychological perspectives for analyzing social identification and group behavior that allows for the distinction between "us" and "them," or in-groups and out-groups.[15] According to such theories, people tend to classify themselves and others into diverse social categories, such as religion, gender, or age group, using different bases of categorization. A self-concept has two components: a personal identity, which includes the idiosyncratic characteristics of the individual, based on physical attributes, abilities, and psychological traits; and a collective identity, which includes the major group classifications in that society.[16] Social behaviors and the process of structuration can be viewed as resulting from the interactions between two or more individuals who are influenced by their personal characteristics or the social groups to which the individuals belong.[17] Social groups and categories determine individuals' behaviors if and only if the individuals identify themselves with the group. Identification develops when agents see themselves as culturally and socially tied to the collectivity and its successes, failures, privileges, and lack of privileges.

The literature lists many factors that contribute to the formation of group identification and specific SIs.[18] The most relevant for our case is the distinctiveness of the group's values and practices compared with those of other groups, which provide individuals with a sense of unique identity;[19] the group's prestige, which may affect the individual's self-esteem;[20] and the salience of the out-group that strengthens the awareness of the in-group.[21] We consider all of these factors as a particular case of structuration, production, and reproduction of collectivities at the various analytical levels, from a nuclear family to an entire society, which the identities define as their boundary.

The factors involved in group identification tend to strengthen social categorizations and augment societal cleavages; especially when they are of a bipolar, either-or nature, they intensify conflicts among groups. According to Turner,[22] when an intense conflict exists between two subcultures, interactions among members of the collectivities will be more strongly influenced by their actual or imaginary membership than when no conflict exists. Consequently, individual members of the collectivities will find it difficult to deal with each other as individuals, and instead tend to treat all members of the out-group uniformly.

However, a person belongs to several collectivities at the same time and may identify with more than one of them. This often leads to complicated relationships among components of social identities that represent different social orders. In each society, the strain among SIs is based on the specific diversifying issues prevalent in the society, but the consequences are the same: Agents must choose among the specific identities that the categorization leads to, thus limiting identification to groups that do not conflict with one another. In some societies, such avoidance is impossible. Israeli Arabs may see themselves as both Palestinian and Israeli; Canadians may see themselves as both French Quebecois and Canadian; before the breakup of Yugoslavia, Yugoslavs could have seen themselves as Slavs, Croats, or

Muslims. At the same time, all such individuals may feel themselves as belonging to a specific locality.

Is one component of identity more central than others? Some researchers[23] claim that class is the most important ingredient of social identity. Others[24] emphasize the pluralistic nature of social identity, claiming that there is no a priori or theoretically based preference for placing class over all others. Priority is determined according to the issue that the agent deals with[25] or the agenda in a particular society.[26]

We expect that, to the extent that a specific identity attracts a cluster of other identities, it becomes a code for a given social order, and thus is located in a central systemic position. In societies in which national rights are unsettled, people tend to define themselves in regional or nationalistic terms and emphasize this aspect of their SI more than class. In societies in which religion is the major basis for social strife, people define themselves by the religious component of their SI—whether the conflict is between religion and secularism, as it is in Spain, or between two religions, as it is for Catholics and Protestants in Ireland and Hindus and Muslims in India.

The Israeli Context

Several somewhat overlapping bipolar cleavages exist in Israel today, including those among political ideologies, religion, ethnic origin, and socioeconomic factors.[27] The cleavages operate in tandem when sociopolitical issues are at stake and form bases for SIs, making the demographic lines of demarcation very clear. Whether or not they are bipolar, cleavage-based identities can exacerbate social conflicts or be the result of such conflicts. Whenever several cleavages overlap, the motivation for agents to produce or reproduce particular social orders is greater than that resulting from a single cleavage.[28] Israeli Jews are deeply divided regarding the peace negotiations in the Middle East. More religious Jews of Mizrahi origin and with lower education and socioeconomic status tend to be right wing and oppose territorial concessions; consequently, they are thought of as agents of an ethnocentric social order. More secular Jews of Ashkenazi origin and with higher education and socioeconomic status tend to be left wing, support territorial concessions, and have a compromising political attitude toward the conflict; they are considered as structuring a civic and universalistic social order. Class is a part of these cleavages, but not a singular or transcending factor as Marshal, Ross, Newby, and Vogler claim.[29]

We posit that the overlaps and centrality of political, religious, ethnic, and class identities, together with a high degree of politicization in a mobilized society,[30] create a tendency toward extremist either-or cleavages. This leads Israelis—Jews and Arabs—to a clash of identities on two levels: between the collectivistic and individualistic dimensions of SI, and among the components within each dimension. As the collectivistic identity and the individualistic identity are inherently antithetical,[31] different, opposing, and competing social orders may be formed.

The collectivistic codes of both Jews and Arabs dictate the precedence of collective over individual needs. All members of the collective society are expected to contribute to attaining the collective's goals as much as they can, with whatever resources they have. Personally attaining wealth and power is regarded as less valuable and important than improving the welfare of the collective, and personal gains are to be made through achieving collective goals rather than individual actions.[32] The individual is seen as a bearer of collective ideals, and commitment to them makes him or her subordinate to their imperative.[33]

Two basic collective identities have formed for both Jews and Arabs, representing two distinct social orders. Jews may identify with a Jewish identity, which excludes from the collectivity all non-Jewish citizens but includes all Jewish people in the Diaspora, and an Israeli identity, which includes all Jewish and non-Jewish citizens of the state. Arabs may identify with an Arab identity, which is related to broader loyalties that imply affiliation with larger entities, and a Palestinian identity, which has territorial and nationalistic connotations. For both Jews and Arabs, the first collectivistic identity represents an ethnocentric and particularistic social order. The second represents a universalistic social order, based on civic virtues.

The dichotomy between particular and universal arises because Israel is not only a self-declared Jewish nation-state of Jewish citizens, but also belongs to Jewish people across the world, which is the essence of Zionist ideology. This feature of Israel is illustrated by the Law of Return, which entitles all Jews and their close relatives to immigrate to the country. Other laws and regulations give the state and the Jewish Agency—the local arm of the World Zionist Organization—authority to enact a series of affirmative action measures that favor the Jewish population in the state.

The individual dimension of SI, however, designates the opposite goals, emphasizing the idea of self-fulfillment that is prevalent in Western societies. According to this ideal, each person strives to develop his or her capabilities to lead a fuller life. A person's major loyalty is to himself, or to his immediate family.[34] All members of the society are meritocratically evaluated, with those who rate higher accorded higher rewards. Material well-being is one of the major indicators of the individual's attaining these goals. As participation in the labor market is the main venue through which the ideal may be attained, it can increase the salience of professional identity. Though self-fulfillment applies more weakly to Israelis than to Americans or Europeans, and is more relevant to professional workers than to blue-collar workers or to the unemployed, it can conflict with the collectivistic identity.

Collective Jewish Identities

Eisenstadt[35] focused on the major components of the collectivistic Zionist identity and the distinction between its particularistic (Jewish and religious) and universalistic (socialist, nationalist, and liberal) principles. One of the salient features of political Zionism is that it purported to be not merely a nationalist ideology, but strove to integrate two value premises that, in principle, conflicted: "the collective particularism of Jewish aspiration to an independent National state, and the universalism of modern Western civilization . . . Both sets of premises . . . become fundamental components of the legitimation of the State of Israel. In political practice, however, they necessarily clashed."[36]

The precarious balance among all of the aspects of collective Jewish identity, always problematic and inherently conflicting, has gradually changed, leading to the weakening of the collectivistic ideology because of demographic transformations, changes in the relative power of different social groups, and the relationship with the Arab world.[37] By the early 1970s, the majority of the Jewish population in Israel was composed of immigrants from Islamic countries or their descendants, and they had not completely assimilated as the Zionist establishment had hoped. The more recent immigrants' estrangement from socialist values, which contradicted their more traditional values, kept growing, as did their dissatisfaction with its institutions.

In the late 1970s, the majority of the Asian-African Jewish voters rejected the socialist Labor Party in favor of right wing or religious parties. In the 1977 elections, the ideological and political situation changed drastically, and the regime was transferred to the basically populist and capitalist[38] Likud Party and its coalition of right wing and religious parties. This switch is considered the result of the Asian and African Jews' disillusionment with the existing sociopolitical system, in which they occupied inferior social, political, and economic positions,[39] or the strengthening of their nationalistic and religious orientations.[40] The right wing and religious coalition, with its pronounced populist and individualist ideology, reflected the social changes that had taken place. The ideology also legitimized and delegated higher status to the Mizrahi culture and value system.[41]

After gaining social legitimacy, Jews from Islamic countries reverted to the more traditional and religious values that the secular socialist ideology tried to force them to eschew as part of its attempt to create the so-called new Israeli man. The strengthening of religious tendencies could not be delegitimized because it translated Zionist aspirations into religious aspirations and fit with the nationalistic premises of the ruling right wing.[42] Kimmerling[43] claims that the strengthening religious trends can be seen even earlier than the 1970s, in the movement of the national-religious strata toward the center of society and in the inclusion of Jewish heritage studies in the secular national schools' curriculum. He shows[44] that in 1974, Jewish identity was already stronger than Israeli identity for both religious and secular Jews.[45] Auron also found a continuous increase in the valence of Jewish identity and a corresponding decrease for the Israeli identity.[46]

The Arab-Israeli conflict has also contributed to the shift in power within Israel that has changed the Israeli identity structure. After the 1967 war, Israel expanded its borders, and nationalists desired to keep and settle the occupied territories. However, the principles upon which the occupation was justified and rationalized undermined the state's Zionist and socialist premises. As the Labor government's ability to reconcile the contradictions deteriorated, the right wing Likud party gained power. Its more pronounced, religion-based nationalistic ideology legitimized the continued occupation. National resources were channeled into housing projects, road construction, and the massive settling of the territories, which became the right wing coalition's highest priority. There are now 120,000 Jews living in the occupied territories, and the proportion of religious people among them is higher than elsewhere in Israel.[47]

The nationalist activities shifted the debate, from the socioeconomic sphere between socialist and capitalist ideologies to the political sphere focusing on the Israeli-Palestinian conflict and the future of the occupied territories. The shift may have important implications for SI and the further strengthening of the bipolarity between Jews and Arabs in the social

structure of Israel. It may have also enhanced the centrality of the primordial Jewish aspect of the collective identity.

Collective Arab Identities

Arabs that remained in Israel after the great exodus from the country in
1948[48] were objects of attempts to shape them into an obedient and loyal
minority. They were separated from their fellow Palestinians outside Israel's
boundaries physically, culturally, and politically, and there was an attempt
to build a separate Israeli-Arab identity[49]—one of the Israeli authorities'
most powerful tools in their efforts to Israelify the Palestinians, mostly by
way of highly selected contents in school curricula.[50]

In the first stage, the attempt to create a new minority, quasi-ethnic but
not national collectivity and identity was impressively successful; until 1967,
the Arabs of Israel tended to adopt the Israeli Arab identity, albeit with
some difficulty.[51] However, after their reunion with the Palestinians of the
occupied territories, Arabs in Israel adopted a strategy of compartmental-
izing their identity among different spheres of activity, adopting, following Hofman and Rohana,[52] "a predominant nationalistic identity combined
with civic aspects of Israeliness." Rouhana[53] distinguished three circles of
identity: an instrumental participatory level in the polity, defined by Israeli
identity; an intermediate-value circle, such as lifestyle, political culture, and
gender relations, which shared both the Israeli and a new Palestinian identity; and a deep sentimental and loyal feeling of common fate, monopolized
by the Palestinian identity. In short, a new Israeli Palestinian identity was
created. Smooha[54] adds what he called a trend of political radicalization
among the Arab minority, accompanied by a new sense of political power,
leading several intellectuals to demand cultural autonomy for themselves,
such as by creating an Israeli-Palestinian university able to teach and study
independently of oppressive Jewish hegemony.

Other Identities

Conflict may arise among individual level identities as well. Research in other
societies has shown several individual identities to be central to individuals:
the family, occupation, gender, locality, and ethnicity. So far, the centrality of
these identities has not been thoroughly examined in the Israeli context, as
research has focused on the relationship between political attitudes and de-

mographic characteristics. Arian and Shamir[55] show that political attitudes such as left versus right have become "super issues," political labels that parties use as cues to motivate people. The left-right distinction, considered by many[56] to be an important generalized frame for political orientation in advanced industrial societies, has a different meaning for each society. In Israel it designates much more than economic ideology. Moore,[57] Peres,[58] and Shapiro[59] point to the strong relationships that exist among class, ethnic origin, religiosity, and education. Religious Jews and working-class people of Asian or African origin, who have less education, tend to vote for right wing or religious parties. Nonreligious European or American Jews who have more education tend to vote for left-wing parties. Peres and Yuchtman-Yaar[60] also show that the same groups who vote for right wing parties tend to be less democratic than those who vote for the left. In this case, we may refer to the voter as another behavioral aspect of agency.

This paper attempts to combine several dimensions of SIs. Acting as agents and structuring the society means, among other things, giving relative weight to diverse SI components in a social order, which is one dimension of the process. Creating different configurations and relations among SI components is another dimension. Combining them emphasizes, first, the different weights of Jewishness versus Israeliness, to the exclusion of all of the other possible components of an agent's identity and the variable combinations among them; then it turns to the interaction among multiple identities.

It remains to be seen which of the identities is more salient in Israeli society, what happens when identities do not overlap or create conflicting loyalties, and how the identities create different and competing—or perhaps hegemonic—social orders. We accept the notion that the relative salience of social identities varies by the issue at stake, but believe that some of the identities attain transcendent stature so that they remain salient and central regardless of the issue at hand, and are produced and reproduced in the basic social order.

Research Method

The Sample

The sample is a national probability sample of the Jewish and Arab population in Israel (excluding kibbutzim) in 1991. The respondents' ages range from twenty to seventy years. The proportions of the categories of gender, ethnic origin, and geographic location in the sample correspond to those of the entire Jewish population in 1991, as reported by the Israeli Bureau of Statistics. Data were collected in structured interviews conducted at the respondents' homes. The sample includes 1,447 respondents (of which 251 are Arab citizens), 45 percent of whom are non-workers (e.g., housewives, pensioners, students, unemployed). Incomplete questionnaires (2 percent) were excluded from further analysis.

Variables and Measures

In addition to the SI components, the relevant questions and measures presented in the paper represent diverse sociopolitical attitudes and a variety of demographic characteristics. These were used to give us additional knowledge about the content of the social order structured by the agents. Table 2.1 specifies these attitudes and demographic characteristics and their frequencies.

Components of SI

Jewish respondents were asked to rank nine components of SI; Arabs ranked eleven. The question for Jewish respondents was stated: "Each person has different things that characterize him. Here is a list of nine characteristics. Please rank those that characterize you most by order of their importance. Write (1) for the most important characteristic, (2) for the second in importance, and so forth. There is no need to rank characteristics that are not important for you." Arab respondents ranked two additional identities, being Palestinian and being a villager or townsperson. For Arabs and other minorities, the religious identity was changed to Muslim, Christian, Druze, or others. Table 2.1 presents the components and their ranks; the frequencies of only the combined first and second ranks and the non-rankings are presented. The value (0) means that the respondent did not rank the specific item at all. Such values were later recoded as 10 (or 12 for Arabs) to create a linear continuum. Thus, the lower the value, the higher the ranking of that component.

Measures of Social and Political Involvement

Assuming that the respondents are agents who produce and reproduce social orders, and that different clusters of attitudes and behaviors define diverse social orders, we presented respondents with questions about social and political attitudes and behavior. One of the cluster of items asked: "In the last 5 years, were you a member in any of the following (whether an active member or not)?" Answers ranged from 1 for active members, 2 for nonactive members, 3 for nonmembers, to 4 for irrelevant. Membership items included 1 for apartment house committees, 2 for parent-teacher associations, 3 for community committees, 4 for workers' committees, 5 for labor unions, 6 for a synagogue, mosque, or church, 7 for voluntary organizations, 8 for economic organizations, 9 for a political movement or group (not a political party), and 10 for a political party. A factor analysis shows that there are two major dimensions of sociopolitical activity. The first represents involvement in public-sphere organizations, such as labor unions, synagogues, mosques, churches, or economic or political organizations, usually falling in the realm of so-called civil society. The second dimension represents activities closer to home, for which the person's involvement contributes directly to his own or family's life, such as household and community committees and parent-teacher associations.

Table 2.1 Measures and their frequencies (percent)

	Jewish frequency		Arab frequency	
Measure	0	1 or 2	0	1 or 2
Social identity components[a]				
Profession	47.3	20.6	39.2	16.4
Being Israeli	28.3	42.6	41.4	8.8
Family	18.5	59.1	36.3	20.4
Being Jewish/Arab	27.0	43.3	21.5	43.0
Place of residence	65.8	6.2	48.6	6.4
Political attitudes				
(left wing or right wing)	72.2	2.9	44.6	10.8
Ethnic origin	75.3	1.9	33.5	21.6
Religious or secularist	63.0	9.2	43.0	10.4
Gender	60.8	10.6	39.8	14.4
Being Palestinian				
(Arab sample only)	25.1	40.6		

Political ideology "To which of the following political/ideological movements do you feel closer?"

1. To the Labor movement	37.2		27.7	
2. To the center	7.1		5.2	

(*continued*)

Table 2.1 Measures and their frequencies (percent) (*continued*)

	Jewish frequency	Arab frequency
3. To right-of-center movements	46.0	3.0
4. To Jewish religious parties	9.7	1.7
5. To Arabic parties (Arab sample only)		62.3

Territorial solution "In general, are you more for territorial annexation as a solution or for territorial concessions?"

1. Tend much more toward annexation	24.3	2.8
2. Tend a little more toward annexation	22.4	1.8
3. Leave the situation as is	18.3	76.9
4. Tends a little more toward concessions	7.5	12.4
5. Tends much more toward concessions	27.5	

Influence "Do you feel that people like you have influence over what is happening in the state?"

1. Have a lot of influence	5.7	4.8
2. Have some influence	23.1	16.4
3. Have very little influence	30.4	32.8
4. Have no influence at all	40.8	46.0

Military capability "In your opinion, to what degree can the Israeli defense forces protect Israel in time of danger?"

1. Very high degree	64.1	36.7
2. High degree	21.8	33.9
3. Quite high	9.5	21.4
4. Quite low	2.1	6.9
5. Low	1.3	0.8
6. Very low or none	0.8	0.4

Social obedience "Some claim it is the duty of citizens to obey the laws of the state in all circumstances. Do you agree with this claim?"

1. Fully agree	39.5	30.0
2. Agree	38.5	40.0
3. Do not agree	17.6	22.4
4. Totally disagree	4.3	7.6

Emigration plans "Do you consider leaving the country for an extended period time?"

1. Yes, intend to leave soon	2.4	1.2
2. Considering it	3.7	4.4
3. Rarely consider it	7.4	9.6

Table 2.1 Measures and their frequencies (percent) (*continued*)

	Jewish frequency	Arab frequency
4. Do not consider it at all	86.5	84.9

Private protection "How much are you willing to pay a private organization to guard your home and neighborhood?" (0. not willing to pay 1. 20 NIS; 7. 500 NIS or more)[b]

	Jewish (percent)	Arab (percent)
	Med = 20–50	Med = 500 +
Gender		
1. Men	46.0	51.4
0. Women	54.0	48.6
Age		
20–24	13.4	11.6
25–29	14.0	11.2
30–34	12.2	15.5
35–39	12.7	13.5
40–44	11.6	7.6
45–49	6.7	13.9
50–54	6.0	10.4
55–64	9.5	10.8
65 +	13.9	5.6
Education		
1. No schooling at all	1.7	–
2. Up to 4 years	1.1	8.4
3. 5–8 years	10.2	18.7
4. 9–10 years	11.4	20.7
5. 11 years	8.1	8.4
6. 12 years	31.6	18.3
7. 13 or more years non-academic education	17.1	11.6
8. 13 or more years academic education	18.9	8.0
Religion "How do you define yourself?"		
1. Orthodox religious	3.9	0.4
2. Religious	11.0	15.9
3. Traditional	26.8	32.7
4. Secular, maintain some of the tradition	23.4	33.9

(*continued*)

Table 2.1 Measures and their frequencies (percent) (*continued*)

	Jewish frequency	Arab frequency
5. Secularist	30.3	15.1
6. Antireligion	4.6	2.0

Family size "How many people live in your household?" (continuous, 1–9)

Employment "Are you employed?"

1. Yes	55.6	50.2
2. No (housewife, student, unemployed, pensioned)	44.4	49.8

Income "To which of the following monthly income categories does the combined income of yourself and your family members who live at home belong?" (scale of 1–9, 1 = up to 700 NIS; 9 = over 5,000 NIS; Med = 27002250)

Father's ethnic origin

1. Asian-African, Muslim	47.6	71.7
2. Israeli, Christian	11.0	16.3
3. European-American, Druze and Cherkess	41.4	12.0

Immigration (not asked in the Arab sample)

1. Born in Israel	53.3	
2. Came before 1940	5.1	
3. 1941–1947	2.9	
4. 1948–1954	14.2	
5. 1955–1960	5.1	
6. 1961–1967	6.5	
7. 1968–1973	4.6	
8. 1974–1979	3.0	
9. 1980 +	5.3	

[a] 0 = did not rank the component. 1 or 2 = first or second choice.

[b] $1 = approximately 2.8 NIS at the time of the research.

Another cluster of questions aimed to reveal respondents' orientations toward the public realm of civil society, that is, the extent to which the agent carried and reproduced the state-produced order. The question read: "Indicate, for each of the following, whether the issue should be dealt with by the citizens or by the state." Answers ranged from 1 for "much better if the citizens dealt with it" and 3 for "should be dealt with equally by the citizens and the state" to 5 for "much better if the state dealt with it." The spheres of the state's authority were tested by situations such as 1 for building kindergartens and day care centers, 2 for helping factories with financial problems, 3 for absorbing new immigrants, 4 for aiding settlers in new settlements far from cities but within the 1948 borders, 5 for aiding settlers in new settlements beyond the 1948 ceasefire line or in the occupied territories, 6 for supporting the needy, such as the elderly or battered wives, 7 for imposing law and order, 8 for dealing with suspects of terrorist actions, and 9 for interfering with groups that attempted to undermine the state. A separate factorial analysis for Jewish and Arab respondents showed that the issues form the same three dimensions: 1 for security issues (items 7–9); 2 for economic issues (items 2, 4, 5); and 3 for social support (items 1, 3, 6). The analysis shows that the state is always expected to shoulder most of the responsibility for the above issues. Responsibility for security is attributed almost totally to the state; economic issues are seen as better dealt with by the state; and social issues as shared by the government and citizens.

Table 2.1 presents all of the additional questions that were used and the response frequency to each of their categories.

Analysis

Overview

Our analysis focused on the central or most often ranked SI components of both groups. Components included family, being Jewish or Arab, being Palestinian (for the Arab sample only), being Israeli, and profession (see Table 2.1). Broadly speaking, the collectivistic identities—Israeli and Jewish for the Jewish sample, Palestinian and Arab for the Arab sample—are highly prominent, and the percentages in both samples are very similar. In the Jewish sample, 43.3 percent ranked Jewish identity in first or second place, and in the Arab sample, 43.0 percent ranked Arab identity as first or second. In addition, 42.6 percent of Jews ranked Israeli first or second, and 40.6 percent of the Arabs ranked Palestinian first or second. Interestingly, 28.3 percent of the sample of Jews ignored being Jewish altogether and 27 percent ignored the Israeli component; among the Arabs, 21.5 percent and 25.1 percent ignored being Arab and Palestinian, respectively. Thus, the generalized collective identities in the two samples seem to be of the same salience. Most of the Arab citizens of Israel do not consider themselves Israelis. This particular identity was ranked highly by very few Arabs (less than 9 percent) and ignored or rejected by many of them (over 40 percent). The Israelification policy of the Arab-Israeli citizen seems to have failed.

Though their meanings are perceived as diametrically opposed or even antithetical, the two collectivistic aspects of SI—the Jewish-Israeli dichotomy and the Arab-Palestinian dichotomy—represent similar facets of the respective SIs. Considering oneself Jewish is not only the more traditional and religion-oriented basis for collectivistic identity, but also one of the major aspects underpinning the meaning of being Israeli.[61] We suspect that this accounts for the surprisingly low ranking of the direct identity of being religious or secular. Jewishness absorbs religiosity and Israeliness covers being secular. The same can be said of the Arab and Palestinian identities: The first is the more traditional and basic identity and the second is the more recent and highly politicized one. Thus, the broader aspect of Jewishness or Arabness somewhat justifies being Israeli or Palestinian and seeing Israel or Palestine as the homeland, which is also the core of the conflict between the two entities.

Examining the other components shows that for Jewish respondents, the most important single component of social identity is not a collectivistic one, but rather the family.[62] Approximately 40 percent of Jewish respondents ranked it as the most important component and about 20 percent ranked it as their second choice. The family component is the least ignored or rejected of all nine components: only 18.5 percent of the respondents did not specify it at all as part of their identity. In the Arab sample, the salience of the family component is much lower: Only 20 percent chose it as one of their major identities, and over 36 percent did not rank it at all.

Professional identity was also ranked higher by Jews than by Arabs, but the differences are not as prominent. Approximately 21 percent of the Jews and 16.4 percent of the Arabs ranked their occupation as first or second in importance. About 47 percent of the Jews and 39.2 percent of the Arabs did not rank it at all. Those who chose their profession as their central SI component also form a distinct group. Choice of this component seems to indicate that in both samples, some respondents have espoused the self-fulfillment and self-enhancement ideologies prevalent in Western societies.

However, most respondents ranked two components or more, so that most of the respondents—67.2 percent of the Jews and about half of the Arabs—chose at least one other major identity in addition to their primary one. Table 2.2 presents these combinations. The analysis of this distribution supports Kerlinger's assumption of attitudinal dualism.[63] In the Jewish sample, identities seem to consist of two sets of juxtaposed components. Jewish and Israeli constitute one continuum, the collectivistic dimension, and family and profession constitute the second continuum, the individualistic dimension. Thus, choosing one component on a specific continuum reduces the probability of ranking the other as very high. In the Arab sample, in which ethnic identity—differentiating among Muslims, Christians, Druze, and Circassians—is more often ranked than either family or profession, the dualistic model is less clear, and the ethnic component seems to represent an intermediate level that is neither individualistic nor entirely collectivistic.

Especially in the Jewish sample, we expected to find that when more than one identity was ranked, the first and most highly ranked identity would be from one continuum and the second from the alternative continuum, so that those who ranked an individual identity, such as family or profession, as their first choice would rank a collective component—Jewish or Israeli in the Jewish sample, Arab or Palestinian in the Arab sample—as their second choice, and vice versa. Table 2.2 shows that this is not always the case. Though it is true for family identity in the Jewish sample, it is less correct for professional identity. Half of the 67.2 percent who ranked two of the major components in the first two places put family together with a collective identity, but less than 10 percent of those who ranked two major components put professional identity together with a collective identity. Instead, professional identity was most often combined with another individual component, namely, the family identity. The combinations are more heterogeneous in the Arab sample. No clear preference can be detected, except the Arab Palestinian combination, as 20 percent of the Arab sample ranked them together.

It is possible that Jews who chose family as the major component did not necessarily reject collective identities and the values they entail, but those who chose profession as the major component did reject collective identities. The familial order is not in competition with the other competing collective identities, and choosing one of the collective or individual components does not mean ignoring the rest of the continuum: The narrower and broader identities can coexist even though they often represent contradictory values. In the Jewish sample, 22 percent of those who ranked two major components chose the two collective identities and 18 percent chose individual components. In the Arab sample, 40 percent chose the two major collective identities together and 6.5 percent chose the two individualist identities. This seems to indicate that the Jewish Israeli collectivity in the 1990s is a less recruited and politicized order than is the Arab Palestinian collectivity.

Table 2.2 Combination of major social identities

Variable	Absolute frequency	Relative frequency
Jewish sample		
Jewish Israeli	15.0	22.0
Israeli family	17.0	25.3
Jewish family	17.0	25.3
Israel profession	3.8	5.7
Jewish profession	2.0	3.0
Family profession	12.0	18.0
Other combinations	32.8	—
	100.0	100.0
Arab sample*		
Arab Palestinian	20.0	40.3
Palestinian family	4.4	8.9
Arab family	3.6	7.3
Palestinian profession	2.0	5.7
Arab profession	4.0	8.1
Family profession	3.2	6.5
Palestinian Israeli	2.8	5.6
Arab Israeli	0.4	0.8
Palestinian ethnicity	1.1	8.9
Arab ethnicity	4.8	9.7
Other combinations	50.4	—
	100.0	100.0

[a] The added categories for the Arab sample capture the differences between the two samples.

The combination of identities leads to espousing less extreme positions on the related sociopolitical attitudes than either of the specific identities espouse alone. It may also indicate the individuals' ambiguous distinctions between these components, or an ability to tolerate partial incongruity to attain a transcendent goal that both identity components, as codes of distinct societal orders, promote.

Structuring the Social Order

The Familial Order. Looking at the correlates of the specific identities (see Table 2.3), we discover additional differences between the two samples. In the Jewish sample, family identity, which is the highest ranked component, is more important for women than for men, and younger people rank it very high. It is salient among the traditional but not highly religious, among those who vote for parties that are in the center of the left-right continuum and oppose territorial annexation, and among those who believe that civil obedience is obligatory in all situations and at all times. More than others who do not consider the family to be an important component of their SI, the family group believes that the state should take care of its underprivileged social groups or classes, such as the elderly, battered wives, and new immigrants.

The carriers of individual identities—family and profession—among the Arab sample also form distinct profiles. However, whereas the professional identity has similar meanings for Jews and Arabs, the family identity is different. The family identity in the Arab sample is politically distinct from both the collectivistic Arabic identities and the Jewish family identity. Arabs who rank family as their major identity component are less committed to living in Israel and show a greater willingness to emigrate. They are also willing to pay more for added private protection. Unlike the other groups, they are not demographically defined. We hesitate to conclude that those who place their family highest believe that the best way to protect their family is to leave the area for other places that offer better opportunities, because we lack information as to why people choose specific identities and not others. Still, the data seem to indicate that such an interpretation is possible. If being family-oriented has the same meaning for Jews and Arabs, then the means to achieve family goals is the exact opposite for the two groups: For the Jews, maximizing life opportunities means living in Israel; for the Arabs, it means leaving Israel.

Jewish Agents

The Jewish Order. The agents of Jewish identity are highly attached to the country and will not consider emigration from it. They also strongly support territorial annexation. It is thus hardly surprising that they are staunch supporters of right wing or religious parties, and that many among them are very religious, more so than those who chose any other SI components. Their sociopolitical attitudes are in accord: They tend to be socially obedient and believe that the law should always be maintained. They do not organize or join protests, and they trust in the ability of the government and the armed forces to take care of their safety. The only social activity they are involved in, if any, is in the synagogues they belong to. They are also a distinct

Table 2.3 Spearman correlations with the major identity components

Variable	Jewish identity	Israeli identity	Family identity	Professional identity
Political ideology				
(left* = 1, else = 0)	0.185***	−0.105***	−0.044	-0.60*
(center = 1; else = 0)	0.84**	−0.090**	0.024	0.71*
(right = 1; else = 0)	−0.116***	0.055	−0.030	−0.047
(religious = 1; else = 0)	−0.256***	0.133***	0.135***	0.172***
Territorial solution				
(1 = yes; 2 = not at all)	−0.071*	−0.059*	−0.031	0.135***
Dedicated to neighborhood				
(1 = very; 4 = not at all)	0.065*	−0.003	−0.018	−0.069*
Private protection				
(1. 20 NIS; 7. 500 NIS or more)	0.064*	0.059*	0.032	−0.059*
Influence				
(1 = yes; 4 = none)	0.040	0.087**	−0.044	0.054
Social obedience				
(1 = yes; 4 = no)	0.065*	0.068*	0.070*	0.011
Protest (1 = yes; 4 = no)	−0.070*	−0.018	0.006	0.017
Religion (1 = orthodox;				
6 = antireligion)	0.384***	−0.157***	−0.078**	−0.238***
Sex (1 = men; 0 = women)	−0.006	−0.040	0.169***	−0.099**
Age (20–65+)	0.011	−0.073*	−0.042	0.223***
Education				
(1 = none; 8 = academic)	0.131***	−0.030	0.002	−0.289***
Employment				
(1 = working; 0				
= not working)	0.109***	−0.083**	−0.004	−0.241***
Income				
(1 = less than 700; 9 = 5000+)	0.138***	−0.050	−0.098**	−0.187***
Family size				
(1.1 person; 9. 9 or more)	−0.093**	0.063*	−0.023	0.121***
Father's origin				
(1 = Eastern; 2 = Israeli;				
3 = Western)	0.140***	−0.051	−0.12	-0.063*
Immigration				
(1 = Israeli born; 9 = 1980 +)	−0.035	0.071*	−0.016	0.083**
Role of the state:				
Factor 1 (security)	0.59*	0.036	0.027	−0.016
Factor 2 (economic)	−0.051	−0.057	0.012	−0.104**
Factor 3 (social)	−0.044	0.040	−0.074	−0.050

Table 2.3 Spearman correlations with the major identity components

Variable	Jewish identity	Israeli identity	Family identity	Professional identity
Social and political involvement:				
Factor 1 (public sphere)				
Factor 2 (private sphere)	0.061* 0.030	0.026 0.070	−0.025 0.007	0.046 −0.52

Variable	Identity	Identity	Identity	Identity	Identity
Political ideology					
(Arab parties = 1, else = 0)	−0.286***	−0.297***	0.170**	0.0.69	0.162**
(left = 1, else–0)	0.130*	0.259***	−0.044	−0.090	−0.183**
(center, right, religious = 1)	0.208***	0.073	−0.241***	0.077	0.085
Territorial solution					
(1 = annexation;					
5 = concession)	0.023	−0.044	0.052	0.116	0.152*
Emigration plans					
(1 = yes; 2 = not at all)	0.094	−0.073	0.035	0.116	0.170**
Dedicated to neighborhood					
(1 = very, 4 = not at all)	−0.123	0.001	−0.112	0.066	−0.125*
Private protection					
(1. 20 NIS; 7. 500 NIS					
or more)	0.118	−0.009	−0.050	−0.121	0.022
Military ability to protect					
(1 = high; 6 = low)	−0.022	−0.118*	−0.064	−0.098	−0.084
Influence					
(1 = yes; 4 = none)	0.134*	0.205***	0.040	−0.041	0.065
Social obedience					
(1 = yes; 4 = no)	−0.019	−0.133*	0.149*	0.006	−0.128*
Protest					
(1 = yes; 4 = no)	0.067	0.188**	−0.081	−0.027	−0.000
Religion					
(1 = Orthodox; 6 = antireligion)					
Sex					
(1 = men; 0 = women)					
Age (20–65+)	0.026	−0.125*	−0.121*	−0.014	−0.206***
	−0.016	−0.061	−0.010	0.061	−0.092
	0.008	0.053	−0.062	0.049	0.206***
Education					
(1 = none; 8 = academic)	−0.175**	−0.147*	0.062	0.002	−0.213***

(continued)

Table 2.3 Spearman correlations with the major identity components

Variable	Identity	Identity	Identity	Identity	Identity
Employment					
(1 = working; 0 = not working)	−0.100	−0.043	−0.131*	−0.072	−0.127**
Income					
(1 = less than 700; 9 = 5000+)	0.019	−0.104	−0.007	0.027	0.015
Family size					
(1 = 1 person; 9 = 9 or more)	−0.104	−0.255***	0.072	0.014	0.035
Ethnic origin					
(1 = Muslim; 0 = Christian,					
Druze, and Cherkess)	−0.107	_ 0.253***	0.160**	0.006	0.013
Immigration					
(1 = Israeli born; 9 = 1980+)	—	—	—	—	
Role of the state					
Factor 1 (security)	−0.088	0.038	−0.049	0.013	−0.071
Factor 2 (economic)	0.083	0.034	−0.040	0.007	0.061
Factor 3 (social)	−0.004	−0.029	−0.153*	−0.076	−0.018
Social and political involvement:					
Factor 1 (public sphere)	0.149*	0.114	−0.154*	0.065	0.045
Factor 2 (private sphere)	0.103	0.150	0.011	−0.031	−0.038

The different categories are in accord with the different patterns of response.

***$p < 0.001$; **$p < 0.01$; *$p < 0.05$.

demographic group, tending to be of Asian or African origin, less educated, with big families and low incomes. Many among them are unemployed.

The Israeli Order. Like those agents who rank Jewish as their most important SI, those who rank Israeli as their most important component are strongly attached to the country, but the bases and justifications for attachment are different. For the agents of the Jewish order, the justification is primordial and religious, that is, it is the land of the Bible or the land of our forefathers. For the agents of the Israeli order, it is a shelter granted to the Zionist Jews by the United Nations in 1948. Like those with a strong Jewish identity, the Israelis trust the ability of the government and the armed forces to protect them, and tend to be passive and obedient citizens.

In all of the other criteria, the two orders based on collectivistic identities vary. Those with a strong Israeli identity tend to be left wing and feel that they have influence and control over national processes. They believe that the state should intervene in national security and economic processes, such as helping factories in financial difficulties, building new settlements, fighting crime, and keeping law and order. They are much more involved in their communities, at home and in schools. Demographically, their social profile is the complete antithesis to that of the Jewish order carriers: they are secular, Israeli-born or of Western origin, in which case they are older and not new immigrants. Most of them are older, employed with mid-level incomes, and have small families.

The Profession-Based Order. The social profile of those who ranked their profession highest seems somewhat alienated. They believe in their ability to influence national processes, but they are not attached to their communities or to the country, and consider emigrating from Israel more than do all of the other groups. Also, they do not trust the government and the armed forces to keep them safe, and their obedience is conditional; they do not believe that people should be obedient under any situation to authority. Politically, they are mostly left-wing. If they are involved in any social activity, it is one from which they or their families benefit directly. Their demographic profile is also different: they tend to be highly educated, Israeli-born or of Western origin, young men, mostly employed and with high incomes. They are also the least religious group, with many more holding active antireligious orientations. It seems that these are the carriers of individualistic orientations, much more so than the other types of agents. As in other societies, this group of younger, highly educated secularists seems to be the harbinger of social and value changes.[64] Those who define themselves in professional terms among the Arab sample are very similar to their Jewish counterparts: They accept the Israeli party system and tend to be leftist, they are considering emigration, and they are less dedicated to their communities and locales. They are also employed, more highly educated, and secular.

Arab Agents

Arab Order. Among the Arab sample, those who ranked the Arab identity as their major identity tend to vote for Arab parties rather than for the larger Israeli parties. They seem to reject the whole spectrum of the political system that is dominated by Jews. The lack of correspondence between this identity and a territorial solution may be because about 90 percent of Arabs desire territorial concessions. People in this category believe in their ability to influence political processes, they do not think that additional (paid) protection is necessary, and they are strongly attached to their communities and locales. The Arab identity is tied to being Muslim, so that Muslims— whether religious or not—place this identity higher than do Christian Arabs. Their education is also higher, and they are active in the public sphere.

Palestinian Order. Those who chose Palestinian as their most salient identity form a different social category. Even more than those who chose Arab as their major identity, they reject the Israeli political parties and favor Arab parties. They are Muslim and highly religious. They also believe in their ability to influence political processes, but unlike those with a strong Arab identity, they actively participate in social and political protest and do not believe that social obedience should always be maintained. Demographically, they tend to have large families, low incomes, and high levels of education. Taken together, these indicators seem to point to a more rebellious order, or to greater frustration with the existing system in which they occupy inferior socioeconomic positions.

Arab Israeli Order. Very few Arabs chose Israeli as their major identity, but they form a distinct group. More among them are Christian or Druze; fewer are Muslims. They tend to have smaller families and be more socially obedient. It also seems that this group is less politically defined than those who define themselves as Palestinian or Arab. Their political attitudes are less clear-cut, and they do not feel that they have social or political influence, or external control over their environment.

Pure Orders

Most of the respondents do not carry single and unambiguous societal orders, but rather mixed and sometimes contradictory elements that differ only by the weight they give them. However, some—and, we guess, the more influential, salient, and active agents—carry, produce, and reproduce pure orders. To detect them, we used a partialed-out analysis in which incongruous choices, such as when two major identities at the polar ends of the same continuum were ranked as first and second choices, were removed from the analysis, so that only those who gave an unrelated identity as their second choice were analyzed. This analysis examines the less conflicting combinations of components in the social order. We performed the analysis for the four major identities of the Jews; for the Arab sample, we considered only the Palestinian Arab combination because they were the only significantly overlapping identities. Table 2.4 presents the new correlations.

Pure Israeli Jewish Orders. Analyzing the Jewish sample shows that the patterns have changed for all of the examined identities, but the profiles of the Jewish and professional identities changed more drastically. Those who ranked family as their major identity but did not choose profession as their second identity are significantly against emigration from Israel. This may be because those with Jewish or Israeli identities are against emigration, and those identities are often chosen as the second-ranking identity by those who ranked family first.

Most of the attitudes of those who ranked Israeli but did not rank Jewish as their second identity have strengthened. Their feeling of control or influence has strengthened, they believe more strongly in Israel's military capability, and fewer among them plan to emigrate. In addition, they tend to be more traditional than those who chose both Israeli and Jewish components. Though they are not religious, they do not reject the religious parties.

The Jewish non-Israeli identity seems to be more extremist than the Jewish and Israeli combination. Those who choose this identity support annexation more strongly and believe in Israel's military capability to a greater degree than those with the combined Jewish Israeli identity. They are also more strongly attached to their communities and oppose emigration from the country more than any other group. In addition, those who rank being Jewish as their major identity but not being Israeli as their second identity feel they have more influence on sociopolitical occurrences in Israel than the Jewish-Israeli identity combination. These changes may be due to the tendencies of the pure identities to carry a more simplistic order.

The most significant changes occurred for those who chose professional identity but did not rank the family as their second identity. In this case, the reduced number of respondents influenced the significance of relationships. But the change seems deeper than that: Those who choose two individual identities tend to opt much more for an individualistic social order than those who choose only one such identity. Hence, the two individualistic trends strengthen and enhance each other. When those who chose family as their second identity are removed from the analysis,

Table 2.4 Spearman correlations with partialed-out identity components

Variable	Jewish identity (N = 687)	Israeli identity (N = 677)	Family identity (N = 949)	Professional identity (N = 630)	Arab identity (N = 149)	Palestinian identity (N = 145)
Political ideology						
(Arab parties = 1, else = 0)	—	—		-0.305***	-0.349***	
(left = 1, else = 0)	0.206***	-0.098**	-0.035	-0.140**	0.072	0.267***
(center = 1, else = 0)	0.088*	-0.057	0.014	-0.095*	0.202	0.131
(right = 1, else = 0)	-0.099**	0.074*	-0.032	-0.013	—	—
(religious = 1, else = 0)	-0.297***	0.046	0.151***	0.206***		
Territorial solution						
(1 = annexation; 5 = concession)	0.233***	-0.085*	-0.064*	-0.007	0.029	-0.075
Emigration plans						
(1 = yes; 2 = not at all)	-0.131***	-0.117**	-0.065*	0.093*	0.096	-0.022
Dedicated to neighborhood						
(1 = very; 4 = not at all)	0.096**	0.026	-0.023	-0.064	-0.133	0.025
Private protection						
(1 = 20 NIS; 7 = 500 NIS or more)	-0.013	-0.003	-0.048	0.088*	-0.072	-0.112
Military ability to protect						
(1 = high; 6 = low)	0.081*	0.89*	0.047	0.010	0.046	-0.179*
Influence						
(1 = yes; 4 = none)	0.091*	0.134***	-0.052	0.065	0.156	0.244**
Social obedience						
(1 = yes; 4 = no)	0.68	0.096	0.103**	-0.044	-0.090	-0.177*

Table 2.4 Spearman correlations with partialed-out identity components

Variable	Jewish identity (N = 687)	Israeli identity (N = 677)	Family identity (N = 949)	Professional identity (N = 630)	Arab identity (N = 149)	Palestinian identity (N = 145)
Protest (1 = yes; 4 = no)	-0.086*	-0.039	-0.022	-0.026	0.131	0.250**
Religion (1 = Orthodox; 6 = antireligion)	0.420***	-0.066	-0.91**	-0.238***	0.151	-0.141
Sex (1 = men; 0 = women)	0.001	-0.036	0.165***	-0.089*	0.012	-0.100
Education (1 = none; 8 = academic)	0.141***	-0.016	0.028	-0.190***	-0.153	-0.074
Employment (1 = working; 0 = not working)	0.090*	-0.052	0.004	-0.231***	-0.084	-0.063
Income (1 = less than 700; 9 = 5000+)	0.126***	-0.056	0.111**	-0.183***	-0.063	-0.162
Family size (1 = 1 person; 9 = 9 or more)	-0.168***	0.018	-0.005	0.025	-0.141	-0.300***
Father's origin (1 = Eastern; 2 = Israeli; 3 = Western) (For Arabs: Muslims = 1, else = 0)	0.144***	-0.040	-0.049	-0.060	-0.182*	-0.384***

(continued)

Table 2.4 Spearman correlations with partialed-out identity components (*continued*)

Variable	Jewish identity (N = 687)	Israeli identity (N = 677)	Family identity (N = 949)	Professional identity (N = 630)	Arab identity (N = 149)	Palestinian identity (N = 145)
Immigration (1 = Israeli born; 9 = 1980+)	−0.002	0.102**	−0.048	0.006	—	—
Age	0.007	−0.086*	−0.063	0.158***	−0.035	−0.026
Role of the state:						
Factor 1 (security)	0.059*	0.036	0.027	−0.016	0.038	0.125
Factor 2 (economic)	−0.051	−0.057	0.12	−0.104**	0.028	0.090
Factor 3 (social)	−0.044	0.040	−0.074	−0.050	−0.082	−0.046
Social and political involvement:						
Factor 1 (public sphere)	0.061*	0.26	0.025	0.46	0.164*	0.112
Factor 2 (private sphere)	0.030	0.070*	0.007	0.052	0.077	0.102

***$p < 0.001$; **$p < 0.01$; *$p < 0.05$.

collective values seem to moderate their alienation: fewer among them consider emigration or doubt the ability of the state and the armed forces to protect them, but at the same time they are the only category willing to pay for private protection agencies. Also, the group that chose profession as their primary identity but not the family as a second choice is less distinct demographically: Family size and ethnic origin are not significant for this group as they were for those who chose both profession and family as their major identities.

Pure Israeli Arab Orders. Among partialed-out identities in the Arab sample, we focus only on the Arab and Palestinian identities. The minimal overlapping in the other identities does not justify the analysis. Comparing the correlations in Tables 2.3 and 2.4, we find that here too, the separated identities tend to represent and reproduce more extremist orders than the combined identities. Both the Arab but not Palestinian and Palestinian but not Arab identities support specific Arab parties more than the combined identities do. The Arab identity holders who did not choose Palestinian as their second identity do not oppose leftist parties as do those with combined identities, though they still reject right wing parties. This may be interpreted as a willingness to cooperate with the Israeli left to attain common goals, and to accept the Israeli order. Also, the Arabs but not Palestinians tend to be more orthodox than those with combined identities, the partialed-out Arab and Palestinian identities are more typical of Muslims, and it seems that Muslims tend to separate these identities more than do Christians.

The Palestinian, non-Arab identity seems even more extremist. Strongly supportive of Arab parties and movements, they reject the Israeli identity, belittle Israeli military capability, and believe in their ability to influence social and political processes. They are also much less obedient and more willing to protest.

In sum, for both Jews and Arabs, an agent who carries two collective identities seems to moderate the sociopolitical order because the combination creates conflicting loyalties and demands. Sociopolitical conflicts are sharpened when people choose less conflicting identities. Choosing two individualistic identities strengthens attitudes and sharpens the demarcation lines among competing orders. SIs exist independently of specific political or social issues and their components are meaningful to individuals even when an issue is not specified. Thus, there is no single identity component that is salient for all Israelis.

Discussion

This paper proposes a synthesis between two distinct sociological traditions—one a general theoretical approach and the other a more empirically based tradition—to deal more meaningfully with the basic problem of sociology, that is, the production and reproduction of the social order. The analyses seem to validate and support our hypothesis that social identity has a broader meaning than is usually given to it in sociological theory, which almost always disconnects identities from their role in the formation of social order and change. Locating the term and essence of the identities in the context of the construction of social orders—and perhaps disorders and changes, topics that we did not touch upon at this stage[65]—we suggest a new way to look upon identities, agency, and the meaning of social order, as well as the methodology of its investigation.

In this case, the question of causality, that is, whether social order determines identity or vice versa, is not so crucial because we assume a continuous interplay between agent and structure. The model assumes that as free-floating identities exist in the system, so the possibility of an agent to adopt some of them exists, giving different weights for specific elements and for diverse combinations of these elements. However, the numbers and combinations of identity elements are limited. Many elements of a unified identity carried by agents, or their mixtures, were not present or were statistically negligible. Such rare configurations did not constitute parts of the social order, but might be the nucleus for formations in future orders and potential structures. We assume that situational constraints, present cultures and structures, and internal and external social control tend to minimize the possible combinations of major identities. A given order probably also attempts to influence the contents of already existing identities, such as the meaning of femininity and masculinity, by rewarding or punishing different ways to perform gender roles.

In conclusion, we have not forgotten that individuals belong by free choice or ascriptive ties to real and concrete social groups and collectivities, and that they are even born into specific identities. Our point is that they can play with other options. We tested a part of our thesis within a very specific context, using a sociologically convenient case, in which an ongoing battle between different components of the society over the preferred order is closely connected with the collective identities, but at the same time, this *kulturkampf* has not erupted into a chaotic civil war (yet?) and the battle over order is still managed within the boundaries of certain accepted rules. The cost of using such a well-defined case seems to be to marginalize the role of additional identities that we suspect in other case studies would be more central to the structure of the system, such as religion, gender, or locality. However, despite the relatively restrictive character of the Israeli case, by examining agency through identities, we have demonstrated how a large margin of possible choices and combinations of diverse identities is given to agents, making possible the constitution of alternative orders.

CHAPTER THREE

The Formation Process
of Palestinian Collective Identities

*The Ottoman and Colonial Periods**

Palestinian history reached a significant turning point with the signing of the Declaration of Principles by Yitzhak Rabin, the late Israeli prime minister, and Yasir Arafat, the late chairman of the Palestine Liberation Organization, on September 13, 1993. More agreements followed, and as they were gradually implemented in a part of historic Palestine—the West Bank and Gaza—they seemed at the time to point toward a full state of self-determination for the Palestinians. About a year before the signing of the Declaration of Principles, within the framework of a larger survey, the Arab population of the occupied territories was asked about their ultimate loyalties, interpreted here as an expression of their major collective identities.[1] The distribution of their attitudes at that time appears in Table 3.1.

From a historical perspective, the most striking finding is the almost complete rejection of a pan-Arabist collective identity, the persistence of fa-

* From Baruch Kimmerling, "Process of Formation of Palestinian Collective Identities: The Ottoman and Colonial Periods," *Middle Eastern Studies* 36, no. 2 (April 2000): 48–81.

Table 3.1 (in percent)

	Men	Women
Arab nation	3	1
Islamic nation	25	12
Palestinian people	30	37
Family	38	50

milial identity, and what seems to be an increase in Islamic identity among men and its rejection by women, in favor of familial identity and Palestinian nationalism. Palestinian identity is not a self-evident identity, just as many types of political nationalism are not self-evident, authentic, and natural, as many nationalist elites and theoreticians would like to argue. Historically, Palestinianism is a recent creation, which even Arab and Palestinian nationalists themselves sometimes admit. Palestinianism is hardly an invented tradition imposed by elites on a group of people without any common past or collective memory, but the past was interpreted differently in various periods in accordance with contradictory group interests.

Whenever an independent Palestinian educational system is built, it along with a more or less consensual national culture and civil religion will legitimize the sociopolitical order by creating a coherent Palestinian historiography. But such a historiography cannot be constructed on an ahistorical, mythological link to the Canaanitees on one side and the martyrs of the current armed struggle on the other. From antiquity to the present, however these are defined, the story of the creation of the Palestinian people resembles a Lego set, constructed and reconstructed from diverse components and colors. From this point of view, the Palestinian case study is excellent for testing theories of nationalism in its embryonic forms.

A collective identity is not necessarily a national identity; however, it is a necessary precondition for it. Collective identities are an essential part of the process of constructing, maintaining, and changing the constitution of different levels of social order, from small groups (familial or local) to large collectivities (class, ethnic, religious, or national) or even transnational entities.[2] They are also an integral part of the makeup of the individual level of identities and feelings of loyalty toward different sociopolitical entities. Collective identities allow individual members, in actual or desired, existing or imagined communities,[3] to make sense of "us" versus "them" and the creation of societal boundaries.[4] Identities are membership cards and social passports, determining the objective and subjective location of individuals and groups within a society and articulating the social goods they are entitled to possess in terms of prestige, power, and wealth.[5] Collective identities are not necessarily mutually exclusive, and individuals and groups can be considered and consider themselves to belong to different collectivities at the same time. Individuals and groups are also tied to a nuclear or extended family, a community, a locality, a region, or a class. For larger collectivities—such as ethnic, racial, or religious entities, states, nations, multinational states, empires, cultures, or civilizations—collective identities craft physical and social boundaries, the domestic social order, and the accepted rules of the game that govern the collectivity. Social change is expressed and reflected by changes occurring within collective identities, and fundamental internal struggles take place around adopting competing collective identities.[6] Hegemonic sociopolitical orders are based on a single unchallenged collective identity, supported by strong political strata, classes, and ethnic groups, among other entities.

Collective identities are not free-floating ideas; they tend to organize themselves within concrete institutional and political arrangements and organizations. Existing societal entities and orders create, adopt, or imagine identities for themselves to gain legitimacy and stability and improve their ability to mobilize the members of a collectivity. Sometimes identities are forcefully imposed on diverse groups, especially subjugated and minority groups, as a part of their surveillance and control. In this spirit, paraphrasing Charles Tilly's famous saying, it is helpful to assume that states make collective identities—nationalist identities or any other type—and that collective identities make states. To expand this idea, it must be presumed that different types of states produce different types of identities, and that different identities will shape different types of collectivities and different degrees of stateness.[7]

The present paper has three main purposes. First, it seeks to analyze the creation, invention, production, and reproduction of the collective identity called Palestinian, as a distinct identity from other Arab identities, in its particular historical, social, cultural, and political contexts, as well as in competition with other competing friendly and alien identities. Second, it aims to understand the role of the rise of an ideology of Palestinism, which politicized and intellectualized the Palestinian collective identity. Finally, it explores the institutional arrangements and institution-building processes that accompanied or blocked the development of Palestinian identity, or perhaps identities. In many ways, the crystallization, failure, and later partial and conditional success of the Palestinian attempt to survive as a distinct collectivity and identity has many parallels among the other new nations of the postcolonial era, but at the same time, the Palestinian case has several unique characteristics.

The Notion of *Asabiyya*

In the fourteenth-century, Arab philosopher Abd al-Rahman Ibn Khaldun developed the concept of *asabiyya*, which in Arab cultures can be interpreted as a solidarity or identity group based on real or imagined blood or primordial ties, strengthened by actual or invented common ancestry.[8] The range (boundaries) and content of the *asabiyya* varied in time, space, and sociopolitical context. In the nomadic context it was interpreted as loyalty toward the tribe. In settlements it is expressed through participation in the *hamule*—the extended family or clan—a local rural or urban alliance for mutual protection.[9] Later *asabiyya* was expropriated for rival identities, such as the Islamic religious versus pan-Arabist secular *umma*, the cultural and sociopolitical equivalent to the European term of nation.[10]

The term *qawm* (people) has a similar connotation, but in a more politicized form, referring to loyalties toward the territorial space of the Fertile Crescent and Arabia, namely, Iraq and Greater Syria, including Palestine, Lebanon, Transjordan and Hijaz. The term *qawn* led to the adjective *qawmiyya*, mainly used as *alqawmiyya al-Arabiyya*, or a kind of a general Arab peoplehood. The complementary yet contrasting term was the adjective *watani*, or the noun *wataniyya*, which referred to loyalty to a local and particular region, standing apart from the *umma* or *qawmiyya*. Sometimes it is regarded in a pejorative form as regionalism (*iqlimiyya*) and condemned as a particularistic and factionalist orientation contradicting the principle of *asabiyya*.[11]

By and large, both concepts of *qawmiyya* and *wataniyya* were initially a direct response to Ottoman rule over the region and its accompanying doctrine, Ottomanism, as well as to the dispersion of European ideas of nationalism among the Arabs. Ottomanism was not just an extension of Turkish nationalism, which added an Islamic dimension, including the protection and control of core Islamic territories, such as Mecca and Medina in Hijaz, Jerusalem, Damascus and Baghdad. It was also an extension of a multiethnic world empire situated between Europe and Arabia. This location opened up even the most peripheral territories of the empire to different winds. Three not necessarily exclusive responses evolved out of the early twentieth-century transformation of Ottomanism into a secular Turkish particularistic nationalism, and its separation from the empire. The first response was political Arabism, which demanded Arab self-determination, but within the framework of the empire. The second response was a political disengagement from the empire, which took diverse forms in the different Arab polities and politics. Despite mixing the notions of *qawmiyya* and *wataniyya*, a wide variety of Arab states or would-be states were constituted. First there was Muhammad 'Ali's modernization, bureaucratization, and state building efforts in Egypt;[12] then Husayn ibn-'Ali Amir of Mecca's success in freeing himself and Hijaz from Ottoman influence and establishing a kind of autonomous state; Faysal ibn-Husayn's attempt to establish a modern enlarged Syrian state;[13] and the establishment of completely new entities, such as Iraq, Lebanon, and a reduced Syria. The third response to Turkish nationalism was the emergence of pan-Arabism, claiming that all Arabic-speaking peoples belonged to one great Arab nation independent of the existing empire. Some were inspired by the vision of recreating an all-embracing caliphate or empire, while others wanted to plant the seed for a local and particularistic nation-state.

The additional ingredient in the process of forming a collective identity on Arab-speaking lands, and the supplier of fuel for political motivation, is Islam. Islam has always been a highly politicized religion and a major force behind Arab conquests and empire building.[14] However, as Islam spread beyond the Arab world, the notion of *al-umma al-islamiyya*, the theory of existence of one organic and indivisible Muslim community, based on religious belief and a social and moral order of total obedience to the Qur'an, its practices (*sunna*), and the ruler (*caliph*) or other local representatives of Allah, replaced the notion of *al-umma al-'arabiyya*, the doctrine of the existence of one Arab nation. The Ottoman sultan, the secular and political ruler of the empire and the highest authority for all Muslims believers, and some court elite groups were the most prominent sources of this doctrine. Non-Arabic political orders, such as the Iranian Khomaynism, also tend to stress an all-embracing Islamic state theocracy, and most of Arab Islam tends to mix Arab local or general nationalism and Islam. Thus, Saudi professor Ahmad Muhammad Jamal asserted that "Arab familiarity with *asabiyya* was an authentic pattern of nationalism *long before* [my emphasis] the historical phenomenon related to this ideology took place in Europe or the Americas."[15] The same arguments are stressed by some Jewish historians, including Anthony Smith, regarding the complete overlapping between religion and ethnic nationalism in Judaism.[16]

On the eve of the birth of contemporary Arab nationalisms, which are considered by many as a revolt or secular replacement for religion, Ottomanism and Islam were considered in the region to be congruent forces. The first Arab nationalist thinkers, such as Muhammad 'Abduh (1849–1905), Muhammad Rashid Rida (1865–1935), and 'Abd al-Rahman al-Kawakibi (1854–1902), accepted the primacy of Islam but tried to harmonize it with the modern notion of nationalism. All Muslims were regarded as a single nation, regardless of ethnic, cultural, and linguistic differences. However, the thinkers argued that Islam was first and foremost an Arab religion, the Prophet was an Arab, and the Qur'an an Arabic book. Thus, an Arab renaissance was a necessary condition to restoring Islamic grandeur.

Geographic and Sociopolitical Boundaries

One of the most significant conditions, although not the only one, for the formation and creation of cultural, social, and political collective identities is the existence of geographic or physical boundaries, facilitating certain types of social and political configurations. Moreover, as stated by Armstrong, "geographic boundaries are not only tangible, they possess other important attributes, they often acquire intense symbolic significance, and the direct impact of political action is frequently earliest and strongest in a geographic context."[17] Even though the precise boundaries of the territory later denoted as modern Palestine were never defined, and from time to time the region was politically or administratively fragmented, the area has since time immemorial been a distinct territory, commonly referred to as the Holy Land (al-Ard al-Muqadassa). This religious territorial identity was mainly reinforced by its indisputable geopolitical and symbolic center, Jerusalem (or al-Quds in Arabic). The Jewish mythological kings, David and Solomon, established the city as their capital there three thousand years ago, making it the site of the Jewish Temple after it was captured from the Canaanites. The Holy Land was the land of Jesus's birth and Christianity's source; Jerusalem was where he preached his final sermon and was crucified. Finally, according to Islamic interpretation (Sura 17 of the Qur'an), Jerusalem was the site of the prophet Muhammad's ascension to heaven.

The territory has several natural boundaries. To the west is the Mediterranean Sea, to the east running north to south is the Jordan River, which

flows into the Dead Sea, and the southern boundary is a vast desert running from Arabia to the Nile. Only the northern boundary is somewhat
blurry, even though the Litani River has usually served as a demarcation
line. The country itself is divided into four natural regions surrounding Jerusalem. The first region is that of the central mountains, Jabal al-Quds,
today commonly known as the West Bank, with its biblical cities of Nablus
and al-Khalil (Hebron). This region was the central area of the ancient Jewish civilizations of the Judean and Samaritan kingdoms, and during the past
three hundred years, it was the core territory of the traditional Arab peasant
society. A narrow coastal plain extends from the small city of Gaza in the
south through Haifa's bay in the north, passing through the Karmil region
up to Sidon. Here the old maritime civilizations, such as the Phoenicians
and Philistines, settled and left the cities of Gaza, Jaffa, Acre, and Haifa. The
coastal area should be seen more as a frontier than as a boundary zone because it places Palestine within the Mediterranean basin's climatic, political,
commercial, and economic system. The third and most fertile zone includes
the valleys and hills of al-Jalil—the biblical Galilee—extending from the
city of Acre to the territory's northern area, which incorporates the valley
of Marj Ibn Amir Baysan (the Jezreel Valley). These lands were the major
agricultural reservoirs of the territory and were cultivated by the mountain
peasants when they felt secure from human predators. Finally, the other
frontier region was the desert extending south from Bir al-Sab'—Beersheba—located on the crossroads of nomadic Bedouin tribes and desert-cross-
ing merchant caravans traveling from Asia to Arabia. All of these regions
served from time to time as bases of sub-identities reinforced by regional
coalitions; however, for a long time, the most important and salient collective identities were built on localities. The small rural localities overlapped
with the larger familial identities, loyalties, and authorities. Within this traditional order, the individual was not considered a distinct social category,
except when one was fulfilling a prominent political or bureaucratic role.

Around 1850, the point from which reasonable estimations based on
available Ottoman records are possible, the territory was populated by
about 340,000 permanent inhabitants[18]—300,000 Muslims, 27,000 Christians, mostly Arabs, and 13,000 Jews. In 1882, when the modern Jewish
colonization of the territory began, there were 462,000 inhabitants, 15,000
of whom were Jews. The most important process in the territory was the
rapid development of the coastal cities, mainly of Jaffa and the new road
that directly connected it to Jerusalem in 1869 and the hinterland with the

world market. The inland hilly villages and traditional townlets, such as Nablus, which competed for primacy with Jerusalem and the coastal urban centers, supplied the coastal cities with their products and crops as well as a growing labor force, which soon created a new semi-urban underclass, the *shabab*.[19] The most important characteristic of this new class was its detachment from the old traditional familial loyalties, without being committed to any new loyalties. As such, it was a stratum without any common identity. In exchange, the city granted occasional economic rewards and a degree of protection from the tyranny of the authorities, as well as a springboard for new opportunities and ideas.

Mutual dependence led to a system of enmity and amity between the coastal region and mountainous hinterland, between a rapidly urbanizing and secularizing area and a more traditional and religious realm.[20] The mountainous peasant society regarded the urban notables and wealthy merchants as influenced by corrupt non-Islamic ideas and practices. Throughout the Ottoman period, except for a very brief period of time,[21] the land was divided administratively,[22] with physical, economic, and social conditions creating the contours of a more or less common stratified system of the country later called Palestine. This common system was reinforced by the rise of a weak but common field of authority. The one source of authority was the legal-religious prominence of the Jerusalemite *'ulama*—the religious learned class—the *shari'a* courts, the heads of the *al-awqaf*, the Muslim religious endowment, and the special position of the *mufti*, which for Jerusalem tended to impose its authority over all of the other local religious authorities in the Holy Land, with accountability to Istanbul alone. At the time, Istanbul was the highest Muslim authority in the world after the conquest of the Fertile Crescent and Hijaz. Especially after the defeat of the Ottomans, the Jerusalemite *'ulama* largely succeeded in acquiring control over the appointments of all of the clerical positions of the territory, including the appointment and dismissal of *quadis* (*shari'a* court judges) or Quar'anic school teachers. The emphasis of the special status of Jerusalem was legally expressed in 1887, when it was declared an independent administrative unit, directly responsible to Istanbul.

The other source of Jerusalem's authority was the concentration of large and notable families within its district. One of the aims of the 1864 District Act was to shift the responsibility for tax collection and conscription from the rural chieftains (*shaykhs*) to the more powerful and rich urban notables (*a'yan*), who in turn gained wealth and power. The Ottoman reforms of

1839–76, the so-called Tanzimat, included a law in 1858 on registering and parceling the land. This introduced into the territory the notion of private titles and the possibility of accumulating land and creating large estates.[23] It also created another precondition for the rise of notions of the individual and individualism.

The institutions appointed to carry out the new policy were the newly established local councils (*majalis al-idra*), which were mainly constituted by townsmen who paid high taxes.[24] The Jerusalem families—such as the Khalidis, Nusaybas, Nashshibis, Husaynis, Dajanis and 'Alamis—on the surface seemed less wealthy than other large families in the country; however, they were better educated, both in religious and civic terms, and were more powerful politically due to their century-long tradition of service in the Ottoman political, bureaucratic, and cultural system.[25] For centuries, these notable families, especially the Jerusalemites, generated an imperial Ottoman collective identity. In this case, Ottomanism meant that the empire was seen as the direct inheritor of the Arab caliphate and an embodiment of the universal Islamic state, which on one hand protected the faithful from European and Western colonialism and on the other hand permitted slow technological changes and administrative reforms to adapt the empire's economic, political, and social fabric to the changing world. Only Muslims were considered as political subjects entitled to full rights, while others, such as Christians (including Arab-Christians) or Jews, were considered as protected minorities (*dhimi*) who had to accept the supremacy of Islam, pay a poll tax (*ferde*), and accept certain social disabilities, such as a prohibition on bearing arms. Thus, the boundary of the collectivity and its identity was sharply defined politically by religious criteria. All subjects of the empire sustained a double loyalty toward the sultan as both a political head of state and the head of the faithful. Ottomanism was of course a very convenient ideology for the notables because, as go-betweens for the local population and the empire, they were the major benefactors of the sociopolitical order. For most of the period, Ottoman rule of the districts in southern Syria (Surya al-Janubiyya), later known as Palestine,[26] was weak enough that it was possible for local clans, strongmen, and even Bedouin chiefs to rule local areas de facto, imposing law and order in the name of the empire in exchange for protection tributes. The authority of Istanbul was mostly exercised within the cities, in some of the hinterland, and along the main roads. The other dimension of this situation was the perpetual political but no less bloody quarrels between the rival clans and rulers of the diverse regions.

The Forgotten Revolt

Starting in 1831 and for approximately ten years, Syria, including the future Palestine, was conquered, taken out of the orbit of Ottoman rule, and placed under the control of an Egyptian ruler, Muhammad 'Ali, a former vassal of the Ottomans, and his son Ibrahim Pasha, the commander-in-chief of the Egyptian army. On May 19, 1834 a meeting of important families and sheiks from Nablus, Jerusalem, and Hebron took the dangerous step of informing the Egyptian military governor that they could no longer supply their quotas of conscripts for military service. The peasants, they asserted, had fled from the villages into the mountainous areas, which were difficult to reach. This group was led by Qasim al-Ahmad, chief of the Jamma'in subdistrict of Jabal Nablus.

Ibrahim, who desperately needed more soldiers after he suffered heavy causalities in previous battles and was planning another round against the Ottomans, saw the notables' declaration as a betrayal and rebellion. The first clash between the local *fellahin* and Bedouin tribes broke out in the Hebron area, where about twenty-five Egyptian soldiers who arrived to impose the conscription order were killed. However, the center of the resistance against the Egyptians was Nablus, from which hundreds of rebels laid siege to Jerusalem, the symbol of the government. The turning point occurred when the Abu Ghush clan, which controlled the road between Jaffa and Jerusalem as well as the surrounding villages, joined the rebel forces. On the last day of May 1834, the Muslims of Jerusalem opened the city's gates and the rebels conquered the city, except for its citadel, where Egyptian troops found shelter. In June, Ibrahim launched a series of counterattacks using heavy artillery and managed to regain control of Jerusalem, but at a cost of thousands of casualties and without quelling the spread of the revolt. The small townlet of Haifa was placed under siege and the ancient towns of Safed and Tiberias fell under rebel control.[27]

Most of the territory of Palestine was removed from Egyptian control, and the defeat of the Egyptian army in Palestine endangered the success of Muhammad 'Ali's state-building project, which forced him to take immediate action. His fleet, including a reinforcement of 15,000 troops armed with cannons and led by Muhammad 'Ali himself, arrived in Jaffa. However, his first move was diplomatic: Through a skilled reading of the sociopolitical map of Palestine, he managed to split the coalition of rebellious notables by guaranteeing amnesty to the Abu Ghush clan and diverse concessions, including positions in the Egyptian administration. From that point on, the roads both to Jerusalem and inland were open and secure for Egyptian troops. On July 4, 1834 the punishment expedition began, first against the Nablus region. Sixteen villages on the road were reduced to ash, and the town of Nablus was conquered on July 15. The last battle leveled Hebron on August 4, and saw the slaughter or conscription of most of the men, the rape of women, and the abduction of about 120 adolescents to serve at the disposal of Egyptian army officers. Parts of the Muslim population, some of the notables of Jerusalem, and all of the Bethlehem notables were removed, held captive, or killed. Ten thousand *fellahin* were recruited and shipped to Egypt, and the local population was disarmed.

The 1834 revolt was triggered by the conscription duties, the gathering of arms from the Muslim population, and the tax collection that was imposed on peasants and city-dwellers by the Egyptians, who were more efficient than was the previous Ottoman system. Other important reasons for the rebellion include the facts that, for the first time, an almost countrywide coalition of Bedouin, *fellahin,* and notables formed, incorporating a wide variety of social and regional segments into a single cooperating movement. The Egyptian central administration's threat to the *a'yans'* traditional political and material power base as tax collectors[28] and administrators was another important reason for the upheaval. Introducing a secular legislature restricted the power of *shari'a* bureaucracy and made bureaucrats dependent on state salaries and rules. The rebels heavily emphasized the Islamic religious meaning of revolt, presenting Muhammad 'Ali as an infidel (*gavur*) and an ally of foreigners—Europeans, Westerners, and others. The Bedouin tribes' primary occupation of protecting merchants and other clients was diminished as a result of the vigorous Egyptian law-enforcement policy, giving them an incentive to join the rebellion.

Thus, the Egyptian conquest of Palestine, according to Shamir,[29] signified "the first application of the concept of territorial state . . . This was the inception of the modern history of Palestine." The 1834 revolt was the result of different segments of the territory's population facing a common threat stemming from the changes that had taken place in the relations between rulers and subjects, the fabric of social stratification and order, and perhaps the cosmic order. Momentary coalitions among the various segments of the population did not instantly create a new kind of *asabiyya* and loyalty, but they may have set the preconditions for a new self-consciousness or collective identity. The geopolitical, economic, and cultural conditions already existed for such an identity, carried by local dialects of Arabic, customs, fellahin clothing, and other factors. These were complemented by a distinct, stratified system in an embryonic state, which facilitated the coalitions and the budding identity consciousness.

Another scholar writes that

> the decade of the Egyptian invasion can now be seen to have cut across the spectrum of Middle Eastern history like a band. The old ways of life were profoundly altered. The balance of power and expectations in which the Druze, Christians and Muslims; the townsmen, villagers, and Bedouins; and the *amirs*, *sheikhs* and peasants had lived was shattered. The relationship of the government to the governed, the market to the producers, the foreigner to the native were radically changed.[30]

Despite this, the Egyptians could not or did not have enough time to provide a sense of collective identity, at least for the notables and other elite groups, which Ottomanism had partially succeeded in doing. Individual or familial loyalties, such as the Abd al-Hadis of Nablus toward Muhammad 'Ali or Ibrahim, only contributed to the depth of the internal cleavages that occurred in this society in the making. The divisions also seem to have been a contributing factor to the revolt, which introduced a bud of a common Islamic identity, disconnected from the original Ottomanism: a prototype of popular Islam, in which Islam provides not only a basis for *asabiyya*, but an organizing principle in which the mosque becomes an institution for mobilization, revolt (at least in Jabal Nablus), and the dissemination of information.

In Palestinian collective memory, this bloody event has fallen by the wayside—in contrast with the contemporary Great Arab Revolt of 1936–39 or the intifada—and is not considered in Arab or Egyptian historiography as anything other than the Syrian Peasant Revolt, even though it focused on the quadrant of Jaffa, Nablus, Hebron, and Jerusalem, with only the ricochets reaching Lebanon, Syria, and the southern desert. But this is not surprising, for until recently, the Palestinians were a people without a codified written history and a highly fragmented collective memory, mainly based on local and regional traditions, a common feature to other developing nations in the world.[31] The 1834 revolt, just as Bernard Lewis described, "is the history of events and movements, that is to say, at some stage and for some reason rejected by the communal memory, and then, after a longer or shorter interval, recovered by academic scholarship—by the study of records and the consequent reconstruction of a forgotten past."[32] The humiliating and traumatic events of 1834 were conveniently erased from the collective memory and were documented mainly by the Egyptian bureaucracy, as the local social and political actors had no interest in remembering and glorification. Once Ottoman rule was restored in 1841, following diplomatic bargaining and arrangements between Muhammad 'Ali, the Ottomans, and the European powers, seemingly no one in the territory had any interest in mythologizing a revolt mainly involving interior hill-region peasants[33] and against taxes and conscription, which continued to be both in the local notables' and Ottoman rulers' interests. The notables of the territory were deeply interested in maintaining a cordial relationship with the neighboring Egyptian power, one of the main commercial and cultural links to the outside world; at the same time, they wanted to readjust themselves to Ottoman rule, which vigorously continued the Egyptian reformist policy under the label of the Tanzimat of the 1840s and 1860s, insofar as they had the power to initiate change.

Identity, Boundary Formation, and World Order

Connections with the outside world—mainly European markets, merchants and their merchandise, missionaries, pilgrims, tourists, consuls, and settlers—had different effects on the native population of the territory. On one hand, especially in a xenophobic traditional milieu, contact with aliens is one of the strongest triggers for forming boundaries between "us" and "them," and a base from which a separate and distinct collective identity can be created. On the other hand, the penetration of local space by strangers can fragment local structures, deepen existing cleavages, and create and encourage particularistic vested interests. In the pre-colonial Holy Land, both trends existed and complemented one another.

The Crimean War (1854–56) and the American civil war (1861–65), though remote, accelerated several developments in future Palestine. Until then, the territory had pretty much escaped the effects of the Industrial Revolution. Short-term consequences of the two wars, however, created shortages in certain raw materials and crops, especially cotton crops, which hurt the English and continental industries and increased the demand for agricultural cash crops, raising prices in the world market. Merchants and investors from the Mediterranean basin expanded their search to the east of the basin, reaching the coasts of Gaza, Jaffa, Acre, Haifa, and Sidon. They found as go-betweens the local rural *a'yan* and merchants. Acquiring crops and cash advances provided incentives for local merchants and notables to accumulate land and establish relatively large estates. A new land-owning self-conscious class, backed by the Tanzimat reforms, was created.

Most of the southern hinterlands around Gaza were devoted to growing wheat, barley, and maize for export. Other parts of the territory, such as the valleys and northern coastal plain, grew cotton and sesame. In more mountainous areas, olives—manufactured as oil and soap—and grapes were cultivated. On the coastal plain between Gaza and Jaffa, orange and lemon orchards appeared, demanding sophisticated cultivation, irrigation, financing, and marketing skills. Cash crops such as olives and sesame had long been known as specialties of the territory, but widespread cotton cultivation and intensive orchard planting, requiring large long-term investments, were a major economic and social innovation.[34] All of them were triggers for major changes in land holding; the rise of a new wealthy urban stratum; the continuous enlargement of the urban underclass of the major coastal cities, especially Jaffa, which became a relatively modern Mediterranean city;[35] and a new Arab leadership, which would stay in power until the collapse of the Palestinian polity in 1948. The Jaffa-Jerusalem railroad connection in 1892 symbolized the opening up of the country to new technologies and communications systems, preceded by the telegraph services from Jerusalem in 1865. The Holy Land had been linked in both directions to the world system.

However, the Holy Land drew the attention of foreign powers less because of its economic importance and more for its religious, cultural, and later, for some of the great powers, strategic significance. After the destruction of the Christian Kingdom by Saladin, Christian interest in the Holy Land lay dormant for an extended period; however, in the mid-nineteenth century, the interest once again rose to the surface. Probably most of the 340,000 inhabitants of the territory were completely unaware of the importance of their locale to the rest of the world, and of how much planning, discussion, and competition among the elites of Christian, Western, and capitalist societies over the Holy Land had taken place.[36] As long as the Ottoman regime was powerful enough to protect the territory from an influx of strangers, it was a screen from the outside world. But as the capitulation system grew, patriarchates such as the Latin-Orthodox, Greek-Orthodox, and Anglican Church were established in Jerusalem in 1845–47, causing frictions between Greeks who were new to the area and native and nonnative Christian Arabs, who began to import Arab nationalistic ideas from Europe reinforced by reform-oriented Muslims.[37] Even more important, between 1838 and 1858, all of the great powers had heavy consular presences in Jerusalem, each of them protecting communities of expatriates, missionaries, churches, and later settlers in the city in particular and the Holy Land in general.

The first modern European settlers in the Holy Land belonged to the German Templar religious sect in the 1870s, followed in the 1880s by the first wave of traditional Jewish immigrants. Both groups primarily established agricultural colonies, and as such, from the local population's point of view, they had limited impact. However, they were a part of a larger cumulative process of the country opening up to aliens, which built a sense of the Holy Land as distinct from other parts of the region. This created imagined boundaries, distinct from the borders of the Ottoman administrative districts:[38] They lacked geographic, social, and political clarity, but had a clear and fixed center, the city of Jerusalem.

The Greater Syria Episode

Except for the development of Arab-Jewish relations as an incipient political conflict, little happened during the late Ottoman period within the territory. Retrospectively, the first wave of Jewish immigration proved to be the first step in a massive colonization enterprise, but at the time, it was small in scope and lacked explicit political aspirations and support. After 1904–05 a very different kind of Jewish immigrant arrived in the country: young, single, mainly male, highly politicized, and very poor. These immigrants turned to the existing Jewish colonies pushing the ideology of Jewish labor and Jewish defense, which entailed excluding Arab workers from the colonies and replacing the local strongman protection system with Jewish armed guards, forming the nucleus of a Jewish army.[39] They talked in terms of modern secular Jewish nationalism—that is, Zionism—about the goal of creating a Jewish political commonwealth. Several years later at the 1919 Paris Peace Conference, Chaim Weizmann, the president of the World Zionist Organization, stated that the Zionist goal was to make sure that "Palestine becomes as Jewish as England is English." For the first time the Jewish presence became noticeable, but because of its very limited scope, not yet threatening. During World War I the country suffered Turkish oppression, conscriptions, and famine, which not only halted Jewish immigration, but also decreased the scope of the Jewish presence in the country. After the British arrival the economic and social situations slowly improved. In general, however, British rule over the country had far-reaching consequences.

Even before the territory's occupation by British forces was complete, the well-known Balfour Declaration of November 1917 was announced, in which the British government viewed "with favor the establishment in Palestine of a national home for the Jewish people."[40] From the point of view of the majority Arab-Muslim population of the country, their own Islamic Ottoman rule had been replaced by an alien European and Christian power, which had a declared policy to transform the land into a Jewish country; the very presence of the British mattered.[41]

On October 5, 1918, Amir Faysal ibn Husayn proclaimed in Damascus an "independent Arab constitutional government with authority over all Syria," that would provide equal rights to its Muslim, Christian, and Jewish subjects. Local British military officers, including General Edmund Allenby, seemed to support the move and perceived it in the same spirit as Sir Henry McMahon's promise to the Sharif of Mecca, but in even greater harmony with British interests.[42] The French were ready to recognize the partial independence of the so-called Syrian nation if it remained under French control and influence, which was agreed after long negotiations in Paris with premier George Clemenceau and officials of Quai d'Orsay. This should have been be a major achievement for Faysal, but the agreement was rejected by most of the young and enthusiastic nationalists in Damascus, such as the members of al-Fatat and al-'Ahd (the Covenant). They would not accept relinquishing the great Syrian Arab national state and losing Palestine to Jewish colonialism and British imperialism.[43] At the end of July 1920, the French concentrated their troops and entered Damascus. Faysal and his men left the city and General Henri Gouraud was appointed high commissioner. The first twentieth-century attempt to establish a modern Arab nation-state failed,[44] but the idea survived.

Faysalism was, for a moment in Arab history, a great new hope—a new *asabiyya*, based on the postwar promise of a new world order and in line with Woodrow Wilson's promise of self-determination for all nations. It was a combination of a Syrian *wataniyya* with an all-Arab *qawmiyya*,[45] achieved by Arab forces. Damascus was "liberated" from the Ottomans not only by British and French troops, but also by the so-called Northern Arab Army, with its Sherifian flags and banners. Faysal's court was filled by the best Arab intellectuals and young professionals of the region, including Syrian,

Iraqi, Palestinian, and former Ottoman officers and civil servants. Even if Faysal's agreement of 1919 with Weizmann was attacked by his own adherents and considered by some to betray the Arab cause, it was an original political move with the aim of freeing Faysal from complete dependence on British and French control, through a limited cooperation with the Zionist movement.

The Palestinian association of al-Nadi al-'Arabi (the Arab Club), established in Damascus in 1918, was a substantial part of the Faysalian regime, together with other local nationalist groups such as al-Fatat, founded in Paris in 1911 by two Palestinian students, Awni Abd al-Hadi and Rafiq Tamimi, and the Arab Independence Party (Hizb al-Istiqlal al-'Arabi). However other groups, such as the local Damascus intellectuals and notables and the Al-'Ahd Iraqi nationalists, had their own agenda, each concentrated around the specific interests of their own territories. On June 3, 1919 the General Syrian Congress assembled in Damascus and included, in addition to the abovementioned groups, delegates from Lebanon, the Druze Mountains, and al-Karak (Transjordan). Faysal sought to exchange the French protectorate for English Mandatory power. The majority of the congress was more extreme, rejecting any idea other than an independent greater Syria, including Palestine, Lebanon, and the eastern region of the Jordan territories, and declared Faysal as the king of the independent state. The congress was still convening when the French troops occupied the city on July 28, 1920 suppressing what they defined as revolt.

Membership in a newly established Arab state was a solution to the desperate situation of the Arab inhabitants of Palestine. Thus the proclamation of the Faysalian state provoked in Palestine a stormier response than the reaction in other places. Implementing the Syrian Congress's aims meant nullifying the Balfour Declaration and the hope of freedom from British colonial rule. Without hesitation the Muslim population of Palestine adopted the identity and political program of Southern Syria and most of the newly created nationalistic feelings and energy.[46] The first public appearance of the young Palestinian leader Hajj Muhammad Amin al-Husayni was the organization of a mass demonstration on March 8, 1920, the day of Faysal's proclamation as King of Syria (and Palestine). Countrywide riots broke out when in April, during the holiday of al Nabi Musa, Amin al-Husayni raised a portrait of Faysal and shouted "Here is our king." The crowd replied with "Allah save the king" and attacked the Jewish quarter of Jerusalem.

During the short period of Faysal's rule in Damascus, thousands of Palestinian notables, teachers, professionals, and intellectuals signed and sent petitions to the British rulers as well as to the representatives of the great powers to express their willingness, in the name of the local population, to be included under Syrian rule, and their belief that the territory was a part of Syria, namely, Surya al-Janubiyya. A newspaper with this title was launched in Jerusalem in September 1919 to propagate the same idea. The other two veteran local newspapers, al-Karmil in Haifa and Filastin[47] in Jaffa, were mobilized for the same purpose. The First Palestinian Arab Congress, held in Jerusalem at the beginning of 1919, stated in its resolution that "we consider Palestine nothing but part of Arab Syria and it has never been separated from it in any stage. We are tied to it by national (*qawmiyya*), religious, linguistic, moral, economic, and geographic bonds."[48] After the fall of Faysal and the disappearance of the pan-Syrian option for the Palestinians, the Surya al-Janubiyya collective identity disappeared almost completely from the local political scene, though from time to time, it was brought back to life briefly.

The British Colonial State and the Building of Palestinism

If one major factor could be singled out that shaped and built the Palestinian collective identity and made the Palestinians into a people, but at the same time contributed to their failure, it would be the role of British colonial power. Not that Zionist colonization, the changing world order, the Arab world, and the Palestinians themselves were not important actors in this process, but the British were the crucial factor. Though somewhat out of the ordinary, the Palestinians were similar to other new and not-so-new nations at the time and a by-product of the colonial system. The British colonial state, in its legalistic mandated dress, gave the country its name— Palestine[49]—and defined for its people its final geographical, political, and social boundaries and identity.

Mandatory Palestine was a minimalistic state that supplied only the basic needs for its subjects: law and order, a monetary and fiscal system, basic but modern communication systems, a postal service, transportation infrastructure, such as roads, railways, telegraph, phone, and broadcasting services, and modest but not insignificant welfare, health, and education services. The welfare services were mainly for Arab subjects.[50] The British made considerable efforts to regulate and rationalize the agrarian and land system, mainly by trying to transform the *mu'sha* communal land holding into parcelized private titles, but also encouraged agrarian marketing cooperatives and the use of fertilizers through material incentives.[51] Municipalities and local self-management were also encouraged. For practical but also symbolic reasons, the colonial state provided to its subjects identity cards, passports, and a limited, conditional sense of citizenship and citizen rights in their Western meaning. In exchange for these services and "goods," the colonial state demanded minimal loyalty: acceptance of its legitimacy to rule, cooperation within the administration, and obedience to its laws.

At the same time, the British state provided the political and administrative umbrella for the creation of the Jewish-Zionist polity within the country, creating favorable conditions for immigrating to the country and purchasing land there. Under the Ottomans, more severe restrictions existed on both Jewish immigration and land acquisitions.[52] After the initial period of British rule, Zionist satisfaction with the scope and the rate of British immigration quotas and land policies ended, as the British began to limit the short-term growth and development of Jewish colonization. The policies were intended to ease the local Arab population's fears of increased development of the Jewish community, and from time to time, increased limitations were imposed on the growth of the Jewish presence in the country. Despite these obstacles,[53] the Zionists managed to create a continuum of Jewish territory, mainly on the coastal plain and the great valleys, with hundreds of new settlements, including a new city (Tel Aviv) and new neighborhoods in old cities (Haifa and Jerusalem). They constructed a viable economy, including industries, intensive agriculture (horticulture, orchards, and vineyards), educational systems (from kindergartens to a university) and their own culture (Hebrew vernacular, newspapers, publishing houses, and theaters). Most impressive was the Jewish immigrant-settler society's success in building separate and parallel political institutions and leadership to the colonial state, based on semi-volunteer participation and mechanisms for resource absorption and distribution, supported by a partially mobilized diaspora.[54]

Perhaps the local Arabs' greatest frustration was the nationalists' inability to wield enough social control over local landlords to prevent the sale of lands to Jews. The high prices that the Jews were able and ready to pay for land was a major temptation for the owners, and a perceived threat to the peasant society. The Arab community thus constantly demanded that the British restrict not only Jewish immigration, but also land transfers from one national group to another. Two institutions were established to combat the Jewish National Fund land purchases: the Arab Bank (1930) and the Arab National Fund (1931). Both failed to recruit enough funds for their purpose because of a lack of external resources. All of the major inquiry commissions on the "situation in Palestine" (Shaw Commission, Strickland's report, John Hope Simpson, Lewis French and Peel Commission reports)[55] found that even though it had not been established that a critical mass of Arab peasants and tenants had lost their holdings as a direct consequence of the Jewish land acquisitions,[56] the issue had become very threatening and had raised anxiety among the Palestinian peasant society. The Jewish land purchases directly reduced the land and territorial reservoirs of the local population, which was growing quickly. Together with the usual xenophobia in any traditional society, the land issue was one of the major causes of the creation of two kinds of consciousness that formed the bases of sub-identities: a popular nationalism rooted in enmity toward Jewish society and a popular class awareness rooted in enmity toward the *a'yan, effendi,* and other urban notables, who not only failed to protect them from British imperialism and Zionist colonialism, but were perceived as partners to the foreign powers, betraying the peasantry and the Arab peoples' interests. Both feelings were strongly expressed during the final stages of the Great Arab Revolt, when the national rebellion against the British and Jewish settlement turned into a bloody civil war of peasant gangs against city dwellers.

Institution Building and New Palestinism

Palestinism is a general belief that the Arab population of the British colonial state of Palestine became a collectivity distinct from the other surrounding states and states-in-making of the region, and at the same time a part of *al-qawmiyya al-Arabiyya,* from which the right of self-determination is drawn within the geographical boundaries of the Mandatory state. This belief appeared within a relatively short period of time, nourished by three factors: the regional political reality created after World War I, that is, the creation of other independent or would-be independent Arab *watani*; the actual creation of the British colonial state; and the rapid development of Jewish settlement, which aspired to the same goal for Jews over more or less the same territorial entity.[57] The development, spread, and penetration of this new *asabiyya* among various strata and groups of the Arab society of

Palestine was accompanied by an accelerated institution-building process in various spheres.

More or less concomitantly with the conquering of the territory by British troops, Muslim-Christian associations (MCAs) were formed in almost every city, town, and major locality. The MCAs sought to express an Arab-Muslim and Arab-Christian solidarity[58] in the face of the new ruler, which, in the Balfour Declaration as well the nomination on July 1, 1920 of a self-proclaimed English Zionist Jew, Sir Herbert Samuel, as high commissioner, appeared to endorse an explicit policy of making the country into a Jewish homeland. Most of the local notables and also considerable segments of the younger, educated professionals and intelligentsia were recruited to the MCAs. The MCAs launched petitions and formed delegations to voice their concerns to the representatives of the new rulers, demanding that Britain change its pro-Zionist policy and pay heed to the political rights of the country's Arab majority. The simultaneous, spontaneous, and grassroots creation of the MCAs exhibited impressive political skill and awareness on the part of the local elite,[59] though the MCAs' most important step was to acknowledge the Jerusalemian MCA as the de facto coordinator and leader of the new movement.

On December 13, 1920 the Third Palestinian Congress was held in Haifa by delegates of MCAs and other local clubs from all over the country, the second congress having been forbidden by the government following the April riots of the al-Nabi Musa feast. The congress elected an Arab Executive Committee, designed to be a unified representative of the Palestinian Arabs to the British authorities, a consensual political leadership for all of the Arabs of Palestine, and a counterbalance to the Jewish Agency.[60] The most important difference between the first and third congresses was not only the establishment of a local institutionalized leadership, but its inward shift of focus. Palestine was no longer regarded as a part of Syria or any other larger identity, but rather as a distinct polity unto itself. Among others resolutions, the Congress adopted one calling upon Britain to establish a national government (hukuma al-wataniyya) responsible to a representative assembly of members that would be chosen from "the Arabic-speaking people who inhabited Palestine until the outbreak of the War." In other words, the resolution was a demand to start the process of building an independent Arab state, within clearly defined sociopolitical boundaries and excluding non-Arabic speaking Ashkenazic Jews and Jews who immigrated during and after World War I.[61]

The Islamic Factor

The other focus of power in the emerging Palestinian society was created by the colonial state in cooperation with some the local leadership, but soon became an almost independent factor. Since the territory was cut out of the Ottoman state, it remained without central religious leadership for the majority Muslim population. To fill this vacuum, the Muslim population was defined as an autonomous religious community, or *millet*. Symbolically this was degrading to the Muslim population, because it meant leveling Muslim status to the status of the minority religious groups: the various Christians and Jewish communities.[62] However, institutionally, redefining the Palestinian Muslims as a religious community allowed the creation of local religious institutions and leadership. The Supreme Muslim Council, created in January 1922, had its presidency unified with that of the *mufti* of Jerusalem, and the young and militant Amin al Husayni was appointed to both of the offices, not without considerable resistance from the old religious and traditional leadership. Al-Husayni was a student at Egypt's most prestigious Qu'aranic institute, al-Azhar, where he was exposed to the teaching of Muhammad Rashid Rida. He was also a son of the powerful Husayni clan, and was suspected to be responsible for the 1920 riots following the Nabi Musa festival.[63]

The council and its president were British civil servants, but they gained a critical power position, creating a new Palestinian Islamic hierarchy. Control of the countrywide *al-awqaf*, the Islamic endowment, and the authority to appoint and dismiss all Islamic officials, such as *shari'a* court judges and clerks or mosque and Qu'ranic school system teachers, made al Husayni the most powerful Arab leader in the newly created colonial state. Sunni Islam held considerable power in the basically traditional Palestinian society, but because of the Ottoman legacy, it was not a dominant politicized ideology, except for a short trial during the reign of Sultan Abdulhamid II (1896–1909), when attempts were made to fight the European powers by using Islamic symbols.

Even before his appointment to the office of *mufti*, to which he added the adjective "the Great," Amin al-Husayni realized the political power of religion[64] and certainly perceived himself as the religious leader of Jerusalem and the Holy Land. He tried with some success to build himself international stature as an Islamic leader, convening an Islamic world conference in Jerusalem in 1931 and launching a successful worldwide campaign to renovate the al-Aqsa mosque in that city—only two of his many activities to accumulate more power within Palestinian society. He also knew that too heavy an accentuation on Islam and Islamic symbols would alienate the very important Arab Christian population from the national movement,[65] and almost from the beginning, al-Husayni tried to use his religious power for nationalist purposes. He launched a *fatwa,* a religious verdict, which entailed excommunicating any believer who sold land to Jews. As was done throughout the Muslim world, he used the mosques for political preaching and as a fast and efficient communication network in a traditional society. However, in the aftermath of World War I, Islam and pan-Islamism was not a salient movement, and its usefulness as a means of political mobilization was limited. Of course, from time to time, violent outbreaks in Palestine were connected with religious feelings and xenophobia, based on the suspicion that the Jews intended to destroy the al-Aqsa mosque and rebuild their ancient Third Temple. Fears such as these fueled Muslim anxiety, Muslim leadership exploited them, and all of the violent outbreaks were in one way or another connected with them. The Great Revolt of 1936–1939 was preceded by a challenge from a small militant Muslim group, using esoteric Islamic slogans and led by the charismatic sheikh Izz al-Din al-Qassam, who was killed in 1935 by British troops. Al-Qassam became the first martyr and hero for the Palestinian national movement.

Generally, Jewish settlement was perceived as a penetration of pure traditional Islamic society and its corruption by *kufrs* (non-believers), who were regarded as secularist, colonialist, imperialist, and communist. It was a general xenophobic and antimodern attitude, of which religion was only one ingredient. The life of the traditional religious peasantry was regarded as healthy and right, similar to the Russian Narodnik movement's views. The Jews and their women, who were pictured as the incarnation of evil, were perceived not only as a national enemy and an intruder on the land, but also as an entity that violated Islamic cosmic order.[66] This led to a binary perception of the sociopolitical world order, of the good, pure, Islamic peasant society versus the Jewish, British, corrupt, evil, yet always tempting wider society.[67] Thus Islam, especially its popular forms, was politicized and used for mobilization and socialization, but at the initial stage of the crystallization of the Palestinian collective identity, it was not a determinant factor. The Muslim Brotherhood, a political party established in Egypt by the sheikh Hasan al-Bana in 1928, spread into Palestine and formed several local branches in the 1930s. The sheikh Izz al-Din al-Qassam and his followers were an offshoot of this movement. However, during the colonial period, they never succeeded in becoming a country-wide political power.

Epilogue

The inner logic of the post–World War II era and the decolonization process was that the framework of the major state institutions and the colonial state's power and authority were usually transferred to the representatives of the majority population group. In Israel, however, this did not happen. When the colonial power left the country in 1948, no authority was officially transferred, either to the majority Arab-Palestinians or to the Jewish state in the making. The reasons for the Palestinians' collapse in this period preceded the 1948 war and are beyond the scope of the present analysis;[68] however, the results were far-reaching. The territory of colonial Palestine was broken up into three parts: Israel, the West Bank annexed to Transjordan, and the Gaza Strip, which was placed under Egyptian control.

Systematic and coercive attempts were made to de-Palestinize at least two of the regions, mainly through harsh political control and surveillance as well as educational attempts to reconstruct Palestinians' collective identity. The Hasemites imposed a Jordanian identity, and the Israelis created an Israeli-Arab identity. The rest of the Arab states preserved the Palestinian identity, but mostly within the framework of pan-Arabism—that is, the solution to the Palestinian problem was to lie only in the framework of a victorious establishment of an all-embracing Arab *qawmiyya*. But the Palestinian identity did not disappear. It was preserved in refugee camps, mainly by belonging to a certain village or city; thus third-generation camp-dwellers still perceive themselves as Jaffanians, Miarians, or Dier-Yassiners. After 1967 the three territorial parts of colonial Palestine were reunited under Jewish-Israeli control, which in many ways recreated the initial Palestinian condition. The major cleavage for the Palestinians was then between those who found themselves in their own country but under hegemonic Jewish rule, and those who remained in *gourba* (exile), out of the historic territory of Palestine and dispersed in different countries and continents. The Palestine Liberation Organization, led by Fatah[69] in its second stage, also contributed to building new kinds of Palestinian identities, mostly connected with the concepts of "armed struggle" and "popular resistance." The last turn in this process was the mutual recognition that has recently taken place between the Israelis and the mainstream of the Palestinian national movement, and the gradual establishment of the Palestinian National Authority in a small part of Palestine, as the territory was defined by the British.

Some Conclusions

The Palestinians are stateless yet working toward an ambiguous autonomy, at least for those who have lived in the territories occupied by Israel since the 1967 war. Like most new nations, the Palestinians' initial collective identity was in great measure shaped by a colonial power, which created for its own convenience the Palestinians' geographical, social, and political boundaries. These boundaries were far less arbitrary than in many other colonial cases, such as most of sub-Saharan Africa. Some contours of the future Arab Palestinian society, located between the Mediterranean coastal plain and Jordan River valley, existed long before the British colonial state. Classic scholars of nationalism perceived Palestinism as a natural and authentic expression of ancient primordial communities. Anthony Smith followed them demonstrating the ancient ethnic bases of political nationalism and the nation-state.[70] Ernest Gellner and Eric Hobsbawm, from very different perspectives, saw any national identity as a fabrication of elite groups and somehow an artificial product of Western modernity. Benedict Anderson refers to nationalism as a "cultural artifact transformed into an imagined community,"[71] which does not necessarily contradict any of the other approaches. This essay does not present an overall alternative thesis about the formation of national identities. The aim is only to present the sociopolitical preconditions and mainly external forces that lead to the formation of such an imagined entity. One of these preconditions in our case was the presence of the Jewish settler society, the effect of which grew as time passed and the Jewish presence became increasingly tangible. Yet Jewish settlement was only a part of the greater British colonial venture. Neither the Jewish settlers nor the British rulers perceived each other as extensions of their own systems, but by and large, the British rulers and Jewish colonizers complemented each other, at least from the point of view of the local Arab Palestinian population. Jewish settlement provided the British rulers with some of the functions of classic settler roles—in the economy, civil service, and in some cases, as a factor for control and surveillance of the local population. The Jews also drew some of the violence of local populations to them rather than to the colonial power. For the Jewish immigrant-settler society, British rule provided a limited political and military umbrella, ensuring within colonial law and order the possibility of growth by purchasing lands and enabling immigration, and the development of a society that was ready to switch from a state in the making to a sovereign nation-state when the colonial state ceased to exist. It was also very helpful for the Jewish polity in 1948 that the British colonial state's bureaucracy and institutions were not transferred to the Arab majority when colonial rule terminated; the Arabs of Palestine were not administratively or politically prepared for such a takeover. The colonial government allowed the Jews to build strong political institutions, but was not as friendly to Arab institution-building efforts. Meanwhile, the Jewish state in the making did not depend on the colonial state, and was institutionally prepared to replace it. This probably caused Palestinian political anxiety, and is one of the reasons that they relied so heavily on the help of the already sovereign Arab brother states, mistakenly transferring responsibility for their own fate to them.

Several Arab and Palestinian social scientists and historians assert that the Palestinian case is exceptional among colonial and postcolonial identities, especially its need to confront the so-called Jewish challenge.[72] However, even if Jewish settlement introduced an additional factor into the institutional and identity building and dismantling processes, in the historical stages that preceded 1948, the Palestinian case was not exceptional and does not significantly differ from the experiences of other colonially produced collectivities of the time. The Palestinians were not merely passive objects of the initiative of others, as they often portray themselves. Immediately after the Egyptian invasion, they manifested an ability for collective action stretching across familial, class, urban, rural, and regional cleavages, without having a distinct collective identity.

Ottomanism was a convenient identity and ideology for the urban elites, merchants, and notables, in that the Ottoman regime supplied fluctuating levels of law and order, the feeling of participation in a sociopolitical order, and offices and other material and status benefits, such as tax collection and other concessions. At the same time, for the peasantry and lower classes, the most meaningful identities were those of the clan, the region, and perhaps the ancient primordial grouping around the Qays and Yaman factions. Islam provided some common denominators to bridge gaps between *fellahin* and *effendi*, poor and rich, ignorant and literate, but it did not offer a sense of being a partner in an all-embracing *umma al-islamiyya*. In short, Islam was a part of the more embracing Ottomanism. The ability to adopt a new kind of modern collective identity—the pan-Syrian identity, which could be interpreted in both a particularistic context of *wataniyya* (near to the nation-state notion) or its more universalistic context of *qawmiyya*, or the first stage toward the integration into *umma al-arabiyya*—proved the flexibility of the embryonic Palestinian society and self-consciousness. The adoption of the Southern Syrian identity as a reaction to Faysal's success and failure, and the formation of an implicit Palestinian identity, have far-reaching implications. They hint that collective identities, at least before they become a kind of secular or civil religion, such as nationalism, should be regarded as an additional sociopolitical strategy of coping with changing threats. They draw and redraw the collective boundaries, constructing loyalties and imagined communities, but all based on changing sociopolitical realities.

CHAPTER FOUR

Between Primordial and Civil Definitions of the Collective Identity

Eretz Israel or the State of Israel?[*]

I

In 1974, Shmuel N. Eisenstadt investigated the nature of the Israeli collective identity with special regard to the extent of its Jewishness.[1] This issue gave rise to questions concerning Israel's links to Diaspora Jewish communities and its status in the Middle East in particular and the world in general. This article analyzes collective identity, separating it into its component factors, seeking its roots, and examining its main trends, indicating therein one of

---

[*] From Baruch Kimmerling, "Between the Primordial and Civil Definitions of the Collective Identity: The State of Israel or Eretz Israel?" in E. Cohen, M. Lissak, and U. Almagor, eds., *Comparative Social Dynamics: Essays in Honor of Shmuel N. Eisenstadt* (Boulder, CO: Westview, 1984), 262–283. Parts of this essay are based upon a lecture delivered at a seminar entitled Rethinking Israeli Sociology, offered by the Department of Sociology and Social Anthropology of the Hebrew University of Jerusalem in 1982. The author expresses his thanks to Menachem Friedman and to Erik Cohen for formulation and discussion of several concepts and ideas appearing in this paper. Responsibility for content, however, rests with the author alone.

the central problems of Zionism. Our primary a priori assumption is that the various elements that constitute the Zionist movement, both ideological and social, render it impossible to avoid constant tensions within the Zionist collective identity. The prominence, intensity, and forms of the social and political expressions of these tensions have undergone constant change, especially because of the influence of three factors: the variable composition of the collectivity, the differing political strengths of its respective component groups, and changes in patterns of relations with the surrounding Arab environment.

The main ideological sources of the Zionist movement, which were partial sources of social recruitment as well, were fourfold: the Jewish religion, a variety of socialist ideals, secular nationalism, and finally, classic liberalism, which included certain elements of a capitalistic spirit. There is thus horizontal differentiation in the elements of the Jewish national movement. Vertical differentiation, the dilemma of every national movement, may be presented as a continuum of various degrees of particularism and universalism, essentially cutting across all four horizontal components. Within the religious component, it is easier to discern the predominance of particularism, whereas universalistic orientations flourished to some extent in the other components, depending upon the period considered. This is hardly surprising, as nationalism, including Jewish nationalism, is often defined as the attempt of a particularistic group, the nation, to integrate itself into the community of nations on an egalitarian basis.[2]

We therefore reformulate the sources of tension within the collective identity as, first, the tensions between universalistic and particularistic orientations within each of the four basic social components of the Zionist movement, and second, the tensions among the four components themselves. The tensions stem both from a desire to determine the characteristics of the collectivity, perhaps even exclusively, as well as from aspirations to determine the rules of the overall social game that would maximize control over economic resources—or the positions that determine their allocation—and political predominance. We begin by analyzing the contributions of each of these components to the Jewish national movement and its collective identity.

Religion

A 1939 Royal Institute of International Affairs report determined that "special historical circumstances caused the Jewish people to assume, at an exceptionally early date, some of the characteristics which have since been associated most closely with the modern concept of a 'nation' and that these characteristics were preserved over the generations through an attachment to religion."[3] Most theoreticians of nationalism consider it to be a modern phenomenon, rooted in the French Revolution and accompanied by processes of secularization and modernization, but one need not consider religion and nationalism to be rivals.[4] We often find partial or total overlap between religion and national ideologies, nationalization of religion—as in the Anglican Church—or the imparting of a religious air to national movements.[5] Nevertheless, though the Zionist movement embodied nationalist elements, it initially met with fierce opposition from many Orthodox Jews,[6] and even tended to define itself as a revolution against the traditional communal life of Diaspora Jews.[7] Most of the formulators and leaders of the Zionist ideology and movement overtly or covertly considered Jewish religious beliefs and the Jewish religious establishment not only a mighty political enemy, but also a factor complementary to anti-Semitism in determining the intolerable situation of the Jews in exile.[8]

In any event, the Jewish religion, knowingly and willingly or not, contributed several elements to the Zionist movement that were needed for its formulation and growth. First, it located the target country, Zion. No other objective or attempt for super-territorial definition of Jewish nationality[9] had the mobilizing power of the Holy Land or the land of Zion and Jerusalem. Second, religious symbolism supplied the first key symbols of the Zionist movement, albeit selectively, skipping over the exile-like layers of Jewish religious creativity. Third, the religion supplied the common denominator of the Zionist collectivity in two dimensions, among various orientations and views (e.g., socialists versus liberals) and among people from various countries and cultures (first between Eastern and Western European cultures, and later between those from developed and developing countries), enabling the bridging of primordial gaps. Fourth, the social boundaries of the collectivity were determined by the Jewish religion. Fifth, the greater the prominence and severity of the Arab-Jewish conflict, the more the Jewish religion assumed a role within the Jewish collectivity as the primary mechanism for legitimizing the very existence of the collectivity as a political entity in the Middle East. It appears that religion was the principal solution to the problem of linking nation to land.[10]

Socialism

The various forms of socialism likewise extended beyond the concrete content and traditionally accepted roles of an ideological and even fundamental movement. First, the socialist component, as a social trend, contributed most of Zionism's human resources—from Eastern Europe—during the decisive, perhaps formative period between the second and fourth waves of immigration (1904–1929). The ideological components that the school contributed were no less significant. Second, the formation of a "new Jew" was demanded through fundamental change in the strata of the Jewish people, or at least those who realized the Zionist ideal. The concrete model for such a Jew was the *halutz,* or pioneer.[11] Third, the socialist component contributed the concept of immediate mobilization of masses of Jews, together with the imposition of individual responsibility, or "realization," upon each one of them, but without such mobilization being contingent on political factors outside the control of the Zionist movement or the individual. There were no preconditions to realizing the immediate goal of realization. All that was required was a decision by an individual or a small group of comrades. Fourth, the adherents to the ideological trends contributed the system of building the Jewish nation, that is, of gathering political, social, economic, and territorial strength, long the hallmark of the Zionist method.[12] The efficacy of this system was proved primarily within a situation of nation-building, in a conflict-ridden context and without the unambiguous backing of a colonial power; during that time, colonialism was already on the wane and subsequently disappeared. Fifth, it is obvious that socialists added to the Zionist movement their own classical demands for social justice, egalitarianism, and a large measure of communalism, expressed primarily in the special social creations of the political movement, such as the kibbutz, the cooperative *moshav,* and the workers' society known as the Histadrut, a unique institution combining a trade union with cultural, economic, medical, defense, and other services for members and the collectivity—the class—at large.

Secular Nationalism

The secular nationalist component contributed the main conceptual system within which Zionism could operate, both among the Jewish people and within the framework of the international rules of the game formulated after the French Revolution. The Jewish religion undoubtedly included many nationalist components, yet it considered all attempts to translate national motivation into contemporary political concepts to be false messianism and a contravention of divine will.[13] Socialism alone did not necessarily lead to national conclusions. Rather, the solution to the Jewish problem was considered a by-product of the better world for which it strived.[14] Only the combination of the Jewish religion, socialism, and secular nationalism could provide the impetus for the Zionist movement, as well as the institutional skeleton for the Jewish political entity and its primary symbols.

Liberalism

The contribution of the liberal component to the Zionist movement and the formation of the Israeli collectivity is summed up in two important and interconnected contributions: introducing universalistic and humanistic dimensions to the components of the Zionist collectivity and influencing the determination of the international orientation and cultural model that the collectivity would adopt. The liberal component has always been a counterweight against the strong particularistic leanings of the nationalistic and religious elements, and its adjunction to socialism impelled those on the left wing within the collectivity, who predominated for about fifty years, toward moderate social democracy. The process was by no means free of struggles and problems, especially in the 1930s and the early 1950s, but it prevented reversion to Marxist radicalism and excessive identification with, and control by, the Soviet Union. The combination of liberal and secular national elements created a familiar version of nationalism, resembling that of Giuseppe Mazzini of Italy, Lajos Kossuth of Hungary, or Jan Masaryk of Czechoslovakia, who sought to link their respective nations to the broader collectivity of the international community without descending to romantic levels or extreme nationalism. Theodor Herzl, the founder of modern political Zionism, undoubtedly adhered to this approach, which enabled modern Jews who had already undergone emancipation and secularized in previous generations to identify themselves, at least in part, with the Zionist movement. This identification led to their economic and political support for the movement. Taken to something of an extreme, the approach gave rise to the spiritual Zionism of Asher Ginsberg, known by his pen name of Ahad Haam.

The social weakness of the approach in Zionism perhaps stemmed from its compromising nature, and even more from the fact that it was primarily the lot of Western European and later American Zionists, who were not an important part of the Zionist collective in Palestine. Zionism was perceived more as a rescue movement for persecuted Eastern Jews than as an imperative requiring immediate personal fulfillment. The Ezrahi[15] sector in Palestine, at least up to the mid-1930s, was not characteristically representative of this approach. Afterward, as German and Central European Jews arrived in Palestine fleeing the rise of Nazism, this orientation, too, was institutionalized, albeit marginally so, within the collectivity.

The liberal approach counterbalanced extremism not so much because it introduced an element of universalism, but because it emphasized individualism against the strong collective demands and emphases of the three other components. Only an individualist orientation, anchored in the ideas of Hobbes, Locke, Hume, Smith, and Mill, could form a collectivity comprising citizens for whom the collectivity exists, rather than people who exist for the collectivity. The basis of this conception is that the system, according to the definition provided by Robert Bellah,[16] "can result from the actions of citizens motivated by self-interest alone when those actions are organized through the proper mechanisms." Despite the political and social weakness of the groups that were supposed to represent the universalistic and individualistic ideologies within the system, such approaches were indeed appended to other components. We may assume that this is because of two factors. First, the system could not ignore Western Jews who integrated into the social, political, and cultural fabric of their native countries and whom the system required for its own legitimization. Or, as an Israeli publicist recently stated in a debate on the social-cultural portrait of the country, "We belong to a culture which was created by Heine, Freud and Einstein,"[17] a list to which Marx's name may undoubtedly be added. Second, when the collectivity is quantitatively small in number—and much more demographically vulnerable in light of the Arab-Jewish conflict—one could not forego the individual entirely; a fortiori, the concept of individual sacrifice upon the altar of grand collective ideals could not be developed to its logical conclusion. Rather, under such conditions, collectivism—national, socialist, and religious—must coexist with liberal individualism.

II

The delicate balance among the components of the Zionist and Israeli collective identity was upset or shifted due to a number of different but interconnected processes: the change in demographic makeup of the collectivity during the 1950s; the consequent changing role of religion, that is, an alteration in the place of the religious strata within the population, and religious symbols among national symbols; shifting patterns in the Israeli-Arab conflict, control of the core territory of Zion after 1967, and the desire to hold this territory, with all of the resulting problems;[18] and finally, because of the preceding processes, the 1977 Israeli elections, which brought to power a political stream different from that which had shaped the collectivity's character continuously from the formative period up to that year.

We have already noted the importance of the religious component to the Zionist ideology and movement, and its status as a necessary though not sufficient condition for Zionism's very creation and existence. However, the religious components per se did not secure a central place for religion, especially not for the religious population and political parties, on the collectivity's political and social map, during either the British Mandate or the 1950s and early 1960s in the sovereign state of Israel. During that period, Orthodoxy had situated itself, but was considered by the system as remaining on the borderline or even outside the Zionist collectivity.[19] Religious nationalism was included within the boundaries of the collectivity, but it was relatively peripheral in both political power and symbolic location. The system could use the symbols borrowed from religion with only a minimal need for legitimization from religious groups. Even if religious participation contributed somewhat to the character of the collectivity, it was very difficult for the religious sector to convert this contribution to centrality within the system. Religious Zionism was engaged primarily in gathering resources to maintain its strength within the system and prevent capitulation to the modern, secular society on one side and the Orthodox, non-Zionist subculture on the other.

The national religious sector therefore focused on preserving its existence and continuity, primarily through maintaining separate educational systems and endogamous patterns and ensuring minimum conditions for observant persons to participate in the Zionist collectivity and protect their religious identity (e.g., through observing Sabbath and Kashrut at public institutions and preserving the religious essence of marital laws). The religious legislation also led to a complex system of political and social exchange between the system and the religious sector known as the status quo.[20]

From the early 1960s on, the location of the national religious stratum within the system changed, with the group constantly moving toward the center of society. Orthodox non-Zionist groups also moved subsequently in the same way. Religious men attributed the cessation of desertion from these strata, whether toward the modern secular society or toward the ul-tra-Orthodox world, in part to the success of religious education and the religious youth movement. One of the key instruments attracting the religious sectors to the center was the increasing salience of the collective participation of religious youth in distinguished army units, which combined Jewish scholastic pursuits with military service. The decisive period, however, resulted from both religious and nonreligious Israelis meeting in the territories of Judea and Samaria taken in the 1967 war and the holy places situated there. Because of the disputes that arose both within the system and in international spheres regarding the right and feasibility of Israel's holding these territories, parts of the religious sector—especially the youth among them—were motivated to be active in the public debate, and later to settle in these territories, in a way creating facts that they assumed would put an end to opposition to Israel's holding the territories by forming a settlement network in the occupied territories. The dispute over the territories constituted both the reason and the means for the outright breaking of the previous rules of the game, in which the national and religious public, as a political power, forswore intervention in administrating foreign policy.

Through the extra-parliamentary movement, Gush Emunim, which was created in the wake of the 1967 and 1973 wars, religious youth became a social and political vanguard that not only participated in determining collective objectives, but to a great extent attempted to determine them exclusively according to its own criteria, which conflicted with those of the majority of the political center itself.[21]

III

The centripetal movement of certain religious strata and even their centrality in the parts of society in which Edward Shills declares that social symbols are determined and interpreted and key decisions are taken was only an individual instance of a broader process—one that might be called a shift toward Judaism, as opposed to Israelism, in the collective identity.[22] The first sign of this turning point occurred as early as 1957, when Jewish "heritage studies" were included in the secular national curriculum.

Although we cannot determine the practical significance of this decision, it is nonetheless a fact that when the collective identity of Jewish youth in Israel was investigated at two points in time—1965 and 1974—there was a most significant tendency toward Jewish rather than Israeli identity. Israeli identity among Ashkenazi youth dropped from 50 to 41 percent and among Mizrahi youth from 30 to 24 percent. Among the Mizrahi youth who defined themselves as traditional (see below), Israeli identification dropped from 35 to 18 percent and Jewish identity rose from 30 to 44 percent. Among the group defining itself as nonreligious, Jewish identity rose from 4 to 14 percent among Ashkenazi youth and from 5 to 21 percent among their Mizrahi counterparts.[23] The increase in self-definition as Jewish and the drop in Israeli identification was consistent in all groups, even those who defined themselves as religious and had already indicated a high incidence of Jewish self-identity in 1965, when the original survey was conducted. An anthropologist who studied Jewish immigration from the United States to Israel found that such immigrants undergo a process of traditionalization, including adoption of a more Jewish collective identity.[24] From this, one could derive a more generalized hypothesis concerning the probability of traditionalization processes of other immigrant groups during their transition into Israeli society (or Eretz Israel) and absorption therein, as either a quality of the immigrants or a characteristic of the system, or both.[25]

Moreover, it is very easy to prove that most residents are not nonreligious, even if they do not define themselves as religious. The religious population of Israel is customarily estimated at 15 percent; however, a series of findings by various researchers leads to a far more complex picture. In 1962, members of the Jewish population in Israel were asked if they maintained religious traditions. Fifteen percent responded that they observe all precepts scrupulously, 15 percent said they did so "to a great extent," and 46 percent (!) considered themselves to be partly traditional. Only 24 percent defined themselves as "completely freethinking."[26] In a 1979 study, other scholars distinguished between the dimensions of faith and religious observance; the Jewish religion stresses the second dimension because faith generally cannot be measured, evaluated, or controlled and is therefore considered less relevant.[27] Nevertheless, the findings on the status of faith indicate several additional features of the population: 36 percent of the population believed in the coming of the Messiah, 47 percent believed that there is something above nature that guides the history of the Jewish people, 56 percent believe that God gave the Torah to Moses at Mount Sinai, 57 percent believe that the Jews are the Chosen People, and 64 percent believe in God. An investigation of the degree of religious observance indicates that a much greater proportion of the

Israeli Jewish population observes religious precepts than is officially declared. Without exaggerating the meaning of these findings, we may conclude that the cumulative data indicate that Israeli society is far more religious or traditional than its public and self-image would seem to imply.

Another interesting macrosociological indicator corroborates the theory that Israel is a collectivity with religious tendencies. Secular circles in the country talk of religious coercion: there is no public transportation on the Sabbath and holidays in most parts of Israel; the religious code, imposed by official national sanction, bars people in many groups from marrying the partners of their choice; and other laws are considered to severely limit individual freedom, a lofty value in Western culture. However, all attempts to organize effective political pressure groups to oppose the laws have failed miserably, recruiting not even the small segments of the population that define themselves as secular.

The phenomenon of religious tendencies becomes even more prominent against the background of the success of religious groups in articulating their political demands, gathering strength within both Zionist and non-Zionist political parties, and integrating with the political-party map of Israel. These groups achieved virtually consistent and impressive success in determining the internal character of the state and acquiring political and economic strength for their constituencies. The structural reason for this success, rooted in Israel's political fragmentation and in the religious parties' role in tipping the electoral balance, only partially explains the phenomenon called "theo-politics"—namely, "attempts to attain theological ends by means of political activity."[28] However, it is easy to see that, in the past, in cases in which a large party had other alternatives, either from an ideological point of view (Mapam) or with respect to convenience in terms of political cost (Liberals), the party nonetheless opted for coalition with the religious groups.

Another proposed explanation for what could be called the religionization of the collectivity and the complex relations between religion and state or society is that it was accomplished through what Bellah has termed "civil religion,"[29] a system of syncretic values that draws its symbolism from both the traditional religious and the secular-national value systems, and which comes to accord overall significance to a social order and components thereof: "It places the collectivity at the center of its meaning system and transfers the ultimate authority from God to society. Even still, God appears as an actor in the cosmic order." However, even those who attempt to explain the Israeli system of values in terms of civil religion admit that "Judaism and Jewishness were central components of all the civil religions [in Israel]. Jewishness is both the cause and the effect of Israel's civil religion."[30] If so, it is far more effective to consider the system and its components as exposed to a differential measure of traditional Jewish religiousness, in all its varied forms and expressions, coexisting with other, essentially secular ideologies and values. At different times and in different sectors of the system, they may complement one another, conflict, or coexist side by side.

IV

When Israel achieved independence, its population consisted predominantly of immigrants from Eastern Europe with small minorities from Central and Western Europe, Asia, and Africa. This population was primarily nonmodern and not entirely secular, even if it defined itself as such. A major portion of it had just begun to undergo processes of change. Despite this, most of its constituents maintained a modern, Western-oriented frame of reference. From 1949 on, mass immigration from Asian and African countries altered the demographic parameters of Israel's population. Nevertheless, the social, political, and cultural predominance of the European-born immigrants, which effectively persists to this day, preserved the relative significance of all of the components in the collective identity. Change occurred in the Israeli collective identity only when Eastern immigrants accumulated political power and increasingly translated it into practical terms during the penetration into the core areas of the country (i.e., Judea and Samaria), but an open struggle erupted over the very character of this identity.

In their countries of origin, Asian and African immigrants had already been exposed to processes of modernization and change. Immigrants from Yemen, who began arriving in Palestine as early as 1882—simultaneous with but virtually unrelated to the first *aliya*—became the prototype of purely religious immigration, free of all modern "isms."[31] This immigration in particular indicates that the Jewish religion alone, free of all political considerations and alien constraints, possesses most of the key elements of Zionism,[32] albeit without the demand or ability to establish and maintain a modern state.

Barring acceptance of the modern elements of socialism, communism, and liberalism, the approach closest in content to the Jewish religion is that of modern nationalism. Judaism is predisposed toward nationalism and includes several important elements of it, thus contrasting somewhat with Christianity and Islam. The first Zionist-movement branch, in which the right-wing Revisionists led by Zeev Jabotinsky won an absolute and consistent majority as early as 1928, was that of Tunis. This occurred in the wake of the publication of a series of articles by Jabotinsky in the local paper *Le Reveil Juif*. As Abitbol relates, "The sharpness of thought, the nationalistic phraseology, the frequent references to Mediterranean 'blood' and Spanish *hidalguia* which were characteristic of Jabotinsky's articles, and his warm letters to his sympathizers, captured the hearts of the Tunisian Zionists."[33]

We may characterize the trend as ostensibly a semantic change in the definition of the collectivity from the State of Israel—the official name since the declaration of independence in 1948—to Eretz Israel, the Land of Israel. This change was not accomplished in a formal manner, as the official title of the collectivity remained the State of Israel. However, from the time of the 1977 change in government, Israeli leaders began to utilize the concept of Eretz Israel for two principal reasons: first, to demarcate the new physical boundaries of the collectivity—a return, that is, to the borders of Mandatory Palestine, which included Judea, Samaria, and the Gaza Strip—and second, to define, though not always in a manifest, conscious manner, the collectivity's identity as Eretz Israel, indicating a desire to change the image of Israeli society from one with a basic character rooted in civility to a moral community based on primordial symbols and ties, as described by Shills and Geertz,[34] in which several rules of the game are altered. These rules are evident in the Jewish religious codex, the *halacha*. The State of Israel is a modern concept with no religious connotation or status whatsoever, at least for certain sectors of the population. But a collective identity defined as Eretz Israel entails an entire system of religious precepts that dictate specific behavioral patterns and attitudes.

Transforming the two alternative definitions of the collectivity into ideal types (see Table 4.1), in the sense used by Max Weber, we may discern the main differences between them. In the State of Israel—hereinafter referred to as Israel—social boundaries are determined by citizenship. Israel was indeed established to be a Jewish nation-state, the fundamental objective of the Zionist movement. Yet there is room for non-Jewish minorities with equal rights and obligations. In Eretz Israel, in which the basic definition of membership in the collectivity is kinship rather than citizenship, "sojourners" or "strangers within our midst" *(gerim)* are conceivable, but their status cannot be equivalent to that of the Jews. This definition of membership implies that Judaism is a necessary and sufficient condition for belonging to the Eretz Israel collectivity, whereas membership in Israel is a mixture of ascriptivity, as in all countries, conditioned by a balance of obligations and privileges of the citizen toward the state and vice versa.

In Israel, the placement of an individual or social group is a function primarily of the importance of the social functions fulfilled by the person or group in building and developing the nation, as well as of the rarity of the person's or group's abilities. In Eretz Israel, this matter is approached ambivalently. On one hand, considering the Shillsian center-periphery continuum, the collectivity may be defined as a society without a periphery.[35] All are Jews and all are in the center; the periphery relates to non-Jews, who are considered an out-group. On the other hand, the more Jewish a group is considered to be—and in this context, Jewishness implies religiousness, traditionalism, or a combination of the two—the more central is its placement. As traditionalism partially overlaps with ethnic origins, it appears that Eretz Israel compensates the ethnic groups, who are more marginally situated in Israel, with a greater feeling of centrality and partnership in the collectivity, contrasting with or ignoring the traditionally elite strata.

The situation also affects the quality of relations between the individual and the collectivity. In Eretz Israel, there is an increased demand for the individual's unqualified, or at least verbally unqualified, affinity for the collectivity. The political center identifies itself with the entire collectivity and its welfare, developing a paternalistic approach and lowering the threshold of tolerance of opinions and behavior patterns defined as deviant. There is a tendency to institutionalize more direct relations between the political center and the people, weakening the secondary groups and discrediting other mediating systems, such as the mass media.

In the original model of Israel, there was an outstanding attempt to synthesize the various components of the Zionist movement in drawing up the formal rules of the game—that is, in designing the constitution or legal system.[36] As a Jewish state, Israel enacted the marital laws of the Jewish sector of the population, as under the Mandate, based on religious decisions determined in accordance with *halacha*. In other areas, the parliament enacted civil legislation, generally guided by modern Western rationalistic and universalistic norms but accounting for the spirit and decisions of Jewish law wherever possible. Eretz Israel seeks to subject all aspects of life to *halacha*, thus posing a formidable challenge to its proponents, who are not faced within the framework of the civil State of Israel, in which *halacha*

Table 4.1

Definition component	State of Israel	Eretz Israel
Physical boundaries	1949 ceasefire lines, plus East Jerusalem and other territory obtained through negotiations.	Divinely promised borders (alternatively: the boundaries of Mandatory Palestine).
Social boundaries	All Israeli citizens.	All Jews in Israel and throughout the world.
Conditions of membership	Dependent upon the balance of citizens' rights and obligations toward the state.	Judaism as a necessary and sufficient condition for membership.
Quality of relations between individual and collectivity	Dependent upon reciprocal relations between the individual and the collectivity. The individual is recruited for ad hoc collective missions (such as military service) and the collectivity assumes concern for his welfare.	Relations resembling unconditional kinship. Blurring of differences between society and the individual, with diffuse mobilization of members of the collectivity.
Quality of relations among members of the collectivity	Reciprocal relations among citizens enjoying equal rights and responsibilities.	Tendency toward relations on the basis of primordial ties. Unconditional but not necessarily egalitarian bonds, emphasizing common destiny.
Determination of place within the system	Determined according to functional importance to the collective and contribution to building the nation (primarily mediated by number of years in the country, education, and ethnic origin). Modern parliamentary laws based upon the Napoleonic Code and guided by contemporary Western criteria.	The extent of Jewishness, whether in traditional religious or patriotic terms or a combination of the two.

Table 4.1 (*continued*)

Definition component	State of Israel	Eretz Israel
Law	Modern parliamentary laws based upon the Napoleonic Code and guided by contemporary Western criteria.	*Halacha*, with minimal adaptation to contemporary technological conditions.
Perceptions of relations with the outside world	Cooperation or conflict in accordance with the respective interests of either side and controlled by weak international norms.	Within the accepted frame of reference demanded in relations between Jews and non-Jews (likewise rooted in *halacha* to some extent). Ethnocentricity and particularism as essential guidelines for determining the rules of the game.

is only quasi-legal: how to base an essentially modern state on a code of laws formulated within a millenia-old social, political, economic, and technological context. The problem is further complicated by the general Orthodox consensus—in contrast to the Reform Jewish trend that developed in the United States—that far-reaching changes cannot be instituted in the codex, which is totalistic in nature and pertains to all aspects of life.[37]

Comparing the Two Ideal Definitions of the Collectivity: State of Israel Versus Eretz Israel

Relations among members of the Israel collectivity are reciprocal, with citizens enjoying equal rights and obligations. In Eretz Israel, relations resemble kinship and tend to be primordial. Ties are unconditional, albeit not necessarily egalitarian. Potential tensions resulting from differential allocation of social resources, which continue to partially overlap with ethnic origins, are likely to lose their significance with emphasis on common Jewish destiny and identity, even if Jewishness is interpreted differently in each segment of society. The argument is not that Judaism is predominantly a tribal brotherhood, contrasting with the modern Protestant "otherhood," as presented by Cuddihy.[38] Like other great traditions, Judaism includes numerous universalistic and civilian components alongside its particularistic and tribal elements. This dualistic spirit presents a problem as to which orientation predominates in response to a given situation. At present, there appears to be a rise in the tendency toward tribalizing and demodernizing the system, supported by selected components and symbols of tribal Judaism that reject the Western *zweckrationalitat,* or purposive rationality. This is precisely the result of a fusion between religion and politics that aimed to recruit internal political support for the government from the more traditional and nationalistic strata, and legitimize control over the territories of Judea and Samaria, taken in the 1967 war.

Finally, the two ideal types maintain different conceptions of relations with the outside world. In the Israeli model, the collectivity is active within a global system, in which relations among the various actors are characterized by varying degrees of cooperation and conflict according to a particular issue, and motivated and subject to change according to respective interests and governed by weak international norms. The Eretz Israel *Weltanschauung* is entirely different: The world is divided into "we" and "they," or Jews versus everyone else. This conception transfers the traditional, natural

Diaspora view of relations between Jews and non-Jews to the situation of a sovereign Jewish state. Such Judeocentricity also includes partially rejecting the Western world, a factor further reinforced by the Holocaust, which constitutes a central motif in the system of collective symbols. It is claimed that because the Jews were the central victims of the Holocaust, the "others"—primarily the Western world—who were active or passive partners therein have no right to dictate any rules of the game perceived as contrary to Jewish interests. Nevertheless, the collective is still considered to be more closely aligned to the modern Western world, albeit in a limited and conditional manner, than to any other broad frame of reference.

V

Just as the State of Israel is geographically located within Eretz Israel, so too is the latter socially and politically situated within the former. The two concepts are not always necessarily in a zero-sum situation, as emphasized by Geertz:

> Primordial and civil sentiments are not ranged in direct and implicitly evolutionary opposition to one another in the manner of so many of the theoretical dichotomies of classical sociology. . . . Their marked tendency to interfere with one another stems not from any irrevocable antipathy between them but rather from dislocations arising from the differing patterns of change intrinsic to each of them.[39]

Tensions among the various components of the identity of the Zionist collectivity were thus always built into the movement itself. It was agreed in principle that certain decisions regarding the ultimate content and image of the collectivity would be postponed for the future, whereas mighty differential struggles would be waged over the remaining issues. Until 1977, despite major demographic changes, there were no significant fluctuations in the relative values of these components within the collective identity. In this respect, we note wide gaps between the orientations formulated and represented by elites with relatively universalistic and civil conceptions of the collectivity and those of considerable sections of the periphery, which tended to be more particularistic and Jewish. The new decision-making political elite thus converged somewhat with the periphery, but diverged from other centrist components in Israeli society.

The differences among the various centrist components underscore tensions in the collective identity to a greater extent than do the gaps between the center and the periphery, which are more empirically acceptable and statistically widespread. Cleavages within the political elite that spill over to the periphery may intensify tensions among various elements and create situations of greater societal fluidity than are generally induced by center-versus-periphery differences. While the Israeli collectivity has not yet institutionalized a polycentric society, several of the characteristics and results of such societies may already be discerned. It is therefore hardly surprising that some of the groups that brought the new political elite to power, and which identify with its Eretz Israel orientations, continue to feel that they are in the opposition, owing to the prominent divergences between the political center and the other elites and within the political center itself. On the other hand, the increasing shift toward Eretz Israel intensified feelings of belonging among the non-Zionist groups, such as Agudat Israel or the recently crystallized Torah Observant Sephardim party, as the increase in the extent of Jewishness rendered the system more familiar. As indicated earlier, Eretz Israel is a *halachic*-religious entity, whereas the State of Israel is not.[40] This situation impelled the non-Jewish components of the system even further toward the periphery and further intensified the conflict between the Jewish system and Arab residents of Judea, Samaria, and the Gaza Strip.

The shift toward a more Eretz Israel-type definition of relations between the collectivity and the Diaspora is similarly ambivalent. Intensifying particularistic factors within the system, which entails a more power-oriented policy toward the surrounding Arab environment, may deter certain sectors of world Jewish intelligentsia, known for their universalistic approach, from supporting the collectivity and immigrating to Israel. In contrast, as Avruch has shown, other sectors may well be attracted to a more family-like and Jewish collectivity and its primordial symbols.[41] From this point of view, the increasing tendency toward the Eretz Israel type is likely to influence differential selection of immigration to and possibly emigration from the collectivity. Such migration, in turn, may further reinforce tendencies toward more primordial definitions of collective identity.

VI

Tensions among the various components of the collectivity, resulting from differing sources of collective identity and motivation for immigration, will apparently persist, as it is difficult to conceive of an unequivocal choice between the two types. Nevertheless, the relative weight of the collective identity's different components may change due to three factors: internal processes, such as the continued accumulation and practical application of political power by the offspring of Eastern immigrants, increases in over-all educational levels, and accelerated ethnic intermarriage rates; economic and external developments, that is, control of the occupied territories, which depends not upon Israel alone, but rather a complex of external factors, developments in the world economy, and the energy crisis, among other issues; and the scope and nature of immigration to and emigration from Israel. Such changes have already taken place several times in the past.

The tensions among the components of the collective identity are expressed in the system's ever-present political, social, cultural, and even economic struggles, such as the struggle over the choice of an economic model to be adopted by the system and consequent allocation of resources. The tensions are translated concretely into Israeli society's familiar foci of conflict: religious and non-religious, hawks and doves regarding the occupied territories, Askenazim and Sephardim, Jews and Arabs, the haves and have-nots, and so on. However, the confrontation between the Israel and Eretz Israel approaches is no longer a part of this series. Rather, it has become a sort of meta-game, determining the rules according to which concrete struggles are to be waged; the nature of collectivity relations with the Jewish world, the world at large, and among themselves; and the location and significance of the collectivity within the cosmic order. Is Israel a nation like all other nations—toward which some sectors of Zionism strived? Or are Israelis the Chosen People, and if so, what is the operative significance of such an identity—ethnocentricity or universality? The struggle between these two spirits—the spirit of Israel and the spirit of Eretz Israel—has in no way been resolved; the pendulum continues to swing between them. Apparently, as one spirit becomes more salient, it stimulates a reaction in the other.[42]

CHAPTER FIVE

State Building, State Autonomy, and the Identity of Society

The Case of the Israeli State*

This article has a twofold purpose. The first is to solve a puzzle that is posed by analyzing the Israeli sociopolitical system. The other is to propose an analytical parameter that might be added to the expanding theoretical field in the sociology of politics and historical sociology, namely, the state–civil society paradigm that brings the state back into sociology, positioning it against or alongside civil society.[1] The puzzle pertaining to the Israeli sociopolitical system arises from contradictory evidence concerning the strength of the Israeli state, its capacity to govern, and its ability to make decisions.

Puzzles

On the one hand, the Israeli state is classified as a strong state[2] with a tremendous capacity to mobilize its citizens (e.g., for wars), considerable law-

* From Baruch Kimmerling, "State Building, State Autonomy, and the Identity of Society: The Case of the Israeli State," *Journal of Historical Sociology* 6, no. 4 (1993): 397–429.

enforcement power that penetrates into almost every social formation and grouping of Jewish citizens, and an ability to maintain surveillance over the Israeli Arab population and noncitizens.[3] The state's ability to regulate is also evidenced by its high capacity to raise taxes.[4] On the other hand, the situation in Israel has been characterized as "trouble in Utopia" in a book of that title, a comprehensive look at Israel's sociopolitical system; as its authors, Dan Horowitz and Moshe Lissak, put it, "the 'ungovernable' tendencies of the system reflect its overburdened condition which stems from [the state's] inability to meet contradictory political demands that are rooted in opposing fundamental ideological positions."[5] Their view implies that the autonomy of the Israeli state tends to be low, placing it at the mercy of rival groups that form what seems to be a civil society.[6]

This article's central argument is that the Israeli state continues to be a more powerful actor than any other societal formation, strata, or group in the collectivity. At the same time, it is less autonomous than certain groups and spheres, resulting from its dual identity, or what Hegel[7] calls a "historically produced sphere of ethical life," rooted in the identities of two rival civil societies (*bürgerliches gesellschaften*), one based on primordial ties and the other on civic orientations. To analyze this dynamic, the article provides a somewhat new approach to the Israeli collectivity and the general theory of the state, altering conventional and orthodox views that have dominated macrosociology, social history, political science, and historiography.[8]

Developing the argument involves introducing an additional dimension to the notion of the state that scholars of the state-society paradigm have neglected.[9] This additional dimension is the collective identity, or the unique fingerprint that distinguishes each state-society complex. Collective identities also tend to impose explicit and implicit rules of the game that establish the perceived degree of freedom permitted by the state as a power container.[10] As powerful and strong as it is, the state cannot be detached from the identities and mythic self-perceptions of the population composing the society, referring in this case to the population that considers itself to belong to the somewhat abstract term of Israel, which cuts across state, family, and civil institutions. We are also dealing with the notion of a nation-state—the term "nation" indicates a generalized kind of identity with some structural implications—wherein the identity of the Israeli state is primarily and ultimately a Jewish nation-state.[11] To understand the major developments of this state, its strengths and weaknesses, and its degree of autonomy, we analyze the diverse meanings of the term "Jewish nation-state," together with the state's structural aspects.

By the term "state autonomy," I refer to the state's ability to prevent the unsolicited intervention of different segments of civil society and the imposition of particularistic definitions of the identity of the collectivity, by one or another segment of civil society. Any specific collective identity may determine the rules of the game and practices—the formal and constitutional as well the informal political culture—or of a certain distributive or coercive policy.[12] The social and political strength and salience of particularistic identities can be powerful enough to destroy states and recreate other strong ties and loyalties, as the dismantling of powerful multinational states, such the Soviet Union and Yugoslav Republic, demonstrate spectacularly. Particularistic groups associate themselves with ideologies that act as alternatives to the officially defined identity of the state. By contrast, with the term "state strength," designated as weak or strong, I refer to the state's ability to impose its own definition of identity on all segments of the society, in addition to its ability to enforce law and order, mobilize the population for war, and manage distributive and extractive fiscal policies.[13] Regarding the first part of the definition of the state, I adopt the traditional Weberian concept[14] that views the state as a corporate body with compulsory jurisdiction and a monopoly on the use of legitimate force over a territory and its population, which extends to all action that arises in the territory under the body's control. The state must have a continuous organizational structure, including at least military and police forces, a tax-collection and resource-redistribution apparatus (the state bureaucracy), a rule-making institution (parliamentary or not), a decision-making institution (rulers and their delegates), and a justice-making body (courts that act based on a written code). However, these traits constitute only one dimension of any state.

The second dimension, a state's collective identity, is what makes each state cognitively and culturally different from other states. The identity is the core that tends to persist when the government or even the state's regime changes.[15] It is not only a matter of convenience that each state has its own name, banner, symbols, and anthem. The puzzle of what makes the French state French and the Swiss state Swiss is much more fundamental. The collective identity determines not only the collectivity's geographical and societal boundaries,[16] basic credo, political culture, civic religion,[17] and civil society,[18] but also the rules of the game, stated or unstated—in short, the state's logic.

I understand a state's logic to mean the basic codes, traditions, rules, and practices that are unaffected by changes of government, administration, or regimes. The logics are imposed by geopolitical constraints rooted in the human and material resources that the state possesses—its identity and political culture—and are carried out mainly through the state's bureaucracy and other state agencies that represent their own and their class interests. Thus, the degree of change when a Tory government in the United Kingdom is replaced by a Labour government, or a Democratic administration in the United States gives way to a Republican one, is basically limited and restricted. Even after the Russian Empire became the Soviet Union and then returned back to the Russian state, some basic practices of the Russian state persisted and were even protected and amplified by the new regimes. This is not to say that the state's logic and the practices derived from the logic cannot change; however, the changes do not necessarily overlap with changes in government or regime. Some changes in regime are connected to previous changes in the state's logic, by and large influenced by the state's position as an actor in the international arena.

Origins of Israeli State and Society

It is generally assumed that the origins of the State of Israel are directly connected to the Zionist idea and its development as a social and political movement.[19] The Jewish state was created through several factors: political mobilization of persecuted Jews; encouragement of their immigration to Zion; and mobilization of the political support of the great powers, which created the political conditions needed to establish an integral Jewish society and polity on the soil of the so-called ancestral homeland. Although the Zionist idea and movement was needed to create a Jewish polity in Palestine, the British mandatory or colonial regime established after World War I was an equally important source of the Jewish state.[20] While the latter was intended to maintain and guarantee British interests in the Middle East, the British administration was also intended to lay the foundations for "the establishment in Palestine of a 'national home' for the Jewish people."[21]

Mandatory Palestine was a typical colonial state. Its residents—a Palestinian Arab majority and a growing Jewish minority—did not have the right to determine policies and could only exert influence through negotiating and bargaining with the colonial power, Great Britain, or through local agencies. Such efforts included the use of controlled and uncontrolled violence or the threat to use it.[22] Like any other state, colonial Palestine maintained a regime of law and order through the mechanism of a local police force and other security agencies. The colonial state was also responsible for establishing a judicial system and passing laws that applied to the area within the colony's territorial boundaries; creating a modern bureaucracy; issuing coins and stamps, developing and implementing monetary and fiscal policies, and collecting systematic taxes;[23] funding typical state activities, such as road construction, telephone, telegraph, postal services, and radio broadcasting, through state revenues; providing education and health services; facilitating normal civilian life and minimal welfare; and granting concessions, including the rights to establish an electric company that rapidly electrified the country.

The British regime also supported both a cooperative marketing system for agricultural products and limited agrarian reform, mainly by encouraging the Palestinian Arab peasantry to redistribute their communal lands among households and registering them as private lands. In addition, it partially protected infant industries, loaned money directed for economic development, and extended credit for agricultural production. Passports and identity cards attesting to Palestinian citizenship were issued, and in only thirty years, the regime created not only a legal Palestinian identity and a limited notion of citizenship, but also a potential political identity for at least some of its Arab residents, who constituted the large majority of the population until the end of the colonial regime.[24] From this perspective, it was a strong state, attaining many of its objectives chiefly in the period up to 1936 until the start of the Arab Revolt.[25]

However, colonial Palestine was also a minimalist state. It intervened directly in only a limited number of areas, preferring to extend wide-ranging autonomy to the two major national communities, Arab and Jewish, under its territorial jurisdiction. Prima facie, following Taylor's definition,[26] both communal entities can be defined as civil societies in the maximalist meaning of the term: there were "free associations, not under tutelage of state power"; the communities as a whole could structure themselves, and in so doing, "significantly determine or affect the course of state policy." However, if we consider Hegel's idea that civil society is the societal space in between the family and the state, we see that both civil societies in the framework of colonial Palestine were much closer to family-like associations, based on primordial ties, than the rational secondary groups that civil-society theoreticians presume, implicitly or explicitly.

Before the creation of Mandatory Palestine and during its initial stage, the British and the Zionist movements operated according to two latent but jointly held assumptions, on the basis of which Great Britain agreed to take upon itself the mission of assisting in the establishment of a so-called Jewish national home. The first assumption was that by creating the necessary political preconditions, massive Jewish immigration—ranging into the hundreds of thousands, if not millions—would begin. This immigration presumed a radical change in the demographic and sociopolitical character of the territory, which would rapidly become an entity with a Jewish majority population. The second assumption was that the Arab population's resistance to the process of massive Jewish immigration would not be firm or organized, or alternatively, it would lack the political and organizational ability and skill to mold such resistance into effective political action.

Within a short period of time both of these assumptions were proved to be wrong. First, the Zionist movement's ability to recruit Jewish immigrants turned out to be limited, so that a fundamental and rapid demographic transformation of Palestine's Jewish population would not take place. Secondly, once Palestinian Arabs learned of the Balfour Declaration's content, they began to organize themselves for political protest and even active resistance, thereby sabotaging the British policy to bring about the creation of a "Jewish national home" and to turn the country's Arab majority into a minority within the context of a Jewish state.[27] Faced with strong Palestinian Arab opposition to Jewish mass immigration, as well as land transfers from Arab to Jewish control,[28] the Mandatory regime suffered from serious instability.[29] The resistance movement moved into high gear with the outbreak of the Arab Revolt of 1936–39.[30] Palestinian Arab demands centered on the issue of the transfer of powers and ultimately sovereignty to the national majority in Palestine. To attain this goal, Palestine's Arabs formulated interim demands: establishing a Legislative Council, elected democratically by the country's residents, that is, with an overwhelming Arab majority; terminating or at least severely restricting Jewish immigration; and enacting legislation that would prevent the transfer of land ownership from one community (the Arabs) to another (the Jews).[31]

When the British realized that their two basic assumptions were wrong, they adapted their policy to suit the reality. The principal objective of British policy in Palestine then became ensuring political stability in the area with the aim of continued control at a lower cost. In the wake of the Arab Revolt of 1936–39, and in view of the heavy economic and political burden

of quelling it, the idea of abandoning Palestine became an alternative option on the British agenda. However, the outbreak of World War II forced
Britain to defer decisions about the future of the Mandate and Palestine.
Eventually, once the British departed, the probable scenario would either
be to transfer sovereignty to the hands of the national majority of the population—the Arabs of Palestine—or partitioning Palestine's territory, which
was first proposed by the Palestine Royal Commission of 1937, better known
as the Peel Commission.[32]Both the Palestinian Arab and Jewish communities, however, rejected partition as a viable option.

The Organized Jewish Community in Palestine
and the State in the Making

Starting in the mid-1920s, the Jewish political settler-immigrant community in Palestine was well aware of the strong possibility that, within a short
period of time, sovereignty of the colonial state would pass into the hands
of the territory's majority population, that is, its Arab residents. To prevent such an eventuality, the Jewish community had to establish a parallel
framework to that of the colonial state; in other words, there was a need
for a Jewish state in the making that could offer to the territory's Jewish
residents most of the essential services provided by any state, such as defense, administrative machinery, education, welfare, health, and employment.[33] The state in the making could also mobilize the exclusive loyalty of
the Jewish community's members without risking a head-on collision with
the colonial state.

The colonial regime provided the Jewish immigrant-settler society with
the security umbrella needed for the community to grow and develop despite the Arab majority's opposition, though the Jews were not always satisfied with the extent of British protection.[34] But for Palestine's Jewish community to exist as a political entity, it needed to accumulate institutionalized
macropower, form an organized machinery of violence from the settler-immigrant society, and develop the ability to mobilize Jews in Palestine and
in the Diaspora for political support. Furthermore, the so-called organized
yishuv—the Palestinian Jewish community—had to provide an immediate
alternative to the colonial state, which was destined to disappear together
with British rule. To create an entity with such considerable political potential, the Jewish community had to concentrate most of its institutions
and strata within an autonomous state in the making. Thus, the boundaries

between state and society, or between the central political institutions and nonpolitical institutions, were completely blurred, and internal social control and surveillance intensified, by the political organizations and leadership of the Jewish community.

Knesset Israel, the quasi-governmental institution of the immigrant-settler community in Palestine, overlapped to a great extent not only with the leadership of the Zionist parties—after 1933, predominantly the Mapai party[35]—but also the Executive Committee of the Jewish Agency, the local operational branch of the World Zionist Organization. Within this political complex was the Histadrut, or the General Labor Federation of Jewish Workers in Palestine, the organization of which paralleled that of a state mechanism. In addition to the usual structure of the trade unions, the Histadrut included manufacturing plants and construction firms (such as Solel Boneh), marketing and purchasing cooperatives, an extensive bureaucracy, a comprehensive system of health and hospitalization services, a bank, an employment bureau, a newspaper and publishing company, a competitive and mass-oriented sports organization, and an entire subculture based on symbols—a red flag, anthems, ceremonies, parades, festivals, and holidays.[36]

Not all of the Jews in Palestine were part of the state in the making. For the local Orthodox Jewish community, including branches of Agudat Israel, the largest religious party in the Jewish world at the time, the colonial state was the sole recognized political authority.[37] The Zionist state in the making also excluded members of the Communist Party and to a certain extent some of those who belonged to the long-established Sephardic Jewish community, who were culturally and politically linked with the previous Ottoman Islamic regime. An issue that produced much controversy in the Jewish community of Palestine was the communal position of the Revisionist Zionist movement, which opposed the socialist-led coalition in the World Zionist Organization by arguing for a more assertive Zionist policy and a larger share of power, positions, and material resources. The municipalities were another highly crystallized and institutionalized portion of the Jewish community in Palestine. Even though they were not fully integrated into the state in the making, they held a central position in the polity mainly because they enjoyed the advantage of independent financial resources. The municipal councils, primarily those with a majority comprising the middle-class, nonsocialist, petite bourgeoisie, such as the municipalities of Tel Aviv and Ramat Gan, were autonomous to some extent from the British and the Jewish political center, and mediated between the colonial state and the organized Jewish community.

The very presence of these excluded groups indicates how clearly the boundaries of the state in the making were demarcated.

Although the organized Jewish community was not without its internal struggles and tensions, the community had evolved unique safety valves to prevent confrontations from intensifying. One mechanism was a coalition of benefactors who raised external capital through national funds, collected by various worldwide Zionist organizations and distributed by the local leadership. This was needed because the Zionist venture was a uniquely nonprofit and noneconomic settler movement that chose its target territory not with a view to wealthy and abundant land and natural and human resources, but instead at the behest of a nationalistic vision of utopia, driven by religious and primordial sentiments.[38]

The State

With its establishment in May 1948, in the course of what is referred to as the War of Independence for part of the territory originally included in the mandate, the State of Israel set two priority goals: to establish clear-cut boundary lines between state and society and to obtain an optimal level of autonomy for state institutions apart from other historical foci of power in society. In the pre-state era, the boundaries between these foci and the state in the making were blurred or, in some cases, nonexistent. The Israeli state established its boundaries gradually and systematically to avoid instability and the weakening of its own position in relation to the colonial power centers. At the same time, it was in the state's best interest to maintain its alliance with groups that could ultimately assist the state to penetrate new areas and peripheries.

The ability to extend state autonomy to and control new peripheries was crucial because Israel was rapidly turning into a country of mass immigration and the political and cultural assumptions of the different groups of new immigrants were strikingly different from those of the pre-1948 Jewish community in Palestine.[39] Additional groups incorporated into the state included about 150,000 Arabs who remained within the territory of the newly established state and the Jewish Orthodox non-Zionist groups, which de jure did not recognize the secular Jewish state.[40] At first glance, it would appear that the state succeeded in controlling the new peripheries and preserving the original distribution of power in society. Both the popular image of that early era in Israel's history and the findings of social science research studies indicate that the state appeared to steer the process while also maintaining a high level of autonomy vis-à-vis other actual and potential foci of power.[41] Control was concentrated in Mapai, which shared power in a coalition with the Histadrut, the Workers' Society (Hevrat Ha'Ovdim, or Meshek Ovdim, the complex of labor union–owned companies),[42] and the Jewish Agency.[43] The power of these four partners appeared to be impregnable.

The leaders of the ruling coalition were members of a veteran elite group with certain salient sociological characteristics: they were all of East European (primarily Polish or Russian) origin and had arrived in Palestine in the second or third wave of Zionist immigration, between 1904 and 1917. Together with their children and with a number of individuals who had been co-opted into the elite group, the leaders constituted an oligarchy with an apparently undisputed and unassailable hegemony over Israeli society.[44] This hegemony was expressed in setting the rules of the game for cooperatives active in agriculture[45] and industry,[46] controlling and allocating state resources, and forming a new Hebrew culture, a hidden and explicit political agenda, as the military was used as a tool of control and Israelization.[47] To legitimate its dominant position, the oligarchy pointed to its successes, real or apparent, in a variety of areas: creating a society based on mass immigration and a common (Hebrew) language;[48] transforming the class structure that had been prevalent in Diaspora Jewry; developing the image of the Zionist pioneer, the *halutz*, and the native-born Palestinian (subsequently Israeli) Jew, the *sabra*, blurring the meaning of the Arab-indigenous population; gathering exiles into a melting-pot process; developing modern armed forces, comprised of skillful warriors; effectively handling the Palestinian Arab challenge; and succeeding on the battlefield in a hostile Arab environment.

To the above impressive accomplishments one must add what the leadership termed the "unprecedented success" of absorbing the waves of mass immigration during the 1950s while maintaining the basic contours of pre-1948 Zionist society, depicted as a unified and almost ideal, if not heroic, society.[49] The elite group also popularized the axiom that the oligarchy's values—Western, modern, egalitarian, achievement-oriented, and Zionist—must be accepted by other groups in Israeli society, even if such groups were not represented in the various power centers, and even if implementing these values was not always in the best interests of outsider, marginal, or marginalized groups. Included as outsiders were the elite cluster of old, established Sephardic families; Palestine's organized non-Zionist Jewish community, which predated the Zionist pioneers' arrival in the country; the members of the pre-Zionist colonies (*moshavot*) founded in the late nineteenth century; most of the urban bourgeoisie; and members of non–East European immigrant groups, that is, immigrants from Central and West Europe, Yemen, and in the post-1948 period, Asia and North Africa.[50] The most completely marginalized group were the Arab citizens of the state.[51]

Among the first practical measures that the fledgling Jewish state undertook was to transfer rapidly most of the key personnel of the Jewish Agency, affiliated with the World Zionist Organization, to leadership roles within the state apparatus, and concurrently to separate the Jewish Agency and the state. In accord with the Status of the Jewish Agency Act, the state assigned to the Jewish Agency functions that were clearly defined and that were, in essence, marginal within the state.[52] In this manner, the state sought to secure its autonomy from both the World Zionist Organization and world Jewry. However, a more complex strategy was required to wrest independence from the institutions and subculture of the Workers' Society, which represented the interests not only of the Histadrut, but also of other organizations: Mapai and the remaining Histadrut-oriented political parties, as well as the pioneering Zionist rural settlement movements. When David Ben-Gurion established the ideology of state autonomy, coined statism or *mamlachtiut*, "kingdomship," in Hebrew—accompanied with some degree of militarism[53]—as both a rallying symbol and an immediate objective, he aimed to transfer control of key institutions from special-interest groups to the state. However, it was still not clear who would be ruling whom. Would the party (Mapai), with its dominant position in the labor union, utilize the powerful new instrument of the state to continue to control Israel's power positions? Or, conversely, would the party and the Workers' Society become the informal operational branch of the state?[54]

In line with the concept of state sovereignty, which became synonymous with the state's autonomy, both the pre-state paramilitary organizations, such as the Haganah and Palmach (affiliated to a fragment of the socialist party system, Mapam), and the rightist revisionists, Etzel and Lechi, were disbanded; 90 percent of the lands, key industries, and the school system were nationalized (or "statized"); as was control over the distribution of external resources, such as donations from world Jewry, reparations from Germany, and at a later stage, foreign aid and grants from the United States. Nonetheless, the struggle for control of Israel's society and economy that ensued between the state and the dominant party, Mapai, did not conclude decisively during the 1950s. There were three reasons that the tug-of-war continued.

First, most of those who occupied key positions in the state apparatus also held key positions in the party. Second, strata totally dependent on the state had not yet been created. Third, the labor union and traditional ruling party held sway over vital mechanisms of control and sociopolitical mobilization and penetrated the new peripheries, which the state could not readily dispense with in light of the waves of nonselective mass immigration.

The symbiosis created between state and party was also a convenient medium for enabling the Arab minority that had remained within the boundaries of the new state to be absorbed within Israeli society and the new economic structure, though such absorption was partial and did not let them compete in the labor market with the protected new Jewish immigrants.[55] Due to the symbiosis, the activities of this minority group could be monitored. Only through the four-way coalition of the state, the Jewish Agency, the party, and the Histadrut, and the cooperative frameworks established between these mechanisms, could a drastic change—that is, the possible chaos of destabilization—in Israeli society be prevented. In addition, both the coalition and the cooperative frameworks ensured the preservation of the pre-state distribution of power, even though the emergence of the new state inevitably posed certain threats to the legitimacy of the previous distributive system, entailing major demographic and cultural changes, a total redrawing of ethnic and national boundaries, and a dramatic alteration in the structure of interests.

Despite the threat, the establishment of the state and the concomitant absorption of a mass immigration that doubled the country's population in only three years initiated an accelerated process of social mobility within the veteran Jewish population, almost totally transforming Israeli society's class structure. In addition to increasing significantly both the power and bureaucratic structures of the state, the influx of immigrants led to an impressive upsurge in the number of citizens that depended directly on the state. The period saw the creation of large state and public bureaucracies that absorbed the overwhelming majority of veteran Jewish members of the collectivity. Thus, many of the collectivity's members became officials with the civilian or government security agencies—that is, civil defense, policing, or intelligence—or they became teachers, police officers, physicians, dentists, lawyers, accountants, academics, mass-media personnel, and career and noncommissioned officers in the Israeli armed forces. Many of these individuals became part of the country's social elite, but other became active economic entrepreneurs, subsidized by the state, who created a new middle class.[56] This new middle class balanced the economic and political power bases of both the Workers Society and the bourgeoisie that was already in place when Israel proclaimed its independence. In contrast with the established bourgeoisie dating back to the pre-state period, however, the new entrepreneurial class, which lacked the necessary financial resources, was completely dependent on the state, and like the Worker's Society, required direct or indirect access to public funds or concessions.

The new immigrants, especially those from Middle Eastern countries and North Africa, were expected to become a part of the working class in rural and urban areas and to be absorbed by the labor market in agriculture, industry, and services. As the immigrants were isolated from the veteran community socially and geographically, they were provided with separate social services that further increased their isolation and dependence. Unlike the other actors in the game, the new immigrant class was powerless, to the extent of being unable to translate its adjustment difficulties into a mythology replete with heroic symbols, as happened for some of the previous waves of immigration.[57] Many of the early Zionist settlers had not only mythologized their struggle, but had gone one step further: They had managed to convert the Zionist pioneer myth into capital, status, and power by establishing multiple institutions and securing the leadership of those institutions.[58]

Social differentiation, gaps, diverse strata, and political subgroups began to form within the new immigrant population as part of the process of ecological and social isolation.[59] The division of the immigrant population into subgroups tended to take place along ethnic lines. The East Europeans usually distanced themselves from the Asians and North Africans in the pace and nature of their social mobility.[60] The state mobilized these newly formed strata in the immigrant population to carry out tasks assigned to them, and in this way, they balanced to the strata of the older, more established segments of the country's Jewish population and contributed significantly to growth in the state's autonomy and power. The ways that new immigrants were incorporated into Israeli society strengthened the symbiotic relationship between the party and the state.

Obviously, all of the above processes were neither planned nor consciously willed into reality, but rather were the outcome of the dynamics of control over various resources or the routes of access to these resources, through language, culture, skills, personal connections, and so forth. In other words, the processes resulted primarily from the inner logic involved in the building of the Jewish nation-state and from the desire to enable the state to function autonomously, without becoming an agent for the interests of other groups. At the ideological level, the concept of Zionism was reduced to the task of building up a strong state,[61] while the other goals of Zionist ideology— welfare, quality of life—became secondary. It was felt that only the state could ensure both the security and the continued existence of the country's Jewish community in the face of the protracted conflict with a hostile environment.

As additional groups came into being in Israel, and as more established groups gradually accumulated power, the link between the state and the party began to weaken. The state was not trying to free itself from the Mapai's support; the party simply lost strength as it became progressively more difficult for the party to rally support among new immigrants. In time, Mapai turned into a financial burden, which the state shouldered.

The fading symbiosis between the state and the party exploded into open conflict with the so-called Lavon Affair (1960–61).[62] When David Ben-Gurion and his young lions were kept from the power centers, the state's strength and autonomy diminished in favor of the party. For a brief period, Mapai seemed to regain its hegemonic position, and Israel was perceived as a party-state that maintained a formal democracy with formal rights, such as the franchise, to the Jewish majority, while ignoring important citizen rights, especially those of minority and marginal groups.[63] Although Israelis voted in free elections and enjoyed certain freedoms, they could not remove the ruling party from its position of power because of the country's sociopolitical structure and the oligarchy's cultural hegemony. As far as the symbiosis between the party (which supported and was supported by the Worker's Society) and the state was concerned, the Mapai-Histadrut establishment partnership appeared to have regained dominance and the country's political situation looked increasingly similar to what had been current in the pre-1948 period, when the state, or rather the state in the making, was run by the party.[64]

In 1977, the situation changed dramatically. The process that began shortly after the 1967 war then reached its culmination, and the new middle class, which had abandoned the patronage of Mapai—in its new guise as Alignment, which included Mapam, a party to the left of Mapai—directed its support to a fledgling party, the Democratic Movement for Change.[65] When Mapai's archrival, Herut, in a joint electoral listing with the Liberal party and other small factions called Likud, formed the government in 1977, the link between the state and Mapai was severed, and both the state and Mapai were weakened.

During Likud's first decade in power, its bloc, consisting of Herut and its junior partners, failed to replace Mapai in an alternative system of linkage with the state. Rather, the state managed to utilize some of Likud's ability to reach socioeconomic strata that had previously been alienated from the state, increasing its base of support primarily among second- and third-generation Israelis of Mizrahi Jewish background.[66] Both the 1973 war and the 1982 war in Lebanon considerably damaged the image of the state as an efficient implementer of rationally formulated policies, diminishing the state's power and, to an extent, its very legitimacy compared with other groups. At the same time, however, this diminution of the state's power and legitimacy did not bring about the concomitant growth of a new dominant political party, social agency, or socioeconomic stratum rooted in civil society that could compete with the state in efficiency and strength to supply citizens' needs, or produce any alternative social order or fundamental changes in Israel's foreign or domestic policy.

The Palestinian uprising of 1987 and its spread into the Jewish territories, the need to absorb about 450,000 new Jewish immigrants from the former territories of the Soviet Union, the economic and social hardships that threaten the delicate fabric of Jewish society, recent changes in the world political system following the collapse of the Soviet superpower and the results of the first Gulf war, and the American pressure to link aid in the form of loan guarantees to the peace process have significantly changed the state's political calculus. These factors led to a change of government in 1992, another upheaval of the Labor (previously Mapai) party, which declared a change in national priorities. This was a code for accelerating the peace talks with the Arab states, accepting the principle of territories in exchange for peace (see Chapter Six), and creating bargaining terms under which Israel could grant autonomy and a degree of self-rule to the Palestinians of the West Bank and Gaza. In fact, the autonomy proposed to the Palestinians does not change substantially the nature of Israeli dominance, and remains fully consistent with the original aims of the control system. Even in peacemaking, the Israeli state still relies on the traditional stance of negotiating from a position of strength, using a military-minded approach,[67] as was demonstrated by the expulsion of the Islamic fundamentalist Hamas activists in December 1992.

From the State of Israel to the Israeli State—and Back?

The process of transition from a nation-state to a de facto binational state began immediately before the 1967 war. During that period, when it became apparent that the sociopolitical structure of Israel's Jewish society was changing, the country's first national unity government was established, and the Herut, whose ideals and institutions were traditionally stigmatized, were instead legitimized. Its members, who had always been considered outsiders, were allowed to become a part of the legitimate power system. Israel's spectacular victory in the 1967 war reinforced the image of the state as an effective actor. The state, and not the party, had reaped victory, created a sense of security, brought about a return to the Land of Israel's historic borders, and bolstered the nation's pride.[68]

A new factor gaining prominence on Israel's stratification map was the rapid buildup of its strength, was tied mainly to the state, rather than to the party. This was evidenced by the country's military-industrial complex, comprising the armed force and its elite of senior officers, officials in the foreign and defense ministries, the country's military industries and big businesses, private and public, such as the Histadrut enterprises, and cultural elite groups, which included members of the mass media.[69] Despite their Mapai roots, the components of the complex were essentially state-oriented. Some were operational arms of the state or part of the state's growing bureaucracy. Others were private economic entrepreneurs who derived their funding primarily from direct or indirect state subsidies, or received concessions or special benefits from the state. What is common to all of the individual and group members of the complex is their ultimate loyalty to the state, rather than to any specific interest group, including the party.

While the locus of power appeared to shift so gradually as to be almost indiscernible, in actual fact the shift was built into the situation and some elements of the initial political culture from the start. Since June 1967, the entire area of colonial Palestine, with slight additions if we take into account the Golan Heights, has been annexed de facto to Israel. This annexation did not come about because of a decision from any authority, but rather because no alternative decision was made, and because no individual group had the strength to make such a decision. From this period onward, Israel was transformed into a de facto binational Jewish-Arab state, in which all political power—political rights, citizenship, human rights, access to resources, and the right to define the collective identity—has been concentrated on one side of the newly created entity. Such hegemonic control (keeping Gramsci[70] in mind), was in the possession of the Jewish state, and the situation marks the difference between a de jure and a de facto binational state. One component of this state, namely, the state's veteran (from 1948) Arab citizens, is accorded rights and access to material resources, but is absolutely never granted a share of the symbolic resources of domination.[71]

The identity of the state was constructed as Jewish by means of various symbols and codes,[72] such as its flag, national anthem,[73] construction of its history, official days of celebration and memorial, and calendar.[74] The right to belong to the Israeli state was extended to Jews all over the world, by definition included in the Israeli collectivity. On the other hand, for the Palestinian inhabitants of the state, human rights are restricted by being conditional on good behavior and loyalty to the state, and conferred in a selective manner.

An immediate reply might be that if not for external constraints, the state might have annexed these territories de jure as well. Such annexation could have been effective immediately after the 1967 war and on various subsequent occasions. With the rise of the rightist Likud Party to power in 1977, many people expected or were apprehensive about a formal declaration of annexation, which would have been consistent with the party's platform. However, it is not accidental that this annexation did not come about, even under the circumstances attendant to the formation of an extreme nationalist government. The state was neither able nor willing to declare annexation, nor could it enact a general law covering the territories conquered in 1967, because this would have opened a Pandora's box, giving rise to the demand for civic and political rights on the part of the Palestinian population of the territories, and to a more subtle and sophisticated struggle for the entire territory of historic Palestine. The management by legal means of a conflict over political and civic rights from within—in a state that defines itself as democratic—is much more complex and uncertain than the continuation of a power struggle, conducted by means of violence, in which the Jewish side enjoys a decisive advantage. It is no wonder, then, that a number of Palestinian intellectuals considered privately the idea of proposing to Israel a formal and complete annexation of the occupied territories,[75] given the absence of any tangible possibility of expelling masses of Palestinians from Israel's spheres of control. From the point of view of state building, a de facto political annexation, accompanied by an autonomous settler movement, as has been going on since 1967, is the optimal solution. The status quo amounts to a more efficient and enabling form of annexation than any legalized, declared sort of annexation does.

Israel's polices have changed since the 1992 elections, but the results of the new policies from the perspective of state building are predictably familiar. Efforts were made to differentiate between occupied territories and administered peoples[76] by including in the autonomy offered to Palestinians only those located in densely populated areas, excluding the Jordan River valley, which was defined as a vital security zone, as well as East Jerusalem. The result would create two overpopulated Palestinian enclaves, each separated territorially from one another and from any other Arab-controlled space, forming a divided Palestinian autonomous entity—a reincarnation of the 1967–1992 state of affairs, in which the Israelis continued to control the entire area of colonial Palestine while refraining from building settlements in the most populated areas, but not in the other territorial spaces. However, the dynamics of the peace process, the need to support the mainstream Palestinian leadership in the face of the emerging Islamic fundamentalist movements, and the changing world order should force Israel toward a much more flexible policy.

The occupied territories that were included within the domain of Israeli control since 1967 do not amount to a conventional colony within Israel, as several scholars and thinkers have claimed.[77] A pure colony is a form of political, social, and territorial arrangement, which, despite the foreign control that is imposed upon it, is located outside the boundaries of the colonial state itself, and the state's relation toward it is essentially instrumental. The West Bank and Gaza Strip are an integral part of the building and expansion efforts of the territorial self-image of at least one of the versions of the collective identity of this immigrant-settler state.[78] In some cases, when a colony begins to be a heavy burden for the colonial power, the forces controlling the state begin to make cost-benefit calculations, and if these parties conclude that the business is not worth it, they leave the territory as fast as possible.[79] However, such parties will never concede control of a part perceived as integral to the state itself, even if maintaining control entails costs greater than any benefit that comes from possession; in this case, the price of maintaining the territory does not matter.[80]

The Dual Collective Identity of the State and Civil Societies

Israel possesses two souls that are in continuous tension but also complement each other. Israel defines itself as a Jewish nation-state that potentially belongs to the entire Jewish people. On one hand, this is a very broad definition of Israel's sociopolitical boundaries, which have expanded to contain large populations. Many of the state's symbolic owners are not even citizens, let alone residents, nor do they live within the boundaries of the state's jurisdiction. One may wonder how many of these extraterritorial potential citizens consider themselves to be symbolic owners at all. On the other hand, the definition also restricts Israel's boundaries by excluding both the non-Jewish citizens within the pre-1967 borders and the non-Jewish citizens of the occupied territories controlled by the community-state. This unique situation arises as a result of two factors: the state in the making's ideological sources and patterns of resource mobilization, and the impact of the waves of mass immigration during the early years of statehood. At the same time, Israel defines itself as a democratic state based on Western types of parliamentary and legislative authority, with participation in the state based on a universalistic liberal citizenship—meaning that all citizens, individually, are equal before the law and have equal citizen rights.[81]

This contradiction results from Zionism's defining itself as the national movement of the Jewish people, while having many and varied sources, from modern nationalism to liberalism to different nuances of socialism. One of its principal sources is the Jewish religion, mainly its nineteenth-century East European version. One can distinguish several ways in which religion influenced both Zionism and Israel. First, while the Jewish religion has always regarded Zion as the target territory of Jewish immigration and redemption, the Jewish people's return was designated only in the utopian messianic era. Zionism's decision to adopt this designation from the Jewish religion in its narrow meaning, or from Judaism as a civilization in its wider meaning, was made on ideological rather than political or material grounds. Zion or Palestine was not chosen for rational economic or political reasons, such as cheap, fertile land, abundant natural resources, political opportunities, or availability of native labor.

Second, Palestine lacked all or most of the factors that attracted immigrants to North and South America, North and South Africa, Australia, or New Zealand.[82] Because it required investments that were totally out of proportion to the expected profits, Zionism's choice of Palestine points to the essentially messianic character of the movement, which had to base itself, at least initially, on highly selective immigration.

Third, many of the key symbols used by Zionism and subsequently the Israeli state were drawn from the storehouse of the Jewish religion. The language that Zionism adopted was Hebrew, the language of the sacred Old Testament, which had a strong theological content. The revival work was carried out by secular Jews who referred to these texts more as historical documents, though at same time, as myth or as folklore.[83]

Fourth, at a somewhat later stage in Zionism's history, the Jewish religion was the sole common denominator among immigrants from various sociocultural backgrounds. In addition, the Jewish religion, in a somewhat more generalized form that is carried also by secular Jews—a contradiction in terms because the Zionist revolution saw Jews as a nation, not a religion—provides a common external and mythical enemy, the Gentile's world, which is commonly suspected of harboring anti-Semitic intentions and plots rooted in a somewhat popular Judaism. According to the Jewish religion, one could divide humanity into two parts: the Jews and the others. This division assigned a deterministic character to the Arab-Jewish conflict, which was perceived as an eternal struggle for survival of the Jewish people, or at least a struggle that would be engaged in until the start of the messianic era.

Fifth, the Jewish religion, adopted by the secular state, was the sole criterion for determining the boundaries of Zionist society. No Israeli civic holiday is commonly celebrated by all of the country's citizens. Intended to be a civic festive occasion for everyone, Israel's Day of Independence is a bitter reminder to Palestinian Arabs of their political and social devastation (*al-Nakba*). All of Israel's other holidays and memorial days are of significance only to Jews. Memorial Day (for Israel's fallen soldiers) focuses on Jewish war dead, although Druze and Circassian war dead are also remembered.[84] Similarly, Holocaust Memorial Day is dedicated to the memory of the Jewish victims of the Holocaust, mainly European Jews. Although aimed at both Jews and Arabs, May Day, which is primarily a class rather than a state holiday, is increasingly fading into the woodwork with the shift to the right of the Israeli center of political gravity, and with the recent collapse of Communist regimes in various parts of the world.

Sixth, as the Arab-Jewish conflict in general, and the Palestinian-Jewish conflict in particular, escalated in the last three decades, the legitimacy of a Jewish nation-state in the Middle East has become increasingly problematic.

With its rallying cry of historical rights to the land, the Jewish religion provides a great deal of legitimacy at the general cultural level and at the level of various religious subcultures that deny the existence of any legitimacy problem whatsoever. According to their ideologies, if the God of Israel promised the Land of Canaan to Abraham and his children, the question of Israel's right to exist is a nonissue. Previously occupying only marginal positions in Israel's political system, the representatives of the country's religious subcultures have begun to move closer to the center, both symbolically and in their position regarding other political power centers.

Other ideologies, primarily socialism in its various forms, secular nationalism, and liberalism, were major factors in developing Israeli identity, and to an extent, they neutralized the religious influence (see Chapter Four). When the country's political system was still in its formative phase, socialism provided asceticism, egalitarianism, and the drive to cooperative effort, primarily through the sociopolitical activism of the "here and now" approach. Nationalism supplied the political framework and the institutional tools for both the religious and socialist elements. Liberalism contributed its universal outlook, giving Israel's evolving culture a Western orientation, enabling the entire system to locate itself within the Western world-system, and ensured a continuing link between Israel and its principal competitor in the Jewish world, the North American Jewish community.[85] At the same time, the claims of liberalism enabled the newly created Jewish political entity to detach itself from its Arab environment and from Eastern Jewish immigrants.

Thus, within the Israeli identity, there was a tense but ongoing dialectic relationship between four components: religion (Judaism), socialism, nationalism, and liberalism. At the political and social levels, however, these four sources became sub-identities, around which various political and social subcultures and segments of civil society and political groups formed. These subcultures carried on a historic struggle among themselves for hegemony within the Israeli political culture. In the initial stages, the state in the making and its society primarily evolved under the control of socialist groups, although the collective identity included nationalist elements and reflected coalitions with groups that articulated universalist ideologies.

The political dominance of the socialist, nationalist, and liberal ingredients of the collective identity led to a weakening of Zionism's religious foundations and encouraged many to promulgate the idea of a secular Zionist society in Palestine. In 1948 the gates opened, and waves of nonselective mass immigration began to arrive, bringing with them a considerable number of immigrants who came to Israel mainly for traditional or religious reasons. This period saw the formation of new potential power foci and societal groups, who were inclined to define the Jewish community in the Holy Land in more religious terms, and in terms of sacred history. Combined with nationalism, these new groups entered the political and social spheres by establishing alliances according to their religious-national orientations. The alliances were essentially a protest against the Mapai–Histadrut–Jewish Agency complex that had kept the traditional religious immigrants on the sidelines of society, far from the sources of power, from access to material resources, and even from the establishment's central symbols.

The Territorial Dimension and the Struggle for Hegemony

Before 1967, the Zionist movement had managed to build up a Jewish political entity on the territorial margins of the Promised Land of Zion, namely, the coastal plain, which biblical mythology suggested belonged primarily to the Philistines. Because of the structure of the local Palestinian society, Jewish immigrants could not reach the central hilly areas excepting the region around Jerusalem, which constituted the historical and mythical territory of the biblical kingdoms of Judea and Israel.[86] The development of the State of Israel alongside the sanctified territory of the Promised Land, but not inside the core territory, helped the Zionist sociopolitical system to create a secular society and protect the state's autonomy from pressure by religious and nationalist groups. With the capture of the West Bank and its redefinition as Judea and Samaria, the situation changed dramatically. The encounter between the sacred and the mundane provided several advantages to groups that could exchange holiness for participation in the system, and these advantages continued to increase within the context of the community-state.

Before the 1967 war, elitist religious groups had been relegated to the periphery of the political and cultural system, even though the source of these groups was identical to that of the country's middle and state-oriented classes. Once the West Bank was under Israeli control, these groups began to move within the system toward the symbolic center, and at the same time, to gather political strength, converting their closeness to holiness into political power. There was also an increase in the prestige and power of the Likud party, the successor of the right-wing Revisionist Zionism and later the Herut party, which knew how to establish attractive alliances with traditional and religious groups and best use overt or covert protest based on Jewish ethnic and religious codes. All of the groups allied with Herut had one common grievance: They had been marginalized by the establishment, which was perceived as class-oriented, socialist, and secular. The Herut-led coalition produced, on the one hand, groups of settlers determined to expand the state's territorial control into the occupied territories, and on the other hand, pressure groups demanding that the state change its basis from a class and socialist orientation to a more religious one. It should be noted that the coalition resulted from the convergence of several struggles—class, ethnic, political, and religious—and was not the outcome simply of a struggle among ideologies and political cultures.

The transformation of the State of Israel into the Land of Israel (see Chapter Four) as the cultural and religious encoding for the new Israeli state[87] did not only transform the nation-state into a binational entity, but also clearly signaled that the power relations within the Israeli Jewish community had changed. The origins of several elite groups that pushed immediately after the 1967 war to redefine the collectivity's boundaries and its basic identity, founding the Land of Israel Movement, were from the mainstream secular activist segments of labor and socialist Zionism.[88] Only when the elites of the old regime were weakened by the 1973 war did the political and symbolic struggle to implement the Land of Israel ideology pass to the national-religious and secular-nationalist elite groups, who then transformed the struggle into an internal struggle over the hegemonic rule of the collectivity.

The state also established a new coalition with new strata, as the inner logic of the state—in terms of both the identity and structural dimensions—necessitated the evolution of a binational situation, defined permanently as temporary. To enable the Jewish state to continue defining itself as a Jewish nation-state, the Israeli state maintains control of these territories without annexing them. At the same time, the state carries out several important activities within the captured territories, controlling land transactions, monitoring how water resources are utilized, and introducing settlers from preferred population groups within the dominant society. The Palestinian residents of the occupied territories constitute both a labor and a consumer market for Israel, concomitantly with the establishment of a dual market alongside the national origins.[89] According to the relevant statistics, the profits to the state and to various socioeconomic groups within the state from controlling the territories exceeded the costs up to the end of 1987.

The State under Pressure

Because of the binational situation, two subcultures have crystallized within the dominant Jewish society to challenge the continuation of the status quo in the occupied territories. Each of the subcultures has its own institutions and set of motives for demanding an end to the binational situation. One subculture wishes to annex the territories; its ultimate goal, sometimes overt, sometimes covert, is to create conditions suitable for transferring all or most of the local Palestinian Arab population to lands outside of the Land of Israel, and to resettle Jews in their place. This subculture only partially reflects the state logic at a given time when faced with the complementary state logic of a voluntary reduction in state control of resources, such as land, natural resources, water sources, markets for products created by dominating another people, and cheap labor, so long as the perceived costs of maintaining control of the territories remain within tolerable limits.

Even if the Israel case does not fit precisely the colonial paradigm, some of the processes are familiar from colonial regimes, such as that France in Algeria and that of England in Ireland. This ultimately produces a situation in which the settlers, who are subsidized and supported by the state and serve as its local agents, force the state to act against its own inner logic and best interests. Thus, the state is forced, either formally or informally, to annex the colony as part of its ongoing state-building efforts, or to continue possession, even when the costs of doing so exceed the benefits, and even when such action threatens the very existence of the mother country.[90] Even when the costs are high, continuing control is generally justified by a mixed bag of pragmatic and security-related rationales and ideological or religious concepts that touch on the very nature of the mother state's collective identity.

Another partial aspect of the Jewish state's inner logic is represented by the second subculture, the basic assumptions of which form a worldview that is more or less antithetical to the orientations of its opponent culture. These assumptions include the idea that peacefully resolving the conflicts between Jews and Arabs, and Jews and Palestinians, is possible though not easily accomplished. The solutions depend, among other things, on the political behavior of Israel. Another assumption is that the Arab-Jewish and Palestinian-Jewish conflicts are not different in nature from other negotiable disputes, and have little in common with the persecution of Jewish people in the past. Third, peace is one of the most desirable collective goals because its achievement is a necessary (though not sufficient) condition for attaining other goals, such as a more egalitarian society, economic growth, immigrant absorption, improved welfare, and technological, scientific, cultural, and artistic progress. Fourth, both civil society and state have a civic basis, and membership is based on citizenship; it is not necessarily a relation of non-particularist attributes, such as religious, ethnic, or racial affiliations. Fifth, citizenship is conditional, as it depends on fulfilling mutual obligations. The state must provide its citizens with internal security, law and order, protection from external threats, well being, and all generally accepted civil and human rights. Citizens are obliged mainly to obey the state's laws, perform military duties if needed, and pay reasonable taxes. Sixth, the existence of the state and membership in the collectivity are not ultimate values, but functions of the quality of life that the state offers its citizens. And finally, Israel is supposed to be a part of Western civilization; as an accepted member in this club, it assures a wide measure of multiculturalism and social pluralism.

The subculture described above basically perceives the world system, especially the Western world and North America, as a friendly reference culture. Yet, as most sectors of Israel's political economy seem to be more like those of developing nations, the culture favors the intervention of forces from the outside world to assure the economic, political, and cultural improvement of Israeli society as the subculture defines it. The world system is perceived as a potential ally in the subculture's struggle to gain more influence in Israeli society.

Each of the subcultures adopts its own methods for recruiting state support for its cause, and believes that the rationale for support lies in the state's own value system. In doing so, each subculture provides an authentic but partial gloss of Israel's collective identity as a Jewish nation-state, ignoring the fact that a significant portion of the state's identity, symbols, and decisions regarding areas targeted for Zionist settlement can be traced to Jewish ethnic religion. That said, both subcultures believe in Israel's exclusive Jewish communal identity, and both are determined to ensure that Israel will not become a multinational state in formal terms, although it is a multinational state in fact. All of the other reasons cited for returning to the status quo ante of the nation-state—preserving democratic values and public morality—are not part of exclusively political considerations, but rather are concerned with the nature and procedures of the state's regime. The reasons a subculture gives for its position can be considered of a purely political nature only when they are directly related to the possible weakening or demise of the state.

At the same time, it cannot be argued that a state's policies will always be determined on the basis of its unique political logic. If changes are evident in the state's cost-benefit balance or in the group's interests on which the statist logic is based, state policies will be altered accordingly. The alteration might even be based on the values represented by one of the two opposing subcultures, based on an alternative definition of identity—as seen, at least on the rhetorical level, in the changes in the priorities of the state following the temporary return of the Labor party to power in 1992. However, policy change does not always occur, even when the circumstances justify it, nor is there any guarantee that the state always adopts a pragmatic policy enabling it to adapt to new circumstances. Like any organization, the state can be the cause of its own weakening in terms of overall position, surveillance ability, or resource mobilization, or even the cause of its own destruction. We have the example of the ruin of the Christian Marionette polity in Lebanon, which was unable to resist the temptation to expand into areas populated by Muslims and Druze, alongside the more recent examples from the Balkans and the former Soviet state.

There are two diametrically opposed ways of reasoning in Israel, each of them derived from an alternative definition of collective identity. Although each of these lines of reasoning represents only one aspect of the state's logic, it is very convenient for the state to have the two existing side by side, as from the perspective of statist logic, they complement and balance each other. When it appears that the opposed sides are deadlocked and that decisions cannot be made even in the matter of resolving internal conflict, the state assumes a position of strength. as the political logic apparently contains, in a dialectical manner, both lines of opposite reasoning, perception, and construction of the sociopolitical reality.

However, in the present situation facing Israel, the amount of stateness is somewhat diminished. The reason for the diminishing effect is that the state has extended its control over a population that is relatively large in proportion to the size of the Israeli population, and which completely rejects the idea of being a part of that state. Furthermore, the population presently under control does not accept the legitimacy of Israeli authority, producing a vacuum of legitimacy in the territorial dimension of the state. Moreover, between 1967 and 1992, the autonomy of the state was continuously diminished, in the face of ideological groups that stressed the primordial Jewish state identity. In addition to producing a profound ideological crisis within the Israeli public, the situation calls into question the authority and efficiency of the Israeli regime in general. The crisis, however, stems primarily from the fact that Israel is a strong state, capable of maintaining the status quo, rather than from any apparent weakness on Israel's part in the areas of making and implementing decisions and resolving internal conflicts.

The state institutionalizes conflicts not because it cannot solve them, but rather because it finds that the conflicts are conveniently suited to its own purposes. When a state institutionalizes conflicts that are not beyond its capacity for resolution, its power is augmented and the other competing agencies on the sociopolitical map are neutralized. The 1992 election was seen as an opportunity for the state-related societal groups again to increase the autonomy of the state vis-à-vis groups associated with primordial parts of its identity. But in fact, the expected slowing down in the process of the state's expansion into Palestinian spaces by freezing settlement efforts, and the reversal of the process of integrating the occupied territories into Israel, was not really implemented—exemplifying the continuous decline of the state's autonomy.

Conclusions

This paper introduced two additional dimensions into the state-society paradigm. The first is the state identity, and the second the state logic, which determines the perceived uniqueness of every state and provides an additional linkage as well as a source of strain and tension between state and society. The notion of state logic made possible a conceptual difference between the state and government, and the possibility of positioning the state against the government. The identities determine considerable parts of the social boundaries of the state and its civil society, as well as the basic assumptions of the rules of the game and the political culture. The autonomy of a state is supposed to be more vulnerable and permeable in the face of ideological interest groups and other societal formations that carry as a banner alternative definitions of state and society, especially identities with primordial connotations, symbols, and discourses. However, the state can also manipulate the different groups that represent alternative identities, or emphasize different parts of the identity.

Within this approach to the Israeli state and its society, I have tried to present, in broad terms, an alternative conceptual context for understanding and analyzing their histories as well as the current domestic sociopolitical changes in the country. Israel is presented as emerging from an immigrant-settler society, institutionally built on the remains of the British colonial state, and adopting a civic and secular collective identity, based on selective ingredients of the Jewish religion. The religious components of the state's identity strengthened with the victory in the 1967 war and the capture of the core territories of the Zionist ideology, reducing the state's autonomy.

Also, including about 1.8 million Palestinians into the Israeli control system transformed the country into a de facto binational state, offering a serious contradiction to the growth of its Jewish nation-state identity. The Israeli state, despite a certain diminishing of its autonomy, remains the determining actor in the Israeli political system, rather than civil society. Thus, all other actors compete with each other for the state's favors, on material and ideological grounds. We noted a previous reduction in the state's autonomy against groups with ideologies based on Israel's Jewish ethno-centric and primordial national identity, but at the present time, the state is increasing its autonomy, which in turn strengthens societal strata that represent and adhere to the more universalistic ingredients of its collective identity. The oscillation between universalist and particularist tendencies will continue, depending on which one contributes a higher payoff for the state, which is by no means a closed system. In an unstable world system, these changes can be rooted also in remote exogenous factors, or in the immediate political environment. The disintegration of the Soviet Union suddenly led to Israel incorporating into the system about 500,000 new immigrants—today, more than 1 million—another critical mass that should change the internal distribution of power and the state logic. At the same time, changes in the balance of power in Jewish-Arab relations can be a trigger for state-logic change.

CHAPTER SIX

Patterns of Militarism in Israel*

Like other issues linked to the Jewish-Arab conflict and Jewish-Arab relations, most of the studies concerned with Israel, such as the place of the
military and militaristic culture in Israeli society, are heavily distorted compared with other themes prevalent in the discourse and debates in the social
sciences.[1] Ideological considerations blur the issue; until the publication of
Uri Ben-Eliezer's *The Making of Israeli Militarism,* even using the term "militarism" in the canonical textbooks was taboo in Israel.[2] The main purpose
of this paper is threefold: to survey briefly the present state of the literature
on so-called civil-military relations in Israel; to revise the overall impact of
the Jewish-Arab conflict and the militarization of Israeli society; and to reformulate the effect of militarization on the institutional and value spheres
of the Israeli collectivity and collective identity.

The puzzle that appeals most to social scientists who deal with Israeli
society centers around one research question: if Israel harbors so much

* From Baruch Kimmerling, "Patterns of Militarism in Israel." *European Journal of
Sociology* 2 (1993): 1–28.

military strength, and its military force constitutes such a central part of its society and is essential to its survival, why has the state not become militarist?[3] Given that in Israel, military elite soldiers enjoy such prestige, the military budget claims about a fourth of the state's expenses, and a military-industrial complex has emerged within the country and accumulated powers of its own,[4] how can it be that Israel has not developed a militarist society? Why has Israel not become a modern Sparta? Answers to this question generally relate to a combination of primary variables. The first is the stability of the political structure and the democratic political culture.[5] Second is the "people's army" nature of the Israeli armed forces, or as they are called officially, the Israel Defense Forces, or IDF. Israel's military is perceived to be a popular army that has undergone a process of routinization, that is, the armed forces are built mainly on civilian reserve units and pass through a process of civilization[6] by which they cannot attain a military status detached from the rest of society and beholden to their own independent interests. Similarly, such researchers claim that a kind of mental and institutional compartmentalization between civilian and military spheres obtains in Israel.[7] Third, a military obliged, constantly and intensively, to tend to real security needs has neither the ability nor the resolve to develop a truly militarist character. Finally, the armed forces' high-ranking officers have become part of the social elite that forms national decisions and allocates resources; owing to this constructive partnership,[8] the military has no incentive to intervene in political and social matters at the expense of democratic norms.

Whenever the military has interloped in civilian spheres, it has been perceived as positive intervention. Such intervention is seen as a role expansion by which the military contributes to the education of deprived population sectors,[9] settlement activities in the country,[10] absorbing immigrants,[11] and developing a consensus culture based on universal conscription.[12] In view of such an analysis, researchers have tended to define Israel positively as a "nation-in-arms,"[13] a country in which civilians serve as soldiers whenever necessary to defend their homeland, and then take off their uniforms when the danger has passed. In a nation-in-arms, such obligatory military service does not encourage the armed forces to acquire more than minimal, unavoidable influence in political, economic, and cultural spheres.[14] This classification is opposed to the garrison-state model proposed by Harold Laswell in 1941—a state run by managers of violence, the existence of which, given the hostile outlying environment, is dependent upon developing the military means to ward off dangers.[15] Israel has also not been regarded as a praetorian state—a state in which the military complex wields decisive powers in the political process because the political institutions are weak.[16] In such a praetorian state, the state might be given directly to military rule and martial law, or the political institutions might be co-opted entirely according to David Rapoport's model.[17]

A considerable body of scholarship thus has endeavored to rid Israel of the stigma of militarism. Lately, however, a number of Israeli researchers[18] have tended to characterize Israel as a militarist society. This definition has supplemented other claims about the society, such as the chauvinistic nature of Israeli nationalism, and the betrayal of socialism by the workers' party, Mapai, the ancestor of the Labor party. Scholars view the turn to militarism as a consequence of the establishment of the state in 1948 and of Israel's incorporation into the Western bloc. In this view, rather than solving the Arab and Palestinian problems through a peace process, Israel perceived as in its interest to externalize the conflict and transform it into a dispute between states, if only to forestall the return of the refugees. In quite a different analysis, Ben-Eliezer[19] reached a similar conclusion. In his view, the roots of militarism in Israeli society reach back to the Jewish political community, the *yishuv*, which developed in colonial Palestine. In this period, the decision that only force could resolve the Jewish-Arab conflict was conclusively adopted and has remained operative ever since. As a result of this social construction of reality, an elite has emerged in Jewish society whose crucial role derives from its military or security functions. Barzilai,[20] using the much softer term of "combatant community," found the "permanent siege" costly in terms of civil rights that were considered inferior to security needs.

In both institutional and conceptual senses, the concept of security in Israel is far more wide-sweeping than the term military; at the same time, the ever-expanding boundaries of security are loosely defined, and almost any sphere or subject can be connected expediently to it. The economy, industry, settlements, and elementary school, high-school, and higher education structures are often incorporated in security-related spheres. Yet if the institutional boundaries of what is called the security network are mapped somewhat more formally, they appear to include the armed forces; the intelligence network and General Security Services; the civil and military administration of the occupied territories; the defense ministry and its governmental bureaucracy; the Knesset (the Israeli parliament) Foreign Affairs and Security Committee; the government's (impermanent) security cabinet;

the many-branched military industry, including research and development sectors, either government-owned, public, or private; and finally, various lobby groups of the branches mentioned above.

Despite the above findings, analyses, insights, and hypotheses, social scientists who examine Israeli society tend to resist classifying Israel as a militarist state or society. Assuming that Israel is not militarist, an analytic riddle indeed remains: How has the state retained an essentially nonmilitaristic nature if objective conditions that urge militarism are constantly at play in Israel, and signs of militant character appear in many of its public spheres? This debate is not entirely semantic. The central claims of the present article are as follows: in contrast to most of the approaches in social science research of Israel, which abjure the state's militarist character, it seems reasonable to argue that militarism has developed to a large degree in Israel, and such militarism has varied from time to time in character and potency, it tends to be one of the central organizational principles of the society.

This phenomenon arises mainly as a response to the situation of protracted conflict that has dominated the Zionist settlement movement since its inception in Palestine,[21] where the surrounding Arab populations have been hostile to the movement's perceived colonial aims.[22] Militarism became a factor in Israel's society when arms and the management of violence came to be perceived as routine, self-evident, and integral parts of the Israeli-Jewish culture, a natural state that could never be changed. Such militarism developed a distinctive character over time. After 1977, it declined, but since the beginning of the 2000s, it appears to have taken shape again. As Shaw put it, "militarism and militarization do not depend simply or directly on the role of the military in society . . . but, to the extent that war preparation becomes central to it, it may become effective through other [societal] institutions."[23] To this one might add the extent to which the state and society is organized institutionally and culturally around managing a protracted external conflict.

Patterns of Militarism

Militarism has three main dimensions. Each dimension can exist separately as an expression of a specific kind of militarism, or a dimension may coexist in some combination with one or both of the other dimensions, and each combination creates another pattern of militarism. It bears mentioning that these are ideal types in the Weberian sense of the term. In reality, not all of the possible combinations of militarism are found, and when they appear, they vary in scope and extent. The first dimension can be called the violent-force dimension; the second is a cultural dimension; the third is a cognitive dimension.

The force dimension takes shape when military rule is established, directly or indirectly, and imposed for a length of time. Military rule comes about when generals or colonels take power, even when they take off their uniforms to create a facade of civilian rule. It is praetorian militarism when the rule is exclusively based on the coercive force of the armed forces' bayonets and its loyalty to the military leadership. In this eventuality, military officers become power brokers; they determine the public agenda, regulate the allocation of resources for the good of the military, and reward the ethnic or national class or group from which they themselves have emerged. This process of military rule is exemplified by regimes established in Africa[24] and Latin America from 1970–90.[25]

The force dimension is assured by evident social mechanisms. It arises when significant civilian portions of the state accept military rule as a self-evident and unchallengeable situation, as happened historically in the revolutionary stages of Latin American regimes, when the armed forces became the flag-bearing, liberating element that assured the overthrow of colonialism,[26] and when civilian politicians were perceived as being inferior at managing the state efficiently, remaining incorruptible, being patriotic, and representing the interests of citizens. In other words, force militarism occurs when the perception of the military regime as a self-evident entity penetrates the collectivity's cognitive map. In this way, the military rule imposed by force acquires a type of legitimacy, as many strata of the population do not consider its very existence to be problematic or a subject for political bargaining. When such legitimacy and hegemony arises, the phenomenon should be classified as a comprehensive military regime rather than transient military rule.

At the same time, force militarism is not yet accompanied by a vast ceremonial expression, except perhaps some personal cult of a leader, and in the final analysis, the armed forces are perceived to be politically instrumental means. In such situations, the military amplifies its power to surveill and control for internal security needs and defend interests connected directly to it and to ethnic, class, and other groups that draw their strength from the armed forces and from which they derive their legitimacy.

In some cases, such as Lebanon, Somalia, Nigeria, Zaire, and Congo, the military becomes embroiled in civil war. At first glance, it would seem that there is not, nor has there ever been, militarism of this type in Israel; such a claim, however, depends on the definitions of the terms used and the manner in which the boundaries of the Israeli collectivity are determined. Most social scientists who study Israel[27] define the collectivity as being basically Jewish and within the Green Line borders of the 1949 ceasefire lines. Under those definitions, Israel can be perceived as a democratic society. However, when the collectivity's boundaries are extended to comprise areas that have fallen under Israel's authority since 1967—that is, the conquered territories of the West Bank and Gaza Strip, and the security zone established by Israel in Southern Lebanon, which represents a settlement and security frontier for the Jewish population and in which 1.8 million Palestinians have lived under an occupying regime for a generation—the role of the Israeli military in the control network is cast utterly differently. The surveillance conducted by the armed forces and an auxiliary force of Arab mercenaries, an army that ministers policing activities aimed to pacify a nationally conscious people, and which strives to stifle a popular uprising that broke out in 1989 and has continued ever since, transforms the very nature not only of the Israeli military, but also of the entire Israeli state.[28] For its part, the military becomes a central agent in the attempt to assure internal security and surveillance. When the boundaries of the Israeli collectivity are marked in this way,[29] it taxes credulity to define the state as democratic in the accepted usage of the term; instead, Israel becomes what can be termed a *Herrenvolk* democracy, and its military is essentially the same as the tribal armies of various African states that assure the hegemony of one part of a collectivity's population and the subjugation of all of the other parts. At least in the Israeli case, Giddens'[30] major distinction between internal and external aspects of pacification and militarization of the nation-state cannot be applied. The same social institutions, with the same ideologies, operate both internally and externally.

Cultural Militarism

Another possible dimension of militarism is the cultural facet, which can be interwoven with the first form of political militarism. When militarism is confined essentially to this cultural form and becomes part of the collective identity, it lacks the coercive power to regulate internal affairs and can thus be termed cultural militarism. Prussian militarism is the prototype of this form, which Vagts[31] terms as "militarism by civilians," as opposed to militarism of soldiers. This form reached its zenith, as it were, with the Nazi regime. In it, the military does not control the decision-making process, which is governed by a political and ideological elite, though this elite might sometimes spruce itself up by donning the dress of generals and marshals. Cultural militarism obtains when the armed forces become essential to the social experience and collective identity—when they rank as one of the collectivity's central symbols and the embodiment of patriotism. Public experience is enveloped in ceremonial endeavor dominated by soldiering, military professionals, and paramilitary groups, such as youth movements that emphasize expressions of power, discipline, and military appearance. The main thrust of the collectivity's goals and orientations are defined in terms of war-making, preparations for wars, wars for peace, and wars to prevent wars.

In such political cultures, wars are perceived to be inevitable and the nation's essence and calling, an attitude reinforced as the soldiers march to battle in patriotic war to the sound of thunderous war plans formulated by ruling civilian elites. Soldiers of all ranks are objects of permanent indoctrination and control by professional political supervisors in uniform—so-called *politruks*. Victories are commemorated by an elaborate array of monuments, songs of glory, and cinema and television films, and a significant portion of private and public discourse applies itself to military matters. Monuments commemorate warriors and war dead,[32] and memorial days[33] and bestowing decorative medals for heroism become manifest in the public realm, if not an integral part of the culture and collective identity.

The necessity and unavoidability of wars extends to both internal and foreign affairs. Each major societal goal—education, industry, technological advance, science, the arts, and even leisure—are perceived to be enlisted to serve the homeland, of which the military is viewed as the purest and most conspicuous embodiment. In such cases, the military tends to be apolitical and ruled by professional criteria. The armed forces are autonomous only regarding their own internal matters, and with respect to decisions in logistical and tactical areas, and they are not always independent even in these areas. The boundaries between the military and political institutions are "integral," in Luckham's [34] terms, whereas the boundaries between the military and the cultural spheres are "permeable," that is to say that, all told, the boundaries between military and society are fragmentary. Military professionals receive esteem and prestige but are not granted political power,[35] which resides precisely in the hands of extramilitary, primarily political institutions that exploit the military, its symbols, and the entire discourse on national security to shape the social and political framework—in other words, to set the rules of the game, norms of public behavior, and priorities in the allocating societal resources, and to amplify their own powers.

A certain measure of cultural militarism can be found in the period soon after the establishment of the Israeli state, and some residual elements of this militarism remain today. In the northern metropolitan city of Haifa in the early 1950s, a military parade was arranged to celebrate the nation's independence day, and marchers hoisted the following slogan: "Israel trusts the IDF [Israel Defence Forces]—it is your defender and saviour."[36] A similar slogan that was quite current in the 1950s and 1960s was "The guardian of Israel neither sleeps nor slumbers." It is superfluous to point out that such expressions were known both to religious and secular Jews; here, in a very palpable sense, the military replaced the role of God. These catchall expressions reflected the spirit of the time. Jews had attained independence, and were expressing a sense that their existence and security depended not upon the will of God, fate, or the a colonial superpower, but on a new muscular Jew, his army, and his soldiers.

The attitude toward military institutions and militarism represents a central, determinative element in the social nexus. At the same time, the collectivity did not define itself as militaristic, as the concept had a stigmatic connotation and was considered to be "not appropriate for Jews."[37] The Israeli militarism is inclusive, embracing everything. At the very least, the phenomenon applies to the main, nonmarginal elements of the collectivity, and military mores are presented here as being universal for the time and place.[38]

A different aspect of cultural militarism is created by a thin, exclusive stratum of civilians, as well as military elite groups, who rank military knowledge and norms as classified, esoteric material. In so doing, they endeavor to maintain hegemonic control over the collectivity, excluding those who cannot access such knowledge and skills. In Israel, expressions of this trend appeared whenever the public agenda and political discourse devoted to subjects defined as in the interest of national security were closed and manipulated by a small, elite circle.[39] Even when the security discourse operated in a relatively public manner, it deployed codes that divided the collectivity into two parts: a small group that knew the secret, and the vast majority that both accepted that the security language was comprised of self-evident yet recondite and unknown truths, and was totally alienated from the discourse.

Such social division of labor in the security realm proceeds due to a prevailing assumption that, as security matters must remain classified, those who settle affairs in the secret-security realm possess extraordinary security and military talents. Such a convention was rehearsed to reinforce a perception that, in contrast to mundane operations in political, social, and economic spheres, decision-making in sensitive security fields required exceptional or extraordinary qualifications. Even though the prestige of the military and armed forces in Israel has continuously decreased since the badly managed 1973 war and, even more so, the 1982 war in Lebanon, the institutional and cultural centrality of security remains the same.

Praetorian Militarism

The type of militarism that corresponds most faithfully to the classic notion of the term is praetorian militarism, which is comprised of all three dimensions: coercive force, cultural-ceremonial, and cognitive. Alfred Vagts defines this militarism as the antithesis of the regular military way, which he describes as

> marked by a primary concentration of men and materials on winning specific objectives of power with utmost efficiency, that is with the least expenditure of blood and treasure. It is limited in scope, confined to one function, and scientific in its essential qualities. Militarism, on the other hand, presents a vast array of customs, interests, prestige, actions, and thought associated with armies and wars and yet transcending true military purposes. . . . Its influence is unlimited in scope. It may permeate all society and become dominant over all industry and arts.[40]

It is also a political situation in which the military, in effect, governs the state. The armed forces penetrate all social and state networks, such as bureaucracy, economy, education, and culture. It occurs when political and civilian institutions are weak and perceived as lacking legitimacy,[41] as in Japan before World War II, the Latin American states of the 1960s and 1970s,[42] some African states, and the Bedouin army of Jordan that rules over the Palestinian majority in the Hashemite Jordan state.[43] The military prohibits the existence of an autonomous civilian society; no autonomous public activities are conducted outside of its purview. The armed forces, the state, and the economy are all interwoven. Also, on the cognitive level, no process of differentiation arises between these spheres; the phenomenon is not limited to the institutional level, as C. Wright Mills[44] theorized, but verges toward the military-industrial state envisioned by Giddens.[45]

Civilian Militarism

The third dimension of militarism is cognitive, and once militarism penetrates it, it suffuses both the structural and cultural state of mind of the collectivity. The situation is liable to be reflected by full or partial institutional or cultural expressions, yet the main expression is a latent state of mind. Civilian militarism arises when civilian leaders and the led both regard primary military and strategic considerations as being, self-evidently, the only or the predominant considerations in most societal and political decisions or priority ordering. Usually, such an acceptance is unconscious. This militarism is what Lukes[46] characterized as the "third dimension of power." In such a situation, the entire social nexus, both in an institutional sense—economic, industrial, and legislative—and mental sense, is oriented toward permanent war preparation to defend the collectivity's very existence. Such preparation becomes part of the social routine; it is far from being an issue for public discussion, debate, or political struggle.[47] Even when military performances or other measures taken by the armed forces are publicly criticized, as has occurred often in Israel, the criticism is made through military experts, which does not challenge but reinforces militaristic orientations and discourse. It may be seen as a total militarism because it encompasses most of Israel's social institutions, and because of the perception that all of the people participate in war preparations and possess military expertise, and a majority is involved in active combat.

Such militarism can be termed civilian militarism, as its main bearers and implementers are the social center, the civil government, civil elites, and all or most of the members of the collectivity. For this type of militarism, it is not necessary that the military, as an institutional structure, governs in the political sphere, nor is the army necessarily stationed at the center of a statist cult. In contrast, the civilian militarism, or what might be called the military mind, is systematically internalized by most statesmen, politicians, and the general public to be a self-evident reality, the imperatives of which transcend political or social allegiances. The gist of civilian militarism is that military considerations, as well as matters that are defined as national security issues,[48] almost always receive higher priority than do political, social, economic, and ideological problems.

Military and national security considerations constitute part of the central organizing principles of the collectivity. In fact, any nonmilitary consideration is liable to be subordinate to the national security rationale and discourse.[49] David Ben-Gurion, former prime minister and minister of defense, once explained to Moshe Sharett, the foreign minister, that "the task of the Ministry of Security is to set security policies, whereas the task of the ministry of Foreign Affairs is to explain them."

Israel is a clear example of this type of militarism, amply underscored by the evident and latent social significance that is attributed to military service,[50] the way in which the entire society orients itself toward constant preparation for war, and what Ross[51] coined as "militarism of the mind." The sociopolitical boundaries of the collectivity are determined and maintained by participation in military service, its manipulation, and sacrifice to support spheres that are classified as areas of national security.[52]

The legacy of the early period of statehood is mixed, and it is perhaps hyperbolic to argue that trends of cultural militarism were entirely dominant. The identity of the state was tied in large part to the military, and the armed forces were central to the complex of "sacred" secular aims, achievements, and symbols associated with the new state, very much a mutation of Charles Tilly's phrase that "wars made the state and the state made war."[53] Yet the militarism was not an exclusive nexus of myths and imperatives connected to the state; opposed to it were symbols of other national imperatives and values, such as statehood, Judaism as a secularized nationalist creed, sociodemocracy, the flowering of the wasteland, and the building of the motherland. In the 1950s, the armed forces themselves were on one hand an elitist organization that had yet to undergo processes of professionalization and rationalization of the chain of command.[54] On the other hand, at least symbolically, their tasks were widened and the mission of building the state ascribed to them.[55] The results of amplifying the armed forces' powers were interesting: the process did not, as Horowitz[56] expected, enhance the civilization of the military; instead, as Janowitz[57] analyzed in his review of the limits of the civilization of professional officers and the military in general, the widening of tasks encouraged a trend by which more and more social domains and subjects were perceived to belong to the realm of national security.

The Social Construction of the Arab-Jewish Conflict

A major social process in Israel was the translation of the Jewish-Arab conflict, or the Jewish-Israeli–Arab-Palestinian conflict, into a particular social construction of reality.[58] A particular version of this dispute came to be accepted as a routine, immutable, and uncontrollable given. One important aspect of the process involved encouraging the perception that the Jewish-Arab-Palestinian conflict must be eternal. It was interpreted as fate, or a kind of Greek tragedy, to which the two peoples were beholden. In May 1956, then–Chief of Staff Moshe Dayan struck this general theme in his famous eulogy to an Israeli settler, Roy Rothberg, who was killed by Palestinian "infiltrators" from Gaza:

> We are a generation of settlers, yet without a helmet or a gun barrel we will be unable to plant a tree or build a house. Let us not be afraid to perceive the enmity that consumes the lives of hundreds of thousands of Arabs around us. Let us not avert our gaze, for it will weaken our hands. This is the fate of our generation. The only choice we have is to be armed, strong and resolute or else our sword will fall from our hands and the thread of our lives will be severed.[59]

These words were uttered by a professional soldier, yet they reflected and in some measure continue to express a basic element of Israeli culture. It is no wonder that Dayan's eulogy was branded on the nation's collective memory. Conflict and war was made routine, a trend especially potent on the institutional level[60] and reinforced by the accumulated experience of combat and war. It turned Israeli society into a polity that could mobilize itself in a very short time to advance two interconnected goals. First, reserve soldiers could be enlisted to serve along with regular conscripts and army career professionals, effecting rapid military advantage and creating a force roughly equivalent to that of a middle-sized superpower—about 500,000 men with 4,000 tanks and 600 combat aircraft in the 1960s. Second, the home front was efficiently mobilized to compensate for the enlistment and departure of the vast majority of adult males. The home front perpetuated the operation of the domestic social economy, though the level of social performance dropped and the provision of many broad social services was deferred, so enabling the most rapid possible restoration of a social order until the end of the general call-up.

But the process did not end with the absorption of the conflict into the institutional construction of the society; on the contrary, it decreased the motivation to do it and created large strata interested in its absorption. As suggested, the conflict became a determining factor shaping a fair measure of the social structure and collective identity of Israel.

The Political Structure

The political sphere tends to lose its autonomy as national security considerations, representatives, and interpreters encroach. In the final analysis, civilian militarism represents the supreme expression of attaining a hegemony as state and society become subordinate to military and national security considerations. Analyzing contacts between elites, Lissak remarks in a somewhat restrained idiom that "there are no really integral boundaries between the defense and civilian sectors."[61] This form of militarism is related to Gramsci's[62] approach, by which hegemony is defined as the struggle over monopolistic control of a set of ideas that exclude all other possible rival conceptions and approaches to society and state power, and which supports the domination of the ruling social groups. Such ideas may comprise not only an entire ideological network that regulates the collectivity's behavior, the rules of the game in the society, and even the perceived cosmological order that governs the world, but such ideas may be expressed in terms of institutional and behavioral arrangements that determine the collectivity's structure and boundaries.

As with other types of militarism, a necessary but insufficient condition for the ascendance of hegemonic civil militarism is to use force as the preferred means of solving foreign policy problems—the distinction between foreign and domestic often being blurred. The important determinant factor is whether or not the military mind turns into an organizing principle in the ideological, political, and institutional state realms, and whether or not strategic considerations, defined as necessities to actual physical survival, become ascendant at the expense of all other considerations. Moshe Dayan summarized this situation when he explained at the start of the 1970s that "it is impossible to bear two banners at the same time," referring to the banner of security as opposed to that of social welfare and other societal goals.[63] It is not so much that the militarist approach prioritized security over other social objectives,[64] but rather that the approach strengthened the perception that there were no alternatives in the political and social worlds to the military approach—a solution termed pragmatic and thought to accord with a given sociopolitical reality that the conflict was an issue of physical survival.

In general, the military-military mind, as opposed to the civilian-military mind, is a Weberian ideal type comprised of several elements. It perceives humankind, especially an enemy, as essentially bad, selfish, and irrational, capable of understanding only the language of force and violence. Allocative or value-centered conflicts can be adjudicated only by the use of violent force, or on the international level, by means of war. Instability and uncertainty rule the international order; the actors in this order are nation-states, and the conflicts between them lead invariably to regional wars, or yet more expansive war. Only the nuclear balance and deterrence reduced this instability to some extent. The supreme duty of army regulars and professionals, as well as those who deal with national security, is to remain constantly vigilant, as they provide security against the potential advent of total war. The security threat to the survival of the state is real, tangible, and immediate, as it is difficult to analyze the probability that certain potential threats will turn into actual violence, and danger is automatically perceived in terms of a worst-case analysis. While this situation requires the constant investment of social resources, material and human, in the security realm, the dividends reaped by the allocation never suffice, and it is always necessary and desirable to escalate such investments and promote a higher level of security. The professional military is necessarily subordinate to the civilian echelon, but at the same time, politicians are typically unable to distinguish between social aims that are desirable and undesirable. For instance, war itself—if it is not imposed upon the country—is not desirable. Unnecessary war, or war waged at the wrong moment, merely weakens the state's power and level of security. The military is not supposed to intervene outright in politics, yet it is supposed to offer professional opinions for the consideration of statesmen, and to resist impulsive policies and aggressiveness that is not warranted by circumstances. Only when needed are recommendations made for preventive war. The elements that glorify war are civilians who have never had firsthand experience of its ardor, tolls, and horror; these include statesmen, philosophers, poets, writers, journalists, social scientists, and natural scientists, a group of amateurs contrasted with a nearly scientific military profession.

Such a description of the military mind emerges in particular from Huntington's[65] analysis. In contrast, Janowitz[66] argues that professionalization is actually liable to make the military less responsive to civilian control, as the armed forces develop an ethos described as "the politics of wanting to be above politics." When civilians adopt these orientations, they take them without the self-constraints that the military ethos imposes on the armed forces. As civilians, they can allow themselves to be more militaristic than the military.

The Economic Structure

The situation becomes yet more evident upon examining the economic structure. From war to war, and especially since 1967, the Israeli economy has undergone an accelerated process of militarization. The theory of the necessity of autarchy and nonreliance on foreign elements to acquire security materials emerged in response to the arms shipment embargo enforced against Israel, which started in 1948. Today, Israel manufactures almost all of its arms, beginning with semiautomatic rifles, submachine guns, sophisticated tanks, several types of ballistic missiles, drone planes, observation satellites, and missile carriers and warheads.[67] As Israel's economy was too limited to cover the costs of developing and producing a military arms industry on the scale of a middle-ranking superpower, a vast program of exporting the products of the Israeli arms industry developed. Israel became one of the largest arms exporters in the world, trailing only the great superpowers. Other sectors in the military economy were financed with American aid and domestic government subsidies. When Israel's expenditures for security and material costs are compared to other states, even in current years, when such expenditures have been reduced drastically, the Israeli state still has one of the highest destructive capacities in using resources to improve security.[68]

Such circumstances bred a military-industrial complex in the pure meaning of the term. The regulation of military production schedules and the scope and character of military expenditures is governed by elite state bureaucratic groups, forces in the private economy, both Israeli and multinational, and the armed forces.[69] In a pioneering study, Bichler[70] found that between 1966 and 1986, security expenditures and the conversion of the economy for security production brought about wide-ranging changes in Israel's economic structure, favoring a trend of concentration centered around large holding groups. When in 1985 internal security consumption was cut and the international market was bogged down by crisis, the arms economy faced an acute problem: It was virtually impossible to convert production for security needs to production for civilian needs.[71] For our purposes, Mintz's remark is even more compelling:

> Public opinion in Israel generally views the activities of the complex with favor and support, often considering them to be essential. Because of the centrality and importance of the security conception in Israel and the broad consensus regarding a tangible danger to Israel's security, expressions such as "military-industrial complex," "new state managers," or "national security managers" do not have the same negative connotation which they are accorded in Western countries . . . Defense production and development is viewed with pride in the ability of and technological might of the small developing state and the "Jewish genius" dwelling therein.[72]

However, since the mid-1980s, almost all of the economic indications for defense consumption were in sharp decline as major societal resources were allocated to the settlement regions of the frontier territories of the West Bank and Gaza. Defense consumption as a percentage of gross national income decreased from 20.2 percent in 1980 to 11.7 percent in 1991, and domestic defense consumption from 14 billion to 8.9 billion shekels.[73]

The Legislative and Judicial Structure

After the establishment of the Israeli state in 1948, the provisional state council declared a state of emergency that has not been annulled, revised, or limited to this day. The declaration provides the constitutional basis for emergency legislation and administration; in theory, such laws and powers, enforced by the government, can suspend or abridge all civil and human rights in the state. Thus, according to clause 9(a) in the Code of Law and Order, "the government retains the authority to oblige the will of the prime minister or any other minister and enforce regulations for a state of emergency." Beyond this, a portion of the emergency laws that applied in the period of the British colonial state, and even throughout the previous era of Ottoman rule, remained valid in Israel, and a series of new Israeli emergency laws was added to them. If this is not enough, the legislative branch can also enact regulations for a state of emergency applicable to a period of three months, with an option to prolong the period without parliamentary approval. Such broad powers are founded upon a specific legal doctrine: Israel is perceived as facing a constant state of emergency, and threat to its very survival is understood to hover around it incessantly. Whenever necessary, the threat sanctions annulling or suspending legislation connected to the welfare or political and civil rights of all persons in the state; the justification for such curtailments is, of course, the state emergency. Such broad powers invariably tempt abuse.[74] In recent years, a number of new laws have been appended to the emergency law code that purport to fortify state security, but arguably, they have really been enacted to prohibit political activity that is normally considered to be legitimate.[75]

Such broad-sweeping emergency legislation is liable to seep through all social and political spheres. Between November 1975 and October 1977, regulations governing rates of exchange of Israeli currency were renewed twenty-two times; each time, the justification was a perceived state of emergency. Later, in July 1985, forcing through a so-called economic program, the government appealed once again to emergency regulations. Its purpose this time was to enforce price ceilings, constrain wage negotiations between workers and employers, and even intervene in private agreements, such as rents for housing and service payments. Historically, the judicial branch in Israel, including the nation's highest court, has demonstrated its friendliness toward suspending rights and liberties couched in arguments about national security. The courts generally rely upon the counsel provided by representatives of the state and its military and security experts. At play here is an implicit or explicit assumption that providing for the very survival of Israel are preconditions that demote all other rights, and rarely is there any serious public meditation about the logical inverse of this social proposition, namely, what is the point of the survival of the state entity if it does not guarantee basic human and civil rights?

Hofnung[76] has completed the most comprehensive analysis of the relation between views of state security in Israel and legislation and adjudication in the state. His conclusions are as follows. Legislation for state of emergency can potentially disrupt altogether, or suspend, civil and human rights in Israel, but during the first two decades of Israeli statehood, government authorities exercised restraint toward applying regulations for states of emergency, especially regarding liberties and protections afforded to Jewish citizens. In the 1970s and 1980s, however, such restraint started to erode. The onus of such legislation and the use of security arguments is selective: Jews are less seldom subjected to such regulations, suffer regulatory burdens less than Arabs do, and Palestinians in the occupied territories are exposed regularly to the arbitrariness of such administrative legislation. Control mechanisms have evolved in Israel that assure in some measure a democratic regime and the rule of law, at least for Jews: the Supreme Court, legislative committees, the institution of the state comptroller, the public ombudsman, electronic and print media, associations for the protection of civil rights, the protection of the right of assembly, and others. Yet perpetuation of so-called temporary emergency regulations continues, along with a broad constitutional sanction to enact them, which makes no particular reference to ruling parties or coalitions, or to the nature of the perceived dangers. The political culture of Israel is characterized by the widespread social endorsement given to broad emergency powers; despite many jurists' acute criticisms, the majority of the public, some portion of the elite groups, and the ruling authorities[77] sanction the emergency code. There can be no doubt that this virtual carte blanche to impose marital law represents one of the clear expressions of civilian-militarism in Israel.

Macho Culture and Gender Domination

Since the beginning of the Zionist venture in Palestine, one of the weakest points of the Israeli nation-building process was the state's great demographic inferiority—simply put, that there were far more Arabs than there were Jews, in Palestine and later in the entire region. This inferiority was translated into security and military-power balance terms. To improve the numbers, the two sources of population increase—immigration and internal birth rate—were sanctified. Alongside immigration, encouraging birth became a major societal goal, and women were perceived as the nation's womb. Since the first years of the establishment of the sovereign Israeli state, considerable material incentives were granted to Jewish women and families through the social security system, and a special, high material prize was granted for the birth of a twelfth child.[78]

However, equality for women remains a myth; it was never really implemented even in the kibbutz movement.[79] During active wars, society is divided basically into two major cultures: the warrior society of men and the home front society of women. During these brief periods of interruption, women take over many of the males' roles and positions in society; however, when the boys come home, women do not take advantage of war profits and in most cases have to forfeit their positions to the males. Gender mobility following wars is prohibited.[80] Young women, like men, are drafted into Israeli military service, but the length of the service is shorter and usually women are not called to reserves.[81] No combat service positions are open to women, and most of the complex and prestigious military occupations exclude them.[82] Most of the young women fill secretarial or other auxiliary roles, and the vast majority of them are under the command of authoritative, older, and higher-ranked men. Thus, within the military, the traditional marginality of women and the stereotypical gender-conditioned division of labor in society is reinforced. The military itself is basically a macho and male-oriented subculture.[83] One of the results of marginalizing Jewish-Israeli women in the the military, the most important Israeli cultural and political institution, is not only that women's marginality in society is reinforced, but also that they are excluded from the most important societal discourse, that of national security; recall the cultural convention by which individuals or groups who do not serve in the military, or who serve in peripheral positions—not in elite units, or not as officers—have no perceived right or expertise to participate in the security dialogue.[84] The case of Israeli women demonstrates another consequence of Israeli militarism and the complex relationship between the institutionalization of the conflict and the distribution of power in Israeli society.

A Political Culture with Primordial Tendencies

Rather far-reaching changes in Israel's political culture ensued between 1977 and 1992, beginning with Likud's rise to power and the formation of a Likud-led nationalist-religious ruling coalition. New models came to challenge the old civilian militarism, which had been built upon a religion, perhaps cult of national security. Competing perceptions of territorial and religious nationalism appeared, which became aligned to a manifest-destiny type of expansionist policy in favor of a greater Israel. The common denominator between the new orientations was the emergence of primordial principles (see Chapter Four). Such elements existed in the sociopolitical military establishment beforehand, but in the new Likud-led era, their potency increased. The major difference between the national religious culture and the national security culture was not a question of fundamental ruling assumptions; it was a matter of emphasis. The new orientation viewed Eretz Israel—a designation for Israel that resounded with Biblical connotations—as a territory rife with holy and national significance. Arguably, this perception endorsed the development of a new national moral agenda to which regular conceptions of rational politics and human rights were sometimes extraneous, and thus the new orientation spawned fringe variants that favored the expulsion of the entire non-Jewish population of the territories, either immediately or as a result of a deliberate program that would create circumstances favorable to such dispersion (e.g., war on a local or regional scale). Jewish settlements were established feverishly in the occupied territories densely populated by Palestinians to guarantee surveillance and control over the conquered area and create irreversible fait accompli. The geographic thrust of the new militarist orientation is instructive: the same movement that aimed ardently to consolidate control over greater Israel was willing to relinquish control of the Sinai peninsula, territory that was holy to the competing national security culture.

Another modification wrought by the national-religious political culture was the amplification of the ideological and political sphere by virtue of abandoning national security considerations that seemed too narrow. Emphasizing political and ideological motivations changed the measure of freedom and autonomy attributed to the political center. The most evident expression of the new powers subsumed by the center was the recognition that the state could now wage a war of choice. Even in rhetorical terms, such a conflict was no longer perceived to be a last resort.[85]

At the time of the 1982 war, Menachem Begin endeavored to deploy the military to attain patently political objectives. He denied overtly the rhetoric of the previous culture of civilian militarism dictating that the people's army should engage only in wars in which there was perceived to be no choice but to fight, splitting the national consensus that had evolved concerning the conduct of war. Begin claimed that a war can be waged by choice, and at the same time be considered to be *jus ad bellum,* a just war. But for the first time in the history of the state, a significant, bona fide protest movement, coupled with suggestions of possible mass resistance to an affirmation of the elective use of war violence, emerged in response to the costly prices of the government's policy and its inability to conclude its operations in a timely manner. This nascent resistance included expressions of dissent within the military itself.

Until Begin's affirmation of the legitimacy of war by choice, each war Israel waged, including the Lebanon war in its formative phase, had been defined as a war of no choice. Begin's claim that the state could use wars to gain political and ideological objectives, as well as his affirmation of the right of the political echelon to make the relevant decisions to this end, helped rupture the constructed reality that had defined each war as a war of no choice.

Analyzing the behavior and attitudes of the core of resistance to the Lebanon war yields unsurprising results. Dissent being a new phenomenon in Israel's political culture, those soldiers who refused to serve in the war continue to perceive military service as a civil duty.[86] In their view, military service is a central Israeli experience and an integral part of Israel's national identity. Society interprets their existence as protesting a deviation from the model of military behavior, and from the goals of the state in using violent force, as unheld by national security policy makers.[87] In other words, the dissent must be seen as a desperate attempt to correct the use of the military; in no way was it a pacifist endeavor to defy any resort to military operations. A similar emergence of dissent is not easily found among soldiers who continued to carry out police and internal security functions among the Palestinian populations of the occupied territories during the Palestinian popular uprising that had broken out.[88] The armed forces have obliged the orders given by the political establishment, accepting a definition of the situation as a type of war of no choice and emphasizing professionalism, military skills, and performance. Thus, even when it was challenged by a political though not cultural turnabout, mainly between 1977 and 1992, civilian militarism in Israel ministered the approach most acceptable to the majority of the Jewish collectivity, and remained dominant though not hegemonic, continuing to contest the competing national religious and pure chauvinistic approaches.

Conclusion

Political culture in Israel varies from period to period, but parts of its core remain immutable, derived from a construction of reality that includes the collectivity's demand for total mobilization—institutional and mental—and continual preparation for war. Historically, this military preparedness has verged precariously on self-fulfilling prophecy. The political culture developed a latent and hegemonic cast of militarism, though its evident manifestations have ebbed slightly as cognitive processes emerged that sublimated militarism. Thus the army did not directly run politics but indirectly had tremendous influence. Civilian militarism was expressed in the main by the circumstance that the political establishment has not been accorded practical or conceptual autonomy. Alternative options in the administration of domestic or foreign policies have been blocked many times, and special social realities and exclusionary discourses have been constructed. The approach represents a part of the political culture that is governed by military-minded civilians. As civilian militarism in Israel is challenged today by many political and ideological orientations, its hegemony may have been broken, though it remains a powerful force in Israeli society.

CHAPTER SEVEN

The Social Construction
of Israel's National Security*

Conceptual Framework:
Contextual Deconstruction of the Constructed

Since Plato's well-known cave fable, philosophers and social scientists have been perpetually troubled by the puzzle of what are hard or objective facts and what are artifacts, and how one can distinguish among them.[1] Today some social scientists argue that any search for objectivity is a lost cause, as all so-called realities are culturally or socially constructed; the experts and scientists themselves are products of hegemonic world-orders, rather than being, say, neutral value-free observers from Mars. Most of them do not deny the existence of objective conditions, even in their extreme manifestations, such as wars, epidemics, or disasters that kill human beings. However, the definition of any such conditions as societal problems depends on the degree that collectivities have defined them as such and feel threatened

* From Baruch Kimmerling, "The Social Construction of Israel's National Security," in Stuart A. Cohen, ed., *Democratic Societies and their Armed Forces: Israel in Comparative Context* (London: Frank Cass, 2000), 215–252.

by them.[2] Others still strongly insist that realities and facts are methodologically detectable and separable from their cultural, social, and political wrappings,[3] or as Goode and Ben-Yehuda put it,

> the objectivists argue that what defines a social problem is the existence of an objectively given, concretely real demanding or threatening condition. What makes a condition a problem is that it harms or endangers human life and well being . . . according to this view, the final arbiter of the reality of social problems is the expert, armed with empirical evidence and scientific insight, and not the untrained general public.[4]

I think every social scientist should feel very uncomfortable with both approaches, especially with such a clear separation and negation of the existence of tangible, observable, and measurable facts in both the physical and social worlds. We have the objective knowledge that immense quantities of what people view as an immutable part of every culture and society are the result of social construction and interpretation. I am not referring just to conscious lies, cynical political manipulations, or social engineering, though even such events should be incorporated into the phenomenon of construction. The birth of beliefs, facts that are not facts, and myths that a large portion of the population of any collectivity consider to be facts are, as any student in our introductory courses learns, an integral part of the dynamics of production and reproduction of any social order. From this, three basic problems arise. Presuming that any social scientist is also a product of a social culture and order—inside or outside the collectivity under investigation—is it possible at all for the observer to be objective, or as famously posed by the Weberians, as "value-freed?"[5] Is it desirable to be so? If so, what are the best techniques to do it?

Let me answer the second question in the affirmative. Because if not, then the social sciences in general and sociology in particular lose any advantages they have over ideological or religious analyses of social phenomena, and the processes of social science lose legitimacy as a scientific body of knowledge. Claims against objectivity also make nonsense of any critical approach to evaluating any text in the world. Without objectivity, denials of the occurrence of the Jewish Holocaust, or the Palestinian Nakba, have the same status as more or less accurate texts that assume that the events occurred. As for the first question, my answer is that it is difficult, but not impossible. The precondition is that every social scientist must be fully aware of her or his own personal values and ideologies, as well as the interests of her or his nationality, ethnicity, religion, class, gender, or other group, all of which, consciously or unconsciously, heavily influence the social scientist's professional output—from the choice of research subject and area, the *problemstellung*, and methods to, particularly, the interpretation of findings. There should be a constant and lifelong tension between social scientists and their research materials and objects. Perhaps a total or pure objectivity is never completely achievable, but it must definitely be our aim and desire.

As for the technique to do it, the profession already provides us with contextual constructionism, an approach that can be summarized briefly as starting with the following presumptions. There is no necessary and complete contradiction between an objective societal problem and its shaping and reshaping as a constructed reality. The role of the social scientist is to deconstruct the constructed reality as much as possible to its objective core, if it exists; to follow the historical paths of the construction process within its sociopolitical context;[6] and to discover and analyze the role of the constructed and invented realities, or societal problems, within their context. Social scientists must also consider constructed and invented realities as social problems that can, in a large measure, shape the objective realities,[7] and detect the dialectical interrelations between objective and constructed societal problems.[8]

National security is a societal problem par excellence, the severity and salience of which varies from society to society. It is directly connected to personal and collective life-and-death existential issues, sometimes to the physical, political, and social existence of the entire collectivity. The raison d'etre of any state, its legitimacy, and its claim on the monopoly on physical violence, are derived directly from the state's unalienable promise to provide security for its subjects—law and order for the inside and security from the outside. Analyzing and deconstructing national security as a societal problem poses an almost unique challenge for any social scientist, not only because the complexity of the issue, but also because of the secrecy that is considered as an inherent demand and condition of this sphere of sociopolitical and sociomilitary activities, even in the most democratic regimes and open societies.[9]

Another derivative of the problem of analyzing national security are the questions about who is entitled authoritatively to create, modify, or challenge national security doctrines; who possess the academic expertise to research ongoing (not historical) "strictly military" issues; and who is entitled to participate in the public discourse on military and security issues. In Israel, the last aspect has opened up in the last decade to a wider public, such as media professionals, academics, intellectuals, interest groups, and even ordinary persons—that is, middle-class Jewish males—but the former two aspects are still almost completely the monopoly of generals and ex-generals.[10] Following the consequences of the 1974 war, a Council for National Security, composed of both civilian and military experts to act as a check on the General Staff, periodically appeared on the public agenda, but the "defense establishment"[11] constantly suffocated its initiatives.

Construction of Doctrines

A national security doctrine is supposed to be an explicit or implicit code of rules and practices for the most efficient operation of the armed forces and utilization of other societal resources at the collectivity's disposal to achieve certain defined military goals and targets. In a narrower sense, as mentioned above, because the major role of any state is to provide its subjects with both protection and the feeling of protection from external threats, a national security doctrine is presumed to be a culturally acceptable way to accomplish this. However, limiting the use of military forces to strictly defensive purposes would be far from the proper approach for a sociological analysis of the phenomenon. In large measure, national security is not only a socially constructed term, but it is difficult to differentiate from the other cultural, economic, political, and social characteristics and ideologies of a given collectivity. National security is often supposed to be an integral part of the national interest, or at least is commonly interpreted to be such, and military forces are frequently used and misused for a wide variety of purposes that actually have nothing to do with a strict, non-manipulative definition of national security. Consequently, national security doctrines sometimes include rules and practices that completely contradict the proper interests of the goals of national security, and preserve and maximize the collectivity's military strength and capabilities, as the present essay demonstrates.

The first military doctrine that can be considered an Israeli military doctrine is the so-called Plan D (*Tochnit Daleth*), launched by Major General Yigael Yadin on March 10, 1948[12] in anticipation of the expected military clashes between the state-making Jewish community of colonial Palestine and the Arab community, as well as the assumed intervention by military forces of Arab states. In the plan's preamble, Yadin stated:

> The aim of this plan is the control of the area of the Jewish State and the defense of its borders [as determined by the UN Partition Plan] and the clusters of [Jewish] settlements outside the boundaries, against regular and irregular enemy forces operating from bases outside and inside the State.[13]

Furthermore, the plan suggested several actions, among others, to reach these goals:

> Actions against enemy settlements located in our, or near our, defense systems [i.e., Jewish settlement and localities] with the aim of preventing their use as bases for active armed forces. These actions should be divided into the following types: The destruction of villages (by fire, blowing up and mining)—especially of those villages over which we cannot gain [permanent] control. Gaining of control will be accomplished in accordance with the following instructions: The encircling of the village and the search of it. In the event of resistance—the destruction of the resisting forces and the expulsion of the population beyond the boundaries of the State.[14]

As in many other cases, in Plan D, what seems at a first glance to be a pure and limited military doctrine proved itself to comprise far-reaching measures that led to a complete demographic, ethnic, social, and political transformation of Palestine through the state-building project. Implementing the spirit of Plan D, Jewish military forces conquered about 20,000 square kilometers of territory, compared with the 14,000 square kilometers granted them by the UN Partition Resolution, and cleansed them almost completely of their Arab inhabitants.[15] From this point of view, the doctrine established by Plan D closely fit both the requirements of the intercommunal war and the subsequent stage of interstate war after the intracommunal enemy was eliminated.[16]

Moreover, the doctrine clearly reflected the local Zionist ideological aspirations to acquire the greatest amount of contiguous territory possible, cleansed of Arab presence, as a necessary condition for establishing an exclusively Jewish nation-state. Until the 1948 war, Jewish public agencies and private investors succeeded in buying only about 7 percent of the land in Palestine, which was enough to build a viable community but exhausted their financial abilities. Afterward, they decided to use the sword instead of money to considerably enlarge their territorial resources.[17] The British colonial regime provided a political and military umbrella under which the Zionist enterprise could develop its basic institutional, economic, and social framework, but it also secured the essential interests of the Arab collectivity. As the British umbrella was removed, the Arab and Jewish communities found themselves face to face in a zero-sum-like situation. By rejecting the British partition plan, the Arab community and leadership were confident not only in their absolute right to control the entire country, but also in their ability to do so. For its part, the Jewish community and leadership appreciated that they did not have enough forces to control the entire territory of Palestine and to expel or rule its Arab majority. They accepted the partition plan, but invested all of their efforts toward improving its terms and expanding their boundaries as far as possible, including as small an Arab population as possible within them.

There is no hard evidence that, despite its far-reaching political consequences and meanings, Plan D was ever adopted or even discussed at the political level. If we were to adopt a soft conspiracy-theory approach, we might conclude that many political and national leaders knew very well that some kinds of orders and plans were better not discussed or presented officially. In any case, the way that the military operations of 1948 were conducted leave no room for doubts that Plan D was the doctrine that Jewish military forces used during the war, or the spirit and perception behind their efforts. To paraphrase Tilly's[18] words, social and cultural conditions make doctrines, doctrines make wars, wars make states, and states continue to make wars.

The military, social, political, and global conditions that led to the formulation of Yadin's doctrine have deeply changed since March 1948, in part because of the plan's success. However, some of the basic premises and ideological perceptions behind Plan D are still valid, deeply rooted within would-be Israeli social and military thought, and more importantly, in the combination of and interaction between them. Three of these premises are as follows.

First, there is a demographic asymmetry between the combatant sides: the Jews are always "the few" and the Arabs are always "the many." Yadin did not explicitly acknowledge that his order to destroy hostile Arab villages[19] over which Jewish forces could not gain permanent control was rooted in the scarcity of human power resources or the inability to form a standing army to exercise direct control over the Arab population fallen under Jewish rule.[20] However, the presumption of demographic asymmetry became the baseline for all further versions of the national security doctrine formulated after Plan D, including the most important one, written by Major General Israel Tal.[21]

Second, the immense demographic discrepancy between the Jewish settler-society and its Arab environment may be the main factual and objective ingredient in the entire Israeli national security discourse. However, even in this case, strategists have large degrees of freedom to play between different boundaries of the Jewish-Arab conflict. These boundaries should be subdivided as follows. The Palestinian circle itself has at least three sub-boundaries: Palestinian citizens of Israel, Palestinians within the 1967 war's occupied territories, and Palestinians all over the world, or in the *gurba*, the Palestinian exile.[22] Next is the circle of the immediate Arab states that encircle Israel: Lebanon, Syria, Jordan, and Egypt. The Arab states that are not immediate neighbors—Iraq, Saudi Arabia, the Gulf states, Libya, and the rest—are included in the next circle, sometimes considered as "the Arab world." When the conflict is perceived as religious warfare, the entire Muslim world—including Iran—should be considered. Before the collapse of the Soviet bloc, it was also considered sometimes as a part of the conflict, but in that case, the conflict should have be considered as a confrontation between superpower blocs. This perspective contains something of the outlook of "the West against the rest," especially in the context of worldwide terrorism efforts. Apart from that should be found, especially among some religious xenophobic subcultures, a metaphysical perception of the cosmic order as aligning most if not all of the gentile world against the Jewish people.[23] Even the most quantifiable, objective, and factual aspects of the conflict can be subject to social construction.

Third, settlements are important as objects to be protected as a part of the nation and state-building effort, part of the defense system, and primarily as a tool to determine the state's geographical and political boundaries.[24] The government made the decision to defend all of the settlements considered defensible,[25] even those located outside the borders of the territories allocated for the Jewish state. This was the military and doctrinal complement to destroying all of the Arab localities that were perceived to endanger access to any Jewish settlement, including those outside of the partition plan boundaries, and to expel their inhabitants. The political system accepted the partition plan, but the military system's doctrine grossly violated the principles inherent in partition.

As is understandable from the above, the overall security doctrine was offensive in nature,[26] at least regarding the Arabs of Palestine. Later, the offensive characteristics of the Israeli military doctrine were largely expanded and elaborated upon. Some military experts added the so-called indirect approach, attributed to the British military expert and analyst B.H. Liddel-Hart, to the offensive character of Israeli war-making practices. The approach calls for concentrations of massive forces, surprise attacks against the enemy's weak points through unconventional means and timing, and then the immediate exploitation of the presumed success. Dan Horowitz added to this strategy an additional dimension of "flexible responsiveness."[27] Horowitz depicted the modern, highly mobile battlefield as a chaotic situation in which the supposed chains of command and communications systems no longer exist. In such a situation, the small isolated unit must operate on its own initiative, guessing what the general command expects from it. Horowitz attributed to "the Israeli soldier" the quality of "flexibility," due to his way of socialization, while the "Arab soldier" usually lacked this, and thus was highly dependent on the ordinary chain of command. Horowitz's perspective is a sophisticated example of the mythologization of the Israeli military and its society, a widespread phenomenon between 1956 and 1973, to explain and construct Israel's military successes and its regional unequivocal superiority. Later, many of Israel's military failures were attributed to the same qualities of undisciplined soldiering, private initiatives, and negligence. Another expression of the same phenomenon was the breakup of the chain of command when after the 1967 war, high-ranking offixers, colonels, and major generals took over the command of small units and were involved directly in the battlefield.[28]

The Humanpower Management Doctrine

The Israeli military almost disintegrated after the 1948 war. Many of its officers were killed during the war, while others left the military or were purged for political reasons.[29] Most of the veteran population felt that they already contributed enough to the country and turned to their own well being. The mass of new immigrants was not considered apt for soldiering with high ability and motivation for combat. Under these circumstances, the political and military establishment began to reconstruct the armed forces and was forced to choose between a military based on small elite units and an all-encompassing popular army.[30] The decision that was made then is still in effect, not only in the military, but also across Israeli society: to build up a military based on a universal compulsory draft of all male and female citizens, but to grant to the minister of defense the authority to exempt from service any category of men or women—Arabs and ultra-Orthodox students, for example—according to his absolute discretion. The length of service for women was shorter than the length of men's service, and women's marginality in the military reinforced their position in society and fixed gender roles.

The decision to favor quantity over quality of soldiers was made because of the perception of the military as the major statist tool for the Israelification of new immigrants, especially those from Arab lands, according to Israel's melting-pot ideology,[31] It was also designed to address the situation of "few against many" described above[32] Universal compulsory conscription was complemented by a system of reserve duty over the course of almost all of a man's, and sometimes an unmarried woman's, active life.[33] This doctrine of using humanpower intentionally located military service at the center of the Israeli experience and consciousness, but also contributed to the construction of the meaning of citizenship, societal boundaries, and stratification, as well as the militaristic cultural setting.[34]

If the military system had its own logic in the 1950s and 1960s, when cohorts were tiny, it was that the military was manpower-hungry and immigrants were perceived as needing de-socialization and re-socialization. By the 1990s, the system was devoid of any economic or social logic. It proved itself to be economically and socially wasteful, as the state expropriated for itself a vast portion of its male Jewish citizens without any proper examination of the armed forces' real needs.[35] The system prevented the military from allocating its manpower rationally or economically, and preserving the military monopoly over human resources distorted careers and professional choices across Israeli society and its labor market. This made the Israeli military a clumsy bureaucratic monster. Only a transition to an all-voluntary force can shake the system from its doctrinal deadlock.[36]

The Doctrine of Preemptive War, 1956–1967

By refusing to deal with the problem of uprooted Palestinians concentrated in refugee camps in surrounding countries, Israel was exposed to increasing Palestinian infiltration activities. The infiltrations slowly developed into a kind of guerrilla warfare and terrorist activity, mainly against civilians settled in frontier settlements established on "abandoned" Arab lands and filled with new immigrants. To Israel, the authorities of the Arab states from where the infiltrators came were responsible for the infiltrations, and Israel responded with an escalating series of retaliations and reprisals against military and civilian targets in Arab countries.[37] This period, labeled by Benny Morris[38] as the period of "Israel's border wars" had several consequences.

First, the border quarrels signaled that the Arab-Israeli conflict was not over, as many hoped immediately after the armistice agreements were signed.[39] The state's existence was not yet ensured even after the victorious 1948 war and the Israeli army's cleansing territory of most of its Arab inhabitants. Even the personal security of Israeli citizens was not ensured. Although some military experts, such as Yigal Allon,[40] distinguished between basic security, or the strategic threat to the collectivity's very existence, and current security (*bitachon shotef*), or tactical activities, for most of the last fifty years, this distinction has tended to be blurred both conceptually and organizationally.[41] Conceptually, the infiltrations and later warfare with Palestinians was constructed as an existential or strategic threat. Institutionally, highly trained combat units were frequently employed to meet current security assignments.

Second, the military continued to be a central institution and symbol in the newly established state. Because the state had the monopoly over the military and the use of violence, the state became the major actor in society and stateness[42] (*mamlachtiyut*) the central pillar of the new national identity and Israeliness. The cults of the state and military became one and the same,[43] which was one of the major sources of Israeli cultural and civilian militarism.[44]

Third, major human, emotional, and material resources were invested and recruited for national security concerns. This became the basis for building and reproducing, from war to war, a highly mobilized society and a larger sense that the conflict was routine.[45]

Fourth, some strategists defined the infiltration-retaliation circle as low-density, controlled hostility and perceived it as a functional equivalent to a full-scale war. This challenge-and-response process constructed the expectations of the international community, internal public opinion, and the military itself that there would be a second round of fighting, perceived as necessary to consolidate the territorial and political achievements of the

1948 war[46] and deal with both internal social and economic strains and the rebuilding of the military's offensive and combat capacities.[47]

A popular argument made by government officials and the press was that Israel was too small and vulnerable to absorb a direct major attack against its territory and population, and lacked strategic depth; therefore the initiative must always be Israel's. In addition, Israel's military might was mainly based on the reserve system,[48] which needed time to mobilize. These claims were the basis for developing an elaborate doctrine that was not just an offensive doctrine, but also a doctrine of preemptive, blitzkrieg-style war, based on deception, surprise, the maneuvering of large-scale armor units, and massive air strikes.[49] The doctrine was first successfully applied, partially, during the 1956 Sinai campaign.

However, even the Sinai campaign was not a full-scale war. It was waged against only one Arab state, Egypt, and against only some of its military forces, as the major portion of the Egyptian military was preoccupied with facing (successfully) an Anglo-French invasion to take over the Suez Canal area.[50] Despite this, Israel constructed the Sinai Campaign as a successful war, proving the efficacy of its preemptive war doctrine. However, Egypt's swift political and military recuperation and the international (Soviet-American) pressures on Israel, as well as England and France, to withdraw from the Sinai Peninsula and Gaza Strip led to two doctrinal conclusions. First, it is very difficult to convert military victories into political achievements. Second, Israel may win many rounds of battles but none can be decisive, because Israel cannot destroy any Arab country or fatally damage it, at least with conventional weaponry. However, a single major Arab victory would decompose Israel and lead to what Yehoshafat Harkabi[51] called the "politicide" of the Jewish state. The Sinai campaign injected many high moral feelings and euphoria into the Jewish population of Israel and granted its military a glorious aura, but from a doctrinal standpoint, it led to some very pessimistic conclusions.

Another fundamental question that arose after the successful military operation and quick withdrawal from Sinai[52] was the issue of which side time favors in the long run. The Arabs compared the Jewish settler-state with the Crusaders and the Latin Christian Kingdom of Jerusalem, founded in 1099 by European powers and settlers and led by religious and ideological passion. In 1187, the legendary Ayubian Muslim leader Saladin finally destroyed the Crusader state, despite its long-term military superiority, following the decisive battle in Hittin. Implicitly the Israel culture became aware of this chilling analogy and tried to learn something from the Crusader case. The primary conclusion was that the Crusaders' failure was caused chiefly by two complementary factors: that the Crusaders intermingled too much within the region, and that, as a consequence, they weakened their cultural, political, and technological relations with their mother societies.[53] Not surprisingly, these two lessons are consistent with three major tendencies within Israeli society and culture: to separate itself physically and culturally from the Arabs, due to anxiety about so-called Levantinization, as well the shadow of becoming a binational entity; to consider itself as a part of the West; and to maintain the sentimental, cultural, political, and economic linkages with the Jewish Diaspora, going as far as to consider Israel as the state for all of the Jews in the world. However, all of these cultural traits were not absorbed into the Israeli military's thinking until the Oslo agreements, which were based mainly on agreements about only one of the above tendencies, namely, the wishes of the population to be separate. Until then, the contradictory idea of territorial depth ruled the Israeli military doctrine.

Territorial Depth, Security, and Sanctification of Land

Despite Israel's relatively non-belligerent period between 1957 and 1967, the Israeli military depicted the situation as a "dormant war," liable to erupt at any moment.[54] From a sociological point of view, such a construction of reality should be considered as a self-fulfilling prophecy, and in June 1967, Israel fully applied its preemptive *blitzkrieg* war doctrine, using large concentrations of military forces against Egypt. Israel argued that Egypt had violated the tacit agreements reached following Israel's withdrawal from Sinai in 1957 by concentrating forces close to the ceasefire lines and closing the Tiran Straits to Israeli navigation, acts considered as *casi belli*.[55] Military strategists argued that Israel's inability to prevent Egypt's unilateral militarization of the Sinai had seriously compromised Israel's deterrence credibility, and there was no choice (*ein breirah*) but to reestablish it by full-scale war. After Israel destroyed the Egyptian air force and armor on the ground, it occupied the Sinai Peninsula and Gaza Strip. As the Arab Legion hesitantly joined the war, Israel also occupied the so-called West Bank, "liberating" the old city of Jerusalem. Syria was not directly involved in moving troops, but had long-running quarrels with Israel concerning both countries' desire to control the Jordan River's sources. Israel exploited the enormous successes of the battles against Egypt and Jordan and the fog of war in the region, capturing the hilly Syrian region later known as the Golan Heights. As a consequence, in just six days, Israel gained control of additional territories totaling about 26,000 square miles, an area more than three times as large as its total territory before the war.

The June 1967 war, defined by Yigal Allon[56] as a "preemptive counter-attack," was an example of how to wage a modern conventional war of movement with minimal casualties for the attacking troops and maximal destruction of the enemy's short-run war capabilities.[57] However, the war also showed how the dynamics of sociostrategic escalation develop and how a "war of no choice" is socially constructed. The 1967 war exemplifies the wide gaps between military-strategic planning and doctrine and the lack of complementary political and social planning and vision, the latter of which turned an illustrious military victory into a political disaster and a social catastrophe even by the values of the initiators of the war themselves.

In May 1967, after the spectacular Egyptian troop concentration, Israel also publicly declared a full mobilization of its reserve system. The social and economic meaning of such a total mobilization is to siphon most of Israel's male population from the civilian system, transforming the entire society into what has been labeled as an "interrupted system," in which there is a moratorium on most routine societal goals.[58] A full mobilization in Israel has heavy economic and social costs and means a strong commitment that the threat is real and warfare almost inevitable.[59]

However, Israel did not strike immediately, but only after about ten days of total mobilization and paralysis of the home front, explained by the international community's efforts to solve the crisis.[60] The "waiting period" caused profound collective anxiety and mistrust in the political center; from the time that total mobilization was declared—and the troops remained mobilized for a long time—an automatic social and cultural device was activated and the war, at least against Egypt, became inevitable, not for military but for sociopolitical reasons.

However, the major strategic problems had just begun. The war, especially the air strikes, had been well planned, but there was no strategy, doctrine, or plans made for the aftermath. A general and vague statement was made about the readiness to return territories in exchange for peace, which was promptly reciprocated by the Arab states' total refusal to deal with Israel at the Khartoum summit. For their part, the Israeli leadership did not even consider a unilateral withdrawal from the occupied territories or a part of them, despite some intellectuals' proposals in this direction. The cabinet rejected even Moshe Dayan's suggestion of a minor retreat from the Suez Canal line to make possible opening it to international navigation. Perhaps it was assumed that the pressures exercised by the superpowers would impose a withdrawal on Israel, as happened in 1957.

As time passed, the feeling that the holding of the occupied territories was temporary became routinized and institutionalized. The territories and their inhabitants were absorbed into the Israeli political, economic, cultural, and strategic self-image, and a new political, economic, and strategic entity, which I have called "the Israel control system,"[61] emerged. But not all of the newly occupied territories had the same cultural and strategic meaning. The almost unpopulated Sinai Peninsula was evaluated chiefly for its strategic and economic values, as it contained an enormous quantity of oil and other important and scarce natural resources.[62] Sinai was considered as the ultimate "strategic depth," and the control of the "impassable" Suez canal, fortified by the Bar-Lev Line—the Israeli equivalent of the Maginot Line—gave the Israelis an unprecedented sense of security, despite the high casualties from Egyptian artillery, reciprocated the Israeli air force.[63]

The far-reaching social, ideological, and political consequences of the 1967 war ripened and became clear only after the 1973 war. The most meaningful event was the reopened access to the heartland of the ancient Jewish holy land. As Moshe Dayan, the purely secular defense minister, expressed: "We have returned to you Shilo and Anatot [the ancient cities of the Hebrew prophets near Jerusalem] in order never to leave you." Deep religious if not messianic sentiments captured most of Israeli society, which perceived the results of the war as a miracle and a direct intervention of a higher power in the course of history. The euphoric power trip, however, was accompanied by a tremendously anomic situation. It was unclear how much, in what form, and if at all the superpowers would allow the Israeli state to maintain its control over the newly acquired territories. Between 1967 and 1973, two basic approaches were developed toward the territories. The Allon plan suggested selective annexation of some territories, including the Jordan valley, accompanied with settlements "for security reasons." Dayan suggested a "functional division of rule" over the West Bank, between the Hashemite Kingdom and Israel. The Jordanians were supposed to maintain control over the population, who would be considered as Jordanian subjects, and Israel was to maintain responsibility for the strategic security of the territory and control over its land and water. The only flaw in Dayan's highly innovative approach was Jordan's refusal to accept it.

Perhaps the most significant sociostrategic process in the region—the reappearance of the Palestinian ethnic and national identity—occurred during this time. Between 1949 and 1967 the international community redefined the Palestinian problem as a refugee issue. The disappearance of the Palestinian nationality was of common interest to both Israel and Jordan, and perhaps other Arab states as well; much energy and effort were invested by both states to de-Palestinize the Palestinians and to make them Israeli-Arabs on one side and Jordanians on the other.[64] However, the reunification of the three parts of historical Palestine—Israel itself, the West Bank, and Gaza Strip—and placing all of their Arab inhabitants under Jewish rule was among the paramount factors in the reemergence of Palestinian nationalism. The continuation of the Israeli conquest was a major trigger for their claim for self-determination and their readiness to wage an independent armed struggle against the Jewish state. The new situation in the Middle East, that is, the military and ideological collapse of Nasserist pan-Arabism following the Israeli military victory, added much legitimacy to the until then–negligible and marginal Fatah organization, oriented only toward Palestine. Under this new regional constellation, Fatah and other guerrilla organizations controlled not only the Palestine Liberation Organization (PLO), but also the Palestinian consciousness inside and outside of historical Palestine.

Thus, one significant unintended consequence of the Israeli military victory was the reemergence of Zionism's principal direct foe and competitor over the same land. The construction of the Palestinian ethnic and national identity was accelerated even more following the increasing oppression, caused by "internal" and "external" resistance, labeled by the Israelis as "terror." Additional accelerating factors were the increasing settlement process of the occupied territories by Jews, especially after 1974, and the feeling of the Palestinians of being dispossessed from their last land and water reservoirs.

From Military to Police:
The Transformation of the Israeli Armed Forces

The Israeli state appeared suddenly as a regional power. As stated above, the boundaries of its control were largely expanded, a large Arab population fell within these boundaries, and large frontier territories were reopened for settlement. The initial official attitude after the 1967 war was to agree to withdraw from all of the territory except Jerusalem in exchange for peace or other kinds of arrangements. However, peace and territory were incommensurable values. Peace was an abstract situation that had not yet been experienced by Israeli society on Israeli territory—land, water, or other natural resources—was a measurable and concrete geopolitical term.[65] Additionally, territories were also considered in terms of providing security, national property, and "holiness."[66] But what really made the situation complicated were the Arab inhabitants that densely populated some of the most central areas. The Syrian Heights were largely the cleanest ethnically, and about 90,000 Syrians had been driven away during the conquest. In the West Bank and Gaza, more than a million Palestinians remained. The two basic long-term options were their mass expulsion or granting them Israeli citizenship in the event of annexation of the desired territories, as was suggested by a group of activists and mainstream intellectuals from the Labor camp. Both options were unrealistic, the first because of its moral and international implications and the second because it would transform the Jewish nation-state into a very unwanted binational polity. This permanent-temporary situation of continued occupation, under all of the internal and external constraints, led to a highly anomic situation and a shortage of ideological solutions and political and moral guides. The old hegemonic Socialist-Zionist ideologies no longer had answers in this rapidly changed world.

Into the ideological and political vacuum stepped a new actor that previously had been located on the periphery of the hegemony. This was the Gush Emunim, or Bloc of the Faithful, a social movement and ideology. Using some central elements of the original hegemonic symbols, identity, and culture, the movement tried to establish a counterculture and a political alternative based on theological premises. Above all, it was a rebellion of the Ashkenazi national religious youth and younger generation against its elder generation, which it regarded as having abandoned its religious and nationalist principles for the socialist-secular Zionists. Recruiting the original theology developed in the 1930s by the first Ashkenazic chief rabbi Isaac Hacohen Kook and then applied and interpreted by his son to the sociopolitical situation after the 1967 and 1973 wars, they decided to reshape the Israeli state and society.

In 1974, Gush Emunim took control of the National Religious Party and made it its political sponsor. This enabled it to create a heterogeneous settler society, including nonreligious and nonideological settlers, primarily in the so-called Judea and Samaria territories. The core of the settler society is based around "holy communities" of observant Askenazic Jews, many of them graduates of elite military units and Hesdery Yeshivas.[67] The cores of the communities are the families, reinforced by the local school system, the youth movement (Bnei Akiva), the synagogue, the local rabbi, and the local council or municipality. Even though many of the true believers live or work outside the settler communities, the communities are constructed as ideologically and mutually supportive bubbles.

Within the bubbles it is relatively easy to recruit people for quick political actions,[68] to exercise internal social control, and to grant mutual spiritual and ideological support. Gush Emunim first operated on the supra-territorial level as a political and social movement and later through Amana as an officially recognized settlement authority. Later, when Gush Emunim declined as a political movement, the leadership of the movement was divided between the political and the ideological-spiritual organs, the council of rabbis.

The Emuni ideology proposed to replace the secular state of Israel with the Land of Israel, a geographic and political entity fully based on an ethnocentric fusion of religion and nationalism. This was the delayed effect of the autonomous national-religious educational system as well as the yeshiva high school and other national-religious yeshiva education. Armed with deep religious conviction and personal commitment, Gush Emunim emerged to settle both the occupied territories and the hearts of the Jewish people, using the major classic practical Zionist symbols and the rhetoric of pioneering, settlement, redemption, national security, self-sacrifice, and conquest of land—from Arabs and nature—to establish a new settler society on the newly conquered lands. The immediate political raison d'etre of the settlements and their geographic dispersion was to establish a fait accompli that would preclude any possibility of abandoning the territories. They would ensure the completeness of the Land of Israel and the title of the People of Israel over them, as an integral part of the redemption that was soon coming. They touched upon the dormant religious elements of secular Israeli identity and the Achilles' heel of the Israeli secular and statist nationalism. The Jewish secular society was enchanted by this new pioneering passion and was almost completely disarmed in the face of the renewed Zionist practices, symbols, and myths, primarily because of the absence of any coherent competing ideologies or social movements.

No less meaningful was the Emuni ideological assault on the Israeli public agenda, way of thinking, cultural code, and terminology. The Emuni double-talk proved to be very effective. Toward their own religious-nationalistic constituency they used the primordial symbols of land and blood. Toward the secularists they used the rhetoric of pioneering, settlement, and security. The secular hard-liners or hawkish elites were never equipped with such an arsenal of emotional terms and abundance of associations as were their religious partners. The West Bank became Judea and Samaria, or Yesha, which is not just an acronym for Judea, Samaria, and Gaza Strip, but also literally means salvation or redemption. In public discourse the term "state of Israel" became frequently interchangeable with the term "Land of Israel," eliding the convention that the entire greater Israel belonged exclusively to the Jewish people. More and more the Israeli secular and civil identity, which had been constructed around state citizenship, was reshaped into a narrative of a primordial Jewish identity in which the criteria for belonging were defined basically in religious terms.[69]

As Meron Benvenisti suggested several times, the grassroots settlement of the West Bank became a critical mass of about 140 settlements with about 180,000 Jewish settlers.[70] These settlements and settlers needed day-and-night protection from Palestinian guerrilla warfare, but the Palestinians needed many more times that protection from extremist settlers or avengers. Slowly, considerable portions of the Israeli armed forces—regulars and reserves, especially the infantry, paratroopers, and military intelligence—became engaged in policing the occupied territories. This process of allocating increasing amounts of military force as well as material, human, emotional, and intellectual resources became even more critical as the Palestinian popular uprising, the intifada, broke out in December 1987.

Like any military, the Israeli military did not have a proper doctrine for fighting against an unarmed (at least not with firearms) civilian population. The Palestinians' major weapons were stones thrown by youth, children, and sometimes women. The Palestinians very cautiously almost never crossed the line to give Israeli troops a pretext to use their overwhelming military superiority. Thus the Israeli troops were forced to employ street warfare without firearms. They used tear gas, truncheons, rubber bullets, administrative detentions, and home demolitions. Many other collective punishments, such as closures and curfew, were frequently imposed, and orders to break the bones of rioters were given and executed. This was a war of attrition[71] and both sides became exhausted, pushed into a no-win corner.

The role of policing the occupied territories, which culminated during the intifada, has had a devastating impact on the Israeli military. Instead of preparing the forces and developing doctrines for the future battlefield within the context of a swiftly changing world order, the military and the general staff were intellectually and morally preoccupied with how to fight children. Yitzhak Rabin, then minister of defense, slowly came to the conclusion that there could not be a military solution to the Palestinian problem, only a political one. When Rabin became prime minister again in 1992, with the return of Labor to power, he was ready to leave most of the occupied West Bank and Gaza. He even eventually agreed to establish a limited Palestinian state to redirect the Israeli military to its major military mission of the strategic defense of Israel. The logic of the Oslo agreements, in addition to separation, was to continue the strategic control over the territory[72] but to grant the Palestinians the political, economic, and symbolic satisfactions of having a state and exchanging the policing over them by the Jewish military with policing by their own Fatah militias.[73] Here, Rabin clearly prioritized military-strategic considerations over political, sentimental, and religious considerations. He tried to clarify the Emuni rhetoric, which blurred the boundaries between national security and sentimental considerations toward the occupied territories.[74]

Camp David and the War of Choice Controversy

In 1977 a political upheaval occurred in Israel when the secular ultranationalist Likud movement[75] overthrew the long domination of the Labor movement. The expectation was that one of the first moves of Menachem Begin, the Likud leader identified for years with the ideology of Greater Israel, would be to annex immediately at least the heartland of Judea and Samaria.[76] Instead, to the enormous surprise of his adherents as well as his opponents, Begin responded positively to Egyptian president Anwar Sadat's initiative to exchange the territory of the Sinai Peninsula for a peace treaty with Egypt, as well as Egypt's recognition of the legitimate existence of a sovereign Jewish state in the region.[77] After a difficult bargaining process, Israel withdrew in stages from all of Sinai, which remained a partially demilitarized area, and dismantled all of the Jewish settlements there. The formula of "peace in exchange for [all] the territories" was created, disproving the meta-doctrinal convention that it was necessary to rely forever on military might because it would be impossible for Arabs to accept the existence of the Jewish settler society. The exit of Egypt from the coalition of Arab enmity toward Israel was a major change in the political, military, and regional power balance, and brought about the collapse of the Arab Western Front, just as later the Jordanian-Israeli peace treaty critically damaged the Eastern Front. Begin's breakthrough also stressed that Arab recognition of the legitimacy of Israel, in addition to demilitarized buffer zones and more or less normalized relationships, should not be a less important component of a secure existence than territorial depth and military divisions. However, the Egyptians conditioned their acceptance on a reasonable solution to the Palestinian national problem, and in the Camp David accords, Begin even agreed to grant full autonomy to the Palestinians, though he did not specify what he meant.

However, it seems that Begin's general plans, inspired by his hawkish and charismatic minster of defense, Ariel Sharon, were much more far-reaching. After the September 1970 clashes in Jordan, the Palestinian guerrilla forces and their headquarters left Jordan for South Lebanon and the Beirut area. From there they waged permanent and harassing guerrilla warfare against Israel. After completing the withdrawal from Sinai, despite some popular protests organized by his own political camp, Begin invaded Lebanon. The goal of the invasion was to destroy forever not just the military ability of the Palestinians but also their national movement, will, and identity.[78] This was the second Jewish-Palestinian war, after the first round of 1947–48, and it was waged not so much for the peace of the Galilee but for the consolidation of Israeli control over Judea and Samaria. [79]An additional purpose of the war was to establish a new Maronite regime in Lebanon friendly to Israel. This was the first time that Israel behaved explicitly as a regional power that wanted to convert its military power into political achievements—to make order, or a Pax Israeliana, in the Middle East.[80] Excluding the 1948 war, all of the other Israeli-Arab wars were caused or intentionally not avoided by Israel.[81] Despite this, none of the conflicts were socially constructed as having been Israeli-initiated. In all of the previous wars the Arabs were presented as having caused the escalation that made the war inevitable, if they were not the direct aggressors. Under Begin, however, for the first time an Israeli leader openly demanded the right to use the armed forces not to avoid an immediate existential threat, but to achieve what a democratically elected leadership considered as long-run national interests.[82] Military strategists also claimed that invading Lebanon would rehabilitate the Israeli deterrence capacity and the military morale lowered as a consequence of the 1973 war. This sincere approach lead to a bitter domestic controversy over the war and its goals, marking the first time in Israel that the Jewish national consensus around waging a war was broken and met with a wide popular opposition. Opponents of the war argued mainly that where the armed forces are based on reserves, that is, on a social contract with the people of the military system, the leadership was not allowed to initiate a war by choice (*milchemet breira*), but only a war of no choice.[83] A war by choice was presumed to damage both the morale of the warriors and the highly desired national consensus in the last domain that still united the Israelis, the sphere of national security. For the first time, conscientious objectors appeared in Israel, and the nature of the previous wars also became a part of public discourse.[84] The subject probably would never have been so acute and central if the war had been successful, fast, "clean," and with much fewer causalities. However, despite the PLO's military defeat and the Palestinian guerrilla movement's expulsion to Tunisia, the Palestinian identity in the occupied territories and the demand for self-determination survived and even increased. The Israeli troops welcomed by the local Lebanese population as liberators soon became conquerors, and militia groups like the Shiite Amal and Hizb-Allah, formed following the Israeli invasion, waged guerrilla war against the Israeli soldiers. For years, the politicians lacked the intellectual integrity and courage to accept that the war was the largest doctrinal fiasco in the history of the Israeli military.[85] The most severe consequence of the Lebanese war was the legitimacy granted to the Syrians to take over control of Lebanon and to institutionalize their presence there. Israeli maintenance even today of the "security zone" in South Lebanon, supported by a militia of mercenaries—the so-called South Lebanese Army—is the continuation of the same war within a narrow scope, but continuing most of the doctrinaire misconceptions related to it, namely military security cordons accompanied by direct or indirect occupation of a populated area.

The Outer Circle and the Parallel Doctrine

Almost unrelated to the conventional military doctrines and perceptions, since the early 1960s, Israel has made efforts to develop its own tactical and strategic capability for nuclear war. A nuclear weapon was considered as the ultimate insurance policy, facing the basic asymmetries between Israel and the Arab and Muslim world according to the "few against many" perception. The basic conception was that Israel must have enough conventional capacity to win any regional war, but also possess a nuclear option for three extreme cases: a complete failure of its conventional defense and deterrence capability, and a real and immediate threat to the existence of the Jewish state; the acquisition of nuclear weapons by close or distant regional foes; and deterrence of a superpower threat against Israel, as happened in 1956 when the Soviets threatened it with nuclear missiles. The nuclear option was also perceived as a psychological, ideological, and cultural need for an ultimate security for an immigrant-settler society unaccepted by its surrounding environment, and for a people that just a generation before had been the victim of a systematic genocide.

Israel opted for a sophisticated, ambiguous nuclear policy. It never performed a nuclear test and never publicly admitted the possession of such weaponry. On the other hand it refused to sign the nuclear weapons nonproliferation treaty or be inspected by international or American agencies.[86] Israel always declared that it would never be the first nation to introduce nuclear weapons in the region, which could also be interpreted as having a "bomb in the basement," meaning that nuclear weapons would be available on short notice, even if not yet technically assembled. It seems that Israel had a tacit agreement with the United States and other nuclear powers, which allowed it to develop its own nuclear capacity as long as such capacity remained undeclared. This also depended on its regional nuclear monopoly, which Israel has tried to preserve at any price. This monopoly is necessary because a balance of nuclear terror and mutual deterrence that was valid between superpowers is perceived as meaningless in a regional context, just as a second-strike capability, while technically possible, is meaningless given the limited territorial scope and dense concentration of population in the region, though some strategists like Feldman[87] or Aronson[88] have argued differently.[89] Thus, when Israel suspected that a France-supplied Iraqi reactor (Tammuz) was close to being operative, it hastened to destroy it by an air raid. Following this act was the so-called Begin Doctrine, which suggested that Israel had to destroy any nuclear reactors in any regional power before they could become operative to ensure Israel's regional nuclear monopoly. However, the nuclearization of the region seems only a question of time, and thus Israel's monopoly may vanish very soon.[90] The prestigious military analyst Ze'ev Schiff[91] has suggested that considering the new international world order and the increasing capabilities of the distant or outer-circle conflict states, such as Iraq, Iran, or even Pakistan, to launch missile attacks against Israel—as was demonstrated so well during the Gulf War—the Israeli military doctrine is completely outdated and irrelevant to the rapidly changing reality. Schiff related this to the politicians' inability for long-term thinking and the fear of the military to become entangled with the politicians. In any case, the real or imagined nuclear power of Israel, intended to offer it a basic sense of power, security, and self-confidence, was used domestically to draw two contradictory conclusions: that Israel was powerful enough to be able to make generous concessions in exchange for achieving a peaceful solution to Jewish-Arab conflict and to reach legitimacy as an accepted society in the region;[92] and that Israel was powerful enough to maintain what it perceived as its natural national rights over its motherland, and to stand fast in the face of the entire world.[93]

The Israeli nuclear capability, the existence of a presumed massive nuclear arsenal and reactor, and its moral, political, social, and environmental implications and consequences never were subjects of systematic public debate. So far the issue seems to be the most, and perhaps the last, consensual tacit agreement about its strict necessity, and most of the leftist and rightist political and intellectual elites in Israel keep public silence about it.[94] The silence intermingles very well with Israel's societal construction of the nuclear aspect of its national security doctrine. Even questions about the safety of nuclear reactors—no less severe an existential problem than national security—are eliminated from the public agenda.

Epilogue: The Military-Cultural Complex

Military doctrines are presumed to determine the modus operandi of the state's military forces to achieve the goals imposed by the collectivity most efficiently, but above all, to ensure its very existence. From this preliminary social analysis of the Israeli military doctrines and behavior at different times and in diverse contexts, it is clear that security, as a societal problem, is not performed within a bubble. National security doctrines are a part of the society's belief system, perceptions of reality, and dominant ideologies, and among the interests of diverse groups and other societal categories. However, the military practices and doctrines both create and construct hard fact and reality. As I have demonstrated in previous works,[95] the military mind and culture, sometimes defined as militarism, intruded so much into the Israeli civilian culture and absorbed it that it is almost impossible to distinguish among them. The other side of this phenomenon was the intrusion of civilian values, norms, and political trends within the military.[96] This intermingling among civilian and military cultures in both the institutional and cultural spheres created what should be could be regarded as a military-cultural complex, penetrating and connecting all of the societal spheres, private and collective, in Israel. Settlement doctrines are translated into military doctrines and vice versa, and both create societal problems that construct social facts and are also constructed by them.

The Israeli state is based on an immigrant-settler society, but state-society relations have not yet been firmly established, in large part because Israel's boundaries are still under dispute.[97] During most of its history, it has been considered a colonial intruder among the peoples of the region and obliged to rely on its own sword. This lead to a construction of a societal reality accompanied by military-doctrinaire conclusions. John Keegan[98] claims that warfare and conflict are primarily cultural constructs. The Jewish–Arab Palestinian conflict, most of the time, has been understood as a routine, immutable, and uncontrollable given, an eternal fate, a kind of Greek tragedy that the two peoples are destined to play. The following well-known eulogy by Moshe Dayan to an Israeli soldier (Roy Rothberg) killed in May 1956 plays on this same theme:

> We are a generation of settlers, yet without a helmet or a gun barrel we will be unable to plant a tree or build a house. Let us not be afraid to perceive the enmity that consumes the lives of hundreds of thousands of Arabs around us. Let us not avert our gaze, for it will weaken our hands. This is the fate of our generation. The only choice we have is to be armed, strong and resolute or else our sword will fall from our hands and the thread of our lives will be severed.[99]

The settler society was not powerful enough to completely exclude the native people that it met on the territory it considered to be its ancient homeland. The local peoples were not powerful enough to prevent the settlers from establishing and successfully developing a viable nation and a regional power, and only recently have some of them begun a fragile process of rapprochement and recognition of it. This required the construction of other cultural and military realities, demanding other national security doctrines.

However, the previous perceptions of realities are not dying and persist alongside the old realities. Even now, Israel is considered to be in a protracted existential conflict, expected at any time to erupt into a total war that will require the recruitment of all its material, human, and emotional resources. The doctrines are built on the principle of a worst-case analysis. On the question of in what measure this presentation of the Israeli condition and the security issues as societal problem are closer to "objective reality" rather than just another "constructed reality"—or just one additional text among other texts—I have no conclusive answer.

However, it is no wonder that, under such circumstances, Israel has developed as a culturally and materially recruited militaristic society, in which national security has shaped the culture, values, and ideologies that require an extensive construction of a convenient social reality. In turn, the ideologies, politics, and culture interfere with professional military and national security considerations, until it is almost impossible to differentiate between them.

CHAPTER EIGHT

Jurisdiction in an Immigrant-Settler Society

The Jewish and Democratic State*

In 1995, a couple by the name of Adel and Iman Qaʾadan from the Arab-Israe-li town of Baqa al-Garbiya made a request to purchase a plot of land to build a home in the Jewish communal settlement of Katzir, in the Wadi Ara area south of Hadera. The council clerk of Tel Eiron refused to sell them the land based on the areaʾs official policy, which prohibits the sale of plots to non-Jews. A petition was filed on the coupleʾs behalf by the Association for Civil Rights in Israel in October of 1995. Chief Justice Aharon Barak, the president of the Supreme Court, tried to avoid making a ruling—a response similar to those made in other "sensitive" cases—and suggested that the sides reach an out-of-court settlement. Four and a half years after the filing of the petition, on March 8, 2000, the High Court of Justice (HCJ) ruled resolutely that discrimination against Arab Israeli citizens in allocating state lands, by either state or state-affiliated agencies, such as the Jewish Agency, was illegal.[1]

* From Baruch Kimmerling, "Jurisdiction in an Immigrant-Settler Society: The 'Jewish and Democratic State,'" *Comparative Political Studies* 35, no.10 (December 2002): 1119–1144. Hebrew version in *Bar Ilan Law Studies* 16, no. 1 (2001): 17–36.

The ruling was regarded immediately as revolutionary, even post-Zionist, and a real turning point in High Court history. Many compared it enthusiastically with the U.S. Supreme Court ruling of *Brown v. Board of Education of Topeka*,[2] the decision that undermined the doctrine of separate but equal education for blacks and whites in the United States. The similarity between the cases rests on the Jewish principles of the Israeli state that include systematic, bureaucratized, and far-reaching discrimination against Arab citizens, denying them access to lands to construct homes or for any other purpose. This, together with the Law of Return, constitutes the main form of legal discrimination against Arabs in Israel, and is based on the cultural, political, and legal principles stating that, first, all the land under the sovereignty of the state is exclusively (Jewish) national land;[3] second, no land may be sold by the state, namely, the Israel Land Authority, or any of its agencies, but only leased for a fixed period; and third, the principal agency entitled to allocate lands for settlement, nominally a non-statist agency, is the Jewish Agency. As a presumed representative of the Jewish people around the world, the agency retains special status in Israel and is not obliged to act according to the principles universally established as the responsibility of a state towards its citizens.[4]

However, a closer analysis of the HCJ decision in the Qa'adan family's case shows that, on a personal level, the court did not furnish the petitioners with any actual remedy to their dilemma, but offered only a general statement against discrimination. The court refrained from ordering the relevant authorities to allocate the requested plot of land to the Qa'adans. More meaningfully, it seems that the court stayed within a well-worn paradigm, recognizing formal equality but only because the circumstances did not involve any competing security concerns (see below). The verdict itself leaves a loophole for the court to avoid supporting equal rights for Arab citizens if the mere specter of national security is raised. Moreover, the court refrained from ordering the authorities to rectify built-in legal and institutional discrimination. As Alexander Kedar commented,[5] the "Qa'adan [verdict] draws a line. The past is to be left unchallenged, untouched and unspoken. Moreover, the story of the Qa'adans is isolated from the collective identity and the needs as Palestinian citizens of Israel."[6] Thus, in spite of its liberal rhetoric, the HCJ's verdict in the Katzir case did not improve the status of Palestinian civil liberties. Ronen Shamir suggested that it was not even a landmark case:[7]

The analysis of [by Shamir of a handful of] cases decided by the Is-raeli Supreme Court suggested that the effect of landmark cases was primarily symbolic. On the one hand, the cases reinforced the court's legitimacy as a solid defender of human rights. On the other hand, all these cases were isolated victories of Palestinian petitioners, which were not followed by similar results in subsequent cases. None of the decisions had any significant effects on later policy. . . . Yet, the significance of the cases was exaggerated allowing them to appear as symbols of justice.[8]

The present essay makes two further additions to Shamir's assertion. First, it demonstrates that the practices of the HCJ function not only to grant legitimacy to the court, but also to generate a façade of legitimacy to the Israeli state's internal and external colonization and territorial expansion efforts. Second, the demonstration is done within a suggested conceptual framework.

Changing Boundaries of the Israeli Polity

Israel was formed as a frontier society[9] and a immigrant-settler state. To this day, it remains an active immigrant society, engaged in an ongoing process of settlement and territorial expansion. Even though its external frontiers are in a continual process of closure, following its peace treaties with Egypt and Jordan and having abandoned its posts in southern Lebanon, Israel presently lacks a finalized border both geopolitically and socially. Despite the Israeli state's tremendously fast and constant transformation, its fundamental attribute, that of being a settler society that must expand and consolidate itself within a given territory, has remained institutionally and culturally constant.

Zionism, the national movement that motivated and was formed by Jewish immigration and settlement, was sophisticated enough to distance itself from traditional global colonialism, the historical matrix from which it developed. Zionism emphasized the uniqueness of the so-called Jew-ish problem—anti-Semitism, persecution and, later, the Holocaust—and offered itself as the sole realistic and moral solution. Thus, the Jewish im-migration movement was able to successfully present itself as a return to Zion, the correction of a cosmic injustice that had gone on for thousands of years and totally disconnected from other European immigration movements to other continents.

However, that Jewish immigration and settlement were construed in Zionist terms could not change the basic social and cultural reality. Early Jewish society, established in Palestine mainly by immigrants with ethnic religious and cultural backgrounds, was vastly different from the broad local population, which perceived itself as a Western society. Within the political context of the postcolonial world order, Israeli society is plagued by the problem of existential legitimacy. It has had to repeatedly defend its existence to the international community and explain why it chose Palestine, renamed the Land of Israel, as its target territory for settlement. Palestine was not chosen for its fertile and abundant soil, its natural resources, its cheap labor force, or its potential markets; it was chosen for ideological and religious reasons. The essential reasoning behind the Israeli state and society's right to exist is embedded in symbols, ideas, and religious scriptures, even if there have been attempts to give them a secular reinterpretation and context.[10]

One especially fascinating phenomenon helps to illuminate Israel's current sociopolitical and political cultural arena: the state's multiple yet simultaneously invoked social and political boundaries.[11] The multiplicity of boundaries includes the pre-1967 borders of the state (the so-called Green Line), the area that the Israeli state actually controls, including the territory captured in 1967, and the social boundaries encompassing Jews, among others. This multiplicity, which facilitates the delineation of various boundaries in various contexts, allows the state to oscillate between them and create a democratic façade that is supported by a rational and legal judicial system and that grants legitimacy to the regime and the state. I want to look closely at four main, partially overlapping boundaries.

First, the boundary of Jewish citizenship includes the Jewish citizens of the state. It is customary within this boundary to consider Israel to be a complete and enlightened democracy. However, given the constitutional mixture of religion and nationality, the nonreligious members of the collectivity, who are supposed to be the majority within this boundary, are subject to a legislative and judicial system that is not based on fundamental democratic assumptions. Thus, even the privileged strata of Israelis—middle-class Ashkenazis, for example—do not receive the benefit of full civil rights. This is due to the existence of a dual judicial system that allows the rabbinical courts to monopolize personal status laws and has grafted a principle of basic inequality between men and women, as well between religious and secular Jews, onto the system. The *halakha* essentially constitute an archaic patriarchal legal doctrine that has consistently preserved the superior status of males over females.[12]

The nature of the dual judicial system powerfully and systematically violates the right to freedom from religion and legally builds in oppression of women, which radiates from the sphere of personal status to many other social and political spheres. The irony is that the vast majority of the Jewish citizens of the state, including most secular citizens, do not perceive the situation as limiting their freedom, but rather expressing Israel's Jewishness.[13] The civil courts, including the HCJ, have never explicitly recognized the distinctiveness of the boundary, arguing that every citizen is equal before the law. This is part of the legitimacy-generating role of the court, demonstrated below and above by the Katzir affair, and is a very meaningful boundary for the judicial system.[14]

Second, the boundary of Israeli citizenship includes Jews, non-Jews,[15] and Arabs (or Palestinians) in Israel. Israel tends to grant Arabs and other minorities citizen's rights equal to those enjoyed by Jews, except for the previously enumerated rights and on an individual rather than a collective basis. It is considered legitimate to allow educational autonomy to ultra-Orthodox, national-religious, other religious, and conceivably even secular Jews, but not Arabs. Despite the tenet that every vote should carry equal weight, votes for parties defined in Israel as Arab parties are worthless in the sense that no meaningful parliamentary decision based on Arab votes is considered politically or morally illegitimate. The judicial system refers to all people within the boundaries as holding completely equal individual rights, but implicitly not collective rights. This is due to the assumption that, as a Jewish state, Jews are entitled to collective rights and non-Jews only individual rights. However, as we may conclude from the Katzir case and innumerable additional cases, the lack of collective rights diminishes and violates the sphere of individual rights. Many times, when cases involving the limitation of individual rights, despite the existence of collective rights, are brought to court, the court tends to protect what is perceived as Jewish national interests, as expressed by liberal rhetoric, that reinforce both the state's legitimacy and its ethno-national boundaries and identity.

Third, the ethnic-religious boundary includes everyone who is defined as belonging to the Jewish people, both in Israel and in the Diaspora. Potentially and with only a few reservations, the state belongs to anyone defined

as a Jew, wherever he or she may be, even if that individual has never considered immigrating to Israel or requesting citizenship. The first and third
categories may be further subdivided into classifications of Jews according
to the *halachic* Orthodox definition and alternatively, Jews accepted as Jews
according to a political or other social definition. Agencies not officially
part of the state bureaucracy, such as the Jewish Agency, operate within this
boundary, as do the Jewish National Fund and the Himanutah Company,
a non-Israeli organization with the purpose of acquiring land from Arabs,
especially in the occupied territories.

Fourth is the boundary of the Israeli system of control. Even today, after
establishment of an autonomous national authority following the partial
implementation of the Oslo accords, the Palestinian population in the occupied territories is still within the control and part of the economic system
of the Israeli state. As long as no final settlement is reached, and as long
as no sovereign Palestinian state has been established, there will be no essential change in this situation. If and when a Palestinian state is established, it is difficult to foresee how the Palestinian and Israeli entities will
be separated. The two entities are highly interwoven in a geopolitical sense,
and there is much asymmetry in their economic and military power and
cultural capital. After twenty-nine years of direct, coercive Israeli rule over
the Palestinian population, the form of government, for the time being, has
become a sort of shared rule, divided between the Palestinian National Authority and Israel. Authority continues to be reinforced by the military and
police, economic means, and settlement. The network of settlements and
the military protection they are afforded constitute a direct expansion of
the Israeli state; the territories of the West Bank and Gaza Strip occupied
in 1967 cannot be considered outside the perimeters of Israel's military and
economic control, even if the level of direct control has declined or has been
passed to a subcontractor. It is a kind of internal colonialism, as, among
other reasons, according to the basic perception of each side, neither people
have an alternative homeland.

At first glance it may seem that we are addressing three different, separate subjects. The first is the deprivation of the universalistic state of certain
of its legislative and judicial powers and the transfer of those powers to the
particularistic field of religion and *halakha*, according to the approach and
interpretation of only one of the denominations within Judaism, Orthodoxy. The state thus facilitates the delineation of its collective identity and
the criteria for membership within it using non-civic criteria. From this

perspective, the state is not simply Jewish, but Jewish Orthodox.[16] The ceding of powers to the religious legal-judicial framework makes Israel a partial theocracy, which cannot be reconciled with any definition of liberal democracy. The regime places severe limitations on women, secular citizens, and citizens who identify themselves as Jews but are not classified as Jews according the Orthodox interpretation of the laws of *halakha*. The second subject is the state's legalized discrimination against non-Jewish, mainly Arab minorities. The third subject is the retention of over two million human beings under occupation for more than a generation, and the creation of a system to control them. The state is expanding its boundaries beyond the limits of its legitimate authority as it includes the occupied territories and their population into Israel's field of power and economic system, as a subsidiary economy and simultaneously reinforcing its underdevelopment. Thus, within the control and economic boundaries of the state, there is a population that is wholly deprived of the rights enjoyed even by its compatriot community, which dwells within the boundaries of Israeli citizenship.

The scope of this essay is limited to two intermingled questions of how the Israeli state, which officially and constitutionally defines itself as Jewish and democratic, relates judicially to two categories of Arabs and their rights on disputed land issues: first, the Arab citizens of Israel, and second, the Palestinians who have resided in the occupied territories since the 1967 war. In other words, it addresses how the immigrant-settler state tries to maintain a democratic identity and image—an important source of legitimacy—and at the same time strives to satisfy its hunger for land and the cultural code of creation of living space, all the while violating most universally accepted human rights and international conventions.[17]

The Futile Periodization

The popular periodization of Israel emphasizes the rupture that allegedly occurred following the outcome of the 1967 war, especially by the so-called Israeli left. Before 1967, in the absence of the fourth boundary, Israel functioned as a moral and heroic society and state, a small nation struggling for its right to exist against the entire world.[18] Since 1967, Israel has become an empire of conquerors, oppressors, and dispossessors. Often, the traumatic change in government in 1977 and the rise of religious-political fundamentalism and Orthodox neo-nationalism have also been explained as dialectical consequences of that same war. Such claims are not completely baseless, but they blot out the innumerable evils committed before 1967 and create the illusion of a mythological past, a lost Garden of Eden that existed in a historical vacuum. Future goals, too, are presented as aspirations to restore a past primarily uncontaminated by Arabs, who were absentees, hidden from sight by mechanisms of the military government that existed until 1966. In short, the legal historiography reveals no direct connection between the distant past, the more recent past, and the present. According to this vision, as Emanuel Sivan has also claimed,[19] it is as if the history of Zionist colonization was initiated, and mobilization of all of the necessary institutional mechanisms—including legal mechanisms—undertaken no earlier than 1967.

An in-depth examination of the past that compares it to the present is likely to point to clues about the future, without being too speculative. The most fascinating legal periodization is that of Chief Justice Aharon Barak. He divides the constitutional history of Israel into two eras. The first includes everything that came before 1992, that is, before the legislation of the two additional basic laws [20] of human dignity and freedom and freedom of occupation. The second includes everything that has occurred following the acceptance of these laws.

All who are involved in the legal institutional arena—judges, legal scholars, commentators, the media, and the general public—are clearly inclined to regard the legal system, especially the HCJ, as an impartial and autonomous body that acts according to universal criteria and some internal logic, disconnected from the interests of the state's ruling factions.[21] This approach is anchored, of course, in the idealist doctrine of separation of powers and independence among the branches of government. It is also assumed automatically to imply a system of checks and balances, with each branch of government critiquing the others on behalf citizens' rights, human dignity and freedom, and weak and minority groups. This impression has been strengthened by the HCJ's increasing role as an activist in different fields, investigating the judiciousness of the actions of the other branches of government and the level of recognition of the standing of public petitioners. Moreover, the HCJ has become a sort of constitutional court, not only interpreting laws but intervening in parliamentary legislation and nullifying laws that appear to contradict the spirit of the Basic Laws or are not "enlightened."[22] The general content and quality of the HCJ's services have never been defined or clarified, but their specific content may be discerned by anyone who examines various court rulings.

The Judiciary and the Management of the Conflict

Closely examining the Israeli judiciary system clarifies that the judiciary protects neither Arab subjects from the arbitrariness of the government nor civil and human rights. It also constitutes one of the most sophisticated tools of repression employed since the state of Israel was brought into being. In this particular field, the judiciary is a central tool in reproducing a hegemonic regime, particularly regarding the inter-ethnic conflict being waged in the land and region, a trend that is likely to continue into the future. The above statement refers to all levels of the judiciary system, but especially the HCJ, the stance of which is not necessarily the result of hardheartedness or prejudice, but due to the fact that the judiciary is an integral part of settler-immigrant society, which maintains its own logic and interests and must retain for itself a territorial living space.

The judicial system and administration in Israel thus make for a fascinating case study. They illustrate how a judicial system with a smug self-image of independence, disconnected from the governing ideology of the local population and the ethnocentric practices customary within it, has refrained from self-critique, and subsequently has had difficulty in maintaining autonomy and universality. Yet, before these topics are dealt with in detail, it is necessary to establish a value-oriented axiom upon which most of the arguments in this essay are built. The framework should be overt rather than covert, as should be the norm. The fundamental assumption is that one of the central functions of a court in general, and of the HCJ in particular, is to extend assistance and protection to minorities and to those who are politically, socially, economically, or otherwise deprived within the structure of the law and its interpretation. The court should do at least this much, and if possible more, without distinguishing which minority groups are entitled to more or less assistance. This is part of a more general approach maintaining that the moral caliber of any government or regime is measured by the quality of its relations with the underprivileged and minorities. Such relations should guarantee at least formal equality before the law and the judiciary and protection against the bias of the majority, the state, and its agents. Rhetoric arguing as much appears in innumerable HCJ verdicts and in the biographies of two prominent chief justices, Simon Agrant[23] and, especially, Aharon Barak.[24] We have no more sensitive a litmus test to exhibit the character of the Israeli government than areas in which the HCJ has intervened, or not, and the ensuing consequences. In this regard, no minority in Israel is less privileged than the Arab minority in Israel, and no population is more oppressed by the Israeli state than the residents of the territories occupied following the 1967 war.

The courts' apparent lack of interest in the fate of ethnic and national minorities is even more obvious in a number of rulings handed down in the past few years in favor of Jewish minorities. These rulings were considered courageous and controversial, and aroused the ire of important sectors of Israeli society, such as the Orthodox Jewish community, bringing them into conflict with the courts. In a case regarding women's rights, army authorities were obligated to invite women candidates to combat pilot courses; excluding women and Reform Jews from religious councils was prohibited; and affirmative action in the form of quotas for female appointments to management and directorate positions in government and public companies was mandated.[25] Similarly liberal rulings were made upon issues of equal rights for homosexuals and lesbians,[26] de facto recognition of the Reform and Conservative movements, and de facto recognition of the rights of single-sex married couples. Each of these decisions was made within Jewish ethnic boundaries.

Judicial Restraint Outside the Ethnic Boundary

In contrast to the judicial activism, the radical restraint, to put it mildly, that the HCJ imposes on itself regarding the rights of Arab citizens of Israel and Palestinians in the occupied territories is even more conspicuous. Even Saban,[27] who is very sympathetic toward the HCJ's general impact on advancing citizens' rights within the Arab population of Israel, admitted that these improvements are a result of "perimetrical radiation." Saban's sophisticated expression cloaks the notion that the court's continuous work to secure civil, human, and citizen rights for the entire population of the state also strengthens and empowers the Arab population's rights, even unintentionally. The argument wrongly presumes that the Arab citizens of Israel are subject to civil rights violations similar to violations against Jewish citizens. Recently the District Court in Beersheba affirmed a ruling of the magistrates' court that called to expel thousands of Bedouin from their homes and land in the Negev Desert (Ramat Hovav)—this after they had been exiled from their original home site and resettled there by the military government fifty years earlier.[28] The Bedouin involved failed to obtain and present evidence of the previous expulsion, which involved documentation that could have only been found in the archives of the military government or the state itself, if such population transfers were even documented during those stormy times. Such cases give the impression that the courts acquire the freedom to criticize the authorities and hand down enlightened and courageous rulings on behalf of Jewish citizens in exchange for accepting the ethnocentric rules of the game and ignoring the human rights of non-Jewish communities.

The HCJ and the Occupied Territories

Strikingly, no international convention or accepted norm requires an occupying power to grant the population under its occupation the right to submit a petition to its courts against its agencies, even regarding actions of the military government or occupational security forces. Israel set a precedent in international practice when it did not prevent inhabitants of the occupied territories from filing a suit in its high court. Presumably, this decision was made based on the first petition submitted to the Israeli HCJ[29] and assuming that the state would object to the court's jurisdiction over the occupied territories, but it did not. In the absence of any objection to the HCJ, the court accepted the petition and set the abovementioned precedent.[30]

By failing to object to the possibility of litigation by the inhabitants of the occupied territories within the HCJ, the Israeli state took a highly sophisticated political step. It not only bestowed upon the occupation an enlightened face and a legitimacy anchored in the modern concept of law and order, but from a judicial standpoint, effectively annexed the territories, producing an image of legality for the occupation itself.[31]

Thus, the HCJ, through its actions and omissions, was one of the central mechanisms for managing the Arab or Palestinian–Israeli conflict. The HCJ defended the Jewish ethno-national interest as constructed and presented by the government, the regime, and Zionist ideology, performing a function no less central and decisive than those performed by the settlers, the military, the bureaucracy, and the rest of the governmental agencies considered to be security and intelligence agencies. The HCJ played its role by commission and by omission, but primarily by the use of a very simple, even simplistic, technique that was astonishingly effective: by not questioning the manner in which the term "security" was used and interpreted. First, any time that the state justified its actions or inactions under the aegis of security, in nearly all cases, the court accepted the explanation without investigating the matter further.[32] Second, the term "security" was almost never examined within the context of the presentation of the petition, and the court gave the state and the executive branch exclusive carte blanche to determine security needs without appeal or restriction. The situation is outrageous, particularly given that the court sees itself as an authority certified to rule on every area of the life of an individual or of the collectivity, including economics and banking, government affairs, medicine and biology, religion, education, and the media. State claims connected to national security are the sole exceptions to court scrutiny. The court can use independent expert witnesses in any field, but in the area of security, the experts recognized almost exclusively are the bodies that the court should consider the most questionable: other state authorities, in particular the army and security agencies. Third, in many cases the court acquiesces to the state's demand to present the testimony of government experts off camera. Such secrecy creates a situation in which testimony and evidence is withheld from the legal representative of the side opposing the state. One has to assume that even when judges are acting in good faith, surely a principle that grants the state exclusivity over security information creates an enormous opening for injustice, highlighting the gaping chasm between the judgments made and true assertions of justice.

The Landmark Case of Eilon Moreh

The Eilon Moreh settlement affair was one of the most famous and exceptional cases that strengthened the status quo. In this case, expropriation writs were presented to the *mukhtar*[33] of the Palestinian village of Rujaib to establish a Jewish settlement near Nablus, the necessity of which was explained, as usual, as being for "reasons of security." However, the landowner appealed to the HCJ; the court accepted the petition and ruled that it was not convinced that "reasons of security" were behind the decision to expropriate private land from its owner.[34] In reality, however, the court was left with no choice but to reject the claim of security needs for two reasons. Among those who testified in the case were the intended Jewish settlers themselves, who declared that they meant to settle the area primarily because of their belief in the nation of Israel's right to return to its land. The state's security officials then gave conflicting evaluations of the situation. Major General Rafael Eitan, the chief of staff, testified that the expropriation was for security needs, but Ezer Weizmann, the defense minister, and

Major General Haim Bar-Lev, the previous chief of staff, rejected the need to establish the settlement for purposes of security. After the ruling, the settlement of Eilon Moreh was established on nearby lands that were not registered as private—or, more accurately, their status was never officially determined. After thirty years of accepting claims of on the basis of security reasons without inquiry or examination, for the first time, and almost for the last, the HCJ deviated from its standard routine. Yet even in the case of Eilon Moreh, no definition was offered as to what sort of situation would constitute a need for settlement for security reasons. On the contrary, given the conflicting testimony, doubts were raised only as to the validity of the specific claim.

Following the Eilon Moreh incident, the state took care not to place the court or itself in similarly embarrassing situations. Following Ordinance 172 of the military government, the state created appeals committees for land expropriation orders in the territories. Menachem Hofnung states that "the establishment of a quasi-judicial tribunal was designed so as to prevent the intervention of the High Court of Justice. The High Court's power to grant relief against state authorities is conditional upon the absence of alternative relief being available to the petitioner."[35] When an additional petition was presented to the High Court, it was rejected on precisely these grounds.[36] It should be noted that the court did not consider in any way international treaties' absolute prohibition against making irreversible, permanent changes on the ground, and against the settlement of citizens of an occupying power within territories that are under occupation.

The situation perhaps opens a portal into the foreseeable future regarding interpretations of the legal status of settlements in the territories occupied by Israel in the 1967 war. From a legal perspective, they were considered to be temporary settlements that might be disbanded according to changes in the so-called security situation,[37] and consequently, Israeli law did not apply to them. However, court-protected appropriation in the name of security began much earlier and within the boundary of Israeli citizenship.

The Nationalization of the Land

After the 1948 war and during the 1950s, the largest expropriation and nationalization of land was carried out under the aegis and with the aid of the military government. At the end of this period, 93 percent of the land in the country had been transferred to the Israel Lands Authority and leased to the Jewish National Fund. Hundreds of Jewish settlements were established on these lands.[38] The lands were not expropriated, as is commonly believed, only from Palestinians who were uprooted from territories conquered by the state's military forces and who became refugees. Lands were also expropriated from Arab residents within the state's boundaries, individuals who became citizens after all of the battles had ended. These included both "present absentees," Arabs who were not on their lands at the time of the census,[39] and those who remained in their villages and their homes throughout. The High Court rejected dozens of petitions from Arab citizens, one after the other, simply because government representatives argued that their cases presented a threat to security.[40] One well-known case, though not the only one of its kind, was that of the Marionette villages of Iqrit and Bir'm. During the battles of 1948, the military requested that residents of these villages temporarily evacuate. When the fighting ceased, the authorities refused to allow them to return. Upon their appeal to the High Court, it was ruled that the residents be allowed to return to their homes subject to security considerations—which, as is well known, have prevented their return to this day.[41]

A lesser-known case that aptly demonstrates the collaboration of the executive, legislative, and judicial authorities is the case of the residents of Al-Jalme, who were expelled from their village on March 2, 1950 by order of the military governor and transferred to the village of Jatt. Their lands were then immediately turned over to the members of Kibbutz Lehavot Haviva. In the first stage of the case, the residents of Al-Jalme lodged a complaint with the defense minister. When they received no reply, they petitioned the High Court. The state did not bother to respond with a claim of security reasons, as might usually have occurred; instead, the state retaliated by passing the Law of Land Acquisition (Validation of Acts and Compensation) which gave ex post facto legality to all prior land expropriations, even those without justification. The state's representative before the High Court, Miriam Ben-Porat, did not try to defend the expulsion, but rather announced that the kibbutz had possessed the land and was unwilling to withdraw of its own accord, and that the new law made removal impossible. Judge Jacob Olshen was only able to remark that "the feeling of elemental justice rises up at hearing the claim . . . but now when there is a need to rectify the wrong for the petitioners, the law stands as an obstacle in their way."[42] The right to property has always been considered sacred in Israeli legislation and jurisprudence. Yet the traditional Arab holdings of land[43] were not recognized as ownership, but as a situation that needed to be put into order, in most cases by expropriation.

Had the legislature and the courts wanted to make order concerning only land matters, as Alexander Kedar mentions,

> there was no need to change the statute of limitations in clause 78 of the Lands Law, nor to reduce the evidentiary tools available to the (the Arab) holders of the lands. In the framework of ordering the lands it was possible to order the rights to the land, to formally register the land in the name of the state, but at the same time to settle the situation of the holders: to grant them leasing rights for generations on the lands that they held and thereby to carry out the Law of Land Leasing (Emergency Order)—1959. This arrangement which was even required by law was never carried out in any meaningful way. The desire to redeem the lands (according to the Zionist ethos) was preferred over the legal logic of searching for order.[44]

In practice, as long as the military government existed, about two-thirds of matters concerning Arab citizens of the state were excluded from the jurisdiction of the civil courts and turned over to military courts, in which not even the appearance of equal justice was maintained. The High Court declared itself restricted from intervening in Arab affairs, which were construed as issues of state security. In this way, administrative detentions, confinements, expulsions, and land confiscation for the military's needs ("live-fire areas") were carried out within the legal bubble of emergency decrees, which remained in effect from the British colonial era. It was thus possible to make the law an additional arm of the state, the intent of which was the Judification of all areas of the state as a supplement to sovereign control. Thus Alina Korn[45] found that about 95 percent of the crimes committed against emergency decrees were administrative crimes by Arab citizens, such as going out and working the fields, or going to markets or workplaces outside of the areas authorized by the military government or without its approval.

Expropriation of the Occupied Territories

The military government was abolished in 1966. By that time there was almost nothing left to expropriate of the lands belonging to Arabs in Israel. A year later, the territorial conflict between the Israeli state and the

Palestinians began afresh with the occupation of the territories in the 1967 war. Once again, legislation and adjudication were used to expropriate land and expand territory for the settler-immigrant society, which viewed territories not yet occupied more and more as a frontier available for occupation, or as they saw it, redemption.[46]

According to clause 55 of the 1907 Hague Convention, occupying powers can act only as temporary managers and beneficiaries of land and other properties in occupied territories; creation of permanent "facts on the ground" that remain in the area after the occupation is not permitted. In the case of the confiscation of the lands for the Beit El settlement, the High Court ruled that it was legal to confiscate private land if the owners were compensated (paid leasing fees) to establish "civilian settlements necessary for security purposes."[47] Thus, establishing a civilian settlement became a security measure without the court ever having to interpret the complex meaning of such a ruling. The issue of how a civilian settlement might serve as a security measure was never discussed or weighed, even though many security experts, whom the High Court has never consulted to clarify the issue, agree that at least some of the Jewish settlements in the occupied territories are actually a military burden and danger, both tactically and strategically. These territories, except for the metropolitan area of East Jerusalem and the Syrian (Golan) Heights, were not annexed by Israel and thereby have remained so-called administered territories, differing only semantically from occupied territories. Israel has always rejected the definition of the territories as occupied, claiming that they were never under the sovereignty of another state, as the annexation of the West Bank by Jordan was never recognized by the international community, with the exception of Britain and Pakistan, and because, Israel maintains, the lands came under its control during a just and defensive war. At the same time, Israel took upon itself to abide by the rules of international law in the territories, including those of the Fourth Geneva Convention of 1949.

Most experts in the field of international law do not accept Israel's approach. They are divided between seeing Israel as an occupying power and seeing Israel as a so-called trustee-occupant, controlling the territory until the dormant sovereignty of the local residents, a distinct and conscious sociopolitical entity, develops into a self-ruling body, which is happening before our eyes.[48]

One of the reasons that every Israeli government evaded annexing the territories—part of the area of historical or colonial Palestine—was to avoid granting citizenship and its accompanying rights to the Arab residents, thereby transforming Israel into a de facto binational state. Political convenience dictated subordinating Arabs to military government laws, army decrees, and military justice. Jewish residents and their settlements, as well as the local Jewish authorities, were subject to Israeli law and justice. This arrangement is an extremely original Israeli invention, providing a personal sovereignty that accompanies each settler wherever he or she goes. Few have expressed an opinion on this issue, but it functions as a kind of selective annexation of the territories without granting the Palestinian residents citizenship. Though some of the processes involved in settling the occupied territories came as initiatives of social and political movements, such as Gush Emunim, if the state and its various agents had not desired that the settlements exist, not a single Jewish settler would live in the occupied territories today. The state granted and continues to grant them protection by means of military and police forces, land allocations, and direct and indirect subsidies, including massive allocations to infrastructure.

However, to avoid foreseeable judicial embarrassments, the Israeli occupying rule began to systematically declare unsettled lands, the lion's share of which was under traditional Arab ownership, as state lands. Legally speaking, between 60 and 70 percent of the territory in the West Bank at the time of occupation was not registered in the land registry. Despite this, all previous regimes—the Ottoman, British, and Jordanian—considered the lands as belonging to individuals, families, or villages who took responsibility for maintenance, according to traditional custom.[49] Israel confiscated the territories according to the military government's standard procedure: seizure for military needs, declaration of natural reserves, restriction from public use, establishment of military camps, and closure of live-fire areas. According to measurements taken by Meron Benvenisti,[50] by 1986, 2.8 million out of 5.5 million dunums of land, that is, 52 percent of the entire area of the West Bank, had been transferred to Israeli state ownership.[51] It is undeniable that Jewish settlement upon these lands occurred without fear of the High Court.

Constitutional Revolution and the Judification of the State's Identity

The codification and ideological apex of exclusion of the Arab citizens from the boundaries of the Jewish polity was reached in the early 1990s. In March 1992, two well-known basic laws were legislated: Basic Law: Human Dignity and Freedom and Basic Law: Freedom of Occupation. Aharon Barak, the president of the Supreme Court, has frequently claimed that, beginning in 1992, Israel embarked upon a constitutional revolution. His unspoken reference is to the democratization of the Israeli regime. In one of his latest and least ambiguous expressions, after splitting the history of Israeli law into four eras, Barak writes:

> At the foundation of this revolution stand the human rights that were given constitutional standing above the regular laws. Israel changed from a parliamentary democracy to a constitutional democracy. At the head of the structure stands the constitution. A law of the Knesset cannot contradict or abolish it.[52] The Court is authorized to declare the law unconstitutional. With the legislation of two Basic Laws regarding human rights, constitutionalization of Israeli law occurred.[53]

The process of constitutionalization certainly sounds like a positive trend, particularly because the two basic laws contain some most welcome clauses. However, Ruth Gavison[54] opposes the continued legislation of additional basic laws. Her reasoning is that, given the internal political power relations of the Israeli state, additional basic laws will only strengthen the status quo. This means not only perpetuating the Orthodox monopoly over personal status policy issues, but also the continuous granting of emergency authority to the military and the various security agencies, as well as the protracted absence of civil equality in the state.

Anyone who followed the process of the legislation of the two basic laws knows that not only were they accepted as a compromise between contradictory ideological approaches and legislative doctrines, but also, as Ruth Gavison argued, they reproduce the existing power structure and social order. The legislative and judicial systems usually perceive democracy as a set of procedures, such as free elections, while Jewishness is regarded as an identity, an overall cultural operational code and organizational principle.[55]

Each of the basic laws' proclaimed purpose is to "anchor in a Basic Law the values of the State of Israel as a Jewish and democratic state."[56] However, despite enormous scholastic and heroic efforts to reach a compromise among the two concepts, according to any definition of Judaism or of democracy, the two terms do not correspond with one another; if anything, they are mutually exclusive.[57] The term "Jewish state," the definition of which the law does not elaborate, may be interpreted several ways, including the desire to approach theocracy[58] as per Justice Menachem Elon[59] and according to the minimalist-demographic interpretation of Gavison.[60] Basic Law: Human Dignity and Freedom contributes the declarative and ideological dimension to the laws of return and citizenship that were instrumental in their foundation. This is one of the most instructive examples in which constitutionalization, in the guise of progressive liberalism, perpetuates basic discrimination on the basis of ideology.

Such a phenomenon occurs because of two polar interpretations of the term "Jewish" that are selective interpretations, such as those of Justices Aharon Barak or Haim Cohen. They view the law as endorsing the selective adoption of values and norms that are a part of Jewish heritage, and which conform with Western culture's idea of what is universal, egalitarian, liberal, and democratic. The less significant consequence of this interpretation is that it empties Israel's definition as a Jewish state of all practical content and certainly contrasts with the legislature's intent as revealed by the process of legislation, during which certain parliament members suggested adding the phrases "Jewish state" and "the state of its citizens,"[61] which were rejected outright by most parliament members. From this we see that the intent of the legislature was to interpret the "Jewishness of the state" as similar to the spirit of the term "Jewish" in the Laws of Return and Citizenship, that is, closer to the polar interpretations of Gavison on one hand and Menachem Elon on the other. Needless to say, the two laws are among the most problematic, ethnocentric, and discriminatory in the Israeli codex. Recently, interpretation of the term "Judaism," which had been relatively liberal in accepting the Orthodox interpretation of Judaism, has become more radicalized and narrower. The Knesset passed a law requiring members of religious councils to accept the authority of the chief rabbis. It is improbable that even Menachem Elon would wish to see the primacy of the Jewish state over the democratic state, though that is indeed the design of legislators working within the framework of the constitutional revolution that Chief Justice Barak declared.

Conclusions

Research of the law, the constitution, and the interpretation of both hold great importance. However, the legal field's analysis and research must not be limited to these three areas. To investigate judicial rulings without an understanding of the ideological background and power dynamic within

society is to work within a judicial bubble that idealizes the state and ignores, deliberately or not, its darker corners. None of the articles or research I found on the constitutional revolution contained any admission
that, after the revolution, rulings related to security issues or to the ethnocentric character of the state continue to be handed down, a fact that bla-
tantly contradicts principles of human dignity and freedom. Even after the
constitutional revolution, detentions without trial, torture, expulsions, and
collective punishments continue, just as the process of creeping annexation
and settlement of the occupied territories continues. Apparently the constitutional revolution will never extend to these areas.

Evidently, such rulings are made because, as David Kretzmer[62] has
pointed out, legislators, judges, and the judicial system are all products of
the national ethos and the political and social regime. The system's façade
of independence has simply strengthened the degree of freedom it has in
functioning as a mechanism of ethnic repression. Addressing such issues
within the legal sphere and with legal rhetoric has had the added effect of
granting legitimacy to the basic codes of this still-expanding immigrant-
settler society.

The confines of the law are not defined within the walls of the courtroom;
they are completely vulnerable and accessible to the influence of political,
national, and other interest group ideologies. This is perhaps justifiable.
If knowledge is power, then legislation and interpretation through adjudication is the ultimate power. If we examine the meaning of Basic Law:
Human Dignity and Freedom within its wider context, we conclude with
no difficulty that the law is applicable only within Jewish ethnic boundaries,
making Israel a constitutionally more exclusive state now than it was before
1992.[63] Missing from this law and from all of the basic and other laws is the
right of each individual, as a citizen, to an equal voice in designating common symbolic goods—the flag, state symbol, anthem, common holidays,
days of mourning—in short, the right to a common civil religion or, alternatively, to full cultural autonomy. In this way, the new basic laws and the
constitutional revolution will surely perpetuate ethnic discrimination for
generations to come.

CHAPTER NINE

Exchanging Territories for Peace

A Macrosociological Approach·

The most outstanding feature of the removal of Israeli settlements from the Sinai Peninsula, especially from the town of Yamit, was the prevailing confusion, disorientation, and uncertainty affecting all parties involved. Up to the last minute before the removal, the government of Israel postponed decisions and contravened previous positions. Furthermore, several of the Sinai settler-evacuees' questions remained unanswered. Should they have resisted the evacuation? What form and quantity of compensation for evacuating the settlements should have been demanded? Should there have been negotiations with the government, and if so, how should they have been conducted? Should they have enlisted the aid of external groups, such as various elements of the Movement to Stop the Withdrawal (MSW) in Sinai and the mass media? Should they have employed violence? If so, of what type and to what extent? Finally, how should the settlers have behaved once evacuation was underway?

* From Baruch Kimmerling, "Peace for Territories: A Macro-Sociological Analysis of the Concept of Peace in Zionist Ideology," *Journal of Applied Behavioral Science* 23, no. 3 (1987): 13–34.

For the first time in the history of the modern state of Israel, the Israeli armed forces, which could not deny that the public political debate had pervaded its ranks, became directly involved in a serious internal political controversy. No one doubted that the armed forces would carry out orders from those in political authority, but nevertheless, uncertainty prevailed as to the precise intentions of those orders and the extent to which the military was to employ force, especially against active and armed resistance. Particularly important to the military was whether to reveal that the political controversy splitting the civilian public had seemingly divided the military to the same extent.

The MSW, which emerged from outside the settlers' ranks, comprised various factions that were unaware of the nature and boundaries of the proposed resistance and of the limits that the authorities would impose upon the application of force and pressure. The MSW also did not know how to recruit support without risking a political backlash, nor did it know how many active and potential supporters it required to transform the movement from a limited and relatively marginal group into a political power capable of threatening, and even implementing, civil rebellion.

Confusion apparently peaked in the general public. Except for narrow marginal sectors with well-formulated, extreme political views, the public was largely incapable of taking an unambiguous stand for or against the removal of settlements from Sinai. Moreover, certain opposition factions halfheartedly claimed that the government had other practical options and that a peace agreement with Egypt could have been attained without removing the settlements. None of the parties actively or passively involved in removing Sinai settlements appeared to be aware of the rules of the game or even of the game's ultimate objective. Sociologists call this situation anomie.[1]

This article attempts primarily to prove that anomie was provoked by two principal factors. The first was conflict between two key values in Israeli society and Zionist ideology. Israel aspired for peace with its Arab neighbors, but at the same time, had a powerful need for both Arab and universal recognition of the Zionist enterprise—in particular, the sanctity of settlement as a dominant component of the pragmatics of Zionism and the danger inherent in reversing any settlement processes. The second were problems and internal contradictions in the Israeli political culture related to the concept of peace itself. I first describe and analyze each component, then examine the components' mutual interaction.

Peace in Israel Political Culture

The Jewish social system in Palestine, subsequently Israel, has never truly experienced total peace, and the constant struggle between the society of immigrant-settlers and the Arabs has been subject to drastic fluctuations in patterns, intensity, and significance. I have elsewhere distinguished between the chronic and extended manifestations of this conflict and its periodic active outbreaks, which have taken the form of riots (in 1921, 1929, and 1936–39) or full-scale warfare (in 1948, 1956, 1967, 1973, and 1982).[2] Most participants in the conflict—the Israelis, Palestinians, Arab states, and even the entire Muslim world and its allies—have tended to perceive it as insoluble, not only because of its duration, but also because of several factors. All parties emphasize the cultural and religious gaps between the Jewish and Arab societies. Many perceive the conflict as being based on incompatible interests, in that both parties want the entire territory of Palestine, at least in the long run; it is considered unlikely that either would settle for the existence of two mutually exclusive entities, one Arab Palestinian and the other Jewish Israeli.[3] The conflict is also perceived as being zero-sum, that is, one side's gains necessarily result in the other's losses, so that from the Zionist point of view all acts of nation building are considered directly connected with the Jewish-Arab conflict. Finally, both Israel and the Arab countries consider war to be the natural state of affairs, with peace—or even the "threat" of peace—considered a crisis situation.[4]

Despite the above factors, or perhaps because of them, peace and aspirations for peace remained a central motif of Zionist ideology and an integral part of Israeli society's collective self-image. The aspirations stemmed from several complementary sources. Virtually all schools of Zionism were perceived as bearing a social revolution with a deep moral message, intended not only for the nation of Israel, but for all mankind.[5] This universal dimension of Zionism could be expressed only in a situation of peace, including peace with those in the surrounding Arab environment; without the Arabs within, alongside, or surrounding Jewish society, doubt was cast upon the very legitimacy of the Zionist enterprise.[6] Two conditions are necessary for the Zionist enterprise to succeed: Most of world Jewry must be gathered within the Jewish state, and the Arabs must accept this society's existence. Because of these conditions, a second source of aspirations for peace was the belief that if peace were not imminent, the Zionist enterprise would face constant danger of physical destruction or political annihilation. However,

Israelis pragmatically recognized that the Zionist enterprise could not be completed unless a situation of peace prevailed, for not all of Diaspora Jewry would immigrate to Israel if such a move would threaten one's survival. Anxiety would deter personal or collective destiny, ideological motivation, or any combination of the two.

Zionist Israeli cultural creations, such as literature and poetry, were consistently replete with both externally and internally directed messages of Israel's quest for peace, especially before the Six-Day War in 1967, although the trend continued for a time afterward. Political or overall social objectives contrasting with this ideology of peace were thrust to the periphery. Casting Israel as a seeker of peace and its enemies as opponents of peace—surely not an original Israeli invention—became an integral part of conflict management, for both foreign and domestic purposes. The political perception that these tactics created, even though it was only partially supported by reality, successfully gained long-term acceptance in most of the Western world—Israeli society's principal reference group—and among most of the Israeli political community. Most of the Israeli public sincerely believed that Israel desired peace, though they did not always agree regarding the methods to use or the sacrifices to be made to attain such peace.

At times in Zionist history, Israelis had hoped and even believed that peace, or at least Arab acceptance of the existence of the Jewish political entity in their region, was either imminent or had been attained de facto. On January 3, 1919, Chaim Weizmann and Emir Faysal ibn Hussein signed an agreement that the Zionists interpreted as the Arabs relinquishing their designs on Palestine as a separate component of a future, greater Arab state, and recognizing the Jewish political entity's exclusive rights to that region. For several years afterward, the Zionist movement considered this agreement the basis for Arab consent to the coexistence of the two nations in the region.

Following the 1948 war, Israel signed ceasefire agreements with most of the Arab states involved in the confrontation. The preamble to each of these agreements included a paragraph declaring the agreement to be temporary and valid only until peace had been established between the state of Israel and the relevant Arab state. At the time, Israeli leaders considered the termination of war with the Arabs to be a close, attainable possibility.

Approximately one year before the 1973 war, the ceasefire lines between Israel and Egypt, Syria, and the Hashemite kingdom of Jordan enjoyed relative quiet. No active hostility took place, although political, psychological, and economic warfare against Israel did not cease. This situation, considered in light of Israel's own powerful self-image, led Moshe Dayan, the minister of defense, to his often-stated conclusion that a de facto peace prevailed between Israel and its Arab neighbors. I emphasize, however, that this conception was unusual; the conflict was generally viewed as defying simple or imminent solutions.

Routinization of Aspirations for Peace

In 1966, Yehoshafat Harkabi, the former head of Israeli military intelligence and an expert in Arab perceptions of the Israel-Arab conflict, wrote the following:

> Obviously, we yearn for peace in the near future. However, willingly or otherwise, Israel must prepare for and adjust to the possibility that the conflict will be an extended one. Turning points, unforeseen phenomena and dramatic events may indeed develop . . . but these cannot be predicted in advance; hence we cannot rely upon them.[7]

Harkabi went on to call for the political socialization of Israeli society, especially the youth, according to this approach. He claimed that a world order anticipating peace at any moment had consistently proven to be a false prophecy, potentially counterproductive to Israeli society. Israeli society's routinization of the conflict was vital to its perseverance. Such routinization meant continuing a normal life and maintaining a social structure not permanently on the alert, either psychologically or militarily, for an extended and seemingly interminable struggle. Society was thus obligated to absorb everything pertaining to conflict management as a permanent societal feature, a destiny, or a natural social phenomenon. Just as a society had gaps among its various social strata, such as disagreements among religious and nonreligious groups, so too did it have periodic wars and constant conflict with its environment, as Dayan stated above. Just as persons died from air pollution and traffic accidents, the results of technological developments, so too did persons die in battle or in the perpetual small-scale war involving Israel. Investing in social resources and emotional energy could help reduce the damage, but the phenomenon could not be eliminated altogether.

Another aspect of this process is the routinization of aspirations for peace, stemming from five perceptions commonly accepted in Israel. First, the desire for peace with all Arab states is a national objective and lofty ideal of the Israeli collectivity.[8] Second, the Arabs as countries, nations, and cultures are perceived as unwilling to accept the existence of Israel in the region because of cultural or religious differences, perceptions of their own interests, or a combination of these factors, and therefore seek Israel's annihilation. Third, Israel cannot control the conflict; at most it may intensify it through initiated activity and strong reactions to Arab provocation, but it cannot diminish the conflict, much less resolve it.[9] Attaining peace thus does not depend on Israel, which cannot influence the situation as long as it remains a Zionist state—that is, the potential homeland of all or most of the world's Jews. Fourth, peace will arrive in the nebulous or Utopian future. It may result from processes and developments taking place in the Arab world as it undergoes modernization and comes to understand the advantage of having the Zionist enterprise in the region. Alternatively, the Arabs may realize that annihilating Israel is impossible, that the conflict only causes material and social damage, and therefore find it more worthwhile to accept Israel's existence. Peace may also result from some indescribable process—a miracle.[10] Fifth, though peace remains a desired objective, Israel's military-strategic conception is based upon a "mini-max" approach that accords security a greater value than any other objective, including peace. This implies that attitudes toward peace or any concessions made in its name must be measured against the perceived contributions to security. If peace lowers the level of security, then it is not worthwhile. Peace may only be agreed to and strived for if it neither diminishes nor endangers security.[11]

The routinization of the quest for peace enabled Israeli society to live with itself and the prevailing situation of conflict. Thus, Israel could continue to invest in conflict management and other overall internal and external social objectives while ritually and declaratively devoting efforts toward peace-oriented activities. Keeping this in mind, one can avoid the moot question of whether Israel could have obtained a peace agreement with the Arab states from 1949–67.

The Incommensurable Values

Many of the abovementioned perceptions changed following the Six-Day War in 1967, as Israel gained control of the Sinai Peninsula, the Gaza Strip, the West Bank, and the Golan Heights. At least during the immediate postwar period, Israelis believed that the Arabs' military debacle was so decisive and their losses of territory so unacceptable to them that they finally would be forced to realize that they could not destroy Israel militarily. Hence, the Arabs would have no choice but to recognize Israel's existence. Israel's defense minister announced that he was "awaiting a telephone call" from Jordan's King Hussein.

Soon, however, it became evident that not all parties involved were ready to accept a simple exchange of the captured territories for peace agreements. Israel's dual assumption was that its proven absolute military superiority would lead the Arabs to conclude they must recognize Israel, and that Israel's control of large Arab-populated territories and military proximity to regions vital to the Arab states—the Suez Canal, Damascus, and key Jordanian territories and populations—was unbearable for the affected states in particular and the Arab world in general, and would thus lead the Arabs to negotiate with Israel. These assumptions proved incorrect.[12] The first signs of this appeared as early as February 1969, when Egypt initiated the War of Attrition along the Suez Canal. The results of the war were unclear, for neither side overcame the other. At the same time, Palestinians increased their small-scale attacks against Israel's urban population as Fatah—the newly consolidated main political arm of the Palestine Liberation Organization—began to increase its notoriety in Israel and throughout the world. In March 1969, Hussein announced the establishment of a joint Jordanian-Syrian "eastern front" command, along with military coordination efforts with Egypt, hinting at the possibility of a war of attrition.

Israel's control of vast Arab territories did not diminish the conflict's intensity, and the situation became even more complex with the emergence of the Palestinian Arabs as participants. For about nineteen years, the vast majority of the original Arab population of Palestine had lived under Jordanian rule. Jordan, the only Arab state to consider the Palestinians to be citizens rather than refugees, attempted to involve them in the Jordanian national economic, social, and—to a partial extent—political systems. Israel's subsequent control of territories where large numbers of Palestinians lived initiated the accelerated process of their de-Jordanization and subsequent re-Palestinization.[13] Increasingly vocal Palestinian Arab demands, issued independently of those voiced in their host countries, were accompanied by guerilla warfare within the occupied territories and Israel, as well as by acts of terrorism abroad. These developments intensified the image of the conflict as a zero-sum struggle between parties with mutually exclusive interests.

Institutionalization of Territories

At the same time, an internal process of a totally different nature began to take place within Israeli society. Since its inception, the Zionist movement has yearned for and sought the return of Jews to the "land of their forefathers," and this focus upon obviously sensitive territorial objectives was a key means to mobilize Jews to immigrate to Zion. Patterns of land ownership by Arabs led the Jewish political community in Palestine, with the exception of the new city of Jerusalem, to establish itself in areas with only peripheral territorial symbolism to the Arabs, such as the Mediterranean coastal plain and the Jezareel and Jordan valleys. Although the penetration of Zionist settlements into the central hill regions, the core of the original Land of Israel, had been minor and sporadic, it was full of religious symbolism, as these regions constituted the infrastructure of national Zionist symbols. Hence, Israel's control of them after 1967 aroused powerful sentiments, and not only among the religious strata of Israeli society. Despite his saying he awaited a telephone call from Hussein, Dayan declared that "we have not returned to [biblical towns] Anatot and Shilo merely to abandon them forever." Israel immediately annexed the old city of Jerusalem, and as time passed, the size of the area that both the government and public of Israel were willing to bargain in exchange for peace or some other political accommodation gradually decreased.

The reduction in the size of the land that Israel was willing to part with did not result solely from the territories' national and religious symbolism. Occupying the territories also seemed to reduce Israel's military vulnerability, for the borders of the state, which extended past the ceasefire lines established in 1949, were long and convoluted, making Israel highly vulnerable from both a tactical and strategic point of view. Moreover, the continued institutionalization of the occupied regions intensified class and economic interests, and had several effects.

The Mizrahi Jews—that is, Jewish immigrants from North Africa and Asia—underwent upward social mobilization as a single unit. Prior to 1967, this group had occupied the lower strata of the Israeli social system. After the Six-Day War, adding the Arab residents of the occupied territories to the labor force immediately moved the Mizrahi Jews to the intermediate strata. The Mizrahi Jews also enjoyed occupational mobility as a result, with their former jobs assumed by Arab workers. Meanwhile, the territories were gradually settled by Jews, partially because of government initiatives—as in the case of Yamit—and partially because of private efforts, which occasionally contrasted with declared government policy. The occupied territories became a sort of frontier zone for the social system,[14] due to a combination of perceptions of Israel's strategic military interests, sentiment toward the territories, and the economic interests of the entire social systems and various strata within it. The influx of hundreds of thousands of unskilled workers from the occupied territories into Israel's economy added unprecedented dimensions to its fifteen-year-long postwar boom.[15] Finally, the territories themselves provided Israel with numerous important natural resources, such as water from the Golan Heights, vast quantities of oil and minerals from the Sinai Peninsula, tourist attractions such as the winter resorts along the eastern Sinai coast, the Gulf of Aqaba, the Gulf of Suez, and Mount Hermon, and a potential land reserve.

Hawks and Doves

All of the above factors intensively changed the Israeli perception of the role and value of peace. Until the Six-Day War, peace was considered a lofty ideal, apparently unattainable at a price that most in the Israeli sociopolitical system would accept. After 1967, however, different conceptions began to develop regarding the possibility of obtaining peace as agreements promoted an absence of belligerence in varying degrees, in exchange for some, most, or all of the occupied territories.[16] Furthermore, differences of opinion arose as to whether the benefits of peace were worth the costs of changes affecting sentiment (e.g., concessions involving sites or areas considered holy), security, the economy, and social factors. The cleavages within Israeli society—right wing versus left wing, religious versus nonreligious, Jews versus Arabs, Ashkenazi versus Mizrahi, and the like[17]—were joined by a split between doves and hawks on the issue of peace, a distinction that partially overlapped with the other cleavages.[18]

The terminology of hawks and doves is borrowed from U.S. political culture. In Israel, the doves tended to believe that a peace agreement—or at least an agreement guaranteeing long-term periods of relative non-belligerence and tranquility—was indeed attainable in exchange for all or most of the territories Israel had occupied since 1967. The doves claimed that, even if there was no immediate possibility of obtaining such an agreement, Israel must refrain from taking steps that would prevent or hamper its attainment. For them, peace was of utmost importance, and Israel's control of vast Arab territories and populations was immoral and perhaps practically impossible. The doves did not wish to see Israel transformed into a binational state with a large Arab minority (according to various calculations, this minority will likely become a small majority by the year 2010),[19] whether or not the Arabs from the occupied territories were accorded full civil and political rights, such as the right to vote and to be elected to the Knesset. Thus was created a demographic left, as opposed to a social left, as well a demographic right.[20]

The hawks' position was predicated primarily on Israel's right to the entire Land of Israel promised in the Bible and various claims that the territories had necessary strategic defense value. The hawks had no consistent response to Israel's demographic problem;[21] instead, they drew upon a basic assumption of Zionism that the majority of world Jewry would one day reside in Israel, at which time the relative ratio of Israeli Jews to Palestinian Arabs would become inconsequential. In addition, the hawks doubted that a genuine peace with the Arabs was possible, even in exchange for major concessions.[22]

Both approaches proved to be problematic. For one, each view expressed desires that could not be substantiated empirically. The doves could not prove that, in return for all or part of the occupied territories, the Arabs would consent to a peace agreement and recognize Israel's right to exist. The hawks could not provide for the maintenance of the basic Jewish character of the state of Israel. This led to a reversal of sorts: Social groups that upheld universalist, humanistic, and democratic approaches employed the particularistic goal of preserving Israel's Jewish character, whereas those with a national-particularistic outlook were bound prima facie by universalistic claims that Jews and Arabs could coexist.

Moreover, virtually no consensus existed among the hawks or the doves with respect to the concrete elements of their respective conceptions. The hawks were divided in their attitudes toward authority and obedience to government decisions and democracy. Whether the entire Land of Israel was to include all of the territories conquered in 1967, or only Judea and Samaria—that is, Jordan's West Bank—and the Golan Heights, remained unclear. The hawks also faced the problem of deciding which attitude to adopt toward peace. Should a concrete and reasonable Arab offer of a peace agreement in exchange for territories be refused? If not, which concessions would be considered permissible, and which territories should be defended? International actors affected the issue, as for many years, Israelis had expressed anxiety that their country could face pressure from abroad—primarily economic pressure from the United States—and not be able to withstand it. Israel had already experienced considerable political pressure. Although many Israelis feared such effects from the outside, some more dovish groups actually hoped for it, especially those who had despaired that Israel's political situation would change through internal social processes only.

The hawks maintained so-called price lists with which to trade off values in response to several questions. How much democracy should be sacrificed to hold on to the territories? What were the locations and extent of territories that could be relinquished under different conditions of economic and political pressure? Which territories demanded confrontation with the Israeli government and the collectivity's rules? What should be the nature and intensity of such a confrontation, and which means should be employed? On the whole, the hawks remained more consistently homogeneous than did the doves, who were divided among themselves as to the locations and extent of territories to be traded for peace and the nature of desired security arrangements—that is, how much peace should be negotiated, and with whom. The doves' price lists were even more varied than were the hawks', leading fringe elements of the two camps to meet in the middle of the polarity and create an intermediate category, the dove-hawks, the most obvious manifestation of which was the Allon Plan. This plan posited that the Jewish military and settlement presence should be established in areas not densely populated by Arabs and of strategic defense significance, such as the Jordan Valley. This plan also opposed future de jure annexation of these territories to the state of Israel.

With respect to trading territories for peace, the main difficulty facing the two camps, and all of the Israeli social system, was that the values to be traded were incommensurable. Territory or land is a real, material object that can be quantified, evaluated, compared, and even sold on the market. Peace is a largely abstract and esoteric concept, dependent on experience and culture, elusive and difficult to control. In the context of international relations, one can hold on to territory by overpowering one's rival, but both sides must cooperate to keep peace. Even groups demanding the exchange of territories for peace generally formulated their ideas in relative terms, such as that of taking a calculated risk. This situation made it difficult to create a trade proposal that a broad cross section of Israeli society would accept in valuing peace over the location and amount of territory exchanged for it.

Another difficulty arose for the doves' claim that peace equaled security, which contrasted with the hawks' call for strategic depth. Moreover, although the Arab states, especially Egypt, began to discuss peace as part of their political strategies for securing the return of territories, particularly after the 1973 war, the hawks declared that no similarity whatsoever existed between Israeli and Arab conceptions of peace. Their view was further reinforced by the traditional Arab conception that the Middle East would see peace, and not specifically peace between Israel and the Arabs, when the "legitimate rights" of the Palestinian Arabs were restored, a phrase inviting a broad and highly flexible interpretation.

Despite the problems aroused by the concept of peace, it remains a key symbol in Israeli society, which so urgently needs recognition and legitimacy by the international community, including the Arabs, and a measure of internal legitimacy in the context of the Israel-Arab conflict. When Egyptian president Anwar Sadat dramatically appeared in Jerusalem and proposed peace, the Israelis found they could not refuse his offer, even though its implications clashed with several other key values of Zionist ideology.[23]

Settlements and Anxiety over the Reversibility of Zionism

Since the beginning of the Zionist enterprise, Jewish immigrant settlers in Palestine have encountered local residents who considered the land their own, though conceptions of collective political and social identity among the Arabs was unconsolidated at first, and would not develop until later. Facing increasing opposition to modern Jewish settlement in Palestine, the Zionist enterprise found itself lacking the political strength or colonial-military power to support settlement and nation building consistently and unambiguously, and sought them to attain their declared objectives.

Zionism represented a combined political, economic, and social approach to creating a territorial base for a Jewish polity through purchasing land and creating facts related to settlement, such as the presence of Jewish settlers upon the land acquired.[24] This nation-building strategy, coupled with promoting immigration, was such a central theme of Zionism that it ultimately became one of the movement's chief symbols. It fostered a virtually total identification of Zionism itself, as a social, political, and cultural movement, with the means for its realization: the accumulation of territory and the creation of settlements upon this territory. One school of Zionist thought, the Revisionist Movement, accorded only marginal importance to such settlement, focusing more on the desire for international political recognition (a charter) and simultaneous and immediate sovereignty over most of the territory defined as the Land of Israel. This group, however, had little political clout and remained permanently opposed to the Zionist leadership, who saw no possibility of accumulating international and local political and social power without creating settlements in Mandatory Palestine. This policy was expressed concisely in the slogan "each additional dunum increases our strength." *

Until the Zionist movement attained actual sovereignty, it realized its territorial aspirations by acquiring land, primarily through national institutions such as the Jewish National Fund. The ownership of this land was secured by prohibiting its sale not only to non-Jews, but also to the private Jewish sector, lest it be resold to non-Jews. Thus, the concepts of public ownership of land, the constant accumulation of publicly owned land, and the attempt to render it irreversible became key components of Zionist practice. The prevailing conflict, lack of sovereignty, and constant political weakness led to a mechanism complementing land accumulation and reinforcing its irreversibility: presence, that is, of Jewish settlements on public land.

As with ownership, presence had a dual significance in Zionist thought. Ideologically, establishing various types of settlements, especially rural frontier settlements, was perceived as the heart of the nation-building process. Tactically, presence by settlement was a tool to manage the conflict with the Arabs and was important to ensuring the irreversibility of ownership of the territories. Presence also helped determine the physical and political boundaries of the collectivity. Eventually, these aspects of ideology and tactics merged, and the concept of settlement was "sanctified" within the "official secular religion" of the collectivity (Bellah, 1980).[25]

The combination of ownership and presence became the functional equivalent of political sovereignty, as the system worked much like a sovereign nation in both domestic and foreign affairs.[26] Even when the Jewish polity eventually achieved sovereignty, it was not recognized by the surrounding Arabs, and so the conflict persisted, albeit in different forms. The collectivity remained loyal to the concept that, despite the achievement of sovereignty, high levels of control should be maintained over all territories.

---

* The most common measure of land area in the Middle East, 4.5 *dunums* equals approximately one acre.

This was manifested in the following three components of territorial control: ownership, as obtained through nationalizing 95 percent of all of the country's land; presence, as expressed in the compulsive tendency to ensure Jewish settlement in all areas, or at least prevent Arab presence in them; and sovereignty itself.[27]

The concepts were rooted in an even more basic concern: anxiety over the possible reversibility of the Zionist enterprise. Such anxiety arose from a perception that the settlement enterprise was an entity in which each point of settlement constituted part of a whole, and the process could move only in the direction of increasing control over territories through intensified presence. Decreasing control was thought to initiate the dissolution of the Zionist enterprise, in a manner similar to the domino theory of the fall of nations. Thus, the Israelis did not allow the residents of two Maronite villages, Bir'im and Ikrit, to return to some of the lands taken by Israel in the 1948 war because they did not wish to set a precedent of returning territory to enemy control.[28] Anxiety increased following the conquest during the 1948 war of some parts of Palestine beyond the borders allocated to the Jewish state by the United Nations resolution of November 29, 1947. Whereas before the war, the Jewish entity gained control of lands by buying them, the new areas were acquired through conquest by force, giving rise to vocal Arab claims.

In sum, all manifestations of Zionist settlement—cities, kibbutzim, *moshavim*, and *moshavot*—constituted an integral, sacrosanct part of Zionist ideology. This sanctity increased with the Jewish-Arab conflict, primarily because of anxiety over the possible reversibility of Zionist settlement. In this context, dismantling or removing an Israeli settlement might be perceived as a threat to the Zionist enterprise as a whole.

Internal struggles among Israel's hawks and doves engendered widespread domestic and external support for the claim that no Jewish settlement should be uprooted, and that Israel must pay any price, or at least a high price, to prevent this from happening. Between 1967 and 1977, struggles within the political center led to the formulation of a map of territories not to be returned under any circumstances.[29] During that decade, settlements were established in the Sinai Peninsula, including the town of Yamit (because of pressure by Dayan), to restrain the collectivity from possibly conceding the territory later. Two types of settlements, military and civilian, were set up. The former, established by Nahal soldiers, were an intermediate stage; liquid points of settlement based on strategic and security considerations, they could be dismantled without arousing anxiety over reversibility or demobilized and transformed into a civilian presence, considered irreversible. Later, the overall strategy of the Gush Emunim movement[30] followed this trend, establishing various types of settlements under the assumption that the Israeli political and social system could not concede territories with a Jewish presence.

When Values Collide

On November 9, 1977, addressing the Egyptian National Assembly, Sadat declared that he planned to go to Jerusalem and reach a peace agreement with Israel. Israeli Prime Minister Menachem Begin immediately transmitted a message through the American embassy in Cairo inviting Sadat to Jerusalem. At the same time, Sadat spoke to the Egyptian people in a radio broadcast, calling for "no more wars, no more bloodshed, and no more threats." On November 19, ten days after Sadat's declaration, the Egyptian president's plane landed in Israel; he addressed the Knesset the following day. This dramatic gesture has been termed a "diplomatic surprise,"[31] the equivalent of a strategic military surprise, such as Operation Barbarossa, the Japanese attack on Pearl Harbor, or the Egyptian-Syrian attack on Israel in 1973, and it received unprecedented coverage in the media both inside and outside Israel.[32] It also shattered many components of the Israeli belief system, if only temporarily. Sadat himself recognized his tactics were seeking to break down what he called "psychological barriers":

> I realized that we were about to be caught up in a terrible vicious circle, precisely like the one we'd lived through over the last thirty years. And the root cause was none other than that very psychological barrier. By a psychological barrier, I mean that huge wall of suspicion, fear, hate and misunderstanding that has for so long existed between Israel and the Arabs. It made each side simply unwilling to believe the other.[33]

Polls taken before and after Sadat's visit point to radical changes in Israeli public opinion regarding relations between Jews and Arabs in general, and between Israel and Egypt in particular. In March 1970 only 8 percent of Israelis believed that the Arab states wanted peace with Israel, but during Sadat's visit, this figure surpassed 80 percent, with 95 percent believing that at least Egypt wanted peace. The figures for this issue fluctuate with each specific event affecting relations between the Arabs and Israel, but they never dropped below 40 percent during the period of the Sinai evacuation (1980–1982).[34]

More deeply, Israel's sociopolitical system changed after Sadat's visit, the ensuing negotiations with Egypt, the Camp David accords, and Israeli withdrawal from the territories specified in the Israel-Egypt peace treaty. For the Israelis, the idea of peace with the Arabs was transformed from a distant, Utopian dream to a real, concrete historical possibility, even though Israel and Egypt clearly differed in their conceptions of the essence and form that peace should have taken and its ultimate political results, which were primarily territorial. Despite the absence of a public consensus on the extent of the transformation, the new situation demanded that Israelis update their beliefs as to which trade-offs of peace for territory they considered acceptable. Among Israel's social groups and strata, views had ranged between two extreme poles. One pole to offer only peace for peace, based on the assumption that Israel should not pay for peace with any territory or security property because its opponents required peace as much as Israel did. The other pole demanded that all territories conquered in the 1967 war, with the possible exception of East Jerusalem, be returned in exchange for genuine peace.

This updating of Israelis' peace price list had two main features. First, most Israelis were willing to trade a greater amount of territory and strategic security property than they had been before Israeli-Egyptian negotiations began. Even during the initial stages, however, no concrete results and prices for peace were stipulated. The first Israeli sector to pay a price for implementing the peace agreements was the military, especially the Israeli air force, which lost several important air bases in Sinai and area used for maneuvers and training. Concessions affecting the oil fields harmed Israel's economy, though this did not constitute a concrete price for most of Israel's residents. However, the dismantling of settlements in Sinai, especially the Yamit region, described vividly by the news media, made clear the price of peace. The so-called trauma of Yamit would remain with the Israelis for many years afterward; the hawks hoped that this would prevent Israel from making additional territorial concessions.

Second, the price of peace increased also because of growing internal struggles. These struggles led to new political movements, such as Peace Now, the demonstrations of which attracted entire strata of the population that had never before been politically active. The movement was established to encourage the government to make sufficient concessions to attain a peace treaty, and thus countered the MSW. In contrast, groups such as the Land of Israel Movement, Gush Emunim, and others formed a broad, hawkish coalition to block withdrawal from Sinai and even to prevent the attainment of peace.

The government was the most important actor in this complex situation; its behavior and decisions largely reflected developments in the overall sociopolitical system and influenced its reactions. Begin was identified with an inflexible national ideology, and so his response to the Egyptian offer of peace, declaring that "all is open to negotiation," perhaps constituted the decisive factor in securing major changes in Israeli public opinion and a readiness to pay for peace with territory. Foreign Minister Moshe Dayan, known for his assertion that the coastal strip along the Gulf of Sinai up to Sharm-al-Sheikh could never be returned to Arab control, even in exchange for peace, apparently changed his mind and urged the government to relinquish the entire Sinai Peninsula.[35]

Even as peace between Israel and Egypt became more possible, the problems associated with the concept of peace discussed earlier were still largely apparent, as was the concept's clash with others, such as territoriality, settlement, and reversibility. The clash, in fact, may have intensified. Between Sadat's visit and the final stages of implementing Israel's agreement with Egypt, the possibility of concluding the endless war and attaining legitimation from the largest of the neighboring Arab states achieved salience and unprecedented weight with both the government and public. Egypt itself promised that other Arab countries would follow its lead. Even the problem of trusting the enemy—as expressed by Israel's chief of staff on November 15, 1977, when he warned that Egypt's suggestions may well constitute a diversionary tactic preceding a military surprise attack like the one that occurred on Yom Kippur in 1973—was cast aside for the chance of obtaining legitimation. When it came time to pay the debt agreed to at Camp David, however, anomie intensified within the Israeli government and extended to the periphery.

Even those who trusted Sadat's sincerity felt somewhat anxious about the political instability that characterized developing countries, especially Arab countries. They feared that after Israel ceded territories and relinquished its presence in them, the Egyptian regime would suddenly change, almost certainly leading to Egypt reneging on its obligations to keep the peace. The remaining Arab states opposed the Egypt-Israel peace treaty, and a question arose as to how long Egypt could remain in political, economic, and cultural isolation from the Arab world. Those supporting the peace treaty advanced two arguments. First, if Israel would not take calculated risks, it would never achieve peace. Second, instead of continuing to fight the process, the other Arab states might follow Egypt in negotiating for peace.

The problems and uncertainty connected with the politics of exchanging territory for peace were even more complex. Only a partial peace was being achieved in at least two respects. At that stage, Israel was at peace with only one Arab state, Egypt, and saw no reduction in hostilities with the other states or the Palestinians. The price Israel was asked to pay was also only partial. Moreover, the peace did not resemble the peace that prevails between France and Switzerland. The Egyptians themselves often clarified that the peace with Israel was only a first step toward the region's acceptance of Israel, which would be contingent upon Israel's future behavior and ability to integrate itself within the Arab Middle East construct.[36]

Thus, as Israel strove for a maximum normalization of relations with Egypt, including opening its borders to reciprocal tourism and the flow of goods and offering economic and political cooperation, the Egyptians stopped at a minimum level of openness, viewing peace with Israel as not only partial, but conditioned upon some solution to the Palestinian problem as well as Israel's ultimate ability to integrate itself culturally and politically with the region. Israel found this highly problematic. There were serious differences of opinion as to the best means of resolving the Palestinian problem and the call for Israel to integrate within the region—perhaps the most difficult of all of the political and territorial demands—affected both the basic identity of the Israeli collectivity and the distribution of power and control within the region.

Peace was therefore accompanied by anxiety over the acceleration of the Levantinization of Israeli society, which could undermine its Western rules and culture. The internal stratificational and political implications of integration with the Middle East, however, were no less complex. These stemmed from a covert assumption that integration would end the cultural and political predominance of Jews from Western countries and create a new ethnic balance within Israeli society. Israel's Eastern Jews would perhaps benefit from blurring Israeli society's Western image. Thus, a new, highly problematic, fundamental contradiction arose: The Israelis sought normal relations with the Arabs, but feared the long-term results. This situation effectively reversed accepted Zionist conceptions, as the Jews, once envisioned as the pioneers of progress and modernization in the Middle East, now feared the Arabization of Israeli society.[37]

The Removal of Yamit

The case of the construction and removal of the town of Yamit dramatically illustrates many of the hypotheses proposed in this essay. The town provoked political controversy at its establishment, as preparations for settlement required the eviction of Bedouin tribes, who traditionally held rights to the region. Israel wished to construct a southern Mediterranean port city, establish a presence there, and thereby preclude returning the territory to Egypt or any other Arab claimant. Yamit itself was not intended to be the site of the future boundary of Israel, as the prevailing conception declared that urban settlements must not be situated in border regions. Hence, the plans for Yamit demanded that it be surrounded by a territorial hinterland of rural settlements constituting a buffer between Yamit's urban population and the intended border. According to Israeli sociomilitary doctrine, only rural settlements could fulfill an immediate security role. Yamit's primary purpose was to establish an Israeli presence in the region at large.

Jewish Israeli historiography records two traumatic incidents of urban evacuation: the flight of the Hebron Jewish community following the killing of Jewish residents in the 1929 riots, and the conquest of the old city of Jerusalem by the Arab Legion in 1948. In both cases, however, the enemy imposed evacuation, and Israelis took some comfort that, while both settlements were symbolically highly important. neither of the locations were integral to the Zionist settlement enterprise. Also, their populations largely belonged to the old non-Zionist *yishuv*. Therefore, one could contend that the evacuation did not signify the reversibility of the Zionist enterprise at that time.

The Camp David accords called for the return of the entire Sinai Peninsula to Egypt, but did not allude to the fate of the settlements there. For some time, Israelis were not certain whether Egypt would consent to having Israeli settlers on its territory, a potential source of conflict and of Israeli and Egyptian claims and counterclaims even after withdrawal. It was also unclear whether the Israeli collectivity in general would agree to withdraw, or whether the Sinai settlers would live in a region controlled by another nation, and if so, under what status.

When the withdrawal approached the final stage, Egypt indicated that it did not distinguish between evacuating the territory and removing its

Jewish settlers. The settlers were asked to pay the price of peace personally. Although they were assured generous material compensation for their
property, they nonetheless lost their homes, and at least some of them bore
emotional and psychological costs. As noted previously, many settlers of
Yamit and Sinai were not motivated primarily by nationalism, but rather
by quality of life, financial well-being, and the availability of relatively inex-
pensive housing. Still, they were initially hailed as pioneers; as in previous
settlement ventures, the Zionist enterprise exploited a combination of collectivistic and ideological motivations and individual vested interests. Following the decision to remove the settlements, some settlers were prepared
to pay the cost of peace, just as Israelis were generally prepared to pay the
cost of war. Most of the bona fide settlers—unlike the outsiders recruited
specifically to stop or at least protest the withdrawal—considered the removal merely a matter of bargaining. This caused the public to label them
as extortionists or peace profiteers.

Like the outsiders who gathered in Yamit and its surrounding agricultural settlements during the final stages of the removal, a minority of the
settlers considered the evacuation and withdrawal to be issues of ideology, values, and even of morality and religion. They declared the settled
regions in Sinai and Yamit to be "an inseparable part of the Land of Israel,"
redefining Israel's borders to include the Jewish settlements. Anxiety over
the possible reversibility of the settlement stemmed from an ulterior fear
that withdrawal from Sinai would lead to withdrawal from the West Bank.
Certain ideological opponents of the withdrawal attempted to sanctify the
settlements and thereby make withdrawing from them a profaning of the
sacred, or at least an anti-Zionist act. A few of Meir Kahane's supporters
locked themselves in a bunker and threatened to "surrender their souls for
the sanctity of God"—that is, commit suicide—if forced to evacuate. Thus,
opponents of the withdrawal attempted to combine religious, national, and
instrumental—that is, national security—symbols to recruit support and
restrain decision makers in the government from removing the settlements.
If successful, such efforts would have sabotaged the peace agreement immediately.

The government's decision to raze Yamit, in contrast to its decision regarding remote Ofira, which was handed over to Egypt in return for some
symbolic compensation, is of particular importance. The reasons given for
destroying Yamit down to its foundations included preventing Jewish settlers from hoping they could someday return,thus reducing the risk of cre-

ating a "myth of return." The decision also considered the justice of handing the area back to Egypt as it was when the Israelis took control of it. Apparently, however, the most significant reason was not expressed publicly, which was the emotional difficulty of giving a Jewish settlement to so-called strangers. Feelings of sheer vengeance also likely played a role, as the Syrian town of Kuneitra had similarly been destroyed by the Israeli army before its return following the ceasefire agreements of 1974.

Even sectors of the population that did not oppose withdrawal or enthusiastically supported it to obtain peace apparently found the removal of the settlements discomfiting. This feeling was intensified by the television coverage of the forced removal of the populace and the razing of Yamit. Only at this stage was the cost of peace tangibly recognized. The fear of reversibility, however, did not seem in the forefront of the public consciousness. Rather, many perceived peace as an opportunity to consolidate the Zionist enterprise in the West Bank territories, and its high price was made palpable even to some of the more hawkish Israelis. The Israeli war in Lebanon, which broke out a mere two months after the end of the Israeli withdrawal from Sinai—undoubtedly as part of Israel's plan to hold onto the West Bank—soon deflected the wider public's attention from the Sinai removal and engaged it in another painful, drawn-out affair.

Conclusions

The evacuation of Sinai and the Yamit region epitomized and intensified the complex problems that the Camp David accords posed for Israeli society. It is not surprising that Israel's sociopolitical system experienced a brief period of functional disability, which included difficulties in making decisions, implementing previous decisions, and recruiting political support from all active participants in this domestic struggle. Implementing the peace treaty, and especially evacuating Israeli settlements, aroused significant existential and identity crises in Israeli society and caused confrontations among key values. Making peace with an Arab state was a new experience for the Israeli system, which previously dealt mostly with conflict and war and therefore had come to excel in both military performance and devising institutional methods of conflict management. The Israeli system was unprepared emotionally for peace soon; peace had been perceived as highly priced—although the perception of which price would be fair differed from group to group—partial, conditional, and of doubtful permanence. Price lists for peace included the exchange of tangible items, such as territory and oil, for abstract concepts, such as peace, security, and recognition, requiring difficult comparisons and assessments to quantify and equate territory and peace. This aroused and intensified public anxiety, which can be placed into the following two categories: political anxiety, as expressed in a fear that the system would be de-Zionized and decolonized; and cultural-primordial anxiety, as expressed over the call for "integration within the region, together with the Arabization of Israel,"[38] which constituted a long-term threat to Israel's collective identity and ethno-political structure.

Despite such fundamental problems, Israel honored the peace treaty, at least with respect to withdrawing from Sinai and the Yamit region, and meticulously adhered to the agreed timetable. No civil war broke out, and only limited violence occurred between the resisting evacuees and the forces evacuating them. The defined limits of the rules of the game were nearly met. The situation did not meet the dire expectations aroused by the mass media or the overt and covert threats of factions that opposed evacuation.

Several of the complex reasons for the turn of events are addressed in this paper, but four factors primarily ensured the successful implementation of the removal and prevention of major political upheaval, despite the anomie and confusion that prevailed during the extended period between the signing of the Camp David accords and the final withdrawal. First, the Egyptian proposal of peace and recognition of Israel—that is, the granting of legitimacy to Zionist settlement by a major participant in the conflict— was an offer that could not be refused. The transformation of peace from a Utopian concept to a real, concrete political process fundamentally altered the price lists for peace within the political center and among the public at large. Second, the main opponents of withdrawal—primarily Gush Emunim and the Land of Israel Movement—had difficulty applying power to the bearers of the primary symbols of Israeli nationalism, the Israeli Defense Force and the elected government, especially one so obviously nationalistic. Third, the difficulty of opposing withdrawal was compounded once the opponents recognized that their protest demonstrations did not attract a broad cross section of the public, even among those strata that were against or at least ambivalent about the evacuation. Fourth, the most decisive factor precluding effective opposition and an active public response was the government's firm decision to cease transmitting ambiguous messages and implement withdrawal. The government's response to Sadat and subsequent invitation to Jerusalem constituted a major breakthrough in Israeli public opinion. The shift toward favoring concessions and flexibility resulted from messages originating in the government and reinforced by the rites of passage noted by Katz and Szecsko.[39] Similarly, public opinion that favored peace with Egypt influenced and encouraged the government to continue negotiations despite—or perhaps because of—the attendant crises and to sign the accords.

The four factors probably will continue to affect political situations in Israel similar to those engendered by the peace treaty with Egypt. One may assume, however, that the extent of opposition to any future territorial concessions will greatly increase in intensity. I assume this because the remaining occupied areas conform far more closely to the definition of core territories than did Sinai and the Yamit region, and because the population of Jewish settlers liable to be involved in any political moves is larger.

Nationalism, Identity, and Citizenship

An Epilogue to the Yehoshua-Shammas Controversy:

A Non-Platonic Dialogue*

On September 13, 1985, the eve of the Jewish New Year, Anton Shammas—the Christian Israeli-Arab writer, essayist, translator, journalist, and author of *Arabesque*,[1] an autobiographical Hebrew novel of a youngster growing up as a hybrid of Jewish-Arab culture and identity in the village Fasuta—aroused bitter controversy among the Israeli elite. His brief article accused Israel of excluding Israeli Palestinians from participation in the common political, cultural, and collective identity and nationality.[2]

His accusations of extreme discriminatory policy against Israel's Arab citizens were by no means a new issue on the Israeli political agenda. Between 1949 and 1966 Israeli Arabs had been subject to crass military rule, which served as a useful umbrella for land confiscation, exclusion from the labor market, and de facto deprivation of most citizen and human rights. Since 1966 the situation has gradually improved, but no Jewish intellectual

* Baruch Kimmerling, "Nationalism, Identity, and Citizenship: An Epilogue to Yehoshua-Shammas Controversy," in Daniel Levy and Yfaat Weiss, eds., *Citizenship and Identity: German and Israel in Comparative Perspective* (New York: Berghahn, 2002).

would deny that Israeli Palestinians have remained an underprivileged ethnic or national minority. Shammas' claim, however, went far beyond the
regular complaints and protests against discrimination of a minority group
within a supposedly democratic and humanistic polity. Shammas called for
space and participation for what he called Israeli Arabs within the Israeli
collective identity and culture.[3]

Faced with such a provocation, even the liberal, so-called leftist, and
dovish writer Abraham B. Yehoshua could not restrain himself. He was not
the only respondent to Shammas, but he was one of the most strident and
certainly the most prominent. "I am suggesting to you," shouted Yehoshua,
"that if you want to exercise your full identity, if you want to live in a state
that has a Palestinian character with a genuine Palestinian culture, arise,
take your chattels, and move yourself one hundred yards eastward, into the
independent Palestinian state, that will be established alongside Israel."[4] Al-
luding to God's commandment to Abraham to leave his home and go forth
into the land God will show him, the Land of Canaan, Shammas angrily
responded that "I have no any intention to leave my motherland and my
father's home, for the country Yehoshua will show me."[5]

Another respondent to Shammas' challenge was the Mizrachi writer
Sami Michael, who stated, "Many Jews from every [ideological] camp understand his pain and identify with his suffering as a member of a minority.
Many are ready to pay a price in order to make it more comfortable for him
[to be a minority], but not to the point where they [the Jews] make themselves into a minority."[6] Here the claim for equal civil and symbolic rights
for Israeli Arab citizens was promptly transformed into restoring the situation in which Jews were a minority in Palestine, as they were anywhere in
the world, and the Jewish nation-state was dismantled.

Shammas never intended to dismantle the state, but rather to challenge
its constructions as a homogenous ethno-national entity and identity. He
wanted to invent and create a new local national identity, or nationality,
common to Jews and Arabs of the country and based solely on ethnicity,
state citizenship, and territory. He stated explicitly,

What I'm trying to do—mulishly, it seems—is to un-Jew the Hebrew
language, to make it more Israeli and less Jewish, thus bringing it back
to its Semitic origins, to its place. This is a parallel to what I think the
state should be. As English is the language of those who speak it, so is
Hebrew; and so the state should be the state of those who live in it, not
of those who play with its destiny with a remote control in hand.[7]

He added,

the State of Israel demands that its Arab citizens take their citizenship seriously. But when they try to do so, it promptly informs them that their participation in the state is merely social, and that for the political fulfillment of their identity, they must look somewhere else (i.e. to the Palestinian nation). When they do look elsewhere for their national identity, the state at once charges them with subversion; and needless to say—as subversives they cannot be accepted as Israelis."[8]

The controversy between Yehoshua and Shammas over the meaning and boundaries of Israeli identity was reopened six years later, in 1992. This time Shammas was much more articulate in his arguments and Yehoshua more defensive.[9]

YEHOSHUA: My problem and debate with Anton are not about equality, but about identity. Because as a national minority in an Israeli state . . .
SHAMMAS: What's an Israeli state? There's no such thing!
YEHOSHUA: What do you mean there's no such thing? . . . For me, "Israeli" is the authentic, complete, and consummate word for the concept "Jewish." Israeliness is the total, perfect, and original Judaism, one that should provide answers in all areas of life.[10]
SHAMMAS: You see Israeliness as total Jewishness, and I don't see where you fit me, the Arab, into that Israeliness. Under the rug? In some corner of the kitchen? Maybe you won't even give me a key to get into the house?
YEHOSHUA: But, Anton, think of a Pakistani coming to England today, with a British passport and telling the British, "Let's create the British nationality together. I want Pakistani-Muslim symbols . . ."
SHAMMAS: Buli [Yehoshua's nickname], the minute a man like you does not understand the basic difference between the Pakistani who comes to England and the Galilean who has been in Fasuta for untold generations, then what do you want us to talk about? I always said that the Zionist state's most serious mistake in 1948 was that it kept the 156,000 Arabs who did not run away and were not expelled. If you really wanted to establish a Jewish state, you should

have kicked me out of Fasuta, too. You didn't do it—so treat me as an equal. As an equal in Israeliness.

YEHOSHUA: But you won't receive one single right more for belonging to the Israeli nation. On the contrary. I'll take away your special minority rights . . . For instance you'll have to study Bible, just as in France all citizens study Moliere and in England Shakespeare.

SHAMMAS: But as a literary text . . .

YEHOSHUA: What do you mean?! We have no Shakespeare or Moliere. We have the Bible, the Talmud, and Jewish history, and you will study them, and in Hebrew.

SHAMMAS: If that's the case, then Judaism also has been separated from Israeliness, and you'll oppose that by force of arms.

YEHOSHUA: But how is that possible? Try, for instance, separating France from Frenchness—it is impossible.

SHAMMAS: France and Frenchness come from the same root, But Judaism and Israeliness is a different matter. That's why I advocate the de-Judaization and de-Zionization of Israel . . . I'm asking you for a new definition of the term "Israeli," so that it will include me as well, a definition in territorial terms that you distort, because you're looking at it from the Jewish point of view . . . [However,] ultimately we are dealing with the question of identity; the identity which is given to us by those who have the power to do so.

YEHOSHUA: I'm not excluding you. My Israeliness includes you and all the Israeli Arabs as partners in the fabric of life here. Partners in that you vote for the Knesset [Israeli parliament], on creation of Israeli citizenship as a whole.

SHAMMAS: You want me to vote for the Knesset so you can show off your democracy to the enlightened world. I'm not willing to be a party to that. I know that all I can do here is to vote and nothing else. I know that my mother would never be able to see me become Israel's Minister of Education.

Shammas had already demonstrated several years before this exchange that he possessed a comprehensive and sweeping understanding of the past and present, and what should be done in the future. Zionism as a national movement, Shammas argued, achieved its historic role with the establishment of the state. Every person then living within the Green Line[11] who was a citizen of the state of Israel should have been defined as an Israeli. The time had come to transform the law of return into a regular immigration law, as existed in Western secular and democratic states. This state would have the authority to decide who could be called Israeli, but Israeliness should no longer be automatic or self-evidently granted only to Jews, and all Israelis should be equal with regard to rights and duties. As the bottom line of his argument, he proclaimed that "we, the members of the Israeli nation, should then wait, with Levantine patience, for the first Jew to proclaim at the head of the camp: 'Zionism is dead, long live the Israeli nation!' That in the hope that the entire [Jewish] camp will follow after him."[12]

Subjects and Citizens

We may grossly divide the states in the world into two categories: subject states and citizen states. As T. H. Marshall argued,[13] subject states emphasize the obligations of the individual toward the state and its rulers, and citizen states emphasize the rights that the state is obliged to grant to its citizens. Pure subject states are characterized by the unconditional status of the state's population as the state's property, lacking a true basis or claim to any rights based on universal and egalitarian membership in the state. Relations between the state and its subjects are akin to patronage: Different groups, such as class, ethnic, gender, religious, racial, or occupational groups, receive favors and privileges according to their closeness to the state's rulers and ruling strata in exchange for loyalties to the state's ruler. This loyalty is usually constructed and camouflaged as patriotism, nationalism, and commitment to the state as motherland.

The citizen state is a sociopolitical order based on an unwritten conditional contract between the state and each individual member. The state promises to grant a package of citizen rights that go beyond the self-evident human rights defined by the United Nation's Charter, and the inclusion of which are inviolable, self-evident citizen rights internalized by the state and its legislative and social welfare systems. All of these citizen rights are provided in exchange for a package of citizen obligations toward the state. The state's minimal obligations are to provide law and order, defend against external threats on the citizen's life, insure property and freedoms, and supply basic needs, such as health services, schooling, and subsistence. The state possesses a legitimate monopoly on exercising violent power within its sovereign territory, that is, the right to make war and peace with other states and external entities. In exchange, the citizen's obligations toward the state are to obey the law, pay taxes, answer the call to military service, and even endanger one's own life as the ultimate sacrifice to the state's demands.

No wonder that Charles Tilly compared state-citizen relations to those of a "protection racket."[14] The citizen has to pay the organization protection fees, and beyond these reciprocal relationships, any expansion of the state's role—for example, the scope of the welfare offered by the state or its redistributive agencies—is the subject of perpetual negotiation and bargaining between the state and various groups of citizens. An additional major principle of the notion of citizenship is its universalistic character, or more simply put, that all citizens of the state possess equal constitutional rights. This means that the same criteria for access to both material and symbolic common goods are indiscriminately assured for all citizens, and the same duties are demanded of all.

The idea of rights and obligations implies the inclusion of an individual or social category within the boundaries of the state. The definition of citizenship as a personal status—even if the status symbolizes membership in a collective of equal citizens or in the nation-state as a membership organization, in Brubaker's terms—presumes the existence of an individual to whom rights and obligations are naturally determined by an invisible social contract.[15] According to Tilly, the definition of citizenship as a legal-personal status is as a series of continuing exchanges between persons of a given state, in which each has enforceable rights and obligations "by virtue." The virtues or traits are based on an individual's membership as an exclusive category, that is, native born or naturalized, and on the individual's relation to the state rather than to any other authority the agent may enjoy.[16] The equation is reversed, however, for an active mass immigrant-settler society, in which the natives are not a part of the nationality of the nation-state and the immigrants claim to be the original natives.

Defining citizenship in terms of the individual-state relationship focuses attention on the juridical, political, and symbolic levels of the mutual relations between individuals and the state.[17] It presumes at least a legal membership in the polity congruent with the liberal theory and approach to citizenship, which defines it as a "set of normative expectations specifying the relationship between the nation-state and its individual members which procedurally establish the rights and the obligations of members and a set of practices by which these expectations are realized."[18] Under such a definition, individuals are not committed to each other and lack "communal" responsibility for their fellow citizens. Rights and duties are fulfilled without the help of intermediaries such as institutions and communities, but rather through a direct link between each person and the state.[19]

More precisely, the state relates and constructs citizenship as individual or collective according to its various interests and internal power structures. Some states tend to delimit different types and degrees of citizenship, for example, ethincized, classized, or genderized citizenship.[20] Thus, within the same state, different patterns of citizenship may coexist according to differential access to the rights and obligations of citizenship. The question is how much the underprivileged or passive citizens consider their lowered level of obligations to the state[21] to be a privilege that compensates them for their lowered rights in other spheres, and not as a symbol of their total exclusion from membership in the state. Are "individual-minority rights" a worthy compensation for a lower degree and quality of citizen rights, as Yehoshua hinted to Shammas in equating citizen rights with minority rights?

Theoretically the problem should be even more acute: Can a claim based on the liberal dogma of unalienable equal citizen rights, which is itself based on the right of an individual, legitimately claim equal collective rights as well? Can individual citizen rights be separated from collective religious, ethnic, or cultural rights? The problematic sounds somewhat familiar, and indeed resembles the nineteenth-century French and German Enlightenment and Emancipator movement slogans, that a Jew as a person should enjoy full citizen rights, but Jews as a collective should not. The Jews rightly considered the formula as covert anti-Semitism and as an attempt to dissolve Jewish identity, culture, religion, and community.

Nonetheless, various patterns and qualities of citizenship that grant different scopes and degrees of rights to different groups reflect how states use citizenship to incorporate social groups into their structures and redefine or re-create social categories. As a consequence, patterns of citizenship and diverse cultural, ethnic, and political identities are shaped, created, or reinforced. The identity of Israeli Arabs, or even Israeli Palestinians, was created rather successfully. This seems to fit with White's[22] and Derrida's claim that self-imposed identity, not to mention that imposed by others, is an act of violence. This is because "the rapport of self-identity is itself always a rapport of violence with the other; so that the notions of property, appropriation and self-presence, so central to logocentric metaphysics, are essentially dependent on an oppositional relation with otherness. In this sense, identity presupposes alterity."[23] On the other hand, Moore and I have showed how minority groups can maneuver among different definitions of self-identity in different social and political contexts as a survival strategy (see Chapter Two).

Different positions within the holy civic communion of the state prescribe what Soysal has conceptualized as "models of membership" or "institutionalized scripts and understandings of the relationships between individuals, the state, and the polity as well as the organizational structures and practices that maintain that relationship."[24] These "scripts and understandings" include cultural assumptions that shape the boundaries of the citizens' collectivity, the different positions within it, and the ways in which access to citizenship is interpreted. The cultural assumptions may be conceptualized as national projects, not because they constitute a desire for a separate political and cultural representation for a collectivity, but because they are shaped through narratives and discourses of the state's interests in the discursive space of citizenship.[25]

The convention is that historical processes shape national projects. These processes and constraints explain the ties between citizenship and national identity that national projects promote. As such, they frame the conception of the links between citizenship and nationality, and define the exclusiveness or inclusiveness of those ties as well as their primordial or civil character. Moreover, the patterns or degree of inclusion—full, partial, differential, or exclusive—in the community of citizens, and the arenas through which inclusion is concretized and symbolized, are central to understanding how individuals and social groups react to the state's practices. Patterns of inclusion, meanwhile, are central to understanding the patterns of social action and identity mobilized in transactions between individuals, social groups, and the state's agents, whether those transactions take the form of bargaining or hostility. Negotiations and bargaining over citizenship are not only related to who gets what, but also to who is what and who can decide who is what. The identities and narratives raised in the process of making claims and negotiating over citizenship, including the terms and degree of participation and membership demanded, are thus central to understanding the identities that claim recognition.[26]

The Israeli State and Identity

Citizenship includes a basic and inherent contradiction (see Chapter One). On one hand, it is a legal status that the modern state grants to its members. On the other hand, the state is not just rationally bureaucratic or indifferent to identity; it is also the embodiment of ethnic and national, and sometimes also religious, attachments. These positions result in the state's dual identity, or what Hegel calls a historically produced sphere of ethical life, rooted in the identities of two rival social entities *burgerliche* and *gesellschaften*—one based on primordial ties and the other on civic-orientations.

The Israeli state takes this contradiction to its logical and sociological end. By its own constitutional definition, Israel is Jewish and democratic, and at first glance nothing is contradictory about it. It sounds precisely like French and democratic or German and democratic. A Jew who is entitled to French or German citizenship, but needed to keep his or her ethnic or religious identity, became a French Jew or Jewish French. The same goes for Turkish German or even Muslim French. Nevertheless, taking into account that Israel is a Jewish state, can we even consider a fusion of Jewish and Christian, Jewish and Muslim, or Jewish and Buddhist? These impossible combinations are almost unthinkable within the Jewish Israeli political culture, including the combinations Jewish Jew and Arab Jew. If Israel is a Jewish nation state, it implies that the Jews are a nation, and that Judaism is actually a Jewish national identity. Thus, the existence of a particular Jewish citizenship within the Jewish nation-state sounds, to be blunt, weird and puzzling.

For most Israelis, however, the puzzle has a self-evident answer. It is not accidental that the inscription on the rubric of my official identification card is "nationality (*leom*): Jewish" and not "citizenship: Jewish" or even "Israeli." This is simply because neither Jewish nationalism in its Zionist incarnation nor the Israeli state could invent or construct a purely secular or a civil national identity.[27]

Zionist nationalism was generally not constructed as a pure ideology, but was intermingled with other ideologies, such as classical liberalism, or with varieties of socialism, including communism.[28] The beginnings of Jewish national thought and activity were shaped at the end of the colonialist era, when Jewish migration was intertwined with large-scale intercontinental population movements. During this era, the formation and construction of immigrant-settler nations was still at its height. European colonialism was the dominant world order, and Eurocentrism was the hegemonic cultural approach.

Jewish religious nationalism, which approximated the European approach, was a negligible and marginal minority within the Jewish religious collectivity because the religious principles did not permit "forcing the End,"[29] or achieving collective salvation without divine intervention, though the religious worldview looked positively on ascendance (*aliyah*) to the Holy Land. The religious-national mixture thus demanded a very great intellectual and interpretive effort, and its theological standing within Judaism is quite shaky and problematic even today.[30] Samuel Mohilever, the first rabbi who can be classified as a Zionist, was more concerned with convincing secular Jews to consider the sensitivities of fervently observant Jews than he was with the theological problems of a return to Zion in his day. Practically, Mohilever failed in his mission to bring about an understanding of religious sensibilities among the founding fathers of Zionism, and played a part in starting the split between the religious and secular components of the movement. This laid the foundations for the beginnings of the Mizrachi movement—short for *mercaz ruchani*, or spiritual center—which in 1902 incorporated the group of Rabbi Isaac Jacob Reines.[31]

Even the absence of a distinction between religion and nation is not, however, the primary cause of the basic nature of the Israeli state, but rather flows from it. The nature of the Israeli state cannot be understood apart from its historical and sociological context. Israel was formed as a society of settler-immigrants, and is still an active immigrant society, engaged in the settlement process to this very day. Two mutually complementary political practices are involved. The first concerns what is referred to as Israel's status as an immigrant-absorbing state; the second concerns the expansion and contraction of its borders, which are still in the process of formation.

Despite the tremendously rapid transformation that Israeli state and society is undergoing, its fundamental character as a settler society that must consolidate itself in a given territory, living by the sword and with a need to create a space for itself, remains constant. Almost from the beginning of Jewish settlement, the Arab inhabitants in whose midst the Jewish immigrants settled have consistently resisted the process with great determination. The Jewish-Arab conflict flows from this. Zionism, the national movement that motivated and was also formed by Jewish immigration and settlement, was clever enough to distance itself from the global colonial context that gave it birth. Zionism emphasized the uniqueness of the Jewish problem, anti-Semitism, persecutions, and later, the Holocaust, offering itself as the sole realistic and moral solution. Thus, the Jewish immigration movement was successfully represented as a return to Zion, correcting an injustice that had lasted for thousands of years and totally disconnected from the movements of European immigration to other continents.

Nonetheless, that Jewish immigration and settlement were construed in these terms was not enough to change their basic social and cultural character. In reality, Israeli society was established mostly by immigrants from an ethnic, religious, and cultural background that differed from the broad local population, and who thought of themselves as part of Western society. In the political culture of the postcolonial world order, Israeli society has been plagued by the problem of existential legitimacy. It has had to explain repeatedly, to itself and to the international community, why it chose Palestine, the land renamed the Land of Israel, as its target territory for settlement. Palestine was not chosen for its fertile soil, its natural treasures, the presence of a cheap labor force, or its potential markets; rather, it was chosen out of ideological and religious motives.[32] This meant that the Zionist project was not only unable to support itself from an economic point of view, but also that it was an essentially religious project, unable to disconnect itself from its original identity as a quasi-messianic movement. The essence of the society and state's right and reason to exist is embedded in symbols, ideas, and religious scriptures, even if there has been an attempt to give them a secular reinterpretation and context. In this sense, the society was held captive from the beginning by its choice of target territory for immigration and nation building. Neither the nation nor its culture could be built successfully apart from the religious context, even when its prophets, priests, builders, and fighters saw themselves as completely secular.

At least three basic laws[33] and one additional regular law state that Israel is a Jewish and democratic state. The definition of Jewishness that the state has adopted, however, makes the two concepts of democracy and Jewishness mutually exclusive in certain areas.[34] As a result, many state practices hardly conform to usually accepted notions of Western, liberal, and enlightened democracy. Israel inherited what is known as the millet system from both the Ottoman Empire and the British colonial administration.[35] This system provides that religious ethnic communities should enjoy autonomy from the state and have sole jurisdiction in matters of personal status litigation. Even before its establishment as a sovereign entity, the Israeli state decided to preserve the institution of the millets and to construct a millet form of citizenship. Therefore, citizens are subjected to two separate legal and judicial systems that operate according to different and even opposing principles. One is secular, Western, and universalistic; the other is religious and primordial, and is mainly run—if we are speaking about Jews—according to the Orthodox interpretation of halakha. The minorities, who were thus defined ab initio as religious minorities, are forced to conduct their autonomous lives in accordance with this dual system. The Israeli parliament has so far given up its authority to legislate in crucial areas and recognized a parallel legal and judicial system outside of its control. The state, meanwhile, has obligated itself to relate to rules of *halakha, shariya*,[36] and diverse Christian denominational rules as if they were its own law.

Jewish religious elements have been incorporated into other areas of legislation as well, such as the Work Hours and Days of Rest Law and the Freedom of Occupation Law. In contrast to these, the Law of Return and Law of Citizenship, immigration laws intended as a sort of affirmative action or corrective discrimination on behalf of world Jewry after the Holocaust, are relatively liberal ordinances. One must of course qualify this characterization, since the laws were indeed discriminatory against both Palestinians who were uprooted from the territory that fell under the rule of the new state and those who remained and were for the most part denied family reunification.

Although the laws of return and citizenship are not based on the theological definition of Judaism,[37] and in practice the laws grant Israeli citizenship and define the boundaries of Judaism more or less according to the broader definition of the Nuremberg Laws, the logic underlying them is internally consistent and justified. The laws were intended to grant citizenship to almost everyone who suffered persecution as a Jew, even if the individual case did not correspond with the *halakhic* definition of Jewishness. If the laws of return and citizenship have been among the most problematic laws in Israel until now, they have nevertheless preserved relatively open boundaries of Judaism. The currently proposed Conversion Law,[38] however, has apparently been intended to heal the breach and give the Orthodox a monopoly on determining the boundaries of the collectivity. Complementing the laws of return and citizenship is the Law on the Status of the World Zionist Organization (of the Jewish Agency), which also facilitates allocating particularistic benefits to Jewish citizens of the state alone. Yet another constitutional arrangement is inherent in the Social Security Law, and for many years, it has been complemented by a set of welfare laws the only eligible beneficiaries of which are so-called former soldiers and their families. This most unsubtle code phrase is intended to construct a broad separation between Jewish and Arab citizens. Similarly, the agreement between the Jewish National Fund and the Israel Lands Administration prevents the leasing of state lands—93 percent of the territory inside the Green Line—to non-Jews.

Conclusions

Israeli national identity or nationalism is based on a mixture of both religious and primordial symbols and orientations and civil and universalistic orientations. These two components of Israeli Zionism complement each other, but also create strains, contradictions, and distortions in the democratic regime. The primordial component is exclusionary and emphasizes Jewish ethnocentrism, while the civil component is inclusive and based on the modern notion of citizenship. On the one hand, the primordial orientation envisions the state as a homogenous Jewish nation-state in which ethnic or national minorities have some protected individual rights as citizens. In this view, citizenship is regarded as a legal status, granted to individuals but limited to certain fields. On the other hand, the civil orientation regards citizenship not as a mere legal status, but also as an all-encompassing dominant cultural and political meta-identity, common to all citizens of the state.

According to the primordial orientation, the people constitute a state, which is entitled to grant different kinds of membership to the population under its control—ranging from full citizenship to partial rights for those who are seen as subjects under state control. The opposite approach perceives citizenship as an absolute right, granted at birth to any member of a democratic state. This citizenship and the rights it supplies are considered to be the ultimate base for a common national identity and as the necessary condition for its very existence.

The debate between A. B. Yehoshua and Anton Shammas over the fundamentals of Israeli society centered around these primordial, civil, and symbolic axes. The liberal Jewish Yehoshua was anxious to preserve the exclusive Jewish ethno-national identity of the state, while the Arab Palestinian Shammas demanded, for his own interest, equal symbolic and cultural shares for his local Arabness under a reshaped universal Israeli nationality based on citizenship. Conceptually speaking, Shammas fused the liberal individualistic approach to citizenship and the communitarian construction of citizenship.[39] His hidden argument is that citizenship can be shaped and reshaped by an interaction between the individual as a part of a community and the community that makes individuals—and that individuals have the right of equal representation within the national identity as a part of a minority community.

CHAPTER ELEVEN

The Power-Oriented Settlement

PLO-Israel:

The Road to the Oslo Agreement and Back?*

Since the Zionist movement's first attempts to settle the territory known by the Jews as Eretz Israel,[1] Zionists and the pan-Arab movement, and before that, the pan-Syrian movement, have shared a common interest: preventing the rise of a distinct Arab people or entity in Palestine. Both nationalistic movements have stressed that the Arabs of Palestine are an indivisible part of the great Arab nation and their problem, no matter how it is defined, must be solved within a framework of Arab nationalism and Arab space.[2]

De-Palestinization of Palestinians

Palestinian identity began among parts of the local Arab population who gradually considered themselves a distinct society and polity (*wataniyya*) though like the Arabs of Syria, Iraq, or Transjordan, they were still part of

* Baruch Kimmerling, "The Power-Oriented Settlement: Bargaining between Israelis and Palestinians," in M. Ma'oz and A. Sela, eds., *The PLO and Israel: From the Road to the Oslo Agreement and Back?* (New York: St. Martin's Press, 1997): 223–251.

the Arab nation (*al-umma al- 'arabiyya*). This dual sense of belonging has made the Palestinian collective identity problematic since its formation.[3]

The geopolitical situation that the colonial powers created after World War I meant that the Arabs of Palestine could not immediately grasp the options of joining the pan-Arab movement or achieving a separate polity, but the problem of dual identity still existed. As the British colonial state was consolidated, the sense of political and even cultural distinctiveness among the Arab population grew, and the colonial state provided them with their final sociopolitical boundaries and identity. The difficulties the local population had in meeting the challenge posed by the growing Zionist settlement contributed to the local Arab population's feeling that theirs was a unique fate.[4]

Yet after the Jewish-Palestinian civil war and the 1948 war, sociopolitical conditions led to an almost complete disappearance of the Palestinians and a separate Palestinian identity. Several factors contributed to this process of de-Palestinization. Transjordan became the Hashemite Kingdom of Jordan, annexing the lands that remained from the eastern hilly parts of colonial Palestine, now known as the West Bank. As Jordan granted citizenship to the population, which included the original inhabitants and a considerable proportion of the refugees, it claimed to be the only successor of the would-be Palestinian state. The Hashemites used the educational system and techniques of coercive control and surveillance to impose a Jordanian identity on the new citizens. The Israelis treated the Palestinians who remained within the post-1948 boundaries in a similar manner, granting the Palestinians formal citizenship and equal rights, redefining them as Israeli Arabs, as Sammy Smooha says, and making a considerable effort at Israelification.[5]

The Jordanians and Israelis, who then controlled most of British colonial Palestine, had a common vested interest to create and maintain a Palestinian-less sociopolitical reality in the Middle East. The world order generally supported the approach, defining the problem of the Palestinians as a refugee and not a national problem. Within the refugee camps under Egyptian control (in the Gaza Strip), in Syria, and to a lesser degree, in Lebanon, the Palestinian identity was preserved and nurtured, but even in the camps of the late 1950s, pan-Arabism was prioritized. Arab unity was seen as a precondition for solving the Palestinian problem, followed by the liberation of all Arab lands, including Palestine, from colonialism and imperialism. In Gaza the short-lived All Palestine Government was dissolved in 1949 and responsibility for the Palestinian population transferred to the League of

Arab States. Under such circumstances the Israeli claim that "there are no Palestinians" came very close to realization. By 1964 the Arab-Israeli conflict was in a great measure de-Palestinized into a conflict between states.

The Making of a Demonic Image

Small Palestinian groups, consisting mostly of young intellectuals, tried to disassociate themselves from the pan-Arab doctrine. One such group was Fatah,[6] formed in Kuwait in 1958 by a group of former Palestinian students of the University of Cairo. They tried to reverse the conventional pan-Arab rhetoric and wisdom that Arab unity needed to precede the liberation of Palestine, maintaining that liberation would come from armed struggle, with the Palestinians themselves as a vanguard, regaining responsibility for their own fate. Such ideas were spread by their periodical *Filastinuna* (*Our Palestine*), which has been published since October 1959. They revived an authentic Palestinian voice, but their ideas nevertheless remained a marginal force in Arab politics, pejoratively perceived as separatist. When the first Palestinian National Council (PNC) was convened in May 1964 and the Palestine Liberation Organization (PLO) was established with the veteran Palestinian diplomat Ahmad al-Shuqairi at its head, the as yet unrecognized Fatah comprised about 10 of the 422 delegates assembled at the Intercontinental Hotel in East Jerusalem.[7] The newly created PLO drew some attention, but did not manage to achieve independent status beyond the traditional patronage of the Arab states, and its internal divisions reflected traditional Arab rivalries.

However, the existence of the PLO provided the impetus for the Fatah leadership to establish its own military wing, al-'Asifa (the Storm), and to declare on January 1, 1965 that it was engaged in an armed struggle, or revolution. In their Communique No. 1, it claimed that guerilla action was needed to prove that "the armed revolution is the way to Return and to Liberty . . . and that the Palestinian people remains in the field . . . has not died and will not die."[8] Fatah gained a degree of publicity among the Palestinians between 1965 and 1967 because of the guerrilla war they waged against Israel, including several attempts to sabotage Israel's water-carrier project.

Paradoxically, Fatah's glory days were in the aftermath of the decisive and degrading defeat of the Arab states in the 1967 war against Israel. For the first time since 1948, the entire territory of the British colonial state was once again under the auspices of a single ruling power. Three substantial parts of the Palestinian people—those living in the West Bank, those in Gaza, and the so-called 1948 Palestinians, or Israeli Arabs—were reunited. From a certain perspective, the colonial situation had been reestablished, this time under Jewish control.[9] Fatah's prediction in the early 1960s of greater Israeli expansion and Arab defeat had come true.

A hinterland population was created that, according to the PLO vision, would support a popular guerrilla war inspired by the doctrine of Vietnamese General Vo Nguyen Giap, the Latin American revolutionary Che Guevara, and the National Liberation Front (FLN) leaders and ideologues of Algeria. Yasir Arafat arrived almost immediately after the war in the West Bank to establish underground guerrilla cells. The initiative, however, was crushed by Israeli security and intelligence, and the leader of Fatah was forced to establish his headqurters in Jordan. Despite this, an armed resistance and guerrilla attacks against Israeli targets both inside and outside the Green Line—the border established in the 1949 armistice agreement—began almost immediately, partially inspired by Fatah. Between 1967 and 1970, 115 Israeli civilians were killed and some 690 wounded in the guerrilla warfare.

However, Fatah's most influential effort, and the event that for Palestinians put it and Arafat at the forefront of the liberation struggle, was the battle of Karamah. Karamah was a Palestinian refugee camp in Jordan, and it was Fatah's headquarters. On March 21, 1968 Israeli troops attacked the camp, but were forced by Fatah guerrillas, supported by Arab Legion artillery, into a day-long battle. The Israeli forces lost some twenty-five soldiers and were only able to continue operations with reinforcements from artillery, armored vehicles, and the air force. If the Palestinians were shamed by the outcome of the 1967 war, they regarded Karamah as a victory over the powerful Israeli armed forces that provided them with a source of pride and hope.[10]

A Palestinian hero also emerged—the *fida'i*, or the warrior ready to sacrifice himself for the cause—and quickly gained mythic proportions, sending thousands of teenagers to join the 'Asifa and propelling Arafat to the front of the Palestinian national movement. In July 1968, at the fourth PNC meeting in Cairo, a coalition of Fatah and other smaller guerrilla groups occupied half of the seats and took over de facto control over the organization, reframing the national charter. In February 1968 Arafat was elected as the PLO's chairman.[11]

To a greater extent than its predecessor, the revised Palestinian National Charter adopted the traditional approach toward the Jewish political presence in the Middle East and the existence of a Palestinian polity. Framing the conflict as zero-sum, the charter stated that

> the establishment of the state of Israel is entirely illegal, regardless of the passage of time, because they are contrary to the will of the Palestinian people and to their natural rights in their homeland, and inconsistent with the principles embodied in the Charter of the United Nations, particularly the right of self-determination. (Article 19)

The charter's theological thesis was that "Judaism, being a religion, is not an independent nationality. Nor do Jews constitute a single nation with an identity of its own; they are citizens of the states to which they belong" (Article 20).[12]

The PLO essentially became an umbrella organization for diverse Palestinian political and guerrilla organizations, with Fatah as the predominant force. For the Israelis, the PLO signified the reappearance and revival of the Palestinians as virtually independent political actors on the scene of the Arab-Jewish conflict.[13] At the Rabat summit of Arab states in October 1974, the PLO was recognized as the sole legitimate representative of the Palestinian people. Internal power and ideological struggles fueled the competition over extremist positions and the need for military success; such struggles appeared within the PLO and its executive committee, and between the mainstream Fatah and the Marxist Popular Front for the Liberation of Palestine (PFLP), headed by George Habash, and the Democratic Front for the Liberation of Palestine (DFLP) of Na'if Hawatmah and several other groups.[14]

Beginning in 1974, one of the controversial issues within the PLO was its so-called external operations, which struck Israeli and non-Israeli civilian targets outside of Israel and in the occupied territories. Airline hijackings were the most visible and popular. Among the more spectacular operations were those at the 1972 Munich Olympics, in which most of the Israeli athletic team was taken hostage and later killed, and the May 1972 collaboration between a Japanese Red Army group and the PFLP in mounting an attack on Ben-Gurion airport, murdering twenty-six civilians. These actions put the Palestinian issue on the top of the world agenda, but at the same time, they left the Palestinians demonized as cruel terrorists.

Inside operations also intensified, leading to an uneasy coexistence between the conquerers and the conquered. After 1971 most of the attacks came from Jordan and later Southern Lebanon. Fatah and other guerrilla organizations exploited the weakness of the Lebanese state by establishing a state within a state, building complex social, political, and military infrastructures.[15] This occurred after the abortive attempt to overthrow the Jordanian Hashemite regime in September 1970. By and large, Palestinian guerrilla warfare met with relative success.[16]

Between 1971 and 1982 the Palestinian guerrillas killed some 250 Israeli civilians and wounded more than 1,500. All of these traumatic events were absorbed by the Israeli collective memory. As a consequence, the basic sense of internal and individual security among Israelis was heavily damaged, and the distinction between strategic versus individual security was blurred. Israeli Jewish society began to see the Palestinian guerrilla organizations as a ferocious enemy whose goal was to destroy the Jewish state and "throw the Jews into the sea." The Jews sometimes equated the Palestinians with the Nazis, who "killed Jews simply because they were Jews." Such a construction of reality was referred to rather elegantly by one Israeli scholar as "politicide."[17] Although overused, the term had some foundation, increasing collective frustration and a tendency toward military solutions.

Under such circumstances, the specific history and tragedy of the Palestinian people were completely erased from Israeli collective memory, history, and awareness, to the point of denying the existence of the Palestinians while at the same time perceiving them as the greatest danger that the Jewish state faced. Such feelings were also used for internal political gain by right wing or hawkish Israeli politicians. Israel conducted one limited military operation—Operation Litani in 1978—and one full-scale, bloody war in June 1982 on Lebanese territory against the Palestinian military and political infrastructure. The objective of Operation Litani was to halt the guerrilla war and the bombing of northern Israeli settlements by establishing a limited buffer zone. The 1982 war was conducted in the hope of destroying the PLO, not only militarily, but politically.

Israeli Political Culture

Usually, both the media and the intellectual community depict the Jewish Israeli political scene, in the context of the Israeli-Arab and Israeli-Palestinian conflict, as divided between right and left, doves and hawks, with the addition of a recent third category of Jewish religious fundamentalists. The discourse of a more subtle sociological analysis describes the scene as uni-

versalistic versus primordial or particularistic orientations.[18] These cleavages certainly exist, but mainly as self-identities in the ongoing domestic
kulturkampf. However, they are highly simplistic, stereotyping a social order and attempting to manage a complex situation of quasi-external conflict
that lacks clear-cut and permanent boundaries or easily identifiable rules.

Israeli political culture is characterized by a mixture of a permanent anxiety and a power-oriented culture. On one hand, the Jewish-Israeli polity is
driven by a code of self-perceived weakness, permanent wretchedness, and
existential threat. A sense of permanent siege and potential annihilation in
a hostile, gentile world of anti-Semites—be they Christians, Muslims, Bud-
dhists, or agnostics—is perceived as the state of nature or the cosmic order.
Two or three thousand years of Jewish persecution, culminating in the Holocaust, are offered as final proof of the eternal relevance of the particularistic interpretation of history and collective memory, and its relevance to
the present.

On the other hand, Jewish Israelis are well aware of their country's status as a military power, with one of the best-equipped and trained armed
forces in the region. Military service is an important component of Jewish
Israeli life, as men and women serve in both regular and reserve duty, or
are the parents of soldiers, and so on. The new Israeli—as opposed to the
Jew of exile, shaped and disdained by Zionist ideology and mythology—is
first and foremost a warrior. Jewish Israelis adore *macht* (action); they are
confident that force, now that they have the ability to use it, will solve most
societal and political problems, making power orientation the touchstone
of their political culture.[19] There is a deep convinction that Arabs in general,
and Palestinians in particular, "only understand the language of force." Former Prime Minister Levy Eshkol coined the expression of the "poor Sam-
son" syndrome to describe this Janus-faced character of the Israeli political
culture.[20] The perceived weakness and power-oriented components of the
culture complement each other, yet they also cause internal strain within
the Jewish-Israeli collective identity.

In Jewish Israeli culture, the Jewish Israeli man—especially the Ashkenazi
native-born man—is depicted as modern, educated, sophisticated, highly
skilled, motivated, and an omnipotent warrior, as opposed to the Arab in general and the Palestinian in particular, who is seen as primitive and backward,
uneducated, unsophisticated, unskilled, unmotivated, disabled, and militarily inferior. Poor work is labeled as Arab work, and the language, especially
Hebrew slang, was once filled with degrading and pejorative stereotypes of

Arabs.[21] The wars of 1948, 1956, and 1967 strengthened these stereotypes. A slight change occurred following the 1973 and 1982 wars, accelerating after the popular uprising in the occupied territories.

Jewish Israelis interpreted the reappearance of the Palestinians as independent actors on the stage of the Jewish-Arab conflict, embodied by the PLO, to fit perfectly with both components of their political culture. Israeli overreaction was one of the factors that helped to both give the Palestinian organizations publicity and reconstruct Palestinian identity and nationalism. Al-'Asifa's first guerrilla attack, an attempt to install a bomb into a reservoir of the Israeli national water carrier, had been preceded by several abortive attempts to infiltrate Israel,[22] which the Israeli government gave a great deal of publicity. On May 1, 1965, Levy Eshkol, the Israeli prime minister and minister of defense, warned the Arab countries not to shelter Palestinian guerrillas, and he filed a complaint to the UN Security Council. Fatah then requested that the United Nations consider its captured gunmen to be prisoners of war, to be treated according to the Geneva Conventions and international law. Fatah not only gained relatively rapid worldwide recognition, but moreover, this small group was presented and constructed by the Israelis as a major danger for Israel. This alone operated as a kind of self-fulfilling prophecy, and lay the foundations for a new Palestinian pride.

The Israeli oversensitivity was not completely baseless. As mentioned above, both Israel and some Arab states sought to de-Palestinize the Palestinians.[23] Any deviation from this process was considered by the Israelis and the Jordanian regime as dangerous; any Palestinian claim as such was perceived in terms of a zero-sum game for both the Israeli and Jordanian polities. Ahmad al-Shuqairi, the founder and first chairman of the PLO and the man who gave the organization its initial shape, declared Jordan to be a part of Palestine.[24]

From a political and institutional point of view, the Israeli reaction to the reappearance of a partially independent, Palestine-centered organization and leadership may have been exaggerated, but from a behavioral point of view, the reason for anxiety was evident. From the outset, the PLO, constitutionally at least, continued the traditional Palestinian denial of any collective political rights for Jews in Palestine.

The PLO's argument with the central assertions of Zionist doctrine is also understandable, given the history of both collectivities and the catastrophic outcome for the Palestinians of the encounter with the Jewish national movement. In view of the Israeli public's acquaintance with the PLO

Charter, Arafat's 1994 call for a *jihad* (holy war), which he later attempted to explain as "jihad for peace," and his definition of the post-Oslo Israel-PLO agreements in terms of Muhammad's Treaty of Hudaybiyya, immediately touched the most sensitive Israeli nerves.[25] The real conflict over a piece of land became a cosmic collision between supernatural powers, uncontrolled by human beings. The Palestinian National Charter's direct assault on the very raison d'être and identity of Jewish collectivity reflected the nature of the communal conflict, based on a mutual game of delegitimation. Later, both the nature of the conflict and the delegitimation drove the partners toward mutual accomodation.

Personification

The Israeli approaches toward the Arabs, the Palestinians, and the conflict were embodied in the personality and figure of Arafat, Fatah's leader and later the PLO's chairman. This perception was fueled by Arafat's self-presentation as an ascetic man of the people, completely dedicated to the revolution. Most of the Jewish Israeli media perceived and presented him as a caricature, an appalling but ridiculous terrorist, a cunning conspirator with a limited performance record, a loser survivalist, an untrustworthy and inconsistent pragmatist, and, above all, the personification of ultimate evil. However, just as Arafat preferred, he remained for most Palestinians and Israelis an enigma. From his installment in Gaza and the attempt to establish and efficiently manage the Palestinian National Authority and its routinization to his death in 2002, Arafat's enigmatic image to a large measure disappeared, with his limitations overemphasized both by the Palestinians and Israelis.[26]

Israeli Policy and the Palestinian Response

According to Israel's original field policy, formulated immediately after 1967, the country was to be that contradiction in terms, an enlightened conqueror. On the West Bank this meant "open bridges" over the Jordan River and what Moshe Dayan called "functional division." Functional division assumed continuous control, surveillance, and co-opting of the Palestinian population by Jordan, with Israeli controlling land and water usage. The rules of the game were explicit almost from the beginning. The Israelis wanted to keep all or most of the territories of the West Bank and Gaza because of, as Eshkol, the pragmatic and dovish premier, put it, "the roots of the Israeli people in this land, as deep as ancient days."[27] However, for the Israelis, formally annexing the occupied territories was out of the question, with the exception of East Jerusalem and the Golan Heights, where most of the Syrian population had left or was forced to leave. Such an annexation would have changed the entire demographic balance between Jews and Palestinians, transforming Israel into a binational political entity. Even the right wing regime that came to power in 1977 was unwilling to fulfill the expectations of elements of its constituency by formally annexing the occupied territories.

However, even though the territories were not formally annexed, they were opened up as settlement frontiers[28] and incorporated within a single economy and military control system. In the first period of Jewish settlement, a grassroots movement sprang up, which the government sporadically supported, or better put, made no serious effort to halt. Later, the government openly supported and encouraged the settlements within the framework of the so-called Allon Plan.[29] From 1977 to 1987 a concentrated effort was made to create an irreversible territorial fait accompli[30] by creating Jewish settlements within a densely settled Arab areas.[31] At that time, the West Bank had about 120,000 Jewish settlers spread over forty major settlements.

One of the Palestinian responses to the invasion of their land reservoir and the attempt to suffocate any possibility of future self-determination was to attempt a process of rapid internal institutional and local leadership building,[32] or what Salim Tamari perceives as the creation of a Palestinian civil society.[33] The new local leadership was also supposed to prevent any possible settlement in the West Bank and Gaza Strip, such as between Israel and Jordan, without PLO involvement. Initially, the process of local leadership formation did not contradict Israeli policy, which tried not to interfere with Palestinian internal affairs, at least on a local or municipal level. The idea of indirect rule was built into the situation from the beginning of the occupation, but the actual nature of its application varied from time to time. Most of the mayors elected in the 1976 municipal elections were "nationalist"[33] supporters of the PLO, replacing the traditionalist pro-Jordanian leadership.[34] Together with other notables, intellectuals, and professionals, the new mayors tried to establish an inside leadership, supposedly subordinate to the outside leadership, by forming the National Guidance Committee (NGC). Israeli outlawed the NGC in 1982, and most of its principal members were dismissed from their offices or exiled. Two others were attacked by a Jewish underground group. In short, the occupiers could not allow the creation of a countrywide independent Palestinian leadership that was perceived as a kernel of state and nation building, and an extension and arm of the PLO.[35]

However, the Palestinians' complete economic dependence on Israel prevented any real development of the economic and social infrastructure of local institutions. Almost no investments were made in economic or social development. In addition, employment in Israel undermined the traditional family structure; youngsters and women were now earning money outside the control of their elders' traditional authority. The hopes of certain intellectuals of building a genuine civil society on the ruins of traditionalism and fueled by the intifada—the uprising that demanded a separation from Israel—also evaporated. The social outcome of the uprising was an internally weakened and divided society.

Under Israeli military government, two kinds of Palestinian heroes developed in the West Bank and Gaza—the abovementioned holy warrior or *fida'i,* ready for self-sacrifice, and the steadfast one *(samid),* who endured the hardship and humiliations the conqueror imposed, staying on the land at all costs to avoid a repetition of the 1948 *nakba.* The invention of *sumoud* (steadfastness) in the 1970s as a response to intensive Israeli settlement, created a limited and conditional legitimacy for cooperating with the conqueror and not escalating guerrilla resistance within the territories.[36]

Despite the asymmetrical relationship between ruler and ruled, Palestinian society received a high level of exposure to Israeli society. Many learned Hebrew, consumed Israeli mass media, were employed by Israelis in Israel or in the occupied territories themselves, and formed business ties with Israelis. In addition, generations of young Palestinians spent varying periods in Israeli jails and detention camps. Jewish Israelis encountered Palestinians mainly as employers or during their army service, policing and maintaining security in Gaza or the West Bank. The Palestinians learned the advantages and disadvantages of the Israeli system, while the Jews strengthened their stereotypes of Palestinians. As the political stalemate continued, the process of Jewish colonization advanced. Palestinians' standard of living rose slightly while the traditional family structure was weakened, and the education level rose dramatically. In addition, the Palestinian resistance to the occupation became more sophisticated. The *sumoud* civil society became more active and viable, reaching the level of a popular uprising and mass resistance by the end of 1987. The images of the *samid and* the *fida'i* merged into the image and social role of *shahid*, the martyr who sacrificed his (sometimes her) life for the sake of national liberation.[37]

The Uprising

A revolutionary situation has existed in the West Bank and Gaza Strip since the beginning of the occupation, as the local population never recognized the legitimacy of the occupier. This was expressed by sporadic violence and resistance directed against Israel. Israelis conveniently interpreted these events as disturbances of public order and marginal phenomena. It took time for the Israelis to understand the nature and scope of the grassroots uprising. The popular uprising, carried out by youth (the so-called children of the stones) exemplified a "paradox of the power":[38] A fundamentally weak partner in a conflict can gain an advantage over a much stronger entity that is limited by the political and moral constraints of its own superior position. The territories became ungovernable and, for the first time since 1967, the cost of holding them exceeded the benefits for most Israelis.[39] Creeping penetration of the guerrilla warfare into the Jewish Israeli territories created a picture of the relations between the Jewish Israelis and Palestinians of the West Bank similar to that of intercommunal warfare in such places as Northern Ireland or the former Yugoslavia. The focus of the armed struggle shifted inward and the salience of external operations decreased correspondingly.

In Israel the difference between front and rear was blurred, with individual members of each collectivity becoming potential soldiers and victims. Israeli men and women on the streets anxiously began to carry weapons routinely, recruiting themselves into the war by expecting sudden involvement at any time. The Israeli Jewish population was thrust onto the same plane of communal warfare that the Palestinians had been living with since the beginning of the Israeli and maybe the Jordanian occupation.

For the first time since 1967, the Green Line boundary reappeared on the cognitive map of the Jewish population because of extended closures and curfews. The necessity of separating Israelis from Palestinians crept into Jewish Israeli awareness, though without a concrete specification of how, where, and when. It simply became a desired political option; yet the first stage was not necessarily linked in the public mind with the possibility of withdrawing from the territories or dismantling the settlements, let alone establishing a Palestinian state.

Within the Palestinian population, the scope of recruitment for the uprising expanded tremendously. One of the most fundamental developments of the popular uprising was the amalgamation of Islamic elements into the violent struggle and the consequent formation of Hamas. Originally the Islamic elements, the most prominent of which was al-Mujamma' al-Islami in Gaza, were an offshoot of the Muslim Brotherhood, which had sponsored sporadic social activities in Palestine following its founding in 1945. The Mujamma' concentrated efforts on religious and social activities, building mosques, community centers, and youth clubs, and fighting against drugs, prostitution, and other social maladies as it defined them. In 1979 the Israeli military government officially recognized it as a religious association, and until 1983 it had tacit support from the Israeli authorities, who first perceived it as a counterbalance against the nationalistic PLO.

Hamas was founded in January 1988 by the charismatic Shaykh Ahmad Yasin as a political movement in Gaza.[40] Its military wing was established at the same time, named after the hero of the Palestinian Great Revolt of 1936–39, Shaykh Izz al-Din al-Qassam.[41] Hamas claims about 30 percent support among the Palestinians of Gaza and the West Bank. The Hamas Convenant, published in August 1988, declares that "the liberation of Palestine in its entirety, from the [Mediterranean] Sea to the [Jordan] River, is the most supreme strategic goal." A smaller rival organization, the Islamic Jihad, founded in Gaza in early 1980, is more interested in pan-Islamism and is influenced by Iranian Khomenism and the Algerian Islamic Salvation Front (FIS). The more militant Islamic Jihad is responsible, in considerable measure, for encouraging Hamas's founders to endorse violent activity.

The 1993 Oslo Agreement and the Palestinian National Authority

The ability of Israeli political culture to adopt an accord with the Palestinians, led by the PLO, with relatively little domestic resistance, was surprising considering that Israeli law prohibited contact with the organization just a short time before. It is even more dramatic if we consider that the consequences of the agreement and its implementation meant not only accepting the PLO and some of its demands, but also entailed a far-reaching change in the political status quo in the occupied territories. The change in the first stage of the interim agreement was in accepting Palestinian autonomy in the Gaza and Jericho areas, then extending that autonomy to most areas of the West Bank and Gaza, encompassing a major redeployment of Israeli troops, as a kind of disengagement between the two collectivities.

Starting in 1985, the first year following Israel's Lebanon war, approximately 20 percent of Israeli Jews, a small but slowly growing minority, supported establishing a Palestinian state. The rate of support grew by more than 10 percent, and in the first euphoric stage of the agreement, reached 40 percent. Support has since stabilized at around 33 percent.[42] The acceptance of the autonomy plan is, of course, also considered a revolutionary change in Palestinian political thinking.

From the Israeli point of view, the very conception of the Declaration of Principles (DOP) and its de facto implementation was possible because, contrary to prevailing common sense, it was well rooted in the Israeli power-oriented culture. From the beginning of the return of the Labor Party to power in 1992, there was a demonstrated stiffening in the policy toward the Palestinians, which included the mass deportation of Islamic activists and extensions of curfews and closures on the Palestinian population. The macho image of the late Israeli premier Yitzhak Rabin was well established by his iron-fist policies in the 1980s and his "break their bones" orders in response to the intifada. He was strongly identified with the power culture.[43] Ironically, the previous right wing, patriotic Likud adminstration, despite some of its rhetoric, was more easily identified with the weakness components of Israeli Jewish political culture; most of its political moves were based on arousing anxiety as opposed to the activist and security themes in Labor's message. The final status of the Palestinian entity was conveniently left for another stage of negotiations, depending on the condition that the Palestinian Authority proves itself through its policies and ability to govern. For the Israelis, the major indicator of Palestinian success was defined in terms of providing security to the Israeli Jewish population. For this reason, most of the Israelis were ready to accept the formation of several militia units and security forces by the Palestinian Authority.

A major concern for the Israeli public and leadership was that, despite Israel's formidable military strength, its power underwent continuous attrition and slow deterioration, resulting from the need to police the occupied territories. As the Palestinian popular uprising continued, the price for the Israeli military system of directly controlling the Palestinian population grew, while the gains for the Israeli economy were decreasing. Many Israeli military units drastically cut their basic and advanced training, but worse was the changing mentality of the entire military body, from an elite corps that could conduct extensive blitzkrieg-style, large-scale wars into a static, internal security militia. The Israeli military quickly learned the limitations of a military power facing active civilian resistance primarily composed of stone-throwing children and youth.

Protecting the small Jewish settlements dispersed among the densely populated Palestinian population has been another heavy burden on the Israeli military. According to an obsolete security doctrine, any Jewish settlement in this space is a part of a regional defense system in case of war, granting territorial depth for defensive forces. Analyzing the present and future battlefields as well as the lessons of the 1973 war in the Syrian (Golan) Heights, shows otherwise. Settlements and settlers hampered the military, limiting large-scale movements of armored troops on the battlefield. However, it seems that the Israeli government estimates that public opinion is not ready to tolerate the dismantling of settlements, including those that could be used as bargaining cards with the Syrians and the Palestinians. Even the Netzarim settlement, isolated in the Gaza Strip and entailing a high military and political cost to maintain, is perceived in such terms.

A power-oriented analysis of the situation concludes that indirect control of the Palestinians is a better and cheaper strategy than is direct control,[44] especially in a completely ungovernable area such as the Gaza Strip. Such indirect rule entails transferring local rule to Palestinian authority, including its police and secret services. These arrangements would take at least five years. In any case, a Palestinian autonomous entity—or in the worst case analysis from the current Israeli point of view, a sovereign state, divided territorially between the Gaza Strip and the West Bank and compressed between Jordan and Israel—is for Israel a greater strategic asset than threat.

However, the Oslo Accord itself contradicted the view of Palestinian autonomy just described. The Palestinian Authority desperately needed to gain legitimacy from the Palestinian population, which could only be obtained by holding general and more or less free elections. Elections were finally held in January 1996, in accordance with the Oslo 2 Agreement of September 28, 1995, after major redeployments of Israeli troops from populated areas. The withdrawal of troops in areas of mixed population left behind the seeds of future conflict, as in Hebron; redeployment there without evacuating the small militant Jewish population was a sure formula for confrontation with the Muslim majority. The Israeli government was too weak to wage an open conflict with such ideological settlers before a comprehensive peace-package deal was presented to the public, and was unwilling to do so in any case. However, the catch-22 was that such a deal was impossible without empowering the Palestinian Authority. As the empowerment process continued, opposition within the Palestinian camp and among its Islamic components escalated the armed struggle against Israeli targets within Israel with the expressed aim of destroying the agreement. A softer interpretation perceives these terror attacks as a signal to the Palestinian Authority, controlled by Fatah, to recognize the Islamic opposition's legitimacy and allow it political freedom as well as the freedom to develop its social and educational activities.

When all is said and done, the Palestinian Authority has been unable to deliver the promised internal security goods to the Israelis, and it has failed to deliver tangible and immediate results for the Palestinian population in improving the quality of life, creating better economic conditions, and providing greater freedom of expression. The Western states, which promised massive financial aid to the Palestinian Authority, have hesitated to fulfill their commitments without clear programs for spending the money for its intended purposes.[45] Much of the aid that arrived was turned over to supporting the various branches of the Palestinian Authority military. The Israeli leadership, too, was unable to supply the much-desired and long-promised internal security, a promise that returned Labor to power following the 1992 elections. Intensifying the Islamic and other guerrilla attacks left the peace process looking fake in the eyes of Israeli public opinion, which returned to its traditional anti-Arab sentiments. The Israeli government's response to attacks—imposing long closures on the occupied territories—only worsened material conditions for the Palestinians, especially the Gazans, as a considerable portion of the population worked inside Israel. However, the Palestinian Authority's relative success in establishing authority and reducing Islamic violence for the most part kept the gradual implementation of the agreement on track.

Pragmatization of Fatah

The PLO, lead by the mainstream Fatah and Arafat, have already made gradual, essential, though sometimes merely implicit moves toward coexistence and recognition of Israel. The first was the twelfth PNC resolution (July 1974) "establishing a Palestinian national authority in any liberated area [from Israel]," the so-called mini-state option. The second move was made in December 1988 when Arafat declared in Geneva that the PLO recognized the rights of all parties in the Middle East conflict, including the states of Palestine, Israel, and other neighbors, to exist in peace and security; denounced terrorism; and accepted United Nations Resolution 181. Even though these were abstract declarations without any concrete policy and institutional application, they managed to arouse strident antagonism among many Palestinian groups. The entire process of accepting the Israeli offer and its accompanying details was a revolutionary move for the PLO, as represented by the Fatah leadership and encouraged by part of the local leadership in the occupied territories.

None of the declarations means that Arafat and his colleagues were unaware of Israel's motives, the unfavorable terms of peace from the PLO's point of view, or the danger of becoming the Israelis' soldiers of fortune rather than their equal partners. Palestinian intellectuals in the West, as well as Palestinians who remained outside Palestine, have become the greatest critics of the agreements, continually reminding Arafat and his colleagues of its faults. The irony is that both Rabin and Arafat have been labeled by elements of their own constituencies as traitors. Only a weakened Fatah leader could be coerced into accepting the near-capitulation terms of the agreement, in order to survive after the major political mistake of supporting the Iraqi invasion of Kuwait without the Soviet superpower's political and military backing and threatened by a growing inside leadership of graduates of the popular uprising and Israeli interrogation methods, jails, and detentions camps.

Nonetheless, the ambiguous deal that the Israelis proposed holds within it the potential to create a small, independent Palestinian state. As a sovereign state, it will have greater possibilities to maneuver and exploit political or military opportunities in the face of its two major potential enemies, Jordan and Israel. No doubt, the prospective state's small size split into two separate territorial units, internal demographic pressures, economic underdevelopment, lack of natural resources, and pressures from a highly mobilized diaspora will lend this state built-in political and social instability.[46]

The PLO-Israel deal included an understanding that the organization would amend the Palestinian National Charter; the preamble of the Washington Declaration stated that

it is time [for Israelis and Palestinians] to put an end to decades of confrontation and conflict, recognize their mutual legitimate and political rights, and strive to live in peaceful coexistence, mutual dignity, and security to achieve a just, lasting, and comprehensive settlement and historic reconciliation through the agreed political process.[47]

Interestingly enough, the agreement was made between the government of the state of Israel and "the Palestinian team representing the Palestinian people," and not with the PLO or one of its organs. In an extensive analysis, Bilal al-Hasan,[48] a brother of Khalied al-Hasan, one of the original founding fathers of Fatah, challenged the legal relations between the newly founded Palestinian Authority and its council, which was to be elected by the Palestinian population, and the PLO organs, questioning the subordination of the latter to the council and the Palestinian Authority. Like many of the Palestinian leadership and intellectuals remaining in *ghurba* (exile), al-Hasan questioned the legality of the amendments to the charter. To make matters more complicated, the Israelis conditioned the holding of elections for a new, locally elected, self-governing Palestinian council upon amendments to the charter, placing the Palestinian Authority in a no-win situation.

The New Rejectionist Front and the Holy Land

In July 1974, when the twelfth PNC adopted the idea of the mini-state option, which was in fact a late acceptance of the 1948 partition plan, it gave up the traditional claim for Greater Palestine, and many Palestinians perceived it as a betrayal of the cause. Important organizations such as the PFLP resigned from the Executive Committee and established the Rejectionist Front, supported mainly by Iraq and Libya. Every deviation from the traditional total Palestinian negation of the legitimacy of a Jewish polity in Palestine sparked harsh disputes and created cleavages and violent conflicts.

Thus, it is no wonder that a good deal of violence and hostility accompanied Arafat's acceptance of the Declaration of Principles and the other agreements with Israel —Cairo, Washington, and so on. Both non-Fatah-affiliated organizations and members of Arafat's immediate entourage, including central figures such as Faruq Qaddumi and Hani al-Hasan, openly criticized the agreement. Other previously strong supporters of Arafat and Fatah, including such intellectuals as Edward Said, Hisham Sharabi, and Elia Zureik, attacked the agreement or quietly withdrew from their positions on negotiation teams established in October 1991 following the Madrid peace talks, arguing that the agreement gave the Israelis too much.

Other prominent Palestinians continued to refuse to accept any recognition of the Jewish state within historic Palestine. Most of the Palestinians who remained in *ghurba* would not benefit from the agreement, and thus had no interest in accepting it. For those in the would-be Palestinian territories, it seemed to be minor compensation for all of the humiliations and frustrations they had endured in the years of occupation.[49] For the younger generations it would be hard to adapt to a routine life after the glory days of uprising and permanent revolution.

Under such circumstances, Arafat and the other Fatah supporters of the agreement relied mainly on the support of the West Bank middle class and the personal loyalty of Fatah military units and security forces brought in from the outside.[50] The most loyal and enthusiastic Arab supporters of the agreements were the vast majority of Israel's Arab citizens, who had long desired a reconciliation between their people (the Palestinians) and their state (Israel). In fact, for both Palestinians and Israeli Jews, the agreement hurt longstanding cognitive maps—of who the perceived enemy is, of the intentions of the other, and of the imperatives of collective memories and amnesia—without any proper preparation.[51] Moreover, for both parties, many vested interests are sunk into continuing the conflict and into the mutual concessions that actually or potentially touched upon the interests of diverse social strata. Intentionally or unintentionally, the tactic of both leaderships was to build quickly a new irreversible social and political reality based on their existing political cultures.

The beginning of the resolution of the conflict between the two national movements, Zionism and Palestinism, exposed the primordial and religious dimensions of the confrontation. For both collectivities, Palestine–Eretz Israel was not only a father or motherland, but the Holy Land.[52] As the conflict's national meanings were reduced, its religious and primordial meanings increased. The trend began much earlier on the Jewish side, when, following the 1967 war and the "reunion" with the "holiness of the national cradlelands," a quasi-millenarian movement arose among the Jewish population focused in the later creation of Gush Emunim and a grassroots settler movement in the West Bank[53] that reshaped Israeli society's social and political boundaries. It remains unclear if a real political threat to the Jewish settlements in the Holy Land will lead to violent resistance, and whether a government will be ready or able to face such a resistance.

From the Palestinian side, the conflict between the rapidly growing, highly politicized, and armed Islamic movements and Judaism as a religion and culture is even more prominent.[54] The conflict always had religious roots, and from the beginning religious symbols and terms, such as *jihad, shahid,* or *fida'i,* were used to mobilize the peripheries for the struggle, but Islam was only one component of conflict management. For the Islamic movement, the religious side of the conflict is the dominant consideration—theologically, to give up an Islamic land to non-Islamic people is prohibited—but it seems that Hamas's hesitation to join the peace process was rooted more in following the initial Palestinian nationalistic approach, together with an internal struggle that left open the option to participate in the new Palestinian polity. Continuing guerrilla warfare against Israel to blow up the PLO-Israel agreement was a fundamental challenge to the Palestinian Authority. At the same time, the challenge can be seen as an Islamic leadership requesting recognition as a partner in the deal and treatment as a legitimate actor in establishing a new polity.

The Palestinian national leadership faces a major dilemma. It must prove its credibility through its ability to implement the agreements with Israel so that the process continues, and deliver the goods by guarding Israel's security. At the same time, it must avoid a major clash—one that could develop into a civil war—with the Islamic movements and the other opposition elements in Palestinian society. As the terms of the agreements with the Israelis are humiliating to it, the Palestinian Authority has to continually test the boundaries of Israeli permissiveness and public opinion in granting the use of additional state symbols, nationalist activities in East Jerusalem, and power and institutions that point toward creating a future independent state.

Epilogue

The Israel-PLO agreements simultaneously fit and contradict both sides' collective memories, cultures, and conventional wisdoms, as well as the interests of different strata and interest groups in each society. They are a kind of political experiment in the making. Social scientists label such an experiment as a social construction of reality, interpreting the sociopolitical facts differently. The move was taken by two leaderships that tried to provide new solutions to old problems and, in large measure, to force on their own constituencies top-down solutions. Both leaderships had enough power to begin the process, but the power eroded as they tried to convert images to institutional arrangements.

During an international conference dedicated to the Arab-Israeli conflict at Tel Aviv University in late 1992, most of the participating experts agreed that the conflict "was ripe for resolution."[55] However, none of the experts could provide any theoretical conceptualization or historical depth beyond wishful thinking and gut feelings. No doubt, at that time, dramatic changes had occurred in the Middle East, beginning with the Camp David accords and later accelerated by the collapse of the bipolar world order and the dismantling of the Eastern bloc—the military, ideological, and political patron of the Arab and Palestinian causes. The hidden agenda behind the ripeness theory at least partially assumed that the Israeli side of the conflict had attained a decisive position of power that enabled it to dictate terms to the Arab side, including recognizing Israel's right to exist. The other component of this theory was the assumption that from such a powerful position, the Israeli side would feel secure enough to give the Arabs such a generous offer that a revolutionary shift would be created in their political and ideological thought, leading to their accepting the Israeli state and settler society in the region.

The ingredients of the ripeness theory formed the background dimensions of the settlement, as conducted by the Israeli power-oriented culture before the Palestinians. However, power is a very elusive notion, and in some cases has a consumer effect: the more that one uses a product, the less it is worth. The Palestinian leadership learned a similar lesson. In trying to convert prestige and image into real power, it discovered that power concomitantly deflates. The results of the 1996 elections demonstrated that the Jewish population of Israel indeed was not ripe for a reasonable settlement; the state of ripeness of the Israeli-Palestinian conflict generally is an open question.

CHAPTER TWELVE

Politicide

Ariel Sharon's Legacy and the Palestinians*

Prime Minister Ariel Sharon's political troubles began when a mainly grass-roots movement rose up inside Israel and demanded the construction of a barrier around major Israeli urban centers. Supporters of the fence—which in some strategic locations, such as Jerusalem, is being built as a wall—hoped it would prevent suicide bombers from entering Israel. The settlers and most of the Israeli far right opposed the fence because it could create an implicit border, repartitioning Palestine and leaving many settlements outside of the state's boundaries. Many feared it would also mean the end of the Greater Israel ideology. Most of Sharon's cabinet strongly opposed the project, as did his fellow Likud party members in the parliament and the party's central committee.

Supporters of the wall were motivated less by ideology than by anxiety about the Palestinian suicide bombings of civilians, which the Israeli military seemed unable to prevent. Sharon, however, saw advantages in

---

* From Baruch Kimmerling, "Politicide: Ariel Sharon and the Palestinians," *Current History* 678 (January 2005): 25–29.

separation or "disengagement," a tactical initiative that included not only building the security barrier in the West Bank, but also withdrawing troops and dismantling settlements in the Gaza Strip as part of a supposed master plan. This plan amounted to nothing less than the politicide of the Palestinian people: a combined military, political, diplomatic, and psychological process with the ultimate goal of dissolving the Palestinians' existence as a legitimate, viable, and independent entity, socially, politically, and economically. Despite losing a Likud party referendum in May 2005, the prime minister has managed to keep his plans on track, partly with support from the opposition Labor party.

Two Zionisms

The split between Sharon and his core constituency is not surprising. Sharon's school of Zionism, Labor Zionism, is the traditional rival of romantic Revisionist Zionism, the historical ancestor of the ruling Likud party. Revisionist Zionists envisioned establishing a Jewish state within the borders of Greater Israel, including what is today the territory of the Hashemite Kingdom of Jordan, without specifying how they would achieve it or how to deal with the fate and reaction of the Arab inhabitants of the country and the region. The basic assumption of the Revisionist school was that the Jewish people had an incontestable historical and moral right to the entire ancestral land and that this right would be self-implementing.

The approach of Labor Zionists to building a Jewish nation in Palestine was completely different. They believed less in rights and more in incrementally established facts on the ground. They considered the changing local and international balances of power between the Jews and the Arabs and among their respective supporters in the international arena. The basic tactic was to acquire by purchase, and later by sword, the maximal amount of territory with the minimal number of Arab inhabitants. Labor Zionism had no fixed or sacred borders, but only loosely conceptualized and changeable frontiers. In the Labor Zionist view, the amount of territory under Jewish control was flexible, always subject to complex calculations balancing the ability to hold on to it as well as political, social, military, and demographic considerations.

Such a pragmatic and sophisticated approach to colonizing Palestine was one of the principal causes of the incredible success of the Zionist project, which, from the start, seemed to be working against all odds. Over the past four decades, the boundaries between the two camps have blurred. Sharon himself, a disciple of Labor Zionism, was elected leader of the rival Revisionist camp. Yet the essential distinctions between the approaches remain, and an aggressive version of the Labor Zionists' vision underlies Sharon's attempt to resolve the central dilemma of the Israeli state.

Israel's Dilemma

Since the 1967 war, Israel has become entangled in an ongoing and deepening existential crisis caused by basic internal contradictions that accompanied the gradual and selective absorption of the occupied Palestinian territories and population into the Israeli state. The absorption created an unprecedented economic boom and increased social mobility, which obscured the crisis and became a part of it. By opening the borders of the West Bank and Gaza Strip, the Israeli labor market was flooded with cheap labor, the Palestinian market was opened up for Israeli products, and Palestinian lands became targets for Jewish colonization.

However, the prosperity was conditioned on the continuing good behavior and total cooperation of the Palestinian inhabitants of the West Bank and Gaza Strip and on their willingness to accept the Israeli policy of fully including them in the Israeli economy while completely excluding them from other spheres of the Israeli state and its Jewish character or identity. For nearly an entire generation, the Palestinians accepted these colonial rules, benefiting from relative economic prosperity while being denied most human and civil rights and deprived of the political satisfaction that derives from self-determination, collective symbols, and the exercise of any ethnic and national identity. Both societies became addicted to this deeply asymmetric situation and grew interdependent. Many Israelis and Palestinians who grew up in this anomalous situation see it as natural and find it hard to imagine other kinds of relationships.

The Israeli colonial system started to crack following the Palestinian popular uprising—the first intifada—which began on December 9, 1987, and was mainly characterized by mass demonstrations and stone throwing by youths at Israeli troops stationed in Palestinian cities and refugee camps. For the first time, Israeli society began to pay some of the costs of the occupation, not only politically and economically, but also socially, through an altered self-image. The first intifada was completely crushed, but neither the Israelis nor the Palestinians won a clear victory or suffered a significant defeat. The second round was an armed uprising that began in September 2000 when it became clear that the 1993 Oslo Accords would not result in an independent and sovereign Palestinian state. On the contrary, the peace process had perpetuated a worsening economic situation while Israel tried to pacify the Palestinians by granting them imaginary self-rule. The Palestinian economy had already started to deteriorate after the first intifada, when Israel began importing foreign workers. Palestinian labor was cheaper, but also perceived as unstable and a potential security risk.

Quite apart from the economic interest in the territories, a new complication arose after the 1967 war, namely, the desire of Israeli society, both left and right, to incorporate into the boundaries of the Israeli state the perceived historic heartland of the Jewish people in the West Bank, without including its Arab residents. However, formal annexation would mean that Israel would no longer have a Jewish majority. This contradiction created a built-in crisis, leaving the Israeli state and society unable to make the political decisions that were necessary to resolve the conflict and also meet domestic challenges in economic reconstruction, education, welfare, state-synagogue relations, democratization, and the demilitarization of society. As time passed, the crisis became more explicit, and the contradictory interests became aligned with political parties and absorbed into personal and collective identities.

In 1977, when the right wing nationalist bloc came to power headed by the Likud party, the descendant of the Revisionist party, it was expected immediately to annex the entire West Bank and Gaza Strip, which are regarded as part of the Land of Israel. This was, after all, the main plank in the party's platform, and Menachem Begin, the party's leader, had advocated it when he was in the opposition. Annexation of the territories was also the reason why Sharon, promptly after leaving the military in 1973, urged some small and medium-sized right wing and centrist parties to unite behind the veteran Revisionist leader.

However, except for East Jerusalem and the Syrian (Golan) Heights, no additional territories were formally annexed, even though they were considered to be the mythical motherland of the Jewish people. This restraint was due to the rapidly growing Arab-Palestinian population in the occupied territories, which together with the Arab citizens of Israel, as mentioned above, would at once transform the Jewish state into a binational entity even if the annexed population was not granted rights of full citizenship, suffrage, and access to social welfare programs. Today, despite the unprecedented immigration of more than 1 million non-Arabs—Jews and non-Jews—from the former Soviet Union, the territory between the Mediterranean Sea and the Jordan River contains about 5 million Jews and non-Arabs and 4.5 million Palestinians, both Israeli citizens and noncitizens. Current demographic projections indicate that by the year 2020, a total of 15.1 million people will live on the land of historic Palestine, with Jews comprising a minority of 6.5 million.

As a result, two deeply rooted existential anxieties exist within Jewish Israeli political culture. One concerns the physical annihilation of the state, an issue that many Israeli politicians and intellectuals frequently use, abuse, and emotionally manipulate. The other concerns the loss of the fragile Jewish demographic majority on which the supremacy and identity of the state rest. The loss of that demographic majority is seen as a prelude to eliminating the Jewish state physically. Thus, Israel has found itself in an impossible situation: the patriotic imperative to possess the sacred land contradicts the patriotic imperative to ensure a massive Jewish majority.

As Aluf Ben asserted, there is an "unspoken but crucial factor" behind Prime Minister Ariel Sharon's decisions to unilaterally withdraw Israeli settlers from the Gaza Strip, build a separation barrier in the West Bank, and approve a controversial law preventing any Palestinian who marries an Israeli from becoming an Israeli citizen. All of these measures aim to preserve the Jewish majority, which is seen as a pillar of long-term national survival, and they force Israelis to address head-on the most fundamental and delicate questions about their national identity. When Israeli Jews mention demography, what they really mean is their fear of becoming a minority due to the Arab population's higher fertility rate. Public threats by their adversaries that "the Palestinian womb" will eventually decide the decades-old contest for Palestine fuel this fear. The recent intifada, the four-year Palestinian-Israeli war of attrition, convinced many Israelis that their country's future as a Jewish state, as opposed to a binational one, depends upon winning the demographic war. Even die-hard right wingers, former believers in Greater Israel, now advocate partition along ethnic lines, with a large Jewish majority on the Israeli side. And in recent years the demographic left has grown stronger, certainly compared with Israel's shrinking ideological left. In the end, it seems, "births have helped the Palestinian cause more than bombs and bullets."[1]

A large portion of the electorate that voted for Sharon twice—from both Zionist schools—expected him to solve these internal existential contradictions. They also expected him to address the renewed Palestinian armed resistance against the Israeli occupation following Prime Minister Ehud Barak's failure in 2000 to negotiate a deal with Palestinian leader Yasir Arafat at Camp David that would end, or at least mitigate, the conflict.

The Military Phase

Palestinian inhabitants of the occupied territories had been successfully pacified by a combination of carrots and sticks until the massacre at the Patriarch's Cave, a site holy to both Judaism and Islam. On February 15, 1994, Baruch Goldstein, a fundamentalist, religious Jew, massacred twenty-nine unarmed, praying Muslims and wounded many others. Until then, expressions of Palestinian armed resistance were rare and lacked broad popular support, despite the growing colonization of the West Bank and obstacles to Palestinian economic growth and foreign investments implemented by Israeli authorities.

The Patriarchs' Cave massacre changed the relationship between Israelis and Palestinians at once and created perceptions of religious warfare. It also triggered a reaction from the Palestinians, who had long been frustrated by their national and economic oppression. After the forty-day Islamic mourning period ended, Hamas and other Palestinian religious groups began their vendetta against the Jewish civilian population inside Israel. This, more than the formally acknowledged start of the second intifada in 2000, was the real beginning of the most recent uprising and its escalating chain of mutual violence.

The use of suicide bombers—martyrs, in the Palestinian conception—was initially considered an appropriate response to the immense disparity in the balance of power between the powerful Israeli military and the powerless Palestinians. The bombers' early success was so great that the mainstream Fatah militias, especially the al-Aqsa Martyrs Brigades, joined in these guerrilla operations. They did so both because the suicide bombings panicked and demoralized the Israelis and because they feared losing internal political support to the Islamists. However, the bombings had two unintended and unexpected consequences. The first was the collapse of the Israeli mainstream peace camp, which went beyond Barak's declaration after the failure of the Camp David talks that there was "no Palestinian partner" for peace. The second unintended consequence was the growing sense among Israelis and abroad that military force against the whole Palestinian people, including excessive force, was legitimate.

In 2001, the newly elected Sharon had his own idea about how to solve the Palestinian problem. His was a concept dating to the 1948 war—namely, to commit politicide against the Palestinians. The process of politicide, in addition to breaking the Palestinians' political identity and institutions, may also (but not necessarily) include their gradual, partial, or complete ethnic cleansing from the territory known as the Land of Israel, or historic Palestine, as was attempted during the 1948 war.

Prime Minister Yitzhak Rabin and the mainstream peace camp tried to solve Israel's demographic dilemma by giving up most of the occupied Palestinian territories together with their inhabitants. Rabin was assassinated for this policy, and during subsequent elections, a majority of the Jewish population seemed to reject or at least be ambivalent toward Rabin's solution, which was regarded as a deviation from the Labor Zionist approach. Sharon's government opted almost explicitly to reverse the approach encapsulated in the Oslo Accords.

Sharon's program included military and political stages. The military stage of Sharon's politicide strategy was implemented after an especially deadly terror attack. During the first night of Passover, on March 27, 2002, a suicide bomber murdered 29 people and wounded 150 others who were attending a seder, the ritual Passover meal, at a small hotel in the coastal town of Netanya. Two days later, Israel called up many of its reserve units and initiated a series of extensive military operations known as Operation Defensive Shield. The actions had been planned long before, but the suicide attack, which had stirred domestic and world public opinion, provided the perfect pretext for beginning operations. The objective was to dismember any organized Palestinian security forces and obliterate the internal foundations of the authority of Arafat's regime. At the same time, and for the same purpose, Israel also systematically attacked most of the Palestinian national and public institutions and infrastructure, even destroying databases such as the Palestinian Bureau of Statistics. There is no doubt that every state has a firm obligation to protect its citizens from indiscriminate terrorist attacks and killings; Sharon, however, has used this obligation to go far beyond self defense and to legitimize Israel's own prosecution of state terror.

The frequent and deep incursions into and sieges of Palestinian towns, villages, and refugee camps, along with the extrajudicial executions of Palestinian military and political leadership, were intended to demonstrate Israel's military might as well as its readiness and political ability to use it. The aim was to prove to the Palestinians that they were vulnerable and defenseless against Israeli aggression. The Arab states and the international community paid only lip service to defending the Palestinians, mainly to silence internal unrest, because they suspected the present Israeli government of harboring a penchant for regional war.

During the military phase, Israel enjoyed nearly unconditional American support. Under the umbrella of U.S. President George W. Bush's administration—whose spirit lies close to Christian fundamentalism—Israel is considered, as never before, a moral and political extension of the United States.

Political Stage of Politicide

During the politicide's military stage, which began with Operation Defensive Shield, Sharon gained immense popularity among most of the Jewish population. However, as he moved to the political phase, namely, disengaging from the Katif bloc of the Gaza Strip and building the separation fence, Sharon faced considerable internal and external opposition. Opposition to the settlement evacuations came mainly from the settler movement and the radical right, but the opposition to the fence was from many and different sources. Palestinians and part of the Israeli left opposed it because it was being built on Palestinian land rather than the Green Line, annexing de facto large amounts of Palestinian land to Israel. Rightist elements perceived it as dividing Israel and the occupied territories, signaling the end of the Greater Israel vision. Sharon also encountered opposition from the International Court of Justice, the legal advisory opinion of which stated that the wall should be dismantled and compensation paid to Palestinian owners of property confiscated to build it. As expected, this nonbinding opinion did not change Israel's decision to build the fence, nor did it affect the route, although construction later slowed down.

All of the Sharon government's activities were designed to lower Palestinian expectations, crush their resistance, isolate them, and make them submit to any arrangement suggested by the Israelis under U.S.-led international auspices. Sharon's various versions of his politicide plan, which are compatible with the pragmatic Labor Zionist approach, are certainly incompatible with the Revisionist and religious messianic dreams of an exclusively Jewish Greater Israel. Nonetheless, according to polls, the majority of Israeli citizens supported Sharon's plan, and many abroad are attracted to the public image, reinforced by mass media, of a breakthrough toward settling the conflict.

Many who are oriented toward compromise are presumably aware of Sharon's real intentions but support his policy anyway for reasons that sound sophisticated. First, the Israeli casualties suffered from protecting the few settlers of the Gaza Strip were disproportionate to their limited geopolitical importance. The settlements were isolated and vulnerable, demanding army protection. Second, dismantling the settlements might set a precedent for dismantling other settlements. Third, Sharon could always convert himself into a peace maker, playing the role that de Gaulle did in Algeria, or de Klerk did in South Africa.

When Sharon implemented the political phase of his politicide project, namely, the disengagement, he did so pragmatically. He was aware that international norms would not accept either large-scale ethnic cleansing or transforming the Hashemite Kingdom of Jordan into a Palestinian state, in accordance with his initial approach that "Jordan should be the Palestinian state." Therefore, he tried a more subtle approach toward controlling the greatest amount of territory possible. He dismantled all of the Jewish settlements in the Gaza Strip, which housed about 9,500 settlers, and evacuated four small, isolated settlements in the northern West Bank. In exchange for this concession, Sharon requested that President Bush and the Likud party support retaining the major Jewish settlement blocs, inhabited by about 400,000 settlers in the West Bank.

Sharon had a clear vision for managing the conflict. He said that, with the implementation of the roadmap—the Bush administration's initiative on the Israeli-Palestinian conflict—Israel would create a Palestinian state on a contiguous area of territory in the West Bank, allowing Palestinians to travel from Jenin to Hebron without passing through Israeli roadblocks or checkpoints. However, Palestinians would be separated by walls and fences from Israel and the Jewish settlement blocs.

The contours of the vision are obvious enough: the Palestinian state would comprise four or five enclaves around the cities of Gaza, Jenin, Nablus, and Hebron, lacking territorial contiguity. The border fence would enclose all of the major settlement blocs containing about sixty settlements, many of which lie deep inside Palestinian territory, such as Kiryat Arba, the settler town near Hebron. According to the 2005 report issued by B'Tselem, the Israeli human rights organization, the fence's total length is supposed to be 423 miles long. As of the end of 2005, 35 percent (145 miles) of the barrier was completed, 25 percent was still under construction, 20 percent was authorized though construction had not yet begun, and a remaining 20 percent had not yet been authorized.[2] The route of the fence, which runs inside the West Bank and joins about 10 percent of its territory to Israel, seriously interferes with the lives of hundreds of thousands of Palestinians and cuts up the West Bank into at least three enclaves in addition to the Gaza Strip enclave.

A large cluster of Arab communities will be located on the Israeli side of the fence, isolating them from other Palestinian communities and contradicting even the presumed security logic of keeping Arabs out of Israel. The plan to connect the Palestinian enclaves with tunnels and bridges means that there will be a strong Israeli presence in most other areas of the West Bank, making the situation there comparable to that in the Gaza Strip, where Israel, after the supposed disengagement, retains control over access to the territory by land, air, and sea.

Dov Weisglass, Sharon's close aide and envoy, divulged the true intent of the plan in an interview with the newspaper *Haaretz* on October 8, 2004. He admitted that

the disengagement is actually formaldehyde. . . . It supplies the amount of formaldehyde that is necessary so there will not be a political process with the Palestinians . . . when you freeze that process, you prevent the establishment of a [genuine] Palestinian state, and you prevent a discussion on the refugees, the borders, and Jerusalem. Effectively, this whole package called the Palestinian state, with all that it entails, has been removed indefinitely from our agenda . . . all with a [U.S.] presidential blessing and the ratification of both houses of [the U.S.] Congress.

On June 30, 2004 the Israeli High Court ordered changes to nineteen miles of the route of the West Bank barrier. The ruling was meant to ease the immense hardships experienced by Palestinians living in the most problematic areas of the fence's route. However, the Israeli court accepted the wall in principle, and affirmed that "the current route adequately represents Israel's security requirements" as part of the so-called unilateral disengagement from the Palestinians. As such, the court supposedly granted to Israel legal legitimacy for the entire enterprise. However, as mentioned above, the International Court of Justice at The Hague ruled in July 2004 that the entire separation fence contravenes international law because it is being built on Palestinian land rather than on the Green Line separating Israel from the occupied territories.

When Sharon encountered strong opposition within the Likud party toward his disengagement plan, he created a new political party, Kadima. Following a quick dissolution of the Knesset, an election was held. Three months before the elections that would have thrown the entire Israeli political system into an unprecedented tailspin, on January 4, 2006, Sharon suffered a massive stroke. He was replaced by Ehud Olmert, Sharon's deputy in his new political party.

The election results reflected the unusual circumstances. The Israeli constituencies were confused and had difficulty forming clear political attitudes in the vertigo-inducing situation they encountered. One result was an unprecedented low rate of voter participation, about 60 percent as opposed to 70 to 80 percent in previous elections. The protest vote for the harmless Pensioner's Party won it seven seats, though it had yet to set a clear agenda. Shinui, a centrist-secularist party, completely disappeared from the map. The ruling Likud party collapsed and was left with only twelve seats. It seems, however, that the most noticeable result is a weakening of the overall power and decision-making capacity of the entire political system. After many generations, the traditional right wing and Orthodox-nationalist parties may have lost their superiority in parliament. The two major parties were reduced to only a medium level of influence and did not win enough votes to have a clear and decisive mandate on any issue; consequently, they were forced to establish a coalition containing considerable internal discrepancies. Further complicating the election was the choice of a controversial Labor candidate, Amir Peretz, whom was not accepted by substantial numbers of the party's traditional supporters, veteran Ashkenazi middle class and elite groups. Except in times of war, the Israeli political arena had never undergone such dramatic and abrupt changes in such a short time.

Arafat's Death and the Palestinian Elections

As mentioned, from the start, all of Sharon's activities were designed to lower Palestinian expectations, crush their resistance, isolate them from the rest of the world, and make them submit to any arrangement suggested by the Israelis under U.S.-led international auspices, or the so-called quartet of the United States, Russia, the United Nations, and the European Union.

At present, it seems that this aim has been at least partially achieved by the crushing victory of Hamas in the January, 25, 2006 elections for the Palestinian Authority legislative council—a victory that supposedly proves again that Israel does not have a partner for a negotiated peace settlement. The Palestinian cause was further harmed by Yasir Arafat's death. Despite his corrupt and oppressive regime and his personal limitations as a political leader, as opposed to his virtues as a guerrilla leader, Arafat's personality symbolized the national revival and unity of the Palestinian people. At present, no one can really replace him. Even the religious fundamentalist factions never openly challenged his authority. Now, the tensions among natural rivals—older and younger leaders, locals and former exiles, Islamists and nationalists, and different local strongmen—are set to become a war of all against all. If these internal struggles cause the Palestinian political leadership to descend into chaos, there is no doubt that the Palestinian people will be even more vulnerable to politicide.

One of the most important rivals in this struggle is Hamas itself. Founded in 1978, Hamas, or the Islamic [Suni] Resistance Movement, is historically closely related to the Egyptian Muslim Brotherhood. Rejecting any Jewish claim whatsoever to the land of Palestine, it seeks to establish an Islamic state in the entire area. To achieve this goal, Hamas claims the right to conduct an armed struggle, or holy war (*jihad*), against the Jewish state established on holy Islamic lands (*waqf*). Hamas is considered to be a terrorist group by most of the Western world and, naturally, Israel. Most human right organizations have condemned its indiscriminate attacks on Israeli civilians and other human rights violations as war crimes. During the al-Aqsa intifada, Hamas took responsibility for most of the suicide bombings in Israel and later for the Qassam rockets that targeted southern localities in Israel. These attacks began before the massacre in the Patriarchs' Cave.

The movement's popularity stems partly from its provision of welfare and social services to the Palestinian poor; it is involved in building community centers, nurseries, schools, and hospitals, and fights against drug dealers. Mainly, however, popular support comes from its continuing armed struggle against Israel and its position that Fatah's accommodation with Israel was a betrayal. Hamas is well funded and known to make generous payments to the families of holy martyrs (*shahids*) and suicide bombers. Its leadership is also not thought to be as corrupt as Fatah's.

Hamas has demonstrated some pragmatism by offering, as early as January 26, 2004, a ten-year truce (*hudna* or *fadya*) conditioned on Israel's complete withdrawal from the territories captured in the 1967 war and the establishment of a Palestinian state. Sheikh Ahmed Yassin, one of the leaders and founders of Hamas, stated that the group could accept a Palestinian state in the West Bank and Gaza Strip. Abdel Aziz al-Rantissi, another of Hamas's leaders and founders, confirmed that Hamas had concluded that it was "difficult to liberate all our land at this stage, so we accept a phased liberation." Israel responded by assassinating Yassin and Rantissi in 2004. These assassinations and others only strengthened the image of Hamas as a hero of the Palestinian resistance and liberation movement. Perhaps ironically, Israeli secret services had initially helped to establish Hamas as a counterweight to Fatah, believing that a religious movement was more convenient for Israel than was a national movement.

The transformation of Hamas from a terror group to a ruling political party will be lengthy. Internal differences need to be resolved and there will no doubt be a power struggle with Fatah, which will not relinquish power easily. The great electoral success of Hamas surprised most parties involved, including Hamas itself. It will take some time before they resolve their dilemmas about what kind of internal regime they want to establish and how they will handle their relations with Israel, the Palestinians of the Diaspora, the Arab states, and European and American donors who provide about 90 percent of PA salaries and expenses. Many Hamas supporters in the West Bank and some of its leaders are not religious zealots, but moderates who voted for Hamas to protest Fatah's incompetence and corruption. It remains to be seen whether or not these moderates can fashion Hamas into a relatively less ideological and more pragmatic ruling party.

Some Concluding Words

A conflict can be thought of as a system in which at least two interdependent players participate, with additional indirect partners in concentric circles around the core partners, including, in many cases, players from the entire world system. In the Israeli-Palestinian case, the outlying players in the conflict, with varying involvement and influence, are the United States and European Union, the Arab states, the Islamic world, Russia, American Jewry, the Palestinian Diaspora, and others. Meanwhile, the two core players are not homogeneous entities, consisting of many groups with different identities and, at times, contradictory interests.

The conflict presented in this paper has many facets, including identities, symbols, prestige, territories, and economic issues within and between the societies. Both the Israelis and the Palestinians have passed through several critical historical phases within a relatively short span of time. Each group's societal developments have shaped not only its own side, but the other as well, even if the other group's reaction was either delayed or not immediately visible.

An additional facet of this seemingly intractable conflict is that both parties participate in a kind of wishful thinking: the delusion that one side will wake up on a clear morning and discover that the other party has miraculously vanished and that the whole situation created during the last hundred years was just a nightmare. This way of thinking is reinforced by the myths and historiographies created by both societies and cultures and it is disastrous for both sides. Such ideological constructs render both peoples, excepting some minorities among each, completely confident in the absolute justice of their cause, and confirm them in their inability to empathize for their counterparts in the struggle.

Epilogue

Collective identities constitute the most basic components of any social order and are products of culture, but they are not fixed social and political variables. They are flexible, oscillating, and changeable, sometimes dramatically and visibly, other times subtly and gradually. They include a wide range of different identities that individuals and collectivities hold simultaneously. The changes in the relative salience and ranking of these various identities may be the result of shifts in political reality or territorial boundaries, but they can also become the causes of social and political changes, including alterations of regimes, although not always in intended or predicted directions. Sociopolitical realities may be altered without changing either the origin of the collective identities or the weight given their different components. Even more interesting, rapid fluctuations in the identities may be because of situational changes. According to surveys, when Israeli Jews are not directly positioned in political conflict with the Arabs or Palestinians, most of them prefer an individualistic family identity. However, this volume deals almost only with the large collective identities of the Jews and Arabs, dealing with ethnicity and nationalism, but always understanding that these identities are not the only or always the most central identities on the maps that construct individuals' social orders. They become so when the two sides meet on the sociopolitical battleground—which they do frequently.[1]

Thresholds of Collective Identities

Recently, the idea of collective identities has come under some conceptual and theoretical criticism. Brubaker and Cooper asserted that identity tends to means too much when understood in a stronger sense, too little when understood in a weak sense or nothing at all because of its sheer ambiguity: "'Identity' is a key term in the vernacular idiom of contemporary politics and social analysis must take account of this fact. But this does not require the use of 'identity' as a category of analysis or to conceptualize 'identities' as something that all people have, seek, construct and negotiate."[2] Just as one can analyze "nation-talk" and nationalist politics without positing the existence of "nations," or race-talk and race-oriented politics without positing the existence of "races," one can analyze "identity-talk" and identity politics without positing the existence of "identities.":

> Reification is a social process, not only an intellectual process . . . We should seek to explain how the political fiction of the "nation"—or of the "ethnic group" or "race" or other putative "identity"—can crystallize at a certain moment as a powerful compelling reality. But we should avoid unintentionally reproducing or reinforcing such reification by uncritically adopting categories of practice as category of analysis.[3]

Brubaker and Cooper accuse a long tradition within the social sciences— one that includes prominent scholars using many different paradigms in their research—of imposing ideological predispositions in favor of groupings on reality through the use of analytical tools.[4]

It is undeniable that all collective identities are socially constructed entities, but they are not necessarily created by social scientists. They may be constructed from the top by intellectuals, politicians, and entrepreneurs, from the bottom, or by rival outgroups and enemies. Whether such identities are partially or completely constructed, they are real social facts and can or must be conceptualized in theoretical and analytical frameworks.

In an interesting rebuttal of Brubaker and Cooper's approach, Craig Calhoun explains ethnic identity as follows:

Identities and solidarities, thus, are neither simple not simply fluid, but may be more fixed or fluid under different circumstances. It is certainly true that many solidarities—and not least of all ethnic ones—have been produced partly to engage in new conflicts, not simply to foster a larger peace. It would be a mistake however to think that this is the only thing that ethnicity or community does for people. They provide networks of mutual support, capacities for communication, and frameworks of meaning. Crucially, differential resources give people differential capacities to reach beyond particular belongings to other social connections—including very broad ones like nations, civilizations, or humanity as a whole. Not only options but needs for solidarities [are] unequally distributed [between different people at different time]. And . . . the idea of escaping particularistic solidarities into a greater universality may look very different for elites and those with fewer resources.[5]

Calhoun's approach to collective identities is too soft for the issues presented and analyzed in this volume, perhaps because I deal with an acute, decades-long interethnic and national conflict usually perceived as an all or nothing, zero-sum game. But it is basically compatible with the Israeli-Palestinian conflict, and I adopted it, with some enlargements, changes, and additions, along with the analyses of most of the chapters included in the present book.

This concluding chapter analyzes how major occurrences in Palestinian and Israeli history (see the chronology) caused changes in each side's view of itself and the other, and how these different views changed patterns of behavior, within each society, between them, or both. At least four basic conundrums are in play. First, how is an ethnic collective identity created or imagined and what basic elements contribute to its emergence? The elements may be internal, encompassing religion, culture, language, and geography, or may be externally imposed through discrimination, persecution, marginalization, social, economic, or political inequality, politicide, or genocide. Second, what forces push an ethnic group to pass, in a progression that is not necessarily linear, from a familial orientation to local, religious, ethnic, and national conceptions, which ultimately lead to a demand for self-determination in the framework of a nation-state within its own territory? During World War I, in the tenth of his Fourteen Points, President Woodrow Wilson promised self-determination for all peoples, and the Arabs and Jews each understood this promise in terms of their own claims and aspirations. Third, are the processes of ethnicization and nationalization of a human group reversible and under what conditions? Fourth, under what conditions do two major collective identities consider the relations among them as mutually exclusive, or as a complete or partial zero-sum game, materially, symbolically, or both?

Self-evidently, because this volume deals with only two interrelated societies and one case study, it is impossible to generalize about the above questions, which have kept social scientists, philosophers, intellectuals, and politicians busy for generations. However, the Jewish and Palestinian cases are so full of events, facts, and processes that no serious scholar of ethnicity and nationalism can ignore them and the evidence they provide, even if their interpretations, as presented in this volume, are not the only ones possible and represent only an exception in the field of scholarship.

There are two interlinked basic dimensions inherent in Jewish-Palestinian relations: the material and the symbolic or cultural. The material dimension is mainly territorial, but also symbolic and central for identity formation and transformation.[6] In every parcel of land settled by Jews, The Palestinians saw a theft of their own patrimony, a loss viewed first in local and communal terms and later in ethnic and national terms, or sometimes supranational pan-Arab terms, depending on their shifting collective identity, as analyzed in Chapter Three. The Jews perceived the land within its varying borders as belonging solely to them; it was their ancestral motherland, in religious, ethno-national, or mixed claims. With few exceptions, they constantly expanded their diverse patterns of control over the land, first by purchasing plots and later by acquiring them through military and political means, establishing facts on the ground with settlements.[7] Sometimes the Jewish territorial expansion was accompanied by changes in collective identity or by tensions among competing identities, as demonstrated mainly in Chapter One.

Zion: Territory and Identity

The symbolic dimension was crucial for the Jewish colonization of Palestine. Theodore Herzl, the founding father of political Zionism, initially did not prefer establishing a Jewish state in the Middle East. As a secular, almost assimilated Jew, he understood that the Palestinian territory lacked natural resources, was nearly uncultivable, had an impossible climate, was inhabited by a people experiencing the first stirrings of ethno-national consciousness, and was controlled by the unstable and unfriendly Ottoman Empire. Herzl favored establishing a state in a rich, barely populated country, such as Argentina.[8] However, European Jews, who mostly originated from religious families and had been educated initially in traditional Jewish schools, were unenthusiastic about finding collective salvation in a region without sentimental, symbolic, or historical and mythical connections with their real or imagined past in Zion.[9] For millennia, Jews have prayed to return to the Land of Zion and Jerusalem, though they are fully aware of the ritualistic and utopian nature of this prayer. However, when establishing a Jewish state became a political issue in the nationalist and still-colonial European world, the idea appealed to some Jews, provided that Herzl could be convinced to establish the Jewish home in the Holy Land.

If Jewish history led Zionists to see the establishment of Jewish communities in the Holy Land as a homecoming, Muslim history led Palestinians to see the project as another crusade. After all, the local Muslim population's first major encounter with hostile European powers was also the first European colonial adventure: the conquest of the Holy Land by the Crusaders and founding of the Latin Kingdom of Jerusalem in 1099. That conquest, which lasted approximately one hundred years, united the local population against the Christians and left them with a certain if undefined sense of collectivity. Saladin's victory over the Crusaders in 1187 imbued Jerusalem with a sense of Islamic holiness, making it a kind of capital of the country that did not yet have a separate name. Since the establishment of Israel, the Crusades have become a major reference point in the history and collective memory of the Palestinians, who perceive the Jews as modern-day Crusaders and wait for another Saladin to banish them from the land.

In 1790, the country was first unified, for a short period, within borders nearly similar to the modern ones under the rule of the Governor of Acre, Ahmad al-Jazzâr Pasha, a successful soldier of fortune and rebellious Ottoman vassal from Bosnia. In 1799, Napoleon Bonaparte invaded the Holy Land but was defeated in Acre by an alliance of local fighters formed by extended peasant and merchants families supported by the Ottomans. In 1834, the local notables and peasantry rebelled against the Egyptian conquest of the territory by Muhammad Ali. The revolt, which encompassed the entire territory of what would become Arab Palestine, was brutally suffocated (see Chapter Three). After the Ottomans retook the country, they tried to introduce agrarian and tax reforms (*tanzimat*) and strengthen the central rule. They also subdivided the country into different districts to blur the notion of a Holy Land, as they feared that various Christian powers wanted to conquer the territory. It is interesting to see the attempt to manipulate territorial identity by administrative means.

The Jewish immigrants and settlers in Palestine never regarded themselves as colonists or their movement as a part of the world colonial system. Rather, they saw themselves as a people returning to their homeland after two thousand years of forced exile. The Jews were confident of their historical and religious rights, entitling them to purchase the land and later conquer it militarily. Like other colonists in other places, they were convinced that their presence signaled material, social, and cultural progress and the liberation of the native inhabitants from ignorance. However, the local Arab population, as well as Arabs throughout the region, saw the Jews as strangers, Europeans, whites, and representatives of alien powers and foreign decadent cultures, a corrupting influence on their moral, traditional society and agents of the Western colonial world order.[10] Thus, while the Jews, Zionists or not, considered their return a solution to the so-called Jewish problem, the Arabs considered themselves victims, people who paid the price for injustices, especially the Holocaust, committed by Christian and secular Europeans.

The ancient Jewish ethno-religious identity has undergone many transformations, reinterpretations, and subdivisions among many streams during the past millennia, but not in such a way that would lead necessarily to a Zionist identity or solution. The ideological and lifestyle opportunities and options presented to Jews in the nineteenth century by the brave new world of sociopolitical emancipation and intercontinental mobility and migration were immense. Even the modern hope of humanity—nationalism—offered a new option for Jewish individuals and families, who could choose to adopt a new collective identity and become loyal solely to their French, German, Dutch, or English nations. Alternatively, they could choose to divide their identity between the private and public spheres, between religion and nationalism; they could be Jewish by religion at home and German by nationality in public. In the context of European nationalism, Zionism had no place. In addition, other ideologies captured the imagination and the public scene. As discussed in Chapter One, some Jews adopted the idea that redemption, brought about by radical revolutions of the entire world order based on socialist, communist, or other universalistic ideologies, would also include personal or collective salvation for the Jews. Later, the prominent historian Simon Dubnow fused nationalism, internationalism, and secular Jewishness into a non-Zionist, non-territorially dependent cultural nationalism.

In 1881–1882, a wave of pogroms directed at Jews broke out along the western frontier of the Russian Empire. At the same time, the Romanian authorities drastically reduced many of the rights previously accorded to its Jewish subjects. Many of the Jews affected by these events immigrated to North America, while a much smaller percentage established associations to prepare for immigration and return to what Jews had always considered their utopian fatherland and patrimony—Palestine, or Eretz Israel. The most well known of these movements was a small group of high school students in Krakow know as the Bilu association, which was supported by a larger organization called the Lovers of Zion, established in Silesia in 1884. Envoys were sent to buy land and establish several agricultural colonies. There is a striking similarity between these immigrants' motives and those of the first Protestant immigrants to the Americas, who were also a people with strongly articulated religious convictions and a history of religious persecution. Later Zionist historiography expropriated this wave of immigration, considering it to be the first wave of Zionist immigration linked to subsequent waves, even though it was not politically driven and the newcomers lacked a coherent ideological vision of the Jewish state and nation building.

In 1897, Herzl called delegations from all European Jewish communities to attend a convention in Basel to found the World Zionist Organization. This convention, which became known as the First Zionist Congress, adopted a program to create a home for the Jewish people in Palestine, secured by public law. Today, Herzl is a Zionist icon, used and abused on festive occasions, a revered figurehead representing the more liberal and humanistic streams of Zionism.

The Formative Period

Although British colonial rule lasted a little less than thirty years, it is considered to be the formative period of both the Jewish-Zionist and Palestinian-Arab polities and identity constructions. The colonial government was a minimalist state, providing basic services for its subjects: law and order, justice through courts, an education system, some basic social and health care systems, a financial and monetary system, and infrastructure such as roads, railroads, electricity, ports, and postal and broadcasting services. However, on the symbolic level, the British colonial state provided the most crucial contribution in distinguishing Palestine as a geopolitical, economic, social, and political entity distinct from the surrounding Arab lands and peoples. As a cause of the crystallization of Arab Palestinian identity, it was nearly as important as the existence of a direct enemy—the Jewish coloniz- ers, with whom the Palestinians had very complex material and symbolic exchanges and interactions, as described in Chapter Four.

Israeli Jewish identity was also invented and began to be constructed during the colonial period. The political and cultural elites made a very interesting attempt to build a new collective identity promptly after the Is- raeli state was established. This was a secular statist identity, designed to homogenize the population of the new state following massive, nonselec- tive Jewish immigration (Chapter Five). The ability to extend state power and control to new peripheries and cultural ethnic groups was of crucial importance, as Israel was rapidly turning into a country of new immigrants with political and cultural assumptions strikingly different from those of the pre-1948 Jewish community in Palestine.[11] Additional groups were in- corporated within the social boundaries of the state, but excluded from the power foci and marginalized. Such groups included about 150,000 Arabs who remained in the territory of the newly established state and the Jew- ish Orthodox, non-Zionist groups who did not recognize the secular Jew- ish state de jure.[12] At first glance, the state seemed successful in its aim of controlling the new peripheries and preserving the original distribution of power in society by creating a bureaucratized hegemony. Both the popular image of that early era in Israel's history and the findings of social science research studies indicate that the state appeared to control the process while maintaining a high level of autonomy regarding other actual and potential foci of power.[13] Israeli society became state centered after Ben-Gurion's call for *mamlachtut*, or statism. Few societal organizations took initiatives in areas such as health, education, or even tourism. However, over time, the initial Israeli identity gradually declined and was superseded by a locally invented version of Jewishness, as Chapter One describes.[14]

The Jewish National Fund

The most important organizations set up by the new Zionist movement were a bank established in 1899 and the Jewish National Fund (JNF), established in 1901 with the aim of raising funds to purchase lands in Palestine and later subsidize settlers and settlements. The lands acquired by the JNF were considered inalienable Jewish public lands, never to be sold to or cultivated by non-Jews. Until 1948, the JNF was the major actor in the Jewish-Arab conflict over Palestine, converting money into nationalized lands. However, by 1948, the Jews succeeded in buying, either privately or through the JNF, only about 7 percent of the total land in Palestine, most of it on the coastal plain at the periphery of the ancient Jewish nation's core territories. Moreover, Zionism remained a fringe and unpopular movement for a long time, enjoying little support among Jews or in the world political arena. For decades, it could not recruit substantial political and financial support for its ideas and failed to attract enough immigrants to change the demographic composition of Palestine into a Jewish land, even after the British colonial power extended its political and military umbrella over the movement.[15]

However, Zionism's major victory was to restrict immigration to the United States in the late 1920s and 1930s as a result of the Great Depression. The new immigration policy was not directed against the Jews, but they suffered disproportionately from it because of their relative share of the immigrant population, the rise of fascism and Nazism, and the Holocaust. The only country gate that remained partially open to Jewish refugees was Palestine's. During and after World War II, the Jewish people's claims became much more vigorous as a result of the Holocaust, in which the German Nazis and their collaborators managed to systematically exterminate about six million European and North African Jews.

In the postwar years, the international community felt a strong obligation to compensate the Jewish people for the horrors of the Nazi genocide and for the fact that the Allies did nothing to prevent or reduce the extermination of the Jews. However, the Palestinians regarded the fact that they had to pay for crimes committed by Europeans and Westerners as highly immoral. Nevertheless, on November 29, 1947, the United Nations General Assembly accepted a Resolution 181 to partition Palestine into a Jewish and an Arab state, excluding an internationalized enclave area of Jerusalem and Bethlehem. The Jews accepted the plan while the Arabs rejected it, demanding the whole country because they were still the majority of its inhabitants and its indigenous people. At this point in time, the majority of Jews crossed the threshold from an ethno-religious or cultural identity to a national and territorial identity, even if they did not obey the basic Zionist imperative of making *aliya* (immigrating) to Palestine.

Following the UN decision, the Jews proclaimed an independent state on May 14, 1948, the day that the mandate was terminated, setting the date as Israeli Independence Day and a historical counterpoint to the Holocaust. A day later, troops from several Arab states—mainly Egypt, Syria, Transjordan, and Iraq—invaded Palestine attempting to nullify the partition resolution, rescue their Palestinian brethren, and commit politicide against the Jewish state. Politicide occurred, but in the reverse direction.

The Military Battle over Palestine

Even before Israeli independence, from December 1947 to May 1948, a bitter intercommunal war was fought between the Palestinian-Arab community and the Jewish community. Jews still made up only about 30 percent of the population, but because Jewish immigrants were disproportionately young and politically committed, they had a demographic advantage of about 1.5 to 1 over the Palestinian population in the decisive age-group for fighting—young men between twenty and forty-five years of age—and were far better organized.[16] The first stage of intercommunal war was marked by the initiative and relative superiority of local Palestinian forces, reinforced by volunteers mainly from Syria and Egypt.

The Jewish military forces operated according to so-called Plan D (see Chapter Seven), which aimed to ensure control over the territories that the United Nations had designated for the Jewish state, and to assure free movement between Jewish settlements on the roads controlled by Arab villages. The plan also considered the inability of Jews to spread their forces among hundreds of Arab villages, the logical consequence of which was to destroy almost all conquered Arab villages and expel their inhabitants from the presumed Jewish state. Jewish military forces often found the conquered Arab villages empty or half empty, as certain portions of the Arab population fled after hearing news and rumors of Jewish cruelty and atrocities.[17] Once most of the Arabs had left the country, they were not permitted to return.

Thus, a de facto ethnic cleansing was carried out. At the end of the 1948 war, the number of Palestinian refugees was estimated to be between 700,000 to 900,000.[18] Most of their villages, towns, and neighborhoods were destroyed or repopulated by Jewish residents, some of whom were long-term residents and others of whom were recent immigrants. Since then, the Palestinians' return to their homes and fields has become a central and irremovable political demand and a key component of the Palestinian identity and constitutive myth. Many Palestinians families hold keys to their homes in Jaffa, Haifa, Ramalla, and hundreds of other destroyed or Israelized villages, as if time froze one day in 1948. The majority of the Jews perceive a full right of return (*al-awda*) in its literal meaning as a certain prescription for the destruction of Israel. However, many Palestinian and Israeli politicians and intellectuals gave a softer meaning to the return, claiming that it would be implemented by repatriation to the newly established Palestinian state, along with compensation and rehabilitation programs carried out by Israel and the international community. Israel would also be required to accept its moral responsibility for creating the situation, which few Israeli Jew are ready to fulfill.

Palestinians refer to the 1948 war and their subsequent exile as a *nakba*, a catastrophe; Israeli Jews regard the same period as a war of independence that has become a fundamental component of their identity and a symbolic compensation for the Holocaust. Both peoples have their own cosmic catastrophes, and both have strong collective memories of being the victims of a colossal injustice—either the Jewish experience of Nazi genocide or the Palestinian experience of politicide and ethnic cleansing.[19] The political behavior of both people is heavily influenced by these events.

The Internal Clash

The relationship between the Jewish state and its Jewish population and the Arab minority that remained within its enlarged borders was never easy. Although the Israeli government granted Israeli Arabs citizenship, they were always considered a security threat and experienced not only severe surveillance and control, but the xenophobia that has been built into the Jewish religion and political culture.[20] Until 1966, harsh military rule limited Israeli Arabs' freedom of movement within the country, enabling the government to confiscate most of their agricultural lands and prevent them from competing in the low-skill labor market with new immigrants. The Israeli government also imposed a curriculum on Arab schools that tried to instill a new ethnic collective identity based on traditional Arab and Muslim (or Christian or Circassian) history and a loyalty to the Jewish state that was completely detached from their Palestinian past and separate roots.[21]

In short, Israeli Arabs became a bilingual and bicultural people educated to obey Israeli democracy, but at the same time were systematically deprived of their land and access to most common social goods—welfare, jobs, housing, and other subsidized merchandise. Except for small groups of Druze, Circassians, and Bedouin volunteers, Israeli Arabs were excluded from compulsory military service, then denied full citizenship rights on the grounds that they had not fully fulfilled their citizenship obligations.

From about 7 percent of the total population in 1949, Israeli Arabs have grown to approximately 20 percent of the population in the new Israeli boundaries as established by the armistice lines. For decades, any national or ethnic Arab political organization or protest movement was suffocated. Only the Israeli Communist Party managed to serve as a major access point to the center; it channeled Israeli Arab protests and fought for their rights as citizen within the Jewish state. The Communist Party was also an intellectual hothouse for a new Arab cultural elite that created an original, local counterculture almost completely isolated from cultural developments in other Arab countries. The party's newspapers, periodicals, and Arabic publishing house hosted and participated in creating opportunities for Israeli Arab poets, writers, thinkers, and journalists; in 1992, the late Emil Habibi, a product of this policy, won the prestigious Israel Prize for literature. Later, especially after Israel conquered the West Bank and Gaza Strip and the Palestinians there came under Israel's unified control system, this cultural capital became part of a general cultural and political renaissance of the Palestinian people. Over time, the Arabs of Israel have accumulated not only cultural wealth, but also considerable material wealth and political power.

Ehud Barak's 1999 victory to become prime minister of Israel was due in no small part to the massive support he received from Arab citizens. However, as Barak was anxious to establish his political legitimacy—and because, practically speaking, Israeli leaders are not considered legitimate if their power depends on the Arab community—he excluded Arabs from the foci of power. Later, when a violent crisis erupted between Israel and the Palestinian Authority in the so-called al-Aqsa intifada, Arab citizens expressed their solidarity with the Palestinian struggle through violent demonstrations. The Israeli police overreacted, killing thirteen Arabs with live ammunition and wounding several hundred others. The response deeply shocked the Arab population, and the events were categorized as another massacre committed by Jews against Arabs, like those that had occurred in the past in Deir Yassin (1948) and Kafar Qassam (1956). Arab anger and frustration only increased when, in the face of this violence, the Israeli authorities and most members of the Jewish public demonstrated indifference and a total lack of empathy. During the February 2001 election, most Israeli

Arabs citizens boycotted the polls, denying Labor party leader Barak their community's traditional support. For the first time, the Arab electorate act-ed independently from the rest of the Israeli electorate.

Some analysts interpreted the boycott as signaling the withdrawal of Is-raeli Arab citizens from the state, their Israeliness, and the political arena. However, the meaning of this collective act was quite the contrary: The boycott aimed to indicate to the Israeli state, and especially the political left—namely, the Labor and Meretz parties—that Arab support of leftist Zionist parties could no longer be taken for granted and that the Arab voter demanded an equal voice in the Israeli polity's critical decision making.

Following the second intifada, relations between the Israeli Arabs and and the Jewish state again became strained. The state tended to emphasize its Jewish character and introduced more legal obstacles and other discrim-inatory measures against the Arabs, including the attempt to formulate a constiti tution that excluded any collective rights for Arabs. The Arabs indi-cated that they would no longer be satisfied with their original demand to make Israel a "state of all its citizens" instead of an exclusively Jewish state, and demanded full ethno-cultural and regional autonomy.[22] These height-ened separatist demands increased Jewish anxiety, resulting in increased Arabophobia and demands for more oppressive measures.

Types of Interaction

Most of the encounters between any two partners in a conflict can be divided into two types: concrete interaction and model interaction. The concrete in-teractions are the systems of exchange, competition, cooperation, and con-flict that exist between the two sides in different spheres. One sphere may contain individuals fulfilling social roles while another sphere is concerned with groups or social strata in each community. A third sphere may involve formulating policies for the entire polity. The model interaction—positive or negative—derives from the attitude of one side toward the very existence of the other side in the interaction over its image, its perception, its essence, and its activities, as described in Chapter Two.

Thus, for different parts of the community, the other side can become a positive or negative reference group, either in its entirety or in differential spheres of action. As it becomes a reference group, the other collectivity may also become a partial or complete model to be imitated or rejected. Completely or partially imitating a perceived model is not to be interpreted as adopting a positive attitude or unconfrontational attitude toward it.[23] Earlier Jewish immigrants in the 1910s and 1920s perceived the local indigenous Arab society, and mainly the Bedouin one, as similar to the ancient Jewish society exiled two thousand years ago from the land, tried to imitate it, and partially made them a positive reference group.

Unlike the Jews, the Palestinians are a new people, created like many others in Asia and Africa following the colonization and decolonization process. However, following their military and political defeat by the immigrant-settler society created during the colonial period, they remained stateless, often in exile or consigned to refugee camps. Between 1948 and 1967, they seemed to have vanished. When they reappeared, they were fragmented more or less according to their territorial dispersal and divisions. Even when Palestinians have been reunified under Israeli rule since 1967, there have been significant differences between Israeli Palestinians (the Arab citizens of Israel, or the so-called Arabs of 1948), the inhabitants of the West Bank and the Gaza, and the Palestinians of Jordan or the *gurba* (exile or Diaspora).[24]

Above all, the territorial reunification of three Palestinian areas in 1967—the West Bank, the Gaza Strip, and Israel itself—under a common government, albeit one controlled by Jews, led to a revival of Palestinianism, even though the collective identity was fragmented. The so-called Palestinian issue, defined from 1949 to 1967 as a refugee settlement and humanitarian problem, was redefined by both the Palestinians and most of the international community as an ethnic or national self-determination issue. In large measure, the situation was analogous to the struggle against British colonial rule and oppression, like the Great Arab Revolt of 1936–39, but this time against the Israelis.

For the Israelis, the 1967 war meant that they had captured the heartland of their mythical ancestral homeland, which propelled Israel's identity more and more toward its primordial components, as analyzed in Chapter One. Only recently did the country partially awaken from its messianic dreams and move toward emphasizing its civil components. However, giving up the Eretz Israel identity was a gradual and painful process connected to the reactions of the Palestinians.

The results of the war also introduced Palestinian workers from the occupied territories into the Israeli labor market. The influx caused rapid economic growth in Israel and was closely linked to the movement of all extant Israeli groups into higher positions within the ethnic hierarchy. Furthermore, when more than one ethnic group stood to benefit from the entry and growth of a lower group, those at the top benefited more than others from the change in the ethnic composition of the labor market.[25] Thus, the Ashkenazi Jews were the major beneficiaries of the ethnic recomposition of the labor market—more so than the Mizrahim, though both were pushed upward from the bottom and enjoyed occupational and social mobility. Israeli Arab citizens also experienced some occupational mobility as noncitizen workers entered the system, but still far less than did the Jewish ethnic groups; the economic and social gaps between Israeli Arabs and other Jewish groups were enlarged.[26] An additional benefit for the entire system was the opening up of a vast export market for diverse Israeli products, such as textiles and electronic appliances, to the inhabitants of the occupied territories, and from there, many times to the whole Arab world, even though it officially boycotted Israeli products.[27]

The Jewish State

Israel was transformed into a de facto binational Jewish-Arab political entity, even though all political power in the state—political rights, citizenship, human rights, access to resources, and the right to define the collective identity—has been possessed by one ethno-national segment, namely, the Jews. The hegemonic situation marks the difference between a de jure and a de facto binational state. After 1967, Israeli's veteran Arab citizens who had been there in 1948 received limited access to material resources provided by the state (See Chapters Eight and Ten) but were never granted a share in the symbolic resources of participation as equal citizens, despite possessing formal citizenship.[28] The identity of the state was constructed as Jewish by means of various symbols and codes.[29] The country's history, flag, national anthem,[30] and official days of celebration and commemoration all emphasize the Jewish character of the state, as does the entire calendar.[31]

The right to belong to the Israeli state was extended to Jews all over the world, which by definition includes them in the Israeli collectivity even if they never intended to immigrate to Israel. However, basic human rights were mostly nonexistent for the Palestinian residents of the occupied territories, a situation described as an ethnocracy.[32] Most of the discrimination was imposed by legislative measures, such as immigration and citizenship laws, and political institutions that had no official links to the state but operated as organs of the Jewish nation, such as the Jewish Agency and the JNF,[33] which possess large amount of lands and other material resources, but unlike the government, are not required to distribute them according to universal criteria (see Chapters Eight and Ten).

After 1967

Between 1967 and 1987, before the first intifada erupted, the Israeli occupation of the West Bank and the Gaza Strip and the resulting colonization project provided economic benefits at almost no cost and enabled the move toward a primordial Jewish identity. The occupied territories became a frontier for Jewish colonization, with Israel and the settlers not having to pay directly for the land. The workers commuting from the occupied territories became the cheapest migrant workers in the world, usually returning to their homes in refugee camps and villages without additionally burdening the Israeli state. Most worked without receiving any of the benefits usually accorded to workers in modern society. Thus, the material benefits and the increasing primordial identities reinforced one another.

This cost-benefit ratio depended on the submissiveness and good behavior of the Palestinians. However, as Palestinian anger mounted at their exploitation and humiliation, the gradual reduction in their living space created by Israeli colonization projects, and the inability of their own leadership to ameliorate their hardships or help them realize their national aspirations, they rebelled.

The occupation as a social order started to collapse only after the first Palestinian uprising began on December 9, 1987. It was crushed completely during the second uprising and the ascendancy of the Islamic movement. It always takes some time for the Israeli and Palestinian people and their leadership to decipher and react to changing situations. During the first intifada, the Israeli political economy adapted and began a kind of disengagement by importing foreign migrant workers mainly from Eastern Europe to replace Palestinian workers, which was disastrous for the Palestinian economy.[34] The foreign workers did not threaten public safety, as Palestinian workers were perceived to do. But they were more expensive, and because they were more permanent than Palestinian laborers who lived outside of Israel proper, they were viewed as a possible threat to the future Jewish identity of the society.[35]

Connected to the economic interest in the territories was another complication that arose after the 1967 war—the desire of Israeli society as a whole, both left and right, to annex the historic heartland of the Jewish people in the West Bank but without annexing its Arab residents. Formal annexation would mean that Israel would no longer have a Jewish majority. Demographic changes would destroy the Jewish character and identity of the state even if the Palestinians were not granted full citizenship, as presented in Chapter Twelve. This contradiction created a built-in crisis, leaving the Israeli state and society unable to make the important political decisions that were necessary to resolve both the Israel-Palestine conflict as well as domestic social issues. As time passed, the crisis became more explicit. Contradictory interests became aligned with political parties and were absorbed into personal, group, and even religious identities, creating cleavages such as hawks versus doves, right versus left, religious versus secular, or Zionists versus post-Zionists.[36]

In 1977, when the right wing nationalist bloc headed by the Likud Party came to power, it was expected immediately to annex the entire West Bank—often called by the Biblical names of Judea and Samaria—and the Gaza Strip, both of which are regarded as part of the Land of Israel. Such annexation never occurred, except for East Jerusalem and the Syrian (Golan) Heights. The reason for not annexing the Palestinian occupied territories is explained in Chapter Twelve.

Even after the Israelis had begun to digest the high economic, social, and political costs of the colonization project, it was politically impossible to halt it. By the end of 2006, about 420,000 settlers, including those in East Jerusalem and its metropolitan area, settled there. However, as time passed, the colonization project raised a deep and bitter controversy within Israeli society, involving fundamental questions of identity and the meaning of a Jewish state and being Jewish, as opposed to being Israeli.[37]

Oslo

The Israeli response to the first intifada was to negotiate the so-called Oslo agreements with Fatah, the mainstream Palestinian leadership. The agreements were a real breakthrough, resulting in each side recognizing the other's right to exist. For the first time, the legitimate representative Palestinian political body, the Palestinian Authority, was granted partial autonomy and self-control over densely populated areas and allowed to form militias.[38] But the accords were vague and ambiguous, and the most problematic issues—borders, water rights, control over East Jerusalem, and the right of return of refugees and settlements—were left unresolved.[39]

One of the main flaws of the Oslo accords was the assumption that the Palestinian Authority would be a subcontractor regime, working to maintain Israel's security while all other issues would be subject to endless rounds of negotiations, with every concession depending on Israeli generosity. There was also to be a long period of trust building that, history has shown, created mainly distrust and offered plenty of opportunities for rejectionist forces to sabotage the agreement.

Even after Fatah and the Israeli government ratified the Oslo accords, settlements continued to expand. Established settlements doubled their number of settlers and, it is estimated, 120 so-called unauthorized settlements were constructed after 1996.[40] Such unauthorized settlements vary in size, but many of them were populated by more than twenty families, had permanent building structures, and were connected to electricity and water and linked by paved roads. These settlements never would have persisted as they did without tacit approval from the civilian authorities and protection from the military.[41]

Obviously, not all of the Israeli Jews and Palestinians were happy with the Oslo accords. For many Israelis, the accords meant the repartition of the Land of Israel. For many Palestinians, the accords waived their rights to most of their homeland, and were therefore treasonous. Palestinian Islamist organizations resumed attacks against Israeli targets and the newly established Palestinian Authority could not prevent them from doing so. The attacks began even before the 1994 massacre by Baruch Goldstein, who killed 29 Palestinians and injured 125 more at the Patriarch's Cave—a common holy site for both Jews and Muslims—and transformed the Israeli-Palestinian conflict from a battle of national liberation into a religious war (*jihad*). After the traditional Islamic forty days of mourning, Islamist extremists began a revenge campaign, and dozens of suicide bombers hit the streets of major Israel cities, detonating their bombs mainly in buses and coffee houses.

Ehud Barak and the Collapse of the Israeli Peace-Oriented Camp

The Israeli streets were filled with massive demonstrations against the agreements and political extremists engaged in wild incitement against the government, which they accused of treason. There was an atmosphere of impending civil war. On November 4, 1995, a religious right wing activist assassinated Prime Minister Yitzhak Rabin. In May 1996, the head of the right wing Likud party, Benjamin Netanyahu, was elected prime minister in his place. After his election, Netanyahu declared his commitment to fulfill all of Israel's previous agreements and negotiated the Wye River Accord with Yasir Arafat. Although this agreement resulted in a minor Israeli withdrawal, after a long delay, from Hebron, Netanyahu basically stalled the peace process and refused to implement the steps agreed to in the Oslo Accords.[42] In 1996, Ehud Olmert, than mayor of Jerusalem, decided to open an exit for the Western Wall tunnel under the Haram al-Sharif. This provoked major Palestinian riots, resulting in the deaths of about a dozen Israelis and a hundred Palestinians.

After the Netanyahu years, Ehud Barak's election as prime minister under the Labor Party in 1999 kindled real hope among certain sectors of the Israeli population and profound anxieties among others, namely, the Jewish settlers in the occupied territories and the ultra-Orthodox, who were alarmed by Barak's campaign promise to "separate religion from politics." However, his victory was warmly welcomed among Israeli Arabs, more than 90 percent of whom voted for him; Palestinians; leaders of the Arab states; and the rest of what is known as the Western world. Barak, however, had an agenda and priorities of his own. He would have preferred to form a government with Likud, headed by Ariel Sharon, for whom he entertained a great admiration following their joint military endeavors. From the outset, the support of the Jewish parliamentary majority was more important to Barak than that of the Israeli Arabs. He acknowledged the latter's distress and pledged to strive for their full equality, but would only seek it after a final settlement with the Palestinians had been reached.

The distinction between Barak's and Rabin's approaches was demonstrated by Barak's decision to freeze the implementation of all interim agreements with the Palestinians arising from the Oslo-Wye accords—among them a partial redeployment of Israeli troops on the West Bank, Palestinian control over three villages near Jerusalem, and the release of pre-1993 prisoners—in favor of a comprehensive, permanent-status agreement. Instead, Barak chose to make an agreement with Syria his first priority, for two reasons. First, such an accord looked relatively simple compared to the emotionally loaded negotiations with the Palestinians. Second, Barak foresaw that isolating the Palestinian leadership through a separate agreement with Syria might force the Palestinians to agree to sign a final settlement on his terms. When the Shepherdstown talks with Syria foundered over a few meters of land along the edge of the Sea of Galilee that were due for demilitarization in any case—Barak's hesitation here was probably caused by anxiety over Syrian access to Lake Kinneret, Israel's main water reservoir—Barak decided to withdraw from Lebanon without an agreement. The withdrawal was considered Barak's only achievement, but because the Israeli-Lebanese border was unsecured, the local Shiite militia, Hezbollah, could launch hundreds of missiles over northern Israel during the so-called Second Lebanese war. Only in the summer of 2000, when the end of President William Clinton's tenure and (retrospectively) his own drew near, did Barak finally find time to hold talks with the Palestinians.

Meanwhile, the Palestinian leadership had been begging for concessions—especially the release of prisoners, the most painful issue for their people—to ease the pressure on it from below. On the one hand, the Palestinian Authority was expected to prevent the creation of parallel and competing Palestinian militias, to behave "like Ben-Gurion" in the "Altalena affair," when he ordered an Ezel Revisionist ship loaded with smuggled weapons to be sunk in 1948, a command that caused uproar among the Jewish population. On the other hand, the Palestinian Authority was unable to provide its people with any sign of success as an incentive to supporting it over rival armed groups. As Israeli intelligence services warned that the Palestinian Authority's control was weakening and Hamas and the Islamic Jihad gaining strength, Barak insisted that there would be no release of prisoners "with blood on their hands" or territorial concessions until a final status agreement had been reached.[43]

By the summer of 2000, the seeds of mutual mistrust between Arafat and Barak had already been sown. Central negotiations conducted at Camp David were preceded by innumerable talks at all levels, but they were unproductive. Arafat was opposed a priori to Barak's approach of freezing the third, more extensive troop withdrawal and other previous Israeli commitments, and moving to talks on the conditions for a final comprehensive settlement. But he still had nothing to show to an increasingly restive Palestinian populace as the fruit of the Oslo accords. All the cards were in Israel's hands, and Arafat had no alternative but to agree to take part in the Camp David talks.

The Camp David Talks

The initial Israeli proposal transmitted to Clinton was quite detailed. The Palestinians were to be offered an 80:20 division of territory: 80 percent of the West Bank and Gaza Strip would be under the control and sovereignty of the Palestinian state and 20 percent annexed to Israel. Israel's 20 percent included seven settlement blocs comprising around 80 percent of the Jewish settler population. Additionally, a viaduct would be built to link the Gaza Strip and West Bank. Earlier, the possibility of Israel holding a long-term lease on an additional 10 percent of the West Bank along the Jordan Valley, for security reasons, had also been discussed. The right of return would be recognized only with respect to the Palestinian state. Israel would help to rehabilitate the refugees, but it would not accept any moral or legal responsibility for creating the refugee problem.

The municipal boundaries of Jerusalem would be expanded, apparently annexing Abu Dis, Azariya, and a few other villages and townlets, so there would be, nominally, something to share. The intention was to leave most of the current area of the city under Israeli sovereignty, selling the additional territory to the Palestinians as their Jerusalem. A bypass road would then be paved around East Jerusalem to allow worshippers to reach the holy shrine of Haram al-Sharif, the Islamic Noble Sanctuary and Jewish Temple Mount.

The Palestinians, from their perspective, had already made the ultimate concession by recognizing Israel's legitimate right to exist and thus were without bargaining chips.[44] After the additional concessions, many Palestinians, mostly outside the country, accused Arafat and Fatah of treason.[45] In the Oslo agreements, the Palestinian delegation had recognized Israel's right to exist in 78 percent of historical Palestine in the hope that, following the peace agreements with Egypt and Jordan and on the basis of the Arab interpretation of Security Council Resolutions 242 and 338, which call for withdrawal from territories occupied in 1967, they might recover the remainder with minor border adjustments. However, even though there was a certain slackening of Israeli demands, talks continued concerning annexing another 12 percent or so of the West Bank to create three settlement blocs, dividing the Palestinian state into separate cantons with very problematic connections between them.

Arafat, who was aware of the coordinated American-Israeli position, came unwillingly to the summit. The Palestinians felt that they were being dragged to the verdant hills of Maryland to be jointly pressured by an Israeli prime minister and an American president who, because of their separate political timetables and concerns about their legacies, had a personal sense of urgency.[46] The Americans repeatedly told the Palestinians that the Israeli leader's coalition was unstable; after a while, they said, the goal of the summit meeting seemed to be as much about rescuing Barak as making peace.

Thus, most of the Palestinian delegation decided in advance to adopt a futile bunker strategy of automatically refusing any proposal.

Arafat's suspicions were confirmed when the short-fused Clinton launched a crude attack on him, impugning his honor.[47] In his account of the Camp David meetings, Barak's foreign minister, Shlomo Ben-Ami, has remarked that the episode reflected the extent to which Arafat was a prisoner of his own myths. What the incident really shows is the extent to which each side was sunk in myths of its own. This is apparently the chief reason why the talks ultimately fell apart over the status of the Temple Mount, even though the Palestinians had already agreed to divide the city and Israeli sovereignty over the Western Wall in exchange for control over the land containing the mosques and the city's Arab neighborhoods.

During the talks, Barak agreed to be flexible about Israeli proposals on various issues and was close to conceding over 92 percent of the West Bank's territory. However, each proposal and each issue was discussed individually, and it was stressed that until everything had been agreed upon, nothing was agreed. Thus, the Palestinians were made discrete offers in many different areas, mainly out of the certainty that all would be rejected outright regardless, while the Palestinians—or so it was reported at the time—made no counter-proposals. Afterward, Barak could group together all of the separate instances and claim that he had made an incomparably generous offer to the Palestinians.

When the summit failed and the remnants of his government fell to pieces, Barak made his fateful declaration that there was "no partner" on the Palestinian side of peace talks. Clinton—also out of a decidedly personal interest—was true to his promise and backed him up. There were further so-called non-talks and non-papers in Taba, where, according to some sources, the parties came closer to agreement than ever before. As far as Barak and Arafat were concerned, however, the game at Camp David was over. After Taba, it was only a matter of time before armed conflict erupted.

The Roadmap

After seven years of futile negotiations failed to advance significantly the Palestinian cause and the Jewish colonization process in the occupied Palestinian territories intensified, the question was not whether but when anger and violence would erupt, and in what form. The Palestinians were aware of the asymmetry in the power relations with Israel, but they changed the paradigm. From an attempt to end the occupation and achieve independence that relied upon diplomatic efforts and depended on the kindness of the Jews and Americans, they moved on to a war for independence. Fueled in part by religious emotions, the struggle became one in which the people were prepared to pay a high personal and collective price to achieve what they saw as a paramount objective.

In this respect, Sharon's provocative visit to the Temple Mount in 2000 was only the match that ignited the stores of fuel that Peres, Netanyahu, and Barak had amassed. Barak had paved the way for Sharon's victory in February 2001 with an unprecedented 52 percent of the vote. The shift was historically reinforced by the general election of January 2003, in which the right wing bloc secured 69 out of 120 Knesset seats and Sharon became the first Israeli prime minister to win a second term since Menachem Begin had done so in 1981.

As Chapter Twelve describes, Israel under Sharon became oriented towards one major goal: the politicide of the Palestinian people. Politicide covers a wide range of social, psychological, political, and military activities designed to destroy the political and national viability of an entire community of people. Its ultimate aim is to destroy a certain people's prospects—indeed, their very will—for legitimate self-determination and sovereignty over land they consider their homeland. It is a reversal of the process suggested by Woodrow Wilson at the end of World War I and since then accepted as a standard international principle. The most commonly used techniques of politicide are expropriation and colonization of land; restrictions on spatial mobility, such as curfews, closures, and roadblocks; murder; mass detentions; the division or elimination of leaders and elite groups; hindrance of regular education and schooling and reeducation; physical destruction of public institutions, infrastructure, private homes, and property; starvation; and social and political isolation. Typically, such actions are taken in the name of law and order; a key aim in the struggle is to acquire the power to define one's own side as enforcing the law and the other as criminals and terrorists. An alternative goal may be to establish a puppet regime that is completely obedient but provides an illusion of self-determination to the oppressed ethnic community.

However, the hard facts are that a Palestinian people exists and it will be almost impossible to commit politicide against it without fatal consequences for Israel. That said, Israel is not only an established presence in the region, but also, in local terms, a military, economic, and technological superpower. Like many other immigrant-settler societies, it was born in sin, on the ruins of another culture that had suffered politicide and partial ethnic cleansing—although the Zionist state did not succeed in annihilating the rival indigenous culture, as many other immigrant-settler societies have done. In 1948, it lacked the power to do so, and the strength of postcolonial sentiment at the time made such actions less internationally acceptable. Unlike the indigenous peoples in Algeria, Zambia, or South Africa, however, the Palestinians were unable to overthrow their colonizers. The Jewish state in the Middle East succeeded in proving its viability and developing its own vital society and culture. Its long-term development and internal normalcy depend, however, on its recognition as a legitimate entity by the other peoples of the region. The peace accord signed with Egypt was, in this sense, Zionism's second greatest victory. Its greatest was the Oslo agreement, in which the Zionist movement's primary victim and adversary recognized the right of a Jewish state to exist in Palestine. Just as Sadat's treaty with Begin was a delayed result of Israeli victory in the 1967 and 1973 wars, the revolutionary change in mainstream Palestinian political thought occurred in the aftermath of American victory in the Gulf War of 1991.[48]

Similarly, the George W. Bush administration issued its new roadmap for Israel in the run-up to its invasion of Iraq. Its goal was to close down all armed resistance to Israel in exchange for the establishment, within temporary borders, of an entity described as a Palestinian state by the end of 2003.[49] This was to be followed by the withdrawal of Israeli forces from Palestinian Authority territories and elections for a new Palestinian Council, leading to negotiations with Israel on a permanent agreement to be reached by 2005. The so-called quartet of the United States, European Union, United Nations, and Russia was supposed to supervise the plan's implementation, leaving all of the matters in dispute—the borders, refugees, and status of Jerusalem, among others—open. This strategy fit well with Sharon's tactic of buying time to continue his politicidal policy, a tactic that rests on the assumption that Palestinian terrorist attacks will continue, drawing forth a correspondingly savage Israeli military response.

The opinions of both communities during this period were attested to by a public opinion poll conducted in early December 2002. More than seven out of ten Palestinians and Israelis indicated that they were ready to undertake a settlement process based on the Palestinians refraining from violence and the Israelis agreeing to a Palestinian state within the 1967 borders. Less than one in five Palestinians and Israelis—in both cases the percentages were remarkably similar—were committed to the idea of regaining historic Palestine or holding on to the occupied territories. However, a large proportion of both the Palestinian and Israeli majorities expressed no confidence in the readiness of the other side to give up violence or make the necessary concessions. Thus, the bulk of Palestinians continued to support using violent methods in the intifada, while a similar proportion of Israelis continued to favor a violent crackdown by the Israeli military.

An able map reader, Sharon found the new Bush plan very convenient. In a speech on July 4, 2002, he outlined a clear vision of how he thought the conflict should be managed. By implementing the roadmap, Israel could create a contiguous area of territory in the West Bank, which, through a combination of tunnels and bridges, would allow Palestinians to travel from Jenin to Hebron without passing through any Israeli roadblocks or checkpoints. Israel would undertake measures such as "creating territorial continuity between Palestinian population centers"—that is, withdrawing from cities such as Jenin, Nablus and Hebron—as long as the Palestinians remained engaged in making a "sincere and real effort to stop terror." Then, after the required reforms in the Palestinian Authority had been completed, the next phase of the Bush plan would come into effect: establishing a Palestinian state within "provisional" borders.

The intention was obvious. The Palestinian state, formed by four enclaves around Jenin, Nablus, Hebron, and the Gaza Strip, would lack territorial contiguity. The plan to connect the enclaves with tunnels and bridges meant that a strong Israeli presence would exist in most other areas of the West Bank. To drive the point home, Sharon added:

> This Palestinian state will be completely demilitarized. It will be allowed to maintain lightly armed police and internal forces to ensure civil order. Israel will continue to control all movement in and out of the Palestinian state, will command its airspace, and not allow it to form alliances with Israel's enemies.[50]

Sharon knew very well that it would be virtually impossible for a Palestinian leader to end the conflict in exchange for such limited sovereignty and territory. However, the very mention of the code words "Palestinian state"—taboo in the right wing lexicon—endowed him with an image of moderation abroad and positioned him at the center of the domestic political spectrum. Such gestures also won him an almost unlimited amount of time to continue his program of politicide. It is not clear how much of Sharon's political legacy will survive his departure from public life, especially as his successors lack his charisma, and leadership crises have hindered their ability to implement his agenda.

Palestinian Leadership Crisis

Arafat's death on November 11, 2004 and the election on January 10, 2005 of Mahmoud Abbas as his successor does not alter any basic Middle Eastern realities. Abbas cannot give up the principles framed by Arafat, the Palestinian National Council, and the consensus that demanded a Palestinian state within the borders existing prior to the 1967 war. By calling for a state within these borders, the Palestinian leadership has signaled its willingness to relinquish its claims to all of historic Palestine and settle for 22 percent of the original territory. In addition to a state with East Jerusalem as its capital, the Palestinians demand the release of all prisoners from Israeli jails and detention camps and the right of return, at least in principle, for Palestinian refugees who fled or were uprooted from the territories under Israeli sovereignty since 1948.

In the aftermath of the Anglo-American invasion of Iraq and the glaring failure to find any weapons of mass destruction, Washington attempted to burnish its image as a peace maker by pushing its roadmap again. The Western media has turned its attention to the *hudna,* or truce agreement, by the leaders of Hamas, Islamic Jihad, and the Palestinian Authority, but few have remarked on the precise wording of Israel's May 26, 2003 statement regarding the plan, which declared: "the Government of Israel resolves that all of Israel's comments, as addressed in the [Bush] Administration's statement, will be implemented in full during the implementation phase of the Road Map." In other words, Israel did not accept the map itself, but the fourteen conditions and reservations, each quite separate from the content of the original document. This allowed Sharon to say that he adopted his own version of the roadmap, giving Bush the chance to issue a statement about a "positive step" and come to the Aqaba summit for a photo opportunity.

The Israeli conditions, however, were based on an incorrect perception of the causality and logic of the conflict: the presumption that the root of the violence lies in Palestinian terrorism, rather than in Israel's generation-long occupation and illegal colonization of Palestinian lands and its exploitation and harassment of an entire people. Thus, the initial Israeli condition stated: "'In the first phase of the plan and as a condition for progress to the second phase, the Palestinians will complete the dismantling of terrorist organizations and their infrastructure, collect all illegal weapons and transfer them to a third party." Were the document's framers to adopt a more accurate perspective on the historical and political causalities, they would propose the prompt termination of occupation and withdrawal of Israeli military forces to the pre-1967 borders as the first rather than the last phase of the process. Under such conditions, it would then make sense to demand that the sovereign Palestinian state cease its resistance against a nonexistent occupation and act, gradually but forcefully, against terrorist organizations that might endanger its own authority or stability.

Finally, Bush's roadmap includes two contradictory demands on the Palestinians as preconditions for a settlement. They are to establish an authoritarian regime to fight dissident terror organizations, but they also must democratize their polity. Again, the understanding of the causality needs to be reversed if the plan is not to be simply a hypocritical pretext for avoiding any agreement. A settlement itself, with popular backing, might be the best means to accelerate the democratization of all parties involved. Without such adaptations, the roadmap merely points the way to the continued politicide of the Palestinian people under the umbrella of a Pax Americana.

Sharon had two aims in the talks over the roadmap. The first aim was the de facto (and later de jure) expansion of Israeli borders by annexing the major settlement blocs and the hinterlands in their vicinity. The second aim was to fragment the remaining territory populated by the Palestinians to prevent the creation of a viable Palestinian state alongside Israel—this time under the umbrella of peaceful steps ("to end the occupation") while gaining support from the international community and mainly the United States. In May 2004, the prime minister managed to keep his plans on track by gaining support from the Labor party and other, smaller parties, under the guise of maintaining Israel's identity as a Jewish state and avoiding the creation of a de facto binational entity. Labor supported this aspect of Sharon's policy when it was both inside and outside the government coalition.

Sharon's approach was a real strategic change. Until then, the view that prevailed in pragmatic circles, both dovish and hawkish, was that determining Israeli and Palestinian borders would be part of the final phase of agreements that ended the conflict, as happened when Israel concluded peace agreements with Egypt and Jordan. Sharon's approach, which apparently won the support of the majority of Israeli Jews, conveniently separated reaching a peace agreement from establishing final borders, even an illusion of established, final borders. The policy has worked for three reasons: Israeli despair over achieving a peace agreement in the near future; the subjective perception that the separation—that is, the fence—increases security; and the desire to achieve the functional equivalent of the desired ethnic cleansing, or transfer, in Israeli parlance, by separating Israel from the Arabs.

This approach smashed to smithereens the ideology of Greater Israel and knocked the Eretz Israel ideological and political infrastructure out from under the feet of Jewish fundamentalism. This in itself has merit, although Jewish fundamentalists have not yet had their final say. However, there is no doubt that a unilateral and coerced determination of borders, even with the support of the United States, will lead to the escalation and deepening of the conflict. The Palestinians, led either by Fatah or Hamas, will become even more frustrated by such land grabbing and increasingly motivated to fight Israel. Such fenced borders would not improve the security of Israeli citizens.

Hamas

Palestine's new leading political party, Hamas, or the Islamic Resistance Movement, was founded in 1978 and is closely related to the Egyptian Muslim Brotherhood. It seeks to establish an Islamic state in the entire area of historic Palestine and rejects any Jewish claim whatsoever to the land of Palestine. To create an Islamic state, Hamas claimed the right to conduct an armed struggle, or holy war (*jihad*), against the Jewish state established on holy Islamic lands (*waqf*). Hamas is considered a terrorist group by most of the Western world and, naturally, Israel. Its indiscriminate attacks on Israeli civilians and other human rights violations have been condemned by nearly all human right organizations. During the al-Aqsa intifada, Hamas took responsibility for the majority of the suicide bombings in Israel and later for the Qassam rockets that targeted localities in southern Israel. These attacks began even before the massacre in the Patriarchs' Cave.[51]

The movement is popular in part because it provides welfare and social services to the Palestinian poor—it is involved in building community centers, nurseries, schools, and hospitals, and fighting drug dealers—but mainly because it continues its struggle against Israel and argues that Fatah's accommodation with Israel was a betrayal. Hamas is well funded and known to make generous payments to the families of holy martyrs (*shahids*) and suicide bombers. It is also popular because its leadership is not thought to be as corrupt as Fatah's.[52]

Hamas has demonstrated some pragmatism in the past. On January 26, 2004, it offered a ten-year truce (*hudna*) conditioned on Israel's complete withdrawal from the territories captured in the 1967 war and the establishment of a Palestinian state. Hamas leader Sheikh Ahmed Yassin stated that the group could accept a Palestinian state in the West Bank and Gaza Strip. Abdel Aziz Rantissi confirmed that Hamas had concluded that it would accept a phased liberation because it could not liberate all of what it considered to be its land. Israel responded by assassinating Yassin and Rantissi in 2004. These assassinations and others only strengthened the image of Hamas as a hero of the Palestinian resistance and liberation movement. It is perhaps ironic that Israeli secret services helped establish Hamas as a counterweight to Fatah, believing that a religious movement was more convenient for Israel than a national one. At any rate, the possible transformation of Hamas from a terror group to a ruling political party will be lengthy, both because internal differences need to be resolved and because there will no doubt be a power struggle with Fatah, which will not relinquish control easily.

Concluding Words

A conflict is an integral system in which at least two interdependent actors participate, with additional indirect partners in concentric circles around the core partners, including in many cases players from the entire world system. In the Israeli-Palestinian case, these outlying players in the conflict, with different involvement and influence, are the United States and European Union, the Arab states, the Islamic world—including Iran, with its imperial aspirations—Russia, American Jewry, the Palestinian Diaspora, and others.[53] Neither the two core players nor the other involved parties are homogeneous entities, as they consist of many groups with different identities and contradictory interests.

New Palestinian identities and sub-identities have been created since 1967, both in Palestine and abroad. These identities have passed through several forms, which have varied from place to place, in a relatively short time. The return of the Palestinian leadership, which had been in exile from the territory since 1938, provided hope and pride, but was accompanied by the painful renunciation of more than 78 percent of the initially desired territory. Ceding this territory was followed by a harsh controversy within the global Palestinian society over whether this was just a tactical surrender or a historical compromise. It created a deep schism within Palestinian society, a division between some versions of Western modernism (represented by the city of Ramallah), traditionalism, relatively moderate Islam (as represented by the ancient towns of al-Khallil and Hebron), and fundamentalist Islam (mainly in the Gaza Strip). As the disappointment with the relatively modernist and secularist nationalist model deepened, the Palestinians moved toward an Islamist collective identity. These internal conflicts were worsened by the Fatah leadership's incompetence, corruption, use of excessive power in internal matters, and ideological divisions between the old guard imported from Tunis and the local new guard that led the first intifada and is most connected to the local inhabitants.

Under Arafat, Fatah failed to transform itself from a guerrilla movement to a sociopolitical ruling party operating according to the minimal rules of the democratic game. Fatah's constituency aspired to build a regime close to that of the Israeli open society, possessing the various human and civil rights they enviously perceived it as having.[54] Of course, wishing to adopt the Israeli model rather than the Arab states' despotic and authoritarian models did not ameliorate the enmity they felt toward the Israeli state.

The Israeli collective identity continues to oscillate between its primordial and civil components, and as a result, violent riots—close to a limited civil war—erupt from time to time. The Israeli legislative system tried to bridge the gap between the two basic contradictory models of identities by defining Israel as a Jewish and democratic state, which is an oxymoron when Judaism is mainly regarded as a religion or an ethno-religious term.[55] The Jewish character of the state is exhibited by Israeli marriage laws, which are administered exclusively by Jewish religious authorities, and courts that operate under different values from those adopted by any other modern state, violating basic principles of democracy and equality. For some religious authorities, democracy is not a Jewish value, but a disgraceful Hellenistic, anti-Jewish, Western concept, although it may be used if it serves the authorities' interests.

However, for most Israelis, democracy, or at least a partial and formal democracy, is a very important component of the collective identity. Many Palestinian elite groups desire it as well, regardless of their attitudes toward Israel. The term "democracy" has neither a conclusive theoretical definition nor an agreed-upon set of empirical manifestations.[56] According to all existing definitions, no actual political regime can be classified as a complete or pure democracy, but rather is located on a continuum between the two poles of democracy and authoritarianism. Multiple paths to democracy exist, but the protracted conflict with the Palestinians is moving the Israeli immigrant-settler state farther away from any ideal type of democratic state.

Israel's forty-year occupation of the West Bank and Gaza Strip created deep changes in both Israeli and Palestinian collective or national identities, as well as in the very content and political behavior and culture of both polities. The geographical proximity of the land and people being occupied, as well as the intimate yet asymmetrical interactions between members of the two groups, have also shaped the identities of both peoples and the internal structures of their societies.

The conflict presented in this volume has many facets, including identities and symbols, prestige, territories, and economic issues within and between the societies. Both the Israelis and Palestinians have passed through several critical historical phases and thresholds within a relatively short period of time, and each group's societal developments have shaped not only its own side but the other as well, although the counter-partner's reaction was either delayed or not immediately visible.

Chronology of Major Events

1200 BCE   According to Jewish mythology, the ancient Israelites, led by Joshua, conquer part of the Land of Canaan, annihilating most of the local inhabitants of the country and establishing the territorial base for a semi-monotheistic religion and civilization as well as a tiny regional empire. This land later becomes known as Palestine, named by the Romans after the Philistines, who settled the coastal plain of the country in 1190 BC and were annihilated by King David in a series of bitter battles. In the modern day, some Palestinians are trying to construct a counter-myth referring to themselves as the remnant of the pre-conquest Philistine population.[1]

1075 BCE   Following the collapse of the Assyrian world, power is supposedly built up under the reign of Kings David and Solomon. The inhabitants are forcefully deported and have ceased to exist as a recognizable group.

587 BCE   Nebuchadnezzar II destroys Jerusalem, the capital of Judea, sending a considerable part of the Judean population—mainly the elite and artisans—into Babylonian exile. In Babylon, the Judeans develop a desire to return. When Cyrus of Persia gains control over the ancient world, the Judeans return to Zion, a synonym for Jerusalem and the Land of Israel, and rebuild the second Temple of Yahweh in 550 BC.

168 BCE   The Judean polity rises again amid struggles between rival candidates for the Jerusalem priesthood and attempts to Hellenize the religious cult. A peasant revolt against the Jerusalem elite and their Seleucid

---

1. For the Hebrew Scriptures as mythology, see, T.L. Thompson. *The Mythic Past: Biblical Archaeology and the Myth of Israel* (London: Random House Basic, 1999).

patrons takes place. The military leader of the revolt, Judah the Maccabee, turns the revolt into a guerrilla civil war, which the Judeans eventually win. His clan takes over the Jerusalem priesthood and, in alliance with the Roman Empire, conquer large territories, converting their populations to Judaism. Quarrels among the Maccabean dynasty lead Rome to crown the Idumaean Herod as King of Judea.

66–135 CE A series of Judean rebellions against the Hellenistic and Roman rulers occur, and the Romans destroy the Second Temple. In 135, the Jewish elites are again exiled, effectively destroying the Jewish polity; the Romans then divide the territory, renaming it as Philistine Prima (Primary Palestine) and Philistine Seconda (Secondary Palestine). Christianity separates itself from Judaism and spreads among the Roman underclass and slave populations. By 391 CE, Christianity has survived countless persecutions to become the dominant religion of the Roman Empire.

70–200 Judaism itself undergoes a major transformation when Rabbi Yohanan Ben Zakai establish a new center in the Judean town of Yavneh, redefining Judaism as a religion as opposed to the previous proto-nationalist orientations. Over the next 130 years, Rabbi Judah and his successors develop the Mishnah, codifying Jewish religious law in the Greco-Roman Diaspora.

500 The Babylonian Talmud, the written codification of Jewish oral law by the Sages of Babylon, is compiled into one body of knowledge dealing with all aspects of behavior required of Jews; its style is influenced by the Platonic dialogues. The Talmud is composed of parts of the Mishnah and the Babylonian Gemara. It is a synopsis of more than three hundred years of analysis of the Mishnah in the Babylonian academies. Tradition ascribes the initial editing of the Babylonian Talmud to two Babylonian sages, Rav Ashi and Ravina. Sages in academies—mainly Tiberias and Caesaria—did a similar project, but the Jerusalemian Talmud is considered inferior.

620 According to Muslim mythology, in one night, Muhammad travels from Mecca to "the furthest mosque," identified as the Temple Mount in Jerusalem, the site of the Dome of the Rock, from which Muhammad ascended into heaven.

630–4 (cir.) In the deserts of Arabia, a new culture and religion, Islam, comes into being when a military leader named Muhammad defeats the city of Mecca at the battle of Badr (630 CE). Muhammad establishes Mecca as the center of the new religion, with himself as prophet. His successors, the Khalifs Abu Bakr and Umar, conquer the Fertile Crescent.

635–37 The Arab tribes capture Jerusalem from the Byzantines, making the province of Palestina Prima into a military district (*jund*) of Filastin; Arabization and Islamization of the region.

641 Arabs conquer Byzantine Egypt.

661 Muawiya, the founder of Umayyad dynasty, proclaims himself caliph in Jerusalem but rules from Damascus, his capital.

685–705 Caliph Abd al-Malik builds the Dome of the Rock to emphasize the holiness of the city, in opposition to his rival who controls Mecca and Medina.

705–715 His son Walid builds the al-Aqsa mosque in Jerusalem.

711–1492 Moslem conquest of the Iberian peninsula (al Andalus); establishment of the Caliphate of Córdoba and its successor kingdoms, and creation of a great and tolerant Islamic culture, developing poetry, philosophy, mathematics, medicine, architecture, astronomy, etc. Jews are full partners (as a privileged minority, *dhimmi*) in developing an Arab-Jewish culture; the period is known in Jewish historiography as The Golden Age.

715–717 Suleiman, the seventh Umayyad Caliph, builds Ramleh as his residence.

1095 The famous scholar Abu Hamid al-Ghazali, from Nizamiyya Academy of Baghdad, resides in Jerusalem, where he begins work on his volume *The Revivification of the Science of Religion,* one of the major works of Islamic theology.

1099–1187 Crusaders invade Palestine and establish the Latin Kingdom of Jerusalem; major massacres of the Arab and Jewish populations of the territory.

1187 Salah al-Din (Saladin) reconquers Jerusalem and creates a new Islamic dynasty; the Ayubidis rule over a part of the region.

1236 Iberia is gradually regained by Christians fighting from northern regions of Spain (the Reconquista); the last Islamic stronghold of Granada falls to the Christian forces of Ferdinand III of Castile.

1260 In the battle of Ayn Jalut (Nazareth) the Egyptian-based Mamluks defeat the Mongol hordes of Hulagu (the grandson of Genghis Khan) and overcome the remaining Crusader fortifications.

1260–1515 The region is under the rule of the Mamluk military caste and its sultans after it deposes the Ayubid dynasty.

June 1492 Partial cleaning of Spain and Portugal from non-Christian inhabitants; expulsion or forced conversion to Christianity of hundreds of thousands of Muslim Moors and Jews and their spread all over the known world, mainly among Muslim lands; appearance of the Spaniard Jewish (Sephardic) subculture.

1515–1917 During the rule of Suleiman the Magnificent (1520–1566), the old city of Jerusalem is walled. With some interruptions, the country is incorporated into Turkish Ottoman rule.

1665 A self-appointed messiah named Shabbtai Zvi appears and provokes mass hysteria among hundreds of thousands of Jews, from the territories of the Ottoman Empire to Poland and Eastern Europe and even to many parts of Western Europe, by proclaiming the Day of Redemption to be June 18, 1666. Despite the opposition of most prominent rabbis, the Jews are ready to march as a mighty army and restore the godly kingdom of David on earth. Eventually, the Ottomans interpret the millenarian movement as a rebellion and put the messiah in jail, where he converts to Islam.

1798 Napoleonic campaign in Egypt; battle of the Nile.

1799 Ahmad al-Jazzar, the governor of Acre, turns back the French army, gaining control over most of Palestine.

1808 Muslim revolt in Jerusalem against the Ottoman governor; more power for local families.

1826 Second rebellion of the Jerusalem Muslims; Christians and Jews attacked.

1830 Ibrahim Pasha, the Ottoman governor, gains considerable control and autonomy over the country.

1831–40 Egyptian conquest of the region, including Palestine, and its incorporation into the Egyptian state.

1834 Major revolt of the region against the Egyptians, focused mainly in Palestine.

1839 Proclamation of a program of reorganization in the Ottoman Empire.

1854–56 Crimean War.

1856 Reform in the Ottoman Empire with a more detailed statement than in 1839, followed by land tenure changes.

1860–61 Intercommunal rifts in Lebanon and Syria.

1861–65 Civil War in the United States.

1863 Creation of the municipality of Jerusalem under Ottoman law, first nucleus of modern local government.

1868–75 Ottoman civil code adopted.

1876 Ottoman Constitution.

1881–82 Pogroms in Eastern Europe against the Jews; Arab revolt in Egypt; British occupation of Egypt.

1882–1904 First wave of modern Jewish settlers immigrate to Palestine.

1878 Establishment of Petah Tikvah, the first Jewish modern colony in Palestine.

1891 Ahad Ha'am (Asher Ginzberg) publishes his article "Truth from Eretz Israel [Palestine]," warning his fellow Jews of the danger of ignoring Arabs' feelings in Palestine.

1892 Establishment of Palestinian branches of Credit Lyonnais in Jaffa and Jerusalem.

1897 First Zionist Congress launches the Basel Program to resettle the Jewish people in Palestine and establish the World Zionist Organization.

1899–1902 Arab-Jewish tension following large Jewish land purchases in the Tiberias region.

1904-14 Second wave of Jewish immigration; Jews demand exclusive use of Jewish labor in Jewish colonies and in Zionist-funded enterprises.

1905 Nagib Azouri publishes his *Le reveil de la nation arabe,* envisioning the conflict between the Arab and Jewish major national movements in the Middle East.

1907 Yitzhak Epstein, a Hebrew teacher from Galilee, publishes an essay in *Shiload* warning the Zionist settlers that uprooting Arab tenants from the land will cause hatred against the colonization and promote the crystallization of a common Arab consciousness that will turn against the Jewish settlement.

1908 Appearance of the first Palestinian newspaper in Haifa, *al-Karmil,* with the major aim of fighting against land transfers from Arab to Jewish ownership. Young Turks revolution in Istanbul. Palestinian delegates, elected to the Ottoman parliament, warn against the Judification of the country, frequent tension between Arabs and Jews.

1911 *Filastin,* a large Arabic newspaper, is launched in Jaffa.

1914 World War I breaks out.

1915–16 Correspondence between the British high commissioner in Egypt (Henry McMahon) and Sharif Hussein of Mecca leads to agreement between the British and the Arabs on establishing an Arab kingdom in the Middle East in exchange for an Arab military revolt against the Ottomans; the Arabs believe that the Arab kingdom includes Palestine.

1916 Secret Anglo-French agreement to divide Ottoman Middle East provinces (Sykes-Picot agreement).

June 1916 Hussein proclaims Arab independence and revolts against the Ottomans.

1917 Ottoman forces in Jerusalem surrender to British forces. The Balfour Declaration: Britain support for establishment of a "Jewish national home" in Palestine.

1918 All of Palestine occupied by British forces. End of World War I; Treaty of Versailles and League of Nations Covenant approved; General Arab (Syrian) Congress held in Damascus, including prominent Palestinians, rejects the Balfour Declaration and considers Palestine part of southern Syria.

1919 Arab Literary Club and Arab Club founded to propagate Arab nationalism. British appoint Kamil al-Husseini as Grand Mufti of Jerusalem. A new Muslim hierarchy emerges in Istanbul.

1919–20 Muslim-Christian associations formed countrywide, protesting against the Balfour Declaration and claiming Palestine as part of Syria.

1920 As part of Arab unrest in Syria against the French, Arab rebels attack two Jewish settlements in northern Palestine. Faysal proclaims the independence of Greater Syria and himself as king; the revolt is suppressed by French troops. Faysal's proclamation excites the Arab population of Palestine; riots in Jerusalem and Jaffa following the Nabi Musa festival; some notables arrested by the British; Amin al-Husseini's flight; Musa Kazim al-Husseini, the mayor of Jerusalem, replaced by Raghib al-Nashashibi.

First Palestinian National Congress meets in Haifa, constituted from delegates from Muslim-Christian associations and other notables; the congress nominates the Arab Executive Committee, which is perceived (and recognized de facto) by the British as the political leadership and representative of the Arab community in Palestine until 1935; the Congress demands independence as well as an immediate halt to Jewish immigration and land acquisition.

San Remo Peace Conference assigns Britain the mandate over Palestine

1921 Riots in Jaffa; Arabs kill forty-six Jews; a British commission of inquiry attributes the disturbances to Arab anxiety about increasing Jewish immigration. Amin al-Husseini is appointed Mufti of Jerusalem and pardoned by High Commissioner Herbert Samuel.

1922 Creation of the Supreme Muslim Council to fill the vacuum left by the end of Islamic Ottoman rule; Amin al-Husseini elected president of the Council. Britain issues a White Paper emphasizing that only a part of Palestine is considered to be the Jewish national home, excluding East Palestine (Transjordan) from the Mandate.

1925 Establishment of Palestinian Workers' Society (PAWS) as a moderate trade union movement led by Sami Taha.

1927 Municipal elections end in a resounding Nashashibi-led opposition victory.

1929 Countrywide riots against Jews, including the massacre of many members of the old non-Zionist community of Hebron, following fears and rumors of Jewish intentions to gain control over the Western Wall; Arab Women's Congress in Jerusalem adopts strong nationalist positions.

1930 The Arab Bank established by the Abd al-Hamid Shuman family, competing with Barclays.

1931 Pan-Islamic Congress held in Jerusalem, attended by 145 delegates from the Muslim world, reinforces Amin al-Husseini's position as an Islamic leader.

1932–36 Waves of middle class, persecuted Jewish immigrants from Germany and Poland change the social and economic fabric of Jewish Palestine.

1932 National Congress of Arab Youth convened in Jaffa; anti-British riots provoked by Arab nationalist groups.

Formation of the first modern Palestinian political party, the Istiqlal ("Independence"); strong pan-Islamic ideology and revival of the idea of Palestine as a natural part of southern Syria; creation of additional quasi-parties: Palestine Arab party (Husseinis), National Defense party (the opposition, or the Nashashibis), and Reform party (Khalidis).

1933 Establishment of the Arab Agricultural Bank to grant loans to *fellaheen*. Starting in the 1940s, it is called the Bank of the Arab Nation.

Meetings of some Palestinian leaders—Musa Alami, Awni Abd al-Hadi, and George Antonius—with the just-appointed chair of the Jewish Agency, David Ben-Gurion, in an attempt to find some accommodation between the contrasting demands of the two national movements; no understanding achieved. Arab Executive Committee declares a general strike and mass demonstrations are held in the major cities; the protest is directed solely against British rule, demanding independence, immediate halt of Jewish immigration and land acquisition, and establishment of a local government based on proportional representation. British police and troops suppress the protest movement.

1935 Sheikh Izz al-Din al-Qassam, leader of a small Islamic guerrilla group and considered to be the first Palestinian *shahid,* or martyr, killed by British forces.

1936 Following minor clashes with Jews, Palestinian national committees are established in all towns and some villages; the Jerusalem committee adopts the slogan "No taxation without representation." Some local leaders call for a general strike, forcefully implemented by the mob. All Arab political parties and organizations merged into the Arab Higher Committee, led by Amin al-Husseini; waves of violence; the British lose control over the country despite reinforcements, and the Great Arab Revolt breaks out.

A Syrian officer, Fawzi al-Qa'uqji, enters Palestine, leading volunteers from Arab countries to conduct guerrilla warfare against the British.

The Arab 175-day general strike exhausts the Arab economy. A general strike occurs in Syria against French rule; the French promise to consider granting independence.

1937 The 175-days Palestinian general strike ends with the appointment of a Royal Committee of Inquiry known as the Peel Commission. Different British inquiry commissions have made several inquiries since British rule over Palestine was established, particularly after riots. Most of the commissions found Jewish land purchases and immigration to be the major reason for Arab unrest. After each report was published, new regulations and laws were issued to restrict the purchase of land and to limit immigration to the absorption capacity of the country, usually quantified by the rate of unemployment. The Peel Commission goes further by recommending partition of the territory between the Arabs and Jews and the establishment of a Jewish state, an Arab state, linked with the Transjordan Emirate, and an international enclave, a corridor between Jaffa and Jerusalem that includes Bethlehem. Both the Arabs and the Jews reject the partition proposal.

1938 Insurgence and counterinsurgence escalate; thousands of *fellaheen* join guerrilla rebel forces; Amin al-Husseini establishes the Central Committee of the National Jihad and the Council of Rebellion in Damascus.

Rural rebels control most of the inland towns, such as Nablus, Hebron, Ramallah, Tiberias, Beersheba, and even parts of Jaffa and the walled portion of Jerusalem; well-to-do families leave Palestine; Palestinian counterinsurgence groups fight the rebels; civil war breaks out among the Arabs.

British military rule over the country; reinforcements from Britain; military pressure on the hilly regions; recapture of the Arab Old City of Jerusalem by British troops; guerrilla groups disbanded and leadership killed or captured. Close cooperation between the Haganah, the mainstream Jewish paramilitary organization, and British forces; Colonel Charles Wingate trains and leads joint counterinsurgence units. Arab opposition leaders organize and fund so-called peace bands, fighting against rebel groups and defending villages and neighborhoods.

The Partition (Woodhead) Commission declares the Peel Commission partition proposal to be "impractical"; proposes an Arab-Jewish-British conference to solve the problem of Palestine; deported Palestinian leaders released.

1939 London Conference convened; talks end without agreement. Malcolm MacDonald, colonial secretary of state, launches a new British policy for Palestine (1939 White Paper): after ten years of a transitional period, an independent, unitary (i.e., Arab-ruled) Palestinian state, annual Jewish immigration of 15,000, and heavy restrictions on Jewish land purchases; de facto withdrawal from Balfour Declaration. The House of Commons approves the new policy.

George Antonius publishes *The Arab Awakening*, the first comprehensive history of the Arab nationalist movement.

World War II breaks out.

1940 Publication of land transfer regulations, restricting official Jewish purchases; de facto sales continue.

1941 Economic prosperity; establishment of the Congress of Workers and Union of Section of Arab Workers, both unions under communist influence.

Formation of Jewish military shock units (Palmach).

German invasion of Soviet Union; British troops sent to overthrow pro-German regime in Iraq, with assistance of Jewish units.

The United States enters World War II.

1942 Following a Nablus conference, the Palestinian Worker Society splits; formation of communist-led Federation of Arab Trade Unions.

Ben-Gurion declares the policy of prompt creation of a Jewish Commonwealth in Palestine; awareness of the scope of the Nazi Holocaust.

1944 Revival of Arab National Fund; new board of directors, replacing Amin al-Husseini's supporters.

Etzel declares an anti-colonial revolt against Britain.

1945 End of World War II; millions of uprooted people, among them hundreds of thousands of Jewish survivors of the Holocaust; Jewish leadership begins a policy of sending ships to Palestine with unauthorized immigrants. Declaration of the "Jewish Revolt" against British by the mainstream paramilitary Haganah; negotiations with other Jewish underground organizations on coordination among them.

Formation of the Arab League. Reconstitution of the Arab (Palestine) Higher Committee. Najjada, a Palestinian paramilitary organization, founded in Jaffa.

New statement of policy (White Paper of 1945) launched by British Foreign Secretary E. Bevin; more restrictions on Jewish immigration; proposal to set up Anglo-American Committee of Inquiry.

1946 Jamal al-Husseini, allowed to return to Palestine, takes control of a reorganized Arab Higher Committee. Amin al-Husseini arrives in Egypt to try to regain control over Palestinians; new attempt at unity by creating an Arab Higher Executive. Transjordan gains independence from Britain.

Full-scale Jewish underground operations, mainly against British targets and infrastructure (railroads and bridges); Etzel blows up the British administration headquarters in a wing of Jerusalem's King David Hotel.

The Anglo-American Committee of Inquiry recommends the immediate entry of 150,000 Jewish immigrants and abolition of the 1940 Land Transfer Regulations.

1946–47 London Conference: Britain submits an autonomy plan based on dividing the country into provinces; first round attended only by Arab states; second round includes participation of Palestinian and Jewish delegations. Arabs demand a unitary state, and conference ends without results.

1947 Prime Minister Bevin submits the problem of Palestine to the United Nations; UN special commission (UNSCOP) appointed and sent to Palestine. In UNSCOP report, a majority recommend partition, a minority recommend a federation.

Organization of a second Palestinian paramilitary organization, the Futuwwa, under the control of Jamal al-Husseini. Arab League meeting in Aley (Lebanon) reaffirms Bludan resolution to use oil as a weapon in the struggle over Palestine.

November 29: The Palestinians and the Arab states reject partition; the Zionists accept.

1948 UN General Assembly adopts Resolution 181, recommending the establishment of Jewish and Arab states in Palestine and the internationalization of the Jerusalem-Bethlehem area.

Arab Higher Committee declares a general strike; full-scale intercommunal war breaks out in Palestine. Abd al-Qadir al-Husseini returns to the country and proclaims himself the chief commander of Palestinian forces. Arab League calls for volunteers for an Arab Liberation Army (ALA) under the command of Fawzi al-Qa'uqji. Brigades of ALA irregulars arrive in North Palestine in January; selective abandonment by middle- and upper-class members from the large cities, and flight from the villages captured by Jewish forces in the coastal plain.

Political Committee of Arab League rejects all of Amin al-Husseini's demands and declares that the Arab Higher Committee does not represent the Palestinian people; all funds allocated to the League's Palestinian Council.

Fawzi al-Qa'uqji establishes his headquarters in central Palestine; ALA irregulars arrive in Jaffa; significant successes for the Arab irregulars; the main roads of the country are blocked; Yehiam, Gush Etzion, Hulda, and Nebi Daniel Jewish convoys destroyed; Jewish Jerusalem under siege.

March: Jewish military forces facing the ALA in the north succeed, capturing and demolishing Arab villages on the coastal plain, including Abu Kabir and Jabalya; Plan D adopted, allowing for securing Jewish settlements and the roads to them even beyond the territories allocated for the Jewish state and destroying Arab localities and expelling their inhabitants if necessary for security reasons.

April: Abd al-Qadir al-Husseini is killed in a counterattack by Jewish forces on the strategic village of Castel, dominating the way to Jerusalem; major demoralization among Palestinian irregulars; massacre in the village of Deir Yassin, about 120 villagers killed; Palestinian leadership tries to halt the flight; Arab Higher Committee calls on Palestinian Arabs not to leave. Battle for Jaffa continues; an ALA unit reinforces its defenders; all Arab neighborhoods of West Jerusalem are captured by Jewish forces and their inhabitants driven out.

Qa'uqji withdraws from Mishmar Haemek; Jewish forces take over Tiberias, Haifa, and additional villages; Arab population flees or is expelled; Jaffa under siege; a Jewish convoy to the Mount Scopus campus of Hebrew University is massacred.

Mass demonstrations in Damascus, Baghdad, Cairo, and Tripoli calling to save the Palestinian brethren; pogroms in local Jewish communities; Arab League committee meets to discuss the ALA failures and the Deir Yassin events.

April: Lebanon and Syria announce their intentions to send troops to Palestine; Iraq concentrates troops in Transjordan.

May: Jewish forces capture Safed and its rural hinterland; Jaffa surrenders and the majority of its Muslim population leaves; the remaining Jewish settlements of Etzion bloc in the mountainous region surrender to the Arab Legion.

May 15: End of the British Mandate. The state of Israel is proclaimed; Egyptian regular forces cross the border into Palestine, Arab Legion (Transjordanian) forces cross the Jordan River westward; Syrian troops move to cross the border; the 1948 war breaks out.

The Soviet Union and the United States recognize Israel; creation of the Israel Defense Forces, unifying various militias.

May–June: Major battles between advancing Arab armed forces and Israeli forces; most Arab villages are evacuated following force movements; Israeli decision prevents Arabs from returning to evacuated villages; formation of refugee camps in Gaza, territories controlled by the Arab Legion and Lebanon.

The All Palestine Government, with a temporary site in Gaza, is established by Amin al-Husseini.

July: End of first truce; major Israeli offensive on three fronts, mainly to clear the Tel Aviv-Jerusalem road including the Lydda-Ramleh region; this action leads to a new wave of about 100,000 Palestinians fleeing to territories held by Arab Legion, ALA, and Egypt; a portion of the Palestinians are evacuated by force.

September: Lausanne peace talks fail, mainly due to Israel's refusal to repatriate the Palestinian refugees. The Jericho Conference in November calls on Abdullah to annex the West Bank to Transjordan.

Continuing battles and expulsion of Arabs from the conquered territories by Israeli armed forces; remaining Arab population is moved from one place to another according to perceived security requirements.

December: UN General Assembly Resolution 194(III) recognizes the right of the Palestinian refugees to return "and live at peace with their neighbors."

1948–52 The Jewish population of Israel doubles by mass immigration of Holocaust survivors and immigrants from Muslim countries; severe economic conditions prevail; distribution of minimal food, housing and labor for the needy Jewish population.

1949 Armistice agreements between Israel and Lebanon, Transjordan, and Syria are signed; Israel holds about 80 percent of the total territories of Western Palestine; the eastern mountain area (the West Bank) is under Transjordanian rule; the Gaza Strip is under Egyptian occupation.

The UN partition has granted the Jewish state 5,405 square miles, yet the territory that remains under Israel's control after the armistice agreements in 1949 is 8,108 square miles.

1949–56 Constant infiltration of Palestinians across the armistice lines causes casualties and unrest in Israel, which adopts a policy of retaliating against the Arab states and the "sources of infiltration"; military clashes along the armistice lines.

1950 Military government imposed on most Israeli Arabs; in April, the West Bank is formally annexed to Jordan; the United Nations Relief and Works Agency (UNRWA) begins operations.

1951 Yasir Arafat reorganizes the Palestinian Students' Union in Cairo. Nationalization of oil in Iran.

George Habash organizes the Arab Nationalists' Movement, with a leftist pan-Arabist ideology; its Palestinian branch will develop into the Popular Front for the Liberation of Palestine (PFLP), initiating sabotage activities against Arab and imperialist targets.

King Abdallah of Jordan killed at prayer in al-Aqsa mosque by a Palestinian nationalist.

1952 The Arab League dissolves the All Palestine Government and empowers the Arab states to represent the Palestinian cause.

Free Officers coup in Cairo; end of monarchy.

1955 Alliance among Iraq, Pakistan, and Turkey (Baghdad Pact) links them to Britain and the Western bloc.

1956 Forty-seven Israeli Arabs massacred in Kafr Qasim village after violating curfew.

Nationalization of Suez Canal; Israel conquers Gaza Strip and most of Sinai Desert; Anglo-French intervention.

1957 Most of the Arab members of the Israeli Communist party (MAKI) split away, forming the almost purely Arab Communist list (RAKAH).

Israeli withdrawal from the Sinai Desert and Gaza Strip.

1958 Formation of Egyptian-Syrian federation, creating the United Arab Republic, arouses pan-Arab sentiment.

1959 Fatah is created by Arafat and associates; al-Ard group starts to publish an Arab nationalist periodical in Israel. In Lebanon, Khalil al-Wazir (Abu Jihad) issues the clandestine Fatah magazine *Filastinuna*; the Arab Higher Committee and Amin al-Husseini are forced to move from Egypt to Lebanon.

   Muammar Qaddafi overthrows the monarchy in Libya.

1962 Civil war in Yemen removes the monarchy; Egypt backs the republicans, sending a military expedition.

1964 Israeli authorities outlaw Al-Ard after an attempt to establish it as an Arab nationalist party in Israel.

January: The first Arab summit in Cairo concludes with a statement about the need to "organize the Palestinian people enabling them to play their role in the liberation of their country and to achieve self-determination."

May: The First Palestinian National Council (PNC) convenes in Jerusalem, chaired by Ahmad Shukayri; it adopts the Palestine National Charter as the Basic Constitution of the Palestine Liberation Organization. A Palestine Liberation Army is also planned.

1965 January: Fatah launches its armed struggle to liberate Palestine; Communique No. 1 of al-Assifa, its military branch, is issued.

1966 Abolition of the military government that had ruled Israeli Arabs.

1967 May 16: Nasser orders United Nations Emergency Forces (UNEF) stationed on the Egyptian-Israeli border to withdraw, removing the international buffer between Egypt and Israel that has existed since 1957.

May 22: Egypt announces a blockade of all goods bound to and from Israel through the Straits of Tiran. Israel has maintained since 1957 that such a blockade justifies Israeli military action to maintain free access to the port of Eilat, supplying Israel a pretext to attack Egyptian forces.

June 5: Israel's (preemptive) surprise attack conquers the Sinai Peninsula and the Gaza Strip. Despite an Israeli appeal to Jordan to stay out of the conflict, Jordan attacks Israel and loses control of the West Bank and the eastern sector of Jerusalem. Israel also captures the Golan Heights region from Syria.

   Following Israel's victory in the June war, the entire territory of the former Palestine Mandate comes under Israeli control, including about 650,000 Palestinians of the West Bank and East Jerusalem and 356,000 in the Gaza Strip; East Jerusalem is annexed to Israel. The rest of the captured territories, including the Golan Heights and Sinai Desert, are put under military administration.

August: Arab states leaders' summit in Khartoum rejects any negotiations with Israel.

Arafat attempts to establish his headquarters inside the occupied territories, trying to provoke and lead a popular uprising; by the end of December, his entire network is destroyed by Israeli intelligence and Arafat has left the territories.

September–November: Teachers and students strike against Israeli occupation in the West Bank; first general strike in Nablus.

George Habash's group joins other small guerrilla organizations to form the Popular Front for the Liberation of Palestine (PFLP).

1968 March: Fatah fighters, supported by Jordanian artillery, repel an Israeli attack on Fatah headquarters at Karamah (in the Jordan Valley). At the fourth session of PNC in July, the guerrilla groups led by Fatah take over the PLO, which becomes an umbrella organization of different streams with Fatah predominating; the National Covenant is revised; an Israeli civilian airliner is hijacked by the PFLP and lands in Algiers.

1969 Naif Hawatma splits from the PFLP and founds the pro-Maoist Democratic Front for the Liberation of Palestine (DFLP). At the fifth session of the PNC in February, Arafat is nominated to chair the ruling Executive Committee (EC). The Cairo Agreement between Arafat and Emile Bustani, the Lebanese Army commander, permits "regulated guerrilla activities" in Lebanon; this agreement will be the basis of the state-in-a-state infrastructure that the PLO builds in Lebanon.

1969–71 Demonstrations against Israeli rule in all major West Bank cities; sporadic Palestinian uprisings and guerrilla activities in the Gaza Strip.

1970 The PFLP initiates a multiple hijacking; planes land in the desert area of Zarqa in Jordan and are blown up.

Jordan armed forces begin to destroy the infrastructure of the guerrilla forces around Amman and the refugee camps; civil war erupts between Palestinians and Jordanian troops; the guerrilla forces are defeated in what comes to be known as Black September, and their headquarters are moved to Lebanon.

1971 Israeli security forces under the command of Ariel Sharon pacify the Gaza Strip.

Assassination of Washi Tal, Jordanian premier and minister of defense; it is the first operation of Fatah-led organization Black September, under the command of Ali Hasan Salamah and Salah Khalaf (Abu Iyad).

1972 The Japanese Red Army guerrilla group, in coordination with Wadi Haddad, PFLP's chief of operations, hits Ben-Gurion Airport (Operation Deir Yassin); Black September takes the Israeli Olympic team hostage in Munich; most of the hostages and terrorists are killed during an abortive attempt by German police to rescue the athletes.

1973 April: Israelis launch a commando action against Fatah headquarters in Beirut, killing several Fatah commanders.

Formation in the West Bank of the Palestine National Front, controlled by the Communist party, challenging the outside PLO leadership.

The October War begins with a surprise Egyptian-Syrian attack on Israel; Henry Kissinger brokers separation of forces agreements to prepare for a Geneva peace conference.

1974 Arab Summit recognizes the PLO as the sole legitimate representative of the Palestinian people; Arafat speaks to the UN General Assembly in New York.

July: the twelfth PNC adopts the idea of establishing "a Palestinian national authority in any area liberated from Israeli control," the so-called mini-state option; George Habash (PFLP) resigns from the PLO Executive Committee, establishing the Rejectionist Front, a pro-Syrian guerrilla organization; faced with the possibility of Palestinian participation in the Geneva Peace Conference, the Rejectionist Front is enlarged to include the PFLP-GC, the Iraqi-backed Arab Liberation Front, and other small guerrilla groups.

Creation of the Committee of the Heads of Arab Local Councils, which becomes the Supreme Follow-Up Committee and acts as the leadership and representatives of the Israeli Arabs.

1975–91 Civil war in Lebanon with PLO participation; Syrian intervention in the civil war leads to gradual Syrian control over Lebanon, except for a small security zone in southern Lebanon dominated by Israel.

1976 Municipal elections in the West Bank lead to PLO supporters being swept into office (Bassam al-Shaka in Nablus, Fahd Qawasma in Hebron, Karim Khalaf in Ramallah, Ibrahim Tawil in al-Bira); the elected mayors and other prominent figures form a nucleus of an internal leadership, the National Guidance Committee.

March 30: The first Land Day includes a general strike and protests of Israeli Arabs against land expropriations; six Arabs are killed. In 1992, it is declared a national holiday.

Christian right-wing militias in Lebanon, supported by Syria, enforce a siege on Tal al-Zaatar, a Palestinian refugee camp; the siege ends with a massacre of the camp inhabitants.

1977 Abu Abbas splits from PFLP-GC and forms the Palestine Liberation Front (PLF).

The nationalist right-wing party Likud comes to power in Israel; settlement of the occupied territories by Jews accelerates.

Formation of the radical nationalist group Sons of the Village among Israeli Arabs.

President Sadat of Egypt visits Jerusalem and speaks before the Knesset.

Israeli-Fatah (Habib) agreement on a ceasefire along the Lebanon-Israel border.

Camp David Egyptian-Israel peace accords signed; Israel recognizes the "legitimate rights of the Palestinians" and commits to granting them "full autonomy" after a transitional period of five years; Israel also commits to withdrawal from the Sinai Desert in exchange for peace with Egypt.

Menahem Milson appointed as civilian administrator of the West Bank; tries to establish a local counterbalance to the PLO by forming the Village Leagues, armed groups headed by Mustafa Doudeen.

Revolution in Iran; a radical Shiite Muslim regime is established, promoting militant Islam throughout the Islamic world.

1982 The Palestinian National Guidance Committee is outlawed; general strike and mass demonstrations in the West Bank and Gaza Strip.

June: Israeli troops invade Lebanon in collaboration with the Maronite-Christian forces; Israel's major aim is to destroy the PLO's quasi-state infrastructure. It is the first large-scale Israeli-Palestinian war since 1948, with heavy battles and casualties on all sides; West Beirut comes under siege and bombardment

August: the PLO evacuates its forces and headquarters from Beirut to Tripoli, with its fighters carrying only their personal arms; new headquarters established in Tunis.

Bashir Gemayel elected president of Lebanon; twenty-two days later, he is killed by an explosive planted by Syrian agents.

September: Christian-Maronite militias, under Israeli protection, massacre Palestinians in the Sabra and Shatilla refugee camps.

1984 Jewish settlements in the West Bank and Gaza Strip increase to about 80,000 settlers.

1985 King Hussein and Arafat sign the Amman Agreement on a confederation between a future Palestinian state in the West Bank, Gaza Strip, and Jordan; after a year, King Hussein voids the agreement.

1987 December 9: a general popular uprising, the intifada, breaks out in the Gaza Strip and spreads to the West Bank; popular committees and a unified leadership of the revolt form inside the territories; their directives are ratified by the outside PLO and are spread mainly by leaflets; power shifts toward inside leadership.

1988 April: Khalil al-Wazir (Abu Jihad), the military commandant of Fatah and one of its founders, is assassinated by an Israeli commando unit led by Ehud Barak.

November: The nineteenth session of the PNC convenes in Algiers and declares an independent Palestinian state; following heavy pressure from the United States, which holds out the possibility of recognition and a dialogue with the PLO, Arafat declares in Geneva that the PLO recognizes the rights of all parties concerned in the Middle East conflict to exist in peace and security, including the state of Palestine, Israel, and other neighbors; Arafat denounces terrorism, and the United States opens dialogue.

1988 The Islamic Movement wins the municipal election in the Israeli Arab town of Umm al-Fahm.

1989 When Arafat refuses to condemn a terrorist attack by a PLO constituent organization, the United States suspends dialogue with the PLO.

1990 December: Seventeen Palestinians are killed and nearly two hundred wounded after jittery Israeli security forces open fire near al-Aqsa mosque.

Iraq invades Kuwait; the United States creates a multinational force.

1991 January: Salah Khalaf (Abu Iyad) is assassinated, probably by the Abu Nidal organization, perhaps at the behest of Iraq.

Massive Jewish immigration from the Soviet Union to Israel.

The intifada turns inward as collaborators and other suspects are killed by Palestinian shock troops or individuals; vigilante activities on the part of Jewish settlers.

The U.S.-led force defeats Iraq in the Gulf War; the PLO is hurt diplomatically by its support of Iraq; the Palestinian community in Kuwait of over 300,000 is reduced to several thousand and is badly persecuted.

November: Peace talks begin in Madrid (continued later in Washington) between Israel and Arab delegations, including Palestinians from the occupied territories as part of a joint Jordanian-Palestinian delegation; the peace talks are the product of U.S. diplomatic efforts and are held under the auspices of the United States and Russia.

1992 December 22: In response to the killing of a border policeman, Israel carries out an executive order to expel 415 suspected Hamas activists to Lebanon. The deportees remain near the Israeli border in difficult winter conditions after the government of Lebanon refuses to accept them. Both the deportation itself and the condition of those expelled cause an international uproar.

The Labor party returns to power in Israel, promising to implement Palestinian autonomy within a year.

Deportations lead to a rise in Palestinian support for the Islamic groups in the occupied territories, with a corresponding drop in support for the PLO.

Emil Habibi wins the prestigious Israel Prize for literature.

Secret negotiations between Palestinian and Israeli officials in Norway.

January 20: Informal talks under Norwegian sponsorship begin between Israeli academics and mid-level PLO representatives, with the aim of exploring possibilities for reconciliation between the Palestinians and Israelis.

Israeli foreign ministry officials join the talks in Norway. As the possibility of interim arrangements grows, the Israeli foreign minister and prime minister, along with top Fatah leaders, become involved indirectly by supervising the talks.

A declaration of principles (DOP) is drafted; the DOP includes Israel's recognition of the PLO as the legitimate representative of the Palestinian people and the agreement to grant full autonomy to the Palestinians under PLO leadership for five years, starting in the Gaza Strip and Jericho. The final status of the autonomous entity will be negotiated later. Palestinians interpret the agreement as an interim stage toward establishing an independent state.

September 13: Yasir Arafat of the PLO and Yitzhak Rabin of Israel formally sign the DOP in Washington (Oslo I). The DOP grants the Palestinian National Authority (or simply Palestine Authority) autonomous status in a small portion of the West Bank (Jericho) and most of the Gaza Strip. The DOP includes an understanding that by December 13, an agreement will be reached on withdrawing Israeli troops from the Gaza Strip and Jericho, and that by April 13, 1994, Israeli troop redeployment would be completed. The PLO would assume civil authority in those regions and deploy its own police forces.

Jordan and Israel conclude a framework for a peace agreement.

Intensification of terror acts by Jewish settlers against Palestinians as part of their political protest movement against the PLO-Israel agreement; with similar motives, Hamas members and other figures step up the murder of Jews in Israel and the occupied territories.

Some progress in the Israeli-Arab multinational negotiations in Washington and other locations; Syria takes a hard line by supporting the groups rejecting the PLO-Israeli agreement.

Most of the non-Fatah elements within the PLO and the Islamic movements reject the DOP; some Fatah leaders express objections to Arafat's concessions to Israel.

December: Difficulties occur in PLO-Israeli talks; the December 13 deadline for the Gaza-Jericho plan is missed and high-level negotiations continue; most of the members of the Islamic movements who were expelled are returned to the occupied territories.

1994 Presidents Bill Clinton of the United States and Hafez al-Assad of Syria meet in Geneva; Syria indicates its readiness to negotiate a full peace with Israel in exchange for full Israeli withdrawal from the Golan Heights.

Several months after missing the December 13, 1993 deadline, Israel and the PLO sign an agreement opening the way for Israeli troop withdrawal from the Gaza Strip and Jericho and the beginning of limited PLO self-rule there.

February 25: A radical religious Jew (Baruch Goldstein) carries out a suicide massacre in the Patriarchs' Cave, a holy place for Judaism and Islam; his aim seems to have been to create a chain of responses that would end reconciliation between Palestinians and Jews; twenty-nine praying Muslims are killed and dozens of others wounded.

Rising fear in Israel in response to growing Islamic terror; demonstrations against the peace process, organized mostly by groups of settlers in the territories, religious radicals, and secular right wing activists, gain momentum in Israel.

The number of Jewish settlers in the occupied territories reaches over 150,000.

October 26: Signing of the Israeli-Jordanian peace agreement; Israel acknowledges Jordanian sovereignty over several border areas in which Israeli presence continues (as a formal lease); Israel grants Jordan special status over the Islamic holy places in Jerusalem.

April–March 1996: A series of about ten terrorist attacks in Israeli urban centers by radical Islamic suicide bombers kill one hundred and wound hundreds of others; expanded closures are imposed on the occupied territories; the Palestinian Authority and its machinery begin to take root and spread over the area; dozens of Hamas and Islamic Jihad leaders and fieldworkers are arrested.

In an economic protocol, the PLO and Israel agree that 75 percent of taxes withheld from Palestinian workers in Israel will be transferred to the Palestinian Authority.

May: the first Palestinian self-government begins with PLO self-rule in Jericho and the Gaza Strip.

An agreement allows initial entry of the Palestinian Authority and its militia forces into most of the area of the Gaza Strip and the Jericho region.

1995 September: Interim agreement (Oslo II) grants rule over all Palestinian cities (except Hebron) to the Palestinian Authority (Area A, about 4 percent of the West Bank) and joint Israeli-Palestinian rule over village areas (Area B); large areas of the Jordan Valley, Jewish settlements, and their access roads remain under sole Israeli control (Area C).

Israel redeploys its military forces in compliance with Oslo II.

November 4: Israeli Prime Minister Yitzhak Rabin is assassinated by a national religious youth hoping to stop the process of transferring territories to Palestinian Authority control; Rabin is blamed for betraying the idea of the Greater Land of Israel.

1996 April 24: The twenty-first conference of the PNC is held in Gaza; an 88 percent majority of the 504 representatives decides to revoke all articles of the Palestinian National Charter that conflict with the Oslo agreements. The PNC Legislative Council is given the responsibility for formulating a new charter within six months.

April: With attacks by the Lebanese Islamic Hezbollah organization, public pressure, and upcoming elections, Shimon Peres announces Operation Grapes of Wrath. This series of air strikes on southern Lebanon causes a massive flight of 200,000 citizens; damage in Kafr Kana causes the death of about one hundred Lebanese citizens.

May 29: Early general elections in Israel produce a razor-thin victory for Binyamin Netanyahu, presiding over a bloc consisting of right wing national-religious, secular, and ultra-Orthodox factions; the new government declares it necessary to implement the Oslo agreements, granting autonomy to the Palestinians, but it toughens its position and demands discussion of final status arrangements concerning the occupied territories—including East Jerusalem, over which the Israelis demand sole sovereignty, with allocation of special status over the Islamic holy sites to Jordan.

September 25–27: Following the opening of a tunnel dug by archaeologists under the area of al-Aqsa (the Temple Mount), large-scale rioting sweeps the West Bank and Gaza Strip; about forty Palestinians and eleven Israelis are killed, and one hundred wounded from each side. The Palestinians attack a site being used as a *yeshiva* near Nablus; Israelis try to rescue soldiers stationed there, using tanks and helicopters in the territories for the first time since the Palestinian Authority's creation.

1997 January 16–17: The Israeli government authorizes the Hebron Agreement; the Israeli army transfers control of the city, with the exception of the Jewish enclave, to the Palestinian Authority.

January 22: Yasir Arafat declares that at the end of the interim agreement period, the Palestinians will unilaterally declare the establishment of a Palestinian state.

February 27: About one thousand Palestinians protest in Bet Sahour against the Israeli plan to build in the Jerusalem neighborhood of Homa (Ras al-Amud).

February 4: Two army helicopters bringing soldiers to Lebanon crash by accident, killing seventy-three soldiers; the accident becomes a turning point in Israeli public opinion on the subject of continued control of southern Lebanon.

March 12: A suicide bomber sets off an explosion in central Tel Aviv, killing three and wounding forty-seven; total closure is imposed over the West Bank and Gaza Strip.

March 19: Netanyahu proposes canceling incremental withdrawal and establishing Camp David–style talks for a final status agreement; Arafat rejects the proposal.

July 30: Two suicide bombers set off explosions in a Jerusalem marketplace; 13 Israelis are killed and 170 wounded. The Izz al-Din Brigades takes responsibility. Abdellaziz Rantisi, the Hamas political leader, denies responsibility. The Israelis respond with expanded closures and many arrests.

August 12: Large demonstrations in Nablus call for Arafat to stand up to Israeli pressure aiming to break the resistance movement.

September 4: Three suicide bombs detonate in Jerusalem, killing 5 Israelis and wounding 192; the Al-Qassem Brigade take responsibility.

1998 September 25: Israeli agents try to assassinate Khaled Mashal, the secretary general of Hamas, headquartered in Damascus at the time, by injecting him with poison; following the furious reaction of King Hussein, Israel supplies the antidote. Mashal is considered Hamas's strongman.

January 21: The World Bank decides to fund an industrial area for export products in al-Muntar (Gaza Strip).

September 27–29: Demonstrations in the Arab-Israeli city of Umm al-Fahm against government intentions to use sixty-two *dunums* of olive orchards as a firing range; the police use live fire, and about one hundred Arabs and fifteen policemen are injured. A general strike among Palestinian Israelis is called to protest police violence.

October 17–23: Wye Plantation talks. In the Wye Plantation Agreements, Israel agrees to initiate the third stage of Oslo II, freeing Palestinian prisoners and detainees. The Palestinian Authority pledges to reduce the scope of armed militias, collect arms from residents, and increase coordination of security forces.

October 19: A hand grenade is thrown at a bus stop in Beersheba, wounding sixty-four.

October 30: The Palestinian Authority working council authorizes the Wye Agreement.

November 16: The Knesset authorizes the Wye Agreement, contingent on the Palestinian Authority's implementation of the agreement to collect illegal arms.

November 20: Israel transfers 1.1 percent of Area C to total Palestinian control and frees 250 prisoners; virtually all Palestinian population concentrations in the West Bank and Gaza Strip have now been transferred to PA control.

November 24: An international airport is opened in Gaza.

December 10: The central council of the PLO meets in Gaza, authorizing Arafat's letter to Clinton canceling articles of the National Charter that deal with the extermination of Israel.

December 12: Eight opposition groups from within the PLO, Hamas, and Islamic Jihad meet in Damascus to reaffirm their opposition to the Oslo process and to the changes in the National Charter.

December 14: In the presence of the U.S. President, the PNC cancels articles of the National Charter that deal with the extermination of Israel and appoints a committee for reformulating the charter.

December 20: The Israeli government halts continued implementation of the Wye Agreement, claiming that the Palestinians are not fulfilling their part of the agreement.

December 28: New elections are set in Israel; Benjamin Begin resigns from the Likud to form a right wing opposition bloc to Netanyahu.

1999 January 20: King Hussein's eldest son, Abdullah, is appointed heir to the throne in place of the crown prince, Hasan.

February 6: Large demonstration in Hebron at the Palestinian Authority offices demanding both an end to cooperation with Israel and the U.S. Central Intelligence Agency, as well as the freeing of prisoners by Israel.

February 7: King Hussein dies; his son Abdullah assumes the throne in Jordan.

February 14: About 200,000 ultra-Orthodox Jews demonstrate in Jerusalem against the Supreme Court decision to draft yeshiva students; counter-demonstration of 50,000 secular citizens.

February 15: Naif Hawatma is expelled from the Rejectionist Front after shaking hands with the President of Israel at the funeral of Jordan's King Hussein.

May 17: Ehud Barak, the Labor party candidate, is elected prime minister; Labor and Likud continue losing power as Shas, a religious-ethnic party of Mizrahi Jews, gains strength. Shinui, a secular party, wins six seats. Barak declares efforts toward a final agreement with the Palestinians and his intention to bring it to a popular referendum, but then bypasses Palestinians in favor of efforts to gain settlement with Syria.

May 23: Israeli army withdraws from the security zone in southern Lebanon.

May 27: Binyamin Netanyahu retires from political life.

June 22: Demolition of an Arab house in Lydda sparks protest; the police open fire using rubber bullets; MK Azmi Bishara and sixteen other demonstrators are injured. Supporters of Fatah and the Islamic movement clash in the Ein al-Hilwa refugee camp (Lebanon) over control of the camp.

July 3: The Palestinian Authority declares a day of wrath to protest settlement expansion; response is minimal.

July 5: The International Covenant for Arab-Jewish Peace based in Ramallah organizes a conference in Cairo on the subject of normalization with Israel; about seven hundred Egyptian intellectuals and public figures organize a counter-conference.

July 6: An expanded government is formed in Israel.

July 15: At a Clinton-Barak meeting in Washington, Barak promises to implement the Wye Agreement, announces that most settlements will remain in place after a final status agreement.

The signers of the Fourth Geneva Convention condemn Israel for violation of human rights and actions in the occupied territories and declare the settlements illegal.

Australia, Canada, the United States, and Israel boycott the conference.

July 27: Israel and the Palestinian Authority open negotiations on the construction of a joint industrial area in the Karmi region (Jenin).

August 2: At reconciliation talks in Cairo between Fatah and the Popular Front, the possibility of coordinating over the final status issue is discussed; George Habash refuses to meet with Arafat.

November 16: Israeli armed forces enter several cave villages in the area of southern Mount Hebron and expel more than seven hundred Palestinian residents.

2000 March 4: About one hundred Palestinians from the Diaspora put forth a call to emphasize the refugee issue and the right of return in talks with Israel.

March 8: The Israeli Supreme Court decides against discrimination in allocating land to an Arab family in a Jewish communal settlement.

March 21: Israel implements the second stage of the interim agreement, transferring 6.1 percent of Area B to Area A; the Palestinian Authority now fully controls 18 percent and partially controls 22 percent of the West Bank.

March 22–26: The Pope visits the Holy Land; among other places, he visits Bethlehem and the Dehaisha refugee camp.

March 27: The minister of interior returns 250 *dunums* of land appropriated for public use to the Palestinian Israeli village of Kafr Qasim.

May 20: Stormy demonstrations in West Bank cities of Hebron, Nablus, Jenin, Ramallah, and Tulkarm; five Palestinians dead and about five hundred wounded.

May 23: Total withdrawal of Israeli troops from southern Lebanon; the Southern Lebanese Army is disbanded, and some of its members take refuge in Israel.

June 10: Syrian President Hafez al-Asad dies; his son Bashir is appointed as his successor. Netanyahu and Barak are seemingly close to an arrangement with Syria, but Asad's demand for access to the Sea of Galilee prevent it.

July 9: The Barak government becomes a minority government when Shas, the National Religious Party, and Israel B'Aliya leave in protest over Barak's agreement to final status talks. Meretz, which had left earlier in protest against Shas's remaining in the coalition, supports the government from the outside.

July 11–25: An attempt to arrive at a final status agreement between the Palestinians and Israel fails (Camp David II); each side blames the other for the conference's failure.

July 27: The Israeli Ministry of Interior announces that the Jewish population of the West Bank and Gaza Strip has grown by 13,000 in the past year and now approaches 200,000 people.

August 2: Israeli foreign minister David Levy resigns from the government, blaming Barak for deceiving his supporters with his promise not to divide Jerusalem.

August 8: Suicide bomb explodes in Sbarros, a Jerusalem pizzeria; fifteen are killed and dozens wounded.

August 15: Construction of Gaza Port begins.

September 28: Israeli opposition head, Ariel Sharon, known to be indirectly responsible for the Sabra and Shattila massacre and other murderous acts against Palestinians, visits the areas of the mosques and Haram al-Sharif (the Temple Mount); his visit awakens a fierce emotional storm, leading to mass demonstrations against the continuing Israeli presence in the Palestinian territories.

September 29: Sharon's visit to Haram al-Sharif is considered a provocation by the Palestinians and insensitively timed during negotiations over arrangements for Jerusalem; demonstrations and riots break out throughout the West Bank, with violence directed mostly toward settlers and the Israeli army. Palestinian militia men join as individuals and groups, using live fire against the Israelis; the escalating violence, which turns into ethnic warfare between Israel and the Palestinian Authority by early 2002, is termed the Al-Aqsa (or Second) Intifada, and is later seen by some as the beginning of a war of independence

September 30: Twelve-year-old Muhammad al-Durrah is killed during an exchange of fire between Israeli soldiers and Palestinian armed forces;

the event is captured by TV cameras, and the young martyr becomes a symbol of the renewed Palestinian struggle.

October 1–8: Palestinian Israelis hold protests identifying with Palestinians in the West Bank and Gaza. They block roads and throw stones; the police react with massive live fire. Twelve Arab citizens and one resident of the territories are killed; hundreds are injured.

October 9: Riots between Jews and Arabs in Jaffa; Jews try to burn down the Hassan Beck Mosque.

October 12: Two Israeli reserve officers mistakenly find themselves in a Palestinian controlled area and are taken to the police station in Ramallah; an angry mob beats them to death. The event, broadcast on television, has a strong impact on Israeli public opinion.

November 15: The Israeli government establishes the Orr Commission to investigate the October events in which thirteen Arabs were killed in Israel.

December 17: Israel initiates a policy of extrajudicial executions or assassinations (so-called focused elimination) of those found responsible for terrorist acts and armed resistance; Tanzim activist Samih al-Malabi is among the first murdered.

December 30: Israeli agents assassinate Dr. Thabat Thabat, Fatah secretary general in the West Bank.

2001 January 5: Israel intercepts and captures *Karine A,* a boat full of armaments bought in Iran and destined for Palestinians in the territories, causing great embarrassment to the Palestinian Authority but also great pride among the Palestinians.

January: George W. Bush assumes the U.S. presidency; he takes a much more hands-off orientation to Israeli-Palestinian issues than did his predecessor, Bill Clinton; his statements through the year are more unequivocally pro-Israel.

January 14: Assassination of Raad al-Karmi, the head of the Tanzim in Tulkaram.

February 1: Two suicide bombers blow themselves up in central Jerusalem: eleven are killed and about ninety wounded.

February 6: Special elections for prime minister in Israel; Ariel Sharon, the Likud candidate, is elected by a large majority, but with the lowest turnout ever, mostly because of the boycott by Palestinian Arab citizens.

April 4: Assassination of Iyad Khadran, leader of the Islamic Jihad in Jenin.

May 15: In a speech to the Legislative Council, Arafat proposes regime reforms, democratization, and new elections.

March 27–28: Supporting a Saudi initiative, the Convention of Arab States in Beirut proposes a full peace agreement with Israel, including normalization of relations, in exchange for withdrawal to 1967 borders and the establishment of a sovereign Palestinian state with Jerusalem as its capital; Israel does not respond to the proposal.

June 1: A suicide bomber blows himself up at the Dolphinarium discotheque in Tel Aviv: eighteen are killed and dozens wounded.

August 25: Assassination of Abu Ali Mustafa, secretary of the Popular Front.

September 11: Al-Qaida's terror attack against U.S. targets destroys the World Trade Center towers in New York and damages the Pentagon. The attacks causes anti-Islamic and anti-Arab sentiment throughout the world; President Bush declares a fierce global war on terrorism.

September 17: Sharon calls Arafat a "Bin Laden" and Israel's responses in fighting Palestinian terror to be a part of the global war on terrorism.

October 17: Rachvam Zeevi, Israel's minister of tourism and head of the Moledet movement, which supports transfer (forcible resettlement) of Palestinians outside the country, is assassinated by a Palestinian hit team.

October: The United States and United Kingdom conduct air and, later, land attacks against Afghanistan—the host regime supporting al-Qaida and its head, Osama Bin Laden—with the aim of destroying the organization's infrastructure, killing its leader, and replacing Afghanistan's theocratic regime.

December 2: Two suicide bombers and a car bomb explode in central Jerusalem; about 10 are killed and 150 wounded.

2002 January: The right wing bloc secures 69 out of 120 Knesset seats and Sharon wins a second term.

March 2: A suicide bomber blows himself up in an ultra-Orthodox neighborhood in Jerusalem; nine are killed and fifty wounded.

March 7: A suicide bomber blows himself up in the West Bank settlement of Ariel; fourteen are wounded.

March 10: A suicide bomb is detonated in the Jerusalem cafe Moment; eleven are killed and dozens wounded.

March 27: On the first night of Passover, a suicide bomber kills 29 and wounds about 150 persons in a hotel in Netanya celebrating the holiday.

March 29: Beginning of Operation Defense Shield; the Israeli army reoccupies parts of Area A in the West Bank under Palestinian Authority control, with the exception of Jericho, claiming to be "destroying the infrastructure of terror"; one after another, the major cities, refugee camps, and some villages are occupied. In most cases, Israeli forces do not face strong resistance; about 8,500 suspects are taken to Israeli prisons for investigation.

Arafat's headquarters in the city of Ramallah (the Muqata) is placed under siege.

March 30: The first female suicide bomber blows herself up in a commercial center in a Jerusalem neighborhood; three are killed and twenty-six wounded.

A suicide bomber blows himself up in a Tel Aviv cafe; thirty-seven are wounded, five seriously.

March 31: A suicide bomber blows himself up in an Arab-owned Haifa restaurant; fourteen are killed and thirty-one wounded.

April 2–19: Israeli forces enter the Jenin refugee camp and face strong resistance; twenty-three Israeli soldiers are killed and more than one hundred wounded in the fighting. Fifty Palestinians are killed; entire quarters of the camp, including five hundred houses, are destroyed as a result of Israeli fighting methods. The Palestinians accuse Israel of carrying out a massacre; the international community is summoned; the UN secretary general appoints an investigation committee, but Israel refuses the committee entry.

April–June: Israeli military actions in areas of the Palestinian Authority stir waves of protest throughout the world, mostly in Europe, accompanied by anti-Semitic statements and incidents.

April 2–May 2: A group of Palestinians on Israel's most wanted list takes refuge in the Church of the Nativity in Bethlehem; fighting in the surrounding area stirs international interest; after extensive negotiations, some of the refugees are deported to Gaza and some to European states.

April 3–21: The Battle of Nablus takes place mostly in the old city (Casbah) and the Balata and Askar refugee camps; the Palestinians report about eighty dead and three hundred wounded.

April 10: A suicide bomber blows up a bus on the way from Haifa to Jerusalem; eight are killed, twenty wounded.

April 13: A suicide bomber attacks the Jerusalem marketplace; six are killed and eighty wounded. Marwan Barghouti, Fatah general secretary, considered one of the most visible and dominant figures in the Palestinian Authority, is arrested by Israel on suspicion of involvement with the Al-Aqsa Martyrs' Brigade, the armed branch of Fatah.

April 21–May 20: Israel retreats from Ramallah, but continues siege on Arafat's headquarters in the city; Israel demands extradition of those inside, especially Zeevi's assassins and Ahmed Saadat, secretary of the Popular Front. After negotiations, the most wanted persons are transferred to a prison in Jericho under Anglo-American supervision; the extradition wounds Arafat's prestige in the eyes of the Palestinians.

May 5: In light of the wave of hostility sweeping the world in the wake of the September 11 events, leaders of forty-two Muslim states gather in Malaysia to crystallize an interpretation of the concepts of jihad and suicide combat; differences of opinion are not reconciled.

May 7: Suicide bomber blows up a pool hall in Rishon L'Tzion; fifteen are killed and fifty wounded.

May 15: Arafat promises the Legislative Council that there will be regime reforms, immediate elections, consolidation of the various security mechanisms, increased efficiency, and democratization.

May 17: The Legislative Council proposes reforms, including abolition of the state security courts.

May 19: A suicide bomber blows himself up in the Netanya marketplace; three are killed and about fifty wounded.

May 23: A suicide bomber blows himself up in Rishon L'Tzion; two are killed and about forty wounded.

June: Israel declares Operation Determined Path, reoccupying all of Area A for an indefinite period.

June 24: President George W. Bush conditions the establishment in an unspecified future of a Palestinian state with ending any terror or resistance activities, the change of present Palestinian leadership by free election, and democratization of the PNA.

July 18: Tanzim, the Palestinian militia connected to Yasir Arafat's Fatah faction, prepares to announce a unilateral ceasefire with Israel; European Union officials lead the effort for the ceasefire, which has intensified over the previous two weeks and is supported by Jordanian and Saudi diplomats; Bush administration officials are informed.

July 22: Sheikh Ahmed Yassin, spiritual leader of Hamas, announces that Hamas is willing to agree to a ceasefire, including a halt to suicide bombings, in exchange for Israeli withdrawal from the areas previously under Palestinian administration under the Oslo agreements.

July 23: An Israeli war plane drops a one-ton bomb, killing Sheikh Salah Shehada, a leader of Hamas' military wing; thirteen other people are killed, including nine children. Suspicions mount that the attack was intended to produce massive rage among Palestinians and to impede or scuttle the ceasefire initiative.

2004 January 26: Hamas offers a ten-year truce (*hudna*) conditioned on Israel's complete withdrawal from the territories captured in the 1967 war and the establishment of a Palestinian state. Hamas leader Sheikh Ahmed Yassin states that the group can accept a Palestinian state in the West Bank and Gaza Strip. Israel responds by assassinating Sheikh Ahmed Yassin and Abdel Aziz al-Rantissi.

June 30: The Israeli High Court orders changes to 19 miles of a total projected length of 423 miles of the route of the West Bank barrier.

July: the International Court of Justice at The Hague rules that the entire separation fence contravenes international law because it is being built on Palestinian land rather than on the Green Line separating Israel from the occupied territories.

2005 December: Sharon forms a centrist party (Kadima) to implement his plans. He is joined by leading political figures in the Likud and other factions.

September 12: The Israeli cabinet formally declares an end to military rule in the Gaza Strip after thirty-eight years of control; all Jewish settlements evacuated; Israel still controls territorial, sea, and air access to Gaza for security reasons.

2006 January 4: Ariel Sharon is hospitalized after suffering a major stroke. He is succeeded by his deputy, Ehud Olmert.

January 25: Hamas wins an electoral victory in the Palestinian Authority Legislative Council. Ismayil Haniya elected as prime minister, heading a new government.

February–November: Waves of Qassam missiles hit southern Israel, especially the small town of Shedort; Israel responds with brutal measures, incursions into the Gaza Strip, and targeted killings of Islamic operatives that injure many Palestinian civilians. Israel describes these casualties as "collateral damages." An Israeli soldier is captured and held hostage by the Palestinians, who demand as a condition for his release the freeing of thousands of Palestinian prisoners from Israeli jails and detention camp.

July 12–September 8: Following the kidnapping of two Israeli soldiers by Hezbollah, Israeli troops invade southern Lebanon using massive air strikes and artillery fire on Lebanese civilian infrastructure, including Rafik Hariri International Airport, which Israel says Hezbollah uses to import weapons. Israel implements air and naval blockades and a ground invasion of southern Lebanon. Hezbollah in turn launches Katyusa rockets into northern Israel and engages the Israeli troops in guerrilla warfare from reinforced positions; more than 1,400 people are killed, most of them Lebanese civilians; Lebanese infrastructure is severely damaged; 900,000 Lebanese and 300,000 Israelis are displaced and normal life is disrupted across all of Lebanon and northern Israel.

NOTES

Chapter 1. A Model for Analyzing Reciprocal Relations Between the Jewish and Arab Communities

1. Yehoshua Porath has done important work on the Arab side. See Yehoshua Porath, "Social Aspects of the Emergence of the Palestinian Arab National Movement," in Menahem Milson, ed., *Society and Political Structure in the Arab World* (New York: Humanities, 1973) and Yehoshua Porath, *The Emergence of the Palestinian Arab National Movement, 1910–1929* (London: Frank Cass, 1974). For the Jewish community, see S. N. Eisenstadt, *The Israeli Society* (New York: Basic, 1972) and Dan Horowitz and Moshe Lissak, *Origins of the Israeli Polity: Palestine under the Mandate* (Chicago: University of Chicago Press, 1978).

2. See Baruch Kimmerling, "The Impact of Land and Territorial Components of Jewish Arab Conflict and the Building of Jewish Society in Palestine (from the Beginning of the Settlement until 1955)," Ph.D. thesis, Department of Sociology, The Hebrew University, Jerusalem, 1974. In Hebrew, unpublished.

3. Edward Shils, "Centre and Periphery," in E. Shils, ed., *The Logic of Personal Knowledge* (London: Routledge and Paul, 1961), 117–130.

4. Shmuel N. Eisenstadt, *Social Differentiation and Stratification* (Glenview: Foresman, 1971).

5. As in all cases of new immigrants founding nations. See, e.g., Louis Hartz, ed., *The Founding of New Societies: Studies in the History of the United States, Latin America, South Africa, Canada, and Australia* (New York: Harcourt, Brace & World, 1964).

6. The fourth main possibility is that the immigrant society absorbs the local population.

7. That is, neither the prices of the merchandise nor their quantities were determined by the laws of supply and demand, but were to a large degree dependent

on political and ideological factors. See ESCO Foundation for Palestine, *A Study of Jewish, Arab, and British Policies* (New Haven: Yale University Press).

8. David Horowitz claims that between 1920 and 1940, lands worth close to nine million Palestinian pounds were sold to Jews, "and this stream of capital necessarily had a great influence on the creation of a middle class within the Arab population." See David Horowitz, *The Development of Palestinian Economy* (Tel Aviv: Bialik Institute, Dvir, 1948) (in Hebrew) and Said Sadek, *Palestine in the Claws of Imperialism* (Cairo: Committee for Editing and Printing, 1946), 61–76 (in Arabic).

9. Karl W. Deutsch, "Social Mobilization and Political Development," *American Political Science Review* 55 (September 1961): 494. Starting in the mid-1930s, in certain areas, a part of the stratum of the fellaheen also reached a high rate of political mobilization.

10. Jewish agriculture was the first sector to become economically profitable; then other spheres received profitable impetus. The port of Tel Aviv replaced that of Jaffa, not only as an organization, but also as a facility based entirely on skilled Jewish labor. The immigration wave of 1938–46 supplied the Jewish workforce in other areas as well, such as construction and citrus growing.

11. See Baruch Kimmerling, *The Economic Interrelationships between the Arab and Jewish Communities in Mandatory Palestine* (Cambridge, MA: MIT Center for International Studies, 1979) and ESCO, *Jewish, Arab, and British Policies*. The Middle Eastern version of these syncretic cultures was designated by the concept of Levantinism. Albert Hourani characterizes it as living according to ethical standards adapted from other sources rather than independently generated. See Albert Hourani, *Syria and Lebanon* (London: Oxford, 1963), 46. A fascinating description of the process of selectively internalizing values imported into the Middle East is given in Daniel Lerner, *The Passing of Traditional Society: Modernizing the Middle East* (Glencoe: Free Press, 1958).

12. Joseph Klausner, *A Word of Truth and Peace about the Arabs' Fear of Zionism* (Jerusalem: al-Salam, 1924) (in Arabic) and Mussa (Moshe) Smilanski, *The Jewish Imperialism and the Fellah* (Jerusalem: Malul, 1940) (in Arabic). Both were published in Arabic to try to reach the educated Arab reader and influence him to see Zionism as a blessing to indigenous Arabs. For the Brith Shalom Group and the idea of binationalism, see Susan Lee Hattis, *The Bi-National Idea in Palestine During Mandatory Times* (Haifa: Shikmona, 1970).

13. See, e.g., Jaber Shibli, *Conflict or Cooperation in Palestine* (Jerusalem, Jordan: al-Umma, 1950), 20 (in Arabic) and Jaber Shibli, Society to Safeguard al-Aqsa Mosque and Other Muslim (Holy) Places, *Proclamation* (Jerusalem: Dar al-Itam, 1934) (in Arabic).

14. See Zvi Sussman, *Wage Differentials and Quality within the Histadrut: The Impact of Egalitarian Ideology and Arab Labor on Jewish Wages in Palestine* (Ramat Gan: Massada, 1974) (in Hebrew).

15. "Youths left their families and the traditional society," Israel Kolatt tells us, "and the young watchmen and laborers have begun to wear Arab dress and conform to the customs of their neighbors." The third wave of immigrants saw this as part of the decadence of the new Jewish society. See Israel Kolatt, "Eliezer Schohat and the Poel HaTzair," in I. Shapiro, ed., *Eliezer Schohat* (Tel Aviv: Am-Oved, 1973), 49 (in Hebrew).

16. Rafiq Jabor, *The Zionist Greed in Palestine—Yesterday, Today, and Tomorrow* (Cairo: al-Fajala, 1923) (in Arabic).

17. Edward H. Spicer, "Spanish-Indian Acculturation in the Southwest," *American Anthropologist* 56 (August 1954): 665.

18. See Yehoshua Porath, *Emergence*. See also M. Sarkis and D. Jalli, *Zionism and the Unification* (Cairo: Raamsses, 1933) (in Arabic).

19. An interesting example of this approach is found in an essay by Bashir Qa'aden and Shafiq Shalani. See Bashir Qa'aden and Shafiq Shalani, *Those Are the Zionists* (Damascus: Dar al-Yakub al-Arabyia, 1946), 266 (in Arabic). Izzat Darwazah, *A Short Survey of the Palestine Problem: Facts and Figures* (Beirut: Palestine Liberation Organization, 1966).

20. See Baruch Kimmerling, *The Struggle Over the Land: A Chapter in the Sociology of the Jewish-Arab Conflict* (Jerusalem: Hebrew University Sociology, 1973) (in Hebrew).

21. Baruch Kimmerling, "The Management of the Jewish-Arab Conflict and the Building of the Israeli Nation State," *Medina, Mimshal ve'Yachasim Benlumiim* 9 (May 1976): 35–66 (in Hebrew).

22. See Dan Horowitz and Moshe Lissak, "Authority without Sovereignty: The Case of the National Center of the Jewish Community in Palestine," *Government and Opposition* 8 (Winter 1973): 48–71.

23. Lewis Coser, *The Functions of Social Conflict* (Glencoe: Free Press, 1956).

24. Moshe Ma'oz, "A Palestinian State—Where?" in M. Curtis et al., eds., *The Palestinians: People, History, and Politics* (New Brunswick: Transaction, 1975), 194.

25. Yehoshua Porath, "The Political Organizations of the Palestinian Arabs under the British Mandate," in Moshe Ma'oz, ed., *Palestinian Arab Politics* (Jerusalem: Academic Press, 1975), 4.

26. Lewis Coser, *Functions of Social Conflict*, 93.

27. The Muslim-Christian associations were political organizations created immediately after the British conquest to emphasize the shared Muslim-Christian opposition to fulfillment of the Balfour Declaration. They were organized into a flimsy federation of branches throughout the country with a shared charter. Usually the association in Jerusalem served as the center. At the Third Palestinian Congress in Haifa on December 13, 1920, representatives of the associations chose the Arab Executive Council. A description and analysis of the growth, activities, and demise

of the Muslim-Christian associations can be found in Yehoshua Porath, "Political Organizations of the Palestinians."

28. See report L/4, file IIB in the Zionist Archives.

29. *Al-Karmil*, December 25,1920 (in Arabic).

30. Yehoshua Porath, *Palestinian Arab National Movement*, Chapter 7.

31. This is the anniversary of Saladin's victory over the Christians in 1187. Thus a report in the newspaper *Al-Jami'a al Arabiya* (August 17, 1932) on the battle of Hittin opined that the time had come for Palestinians to be reliberated.

32. Tom Bowden, "The Politics of the Arab Rebellion in Palestine, 1936–39," *Middle Eastern Studies* 11, no. 2 (1975): 147.

33. Robert Szereszewski, *Essays on the Structure of the Jewish Economy in Palestine and Israel* (Jerusalem: M. Falk Institute for Economic Research, 1968), 9.

34. Zvi Sussman, *Wage Differentials and Quality within the Histadrut*, 51.

35. John Marlowe, *Rebellion in Palestine* (London: Cresset, 1946), 139.

36. Zvi Elpeleg, *The Disturbances of 1936–1939—Riots or Rebellion?* (Tel Aviv: Schiloach Institute. Tel Aviv University, 1977), 40 (in Hebrew). For an attempt at an early sociological analysis, compare Sa'ad Adin Ibrahim, *The Sociology of the Arab-Jewish Conflict* (Beirut: al-Tali's Press, 1973) (in Arabic).

37. Baruch Kimmerling, "The Impact of Land and Territorial Components of Jewish Arab Conflict."

38. See Haim Arlozoroff in his letter of June 30 to Dr. Weizmann. Haim Arlosoroff, *Jerusalem Diary* (Tel Aviv: Mifleget Poalei Eretz Israel, n.d.), 334 (in Hebrew). Arlozoroff was the most prominent leader of the Jewish polity The opposite side reached similar conclusions, and Amin al-Hussaini and other leaders even expressed them publicly. See, e.g., *Al-Jami'a al-Arabiya*, September 23, 1931.

39. See Yehuda Slotzky, *History of the Haganah: From Defense to Struggle*, vol. 2 (Tel Aviv: Am Oved, 1964) (in Hebrew).

40. Yehoshua Porath, *Palestinian Arab National Movement*, 132.

41. Majib Sudfa, *The Problem of Palestine* (Beirut: Dar al-Qitab, 1946), 72–73 (in Arabic).

42. Saadi B'seyso, *Zionism—A Critical Analysis* (Jerusalem: Commercial Printing House, 1945) (in Arabic).

43. Joel Migdal and Baruch Kimmerling, *The Palestinian People: A History* (Cambridge, MA: Harvard University Press, 2003).

44. Joel Migdal and Baruch Kimmerling, *Palestinian People*, 184.

45. Istiqlal, *The Rules of Hizb al-Istiqlal* (Jerusalem: al-Arab, 1932) (in Arabic).

46. G. Z. Israeli (pseudonym), *M.P.S.—P.C.P.—Maki: The History of the Communist Party in Israel* (Tel Aviv: Am-Oved, 1953).

47. G. Z. Israeli claims that one of the reasons that the Arabs joined the Communist Party was "the chance to meet Jewish girls." The same author claims that many of the active party workers married Jewish women, including

"Mussa," Abd al-Jani al-Karmi, and Jabra Nicola. See G. Z. Israeli, *M.P.S.—P.C.P.—Maki*, 177.

48. Of course other questions can be raised about the changes in the mode of interaction, such as the pace of the change, degree of suddenness, and many other questions about social change.

49. Usually in concrete situations the choice of a behavioral strategy toward the opposing side is not made according to rational considerations, as game theory would have it, but also by accounting for social restraints and basic codes that are profitable in the system. It is also difficult to generalize from the decisions of an isolated player in a multi-round game to those of an entire social system.

50. Anatol Rapoport, *Strategy and Conscience* (New York: Schocken, 1964), 309.

51. Concrete contact was also minimal. Thus Assaf points out that "of all the extensive Hebrew literary activity which has developed in this period (the Mandatory period), only one book has been translated into Arabic, and this is a book on child care." M. Assaf, *Arab-Jewish Relations in Palestine (1860–1948)* (Tel Aviv: Educational and Cultural Projects of the Histadrut, 1970), 281 (in Hebrew).

Chapter 2. Collective Identity as Agency and Structuration of Society

1. See Talcott Parsons, *The Social System* (Glencoe: Free Press, 1951); Robert King Merton, *Social Theory and Social Structure* (Glencoe: Free Press, 1957).

2. Others who tried less systematically to meet this challenge are Pierre Bourdieu, *Outline of a Theory of Practice* (Cambridge: Cambridge University Press, 1977); Roy Bhaskar, *The Possibility of Naturalism: Philosophical Critique of the Contemporary Human Sciences* (Brighton: Harvester, 1979); and Randall Collins, "On the Microfoundations of Macrosociology," *American Journal of Sociology* 86, no. 5 (March 1981): 984–1014.

3. Anthony Giddens, *The Constitution of Society: Outline of a Theory of Structuration* (Berkeley: University of California Press, 1984), 71.

4. John B. Thompson, "The Theory of Structuration," in David Held and John B. Thompson, eds., *Social Theory of Modern Society: Anthony Giddens and His Critics* (Cambridge: Cambridge University Press, 1989), 58. See also Alan Swingewood, *A Short History of Sociological Thought* (London: Macmillan, 1984).

5. Anthony Giddens, *New Rules of Sociological Method: A Positive Critique of Interpretative Sociology* (New York: Basic, 1976), 56; and Anthony Giddens, *Central Problems in Social Theory: Action, Structure, and Contradiction in Social Analysis* (Los Angeles: University of California Press, 1979), 17.

6. Anthony Giddens, *Central Problems in Social Theory*, 4.

7. William H. Sewell points to additional problems, such as rigid determinism. See William H. Sewell, Jr, "A Theory of Structure: Duality, Agency, and Transformation," *American Journal of Sociology* 98, no. 1 (July 1992): 1–29.

8. Ira .J. Cohen, "Structuration Theory and Social Praxis," in Anthony Giddens and Jonathan Turner, eds., *Social Theory Today* (Stanford: Stanford University Press, 1987) 273–308. This is a very brief and superficial summary of Giddens' rich and innovative approach, but due to the limitation of space we cannot do justice to his theoretical work.

9. Anthony Giddens, *New Rules of Sociological Method* and *The Constitution of Society*.

10. That different individuals assign different meanings and interpretations to the same identity, or that the same identity assumes different content in any culture, does not weaken the identity's importance. Such ambiguities are built into any cultural term and make its togetherness possible; at the same time, they help us to explain social changes that are the basis for many *kulturkampfs*.

11. Sharon Hays, "Structure and Agency and the Sticky Problem of Culture," *Sociological Theory* 12, no. 1 (March 1994): 57–72.

12. See Abraham Tesser and Jennifer Campbell, "Self-Evaluation Maintenance and the Perception of Friends and Strangers," *Journal of Personality* 50, no. 3 (September 1982): 261–279; Henri Tajfel and John C. Turner, "The Social Identity Theory of Intergroup Behavior," in S. Worchel and W. G. Austin, eds., *Psychology of Intergroup Relations* (Chicago: Nelson-Hall, 1986), 7–24; Blake E. Ashforth and Fred Mael, "Social Identity Theory and the Organization," *Academy of Management Review* 14, no. 1 (January 1989): 20–39; and M. Diehl, "Justice and Discrimination between Minimal Groups: The Limits of Equity," *British Journal of Social Psychology* 28, no. 3 (September 1990): 227–238.

13. See Gordon Marshall, Howard Newby, David Ross, and Carolyn Vogler, *Social Class in Modern Britain* (London: Unwin Hyman, 1998); M. Emmison and M. Western, "Social Class and Social Identity: A Comment on Marshal et al.," *Sociology* 24, no. 2 (1990): 241–253; and Fiona Devine, "Social Identities, Class Identity, and Political Perspectives," *Sociological Review* 40, no. 2 (1992): 229–252.

14. See Donald R. Kinder and David O. Sears, "Public Opinion and Political Action," *Handbook of Social Psychology* (Reading, MA: Addison-Wesley, 1983); Richard G. Niemi and Herbert F. Weisberg, *Controversies in Voting Behavior* (Washington, DC: CQ Press, 1984); and Anothony Heath, Roger Jowell, and John Curtice, *How Britain Votes* (Oxford: Pergamon, 1985).

15. Henri Tajfel, *Human Groups and Social Categories: Studies in Social Psychology* (Cambridge: Cambridge University Press, 1981); John C. Turner, "Social Identification and Psychological Group Formation," in Henri Tajfel, ed., *The Social Dimension: European Developments in Social Psychology*, vol. 2 (Cambridge: Cambridge University Press, 1984), 518–538; John C. Turner, "Social Categorization and the Self-Concept: Cognitive Theory of Group Behavior," in Edward E. Lawler, ed., *Advances in Group Processes* (Greenwich, CT: JAI Press, 1985), 77–122; and N. El-

2. Collective Identity as Agency and Structuration of Society 341

lemers, "Identity Management Strategies: The Influence of Socio-Cultural Variables on Strategies of Individual Mobility and Social Change," Ph.D. dissertation, University of Groningen, The Netherlands, 1991.

16. John C. Turner, "Social Categorization"; Blake E. Ashforth and Fred Mael, "Social Identity Theory."

17. John C. Turner, "Social Identification"; Henri Tajfel and John C. Turner, "The Social Identity Theory of Intergroup Behavior."

18. See Blake E. Ashforth and Fred Mael, "Social Identity Theory."

19. Dennis N. Perkins, Veronica F. Nieva, and Edward E. Lawler, *Managing Creation: The Challenge of Building a New Organization* (New York: Wiley, 1983); P. Oakes and J. C. Turner, "Distinctiveness and Salience of Social Category Membership: Is There an Automatic Perceptual Bias toward Novelty?" *European Journal of Social Psychology* 16, no. 4 (October/December 1986): 325–344.

20. Jennifer A. Chatman, Nancy E. Bell, and Barry M. Staw, "The Managed Thought: The Role of Self-Identification and Impression Management in Organizational Settings," in H. P. Sims and D. Q. Gioia, eds., *The Thinking Organization: Dynamics of Organizational Social Cognition* (San Francisco: Jossey Bass, 1986), 191–242; Fred Mael, "Organizational Identification: Construct Redefinition and Field Application with Organizations Alumni," Ph.D. dissertation, Department of Psychology, Wayne State University, Detroit, MI, 1988.

21. Noah E. Friedkin and Michael J. Simpson, "Effects of Competition on Members' Identification with their Subunits," *Administrative Science Quarterly* 30, no. 3 (September 1985): 377–394.

22. John C. Turner, "Social Identification."

23. See Gordon Marshall, Howard Newby, David Ross, and Carolyn Vogler, *Social Class in Modern Britain.*

24. See M. Emmison and M. Western, "Social Class and Social Identity."

25. Ernesto Laclau and Chantal Mouffe, *Hegemony and Socialist Strategy* (London: Verso, 1985).

26. P. Sanders, *A Nation of Home Owners* (London: Unwin Hyman, 1990).

27. Dan Horowitz and Moshe Lissak, *Troubles in Utopia* (Albany, NY: State University of New York Press, 1989).

28. Peter McDonough, Samuel H. Barnes, and Antonio Lopez Pina, "Social Identity and Mass Politics in Spain," *Comparative Political Studies* 21, no. 2 (1988): 200–230.

29. Gordon Marshall, Howard Newby, David Ross, and Carolyn Vogler, *Social Class in Modern Britain.*

30. Baruch Kimmerling, *The Interrupted System: Israeli Civilians in Wars and Routine Times* (New Brunswick, NJ: Transaction, 1985); see also Chapter Six in present volume.

31. See Chapter Four.

32. Moshe Lissak, "Images of Class and Society in the Yishuv and Israeli Society," in S. N. Eisenstadt, H. Adler, R. Bar-Yosef, and R. Kahana, eds., *The Social Structure of Israel* (Jerusalem: Academon Press, 1969) (in Hebrew).

33. Dan Horowitz and Moshe Lissak, *Origins of the Israeli Polity: Palestine under the Mandate* (Chicago: Chicago University Press, 1978).

34. In the case of Arab society in Israel, we may consider loyalties to the extended family (the *hamula*) as a semi-individualistic orientation because of the interchangeability of the two types of families.

35. Shmuel N. Eisenstadt, *Change and Continuity in Israeli Society* (New York: Humanities Press, 1974).

36. Erik Cohen, "Ethnicity and Legitimation in Contemporary Israel," in E. Krausz, ed., *Politics and Society in Israel: Studies of Israeli Society* (New Brunswick, NJ: Transaction, 1985), 322.

37. Baruch Kimmerling, *Zionism and Territory: The Socio-Territorial Dimensions of Zionist Politics* (Berkeley, CA: Institute of International Studies, 1983).

38. We use the term populist capitalism following Shapiro's definition: "Populism is composed of a distinct political ideology and a political structure. Populism is not an ideology of social change. It is designed for groups that feel deprived and cut off from the dominant culture . . . Populism is against the establishment, not against the state." Yonathan Shapiro, "Political Sociology in Israel: A Critical View," in E. Krausz, ed., *Politics and Society in Israel* (New Brunswick, NJ: Transaction, 1985), 24.

39. Yonathan Shapiro, "Political Sociology in Israel."

40. Though of immense importance, the militarist aspect of the ideology has less direct bearing on the labor market in this context, and thus, it is not elaborated here; see Chapter Five in the present volume for an extended discussion of militarism.

41. Baruch Kimmerling, *Zionism and Economy* (Cambridge, MA: Schenkman, 1983).

42. Asher Arian and Michal Shamir, "The Primarily Political Functions of the Left-Right Continuum," *Comparative Politics* 15, no. 2 (January 1983): 139–158; Erik Cohen, "Israel as a Post-Zionist Society," unpublished manuscript, Hebrew University, Jerusalem, 1991. However, despite the tremendous political and ideological changes and the greater participation of Asian African Jews in the political power structure, their economic and social status deteriorated. See Sammy Smooha and Vered Kraus, "Ethnicity as a Factor in Status Attainment in Israel," in R. V. Robinson, ed., *Research in Social Stratification and Mobility*, vol. 4 (Greenwich, CT: JAI, 1985), 151–176; Yossi Shavit and Jennifer L. Pierce, "Sibship Size and Educational Attainment in Nuclear and Extended Families: Arabs and Jews in Israel," *American Sociological Review* 56, no. 3 (June 1991): 321–330.

43. See Chapter One of the present volume.

44. Based on Uri Farago, *Stability and Change in the Jewish Identity of Working*

Youth in Israel: 1965–1974 (Jerusalem: Levi Eshkol Institute for Economic, Social, and Political Research, Hebrew University, 1977) (in Hebrew).

45. See also Simon N. Herman, *Israelis and Jews: The Continuity of an Identity* (New York: Random House, 1970); Kevin Avruch, *American Immigrants in Israel: Social Identities and Change* (Chicago: University of Chicago Press, 1981).

46. Yair Auron, *Jewish-Israeli Identity* (Tel Aviv: Sifriat Poalim, 1993) (in Hebrew).

47. Central Bureau of Statistics, *The Statistical Yearbook* (Jerusalem: State of Israel, 1992).

48. Benny Morris, *The Birth of the Palestinian Refugee Problem, 1947–1949* (New York: Cambridge University Press, 1987).

49. Baruch Kimmerling and Joel Migdal, *Palestinians: The Making of a People* (Cambridge, MA: Harvard University Press, 1994), Chapter 6.

50. Sami Khalil Mar'i, *Arab Education in Israel* (Syracuse: Syracuse University Press, 1978).

51. Y. Peres and N. Yuval-Davis, "Some Observations on the National Identity of Israeli Arabs," *Human Relations* 22, no. 6 (1969): 219–233.

52. John Hofman and Nadim Rouhana, "Young Arabs in Israel: Some Aspect of a Conflicted Social Identity," *Journal of Social Psychology* 99 (1976): 75–86.

53. Nadim Rouhana, "Palestinization among the Arabs in Israel: The Accentuate Identity," paper for the conference Arab Minority in Israel: Dilemmas of Political Orientations and Social Change, The Dayan Center, Tel Aviv University, Tel Aviv, June 3–4, 1991.

54. Sammy Smooha, *Arabs and Jews in Israel: Continuity in Mutual Intolerance* (Boulder, CO: Westview Press, 1992).

55. Asher Arian and Michal Shamir, "The Primarily Political Functions of the Left-Right Continuum."

56. Scott Flanagan, "Changing Values in Advanced Industrial Societies," *Comparative Political Studies* 14, no. 4 (1982): 403–444; Scott Flanagan, 'Measuring Value Change in Advanced Industrial Societies," *Comparative Political Studies* 15 (1982): 99–128; Ronald Ingehart and Scott Flanagan, "Value Change in Industrial Societies," *American Political Science Review* 81, no. 4 (December 1987): 1289–1319; Ronald Inglehart, "Changing Values in Japan and the West," *Comparative Political Studies* 14, no. 4 (1982): 445–479; and Ronald Inglehart, "New Perspectives on Value Change," *Comparative Political Studies* 17, no. 4 (1985): 485–532.

57. Dahlia Moore, *Labor Market Segmentation and its Implications: Social Justice, Relative Deprivation, and Entitlement* (New York: Garland, 1992).

58. Yochanan Peres, "Religious Adherence and Political Attitudes," *Sociological Papers* (1992): 1–20.

59. Yonathan Shapiro, "Political Sociology in Israel."

60. Yochanan Peres and Ephraim Yuchtman-Yaar, *Trends in Israeli Democracy* (Boulder, CO: Lynne Rienner, 1992).

61. Shmuel N. Eisenstadt, *Change and Continuity*; B. Kimmerling, *The Interrupted System*.

62. See also Baruch Kimmerling, "Yes, Back to Family," *Politika* 48 (1993): 40–45 (in Hebrew).

63. See Fred N. Kerlinger, *Foundations of Behavorial Research* (New York: Holt, Rinehart and Winston, 1986).

64. Ronald Inglehart and Scott Flanagan, "Value Change in Industrial Societies."

65. A longitudinal study is necessary for that, though such research could tell us the possible implications of such changes. Also, further research is necessary to ascertain which factors influence choices of specific identity combinations, or in line with our approach, how the social order is constituted in the field, rather than being simply the presumption of a circular process between the individual and the order.

Chapter 3. The Formation Process of Palestinian Collective Identities

1. The extensive survey was carried out in June, July, and August 1992. The representative sample included 2,500 Palestinian households in the Gaza Strip, the West Bank, and Arab Jerusalem. See Marianne Heiberg, "Opinions and Attitudes," in Marianne Heiberg and Geir Ovensen, eds., *Palestinian Society in Gaza, West Bank, and Arab Jerusalem: A Survey of Living Conditions* (Oslo: Fagbevegelsens, 1993), 249–312. The survey did not include Israeli Palestinian citizens or Palestinians in the diaspora. The great discrepancies between men and women regarding their identities are almost self-evident. Islam appears to impose great restrictions on women, who are divided between the two major competing components of the Palestinian collective identities: the traditional family and Palestinian nationalism. The same level of strength of the familial identity was found in a Jewish Israeli sample, but not among the Israeli Palestinians who expressed a strikingly different structural pattern of their collective identity, preferring Arabism and Palestinism, and pushing the familial identity into a relatively marginal position. See Chapter Two.

2. See Harrison C. White, *Identity and Control: A Structural Theory of Social Action* (Princeton: Princeton University Press, 1992).

3. Benedict Anderson, *Imagined Communities: Reflections on the Origin and Spread of Nationalism*, revised ed. (London: Verso, 1983).

4. N. Ellemers, "Identity Management Strategies: The Influence of Socio-Cultural Variables on Strategies of Individual Mobility and Social Change," Ph.D. dissertation, University of Groningen, The Netherlands, 1991. See also Dahlia Moore and Baruch Kimmerling, "Individual Strategies in Adopting Collective Identities," *International Sociology* 10, no. 4 (1995): 387–408. Baruch Kimmerling, "Boundaries and Frontiers of the Israeli Control System," in Baruch Kimmerling, ed., *The Israeli State and Society* (Albany: State University of New York Press, 1989), 265–284. For

what and how national identities are constructed, see Benedict Anderson, *Imagined Communities*.

5. J, Sidanius, R. M. Brewer, E. Banks, and B. Ekehammar, "Ideological Constraint, Political Interest, and Gender: A Swedish-American Comparison," *European Journal of Political Research* 15, no. 4 (1987): 471–492; or J. Sidanius and G. Duffy, "The Duality of Attitude Structure: A Test of Kerlinger's Critical Referents Theory within Samples of Swedish and American Youths," *Political Psychology* 9, no. 4 (December 1988): 649–670.

6. Changing identities are also a way to recruit people to cope with hardships, such as foreign rule, uncertainties of social change, and modernization. Thus, Liah Greenfeld perceived nationalism as a tool for political modernization, contrary to Gellner, who saw nationalism as outcome of modernity. It is the elites' privilege to be sovereign first; later, it is extended to the entire people. See Liah Greenfeld, *Nationalism: Five Roads to Modernity* (Cambridge, MA: Harvard University Press, 1992); Ernest Gellner, *Nations and Nationalism* (Oxford: Blackwell, 1983).

7. Recent literature examines the state as a conceptual variable, measured by its roots in a particular society's culture and tradition. See J. P. Nettl, "The State as a Conceptual Variable," *World Politics* 20, no. 4 (July 1968): 522–559.

8. In his monumental work *Muqaddima* (Prolegomena). See Abd alRahman Ibin Khaldun, *The Muqaddimah: An Introduction to History*, trans. Franz Rosenthal (London: Routledge and Kegan Paul, 1958). For an innovative discussion on the term, see Bassam Tibi, *Arab Nationalism: A Critical Inquiry* (London: Macmillan, 1990), 138–141.

9. For Qays and Yaman factions in the Jabel Nablus area, see Miriam Hoexter, "The Role of Qays and Yaman Factions in Local Political Division: Jabal Nablus Compared with Judean Hills in the First Half of the Nineteenth Century," *Asian and African Studies* 9, no. 3 (1973): 245–259. Compare this with Salim Tamari, "Factionalism and Class Formation in Recent Palestinian History," in Roger Owen, ed., *Studies in the Economic and Social History of Palestine in the Nineteenth and Twentieth Centuries* (Carbondale: Southern Illinois University Press, 1982), 181–186. Tamari called them "fictive alignments" (p. 181) because they were used as a principle of legitimacy for coalition formations.

10. Originally, the *umma* was used to denote a man's tribe, community, kinfolk, or people, and was later accepted as the Islamic concept of the "community of all the believers in God and his prophet Muhammed." The notion was juxtaposed to the individual person, the concept of which does not exist without being a part of the organic moral community of the *umma*. However, Sylvia Haim's analyses of modern Arab nationalist thought, especially that of Sati' al-Husri, who was influenced by German Romanticism, asserted that the notion has been modernized and Westernized and can unequivocally be understood as a nation in the European sense. See Sylvia G. Haim, "Islam and the Theory of Arab Nationalism," in Walter Z.

Laqueur, ed., *Middle East in Transition* (London: Routledge and Kegan Paul, 1958), 287–298. See also Sylvia Haim, "Introduction" in Sylvia G. Haim, ed., *Arab Nationalism: An Anthology* (Berkeley: University of California Press, 1976), 3–74; Eric Hobsbawm, *Nations and Nationalism since 1780: Programme, Myth, Reality* (Cambridge: Cambridge University Press, 1991); Eric Hobsbawm and Terence Ranger, eds., *The Invention of Tradition* (Cambridge: Cambridge University Press, 1983). The Qur'anic word *umma*—"the people" or "community"—is sometimes connected with *umm* (mother) and seems to be a word taken from Hebrew or Aramaic for motherhood. Today there is also a difference between *sha'b* (people) and *umma* (nation). See Bernard Lewis, *The Political Language of Islam* (Chicago: University of Chicago Press, 1988), 17.

11. See C. Ernest Dawn, *From Ottomanism to Arabism: Essays on the Origins of Arab Nationalism* (Urbana: University of Illinois Press, 1973); Sylvia G. Haim, *Arab Nationalism*, 39; and Bernard Lewis, *The Political Language of Islam*, 40–41. See also William L. Cleveland, *The Making of an Arab Nationalist: Ottomanism and Arabism in the Life and Thought of Sati al-Husri* (Princeton: Princeton University Press, 1971).

12. The Asian Arab nationalism—mainly a venture of Syrian Lebanese and Christian intellectuals—was different from Egyptian and North African Arab nationalism. Only the Egyptian occupation of Syria and Palestine created some connections among these entities. See Henry H. Dodwell, *The Founder of Modern Egypt: A Study of Muhammad 'Ali* (Cambridge: Cambridge University Press, 1967 [1931]). However, the initial Egyptian nationalism lacked many Arab components and stressed Egyptian distinctiveness. James Janowski, "Egypt and Early Arab Nationalism, 1908–1922," in Rashid Khalidi, Lisa Anderson, Muhammad Muslih, and Reeva S. Simon, eds., *The Origins of Arab Nationalism* (New York: Columbia University Press, 1991), 244–245.

13. The Syrian General Congress, claiming to be the representative of Greater Syria (i.e., Syria, Lebanon, and Palestine, including Transjordan), declared independence on March 8, 1920. The declaration also demanded a federation between Iraq and Syria, because they "possess linguistic, historical, economic, natural and racial ties, which make the two regions dependent on each other." See Sati' al-Husari, *The Day of Maysalun* (Beirut: al-Maqsuf, 1945), 246–273 (in Arabic). Al-Husri himself was a prominent ideologue of a secular pan-Arab nationalism. This was a clash with French imperial power, which, following the post–World War I armistice among the great powers, was supposed to rule the territory. Al-Husri was very close to Amir Faysal during his abortive trial to establish the Syrian state in 1918–1920; see also Muhammad Muslih, "The Rise of Local Nationalism in the Arab East," in *The Origins of Arab Nationalism*, 189–203.

14. See Andrew Rippin, *Muslims: Their Religious Beliefs and Practices. Volume 1: The Formative Period* (London: Routledge, 1990), 47–58. The Muslim Ottomans

incorporated the territory into the empire in 1516 after taking it from the Mamluks. During the reign of Suleyman the Magnificent and Selim II (1520–1574), there was a temporary economic revival, including renewal of Jewish settlement in Tiberias by Don Joseph Nasi, a banker and counselor of Selim.

15. Bassam Tibi, *Arab Nationalism: A Critical Inquiry*, second ed. (London: Macmillan, 1990), 6. Many modern Jewish thinkers claim the same about the Judaism, which is perceived as a religion that has hidden within it, since the first exile of the Jews, strong ingredients of modern nationalism. Many other nationalistic ideologies—e.g., Irish, Polish, Italian—include strong religious ingredients.

16. Jacob Katz, *Jewish Nationalism* (Jerusalem: World Zionist Organization, 1983).

17. John A. Armstrong, *Nations before Nationalism* (Chapel Hill: University of North Carolina Press, 1982), 9. See also Elie Kedourie, *Nationalism* (London: Hutchinson University Library, 1961); Anthony Smith, *Theories of Nationalism* (New York: Harper and Row, 1972); Ernest Gellner, *Nations and Nationalism* (Oxford: Basil Blackwell, 1989); and Ernest Gellner "Tribalism and the State in the Middle East," in Philip Khoury and Joseph Kostier, ed., *Tribes and State Formations in the Middle East* (London and New York: I.B. Tauris, 1991).

18. See Justine McCarthy, *The Population of Palestine: Population History and Statistics of the Late Mandate Period and the Mandate* (New York: Columbia University Press, 1990), 10. In 1860, in the twelve cities of Palestine, there were an estimated 90,000 city dwellers. Twenty years later, there were 120,000 city dwellers. Yehoshua Ben-Arieh, "The Population of the Large Towns in Palestine during the First Eighty Years of the Nineteenth Century According to Western Sources," in Moshe Maʾoz, ed., *Studies on Palestine during the Ottoman Period* (Jerusalem: Magness, 1975), 68 (in Hebrew).

19. *Shabab* literally means "youth"; however it was generalized for people who cut their traditional familial loyalties and became an urban underclass.

20. Baruch Kimmerling and Joel S. Migdal, *Palestinians: The Making of a People*, second ed.(Cambridge, MA: Harvard University Press, 1994), 36–63. For the classic analysis of the distinction between Mediterranean coast and hinterland and the interplay between the regions, see Fernand Braudel, *The Mediterranean and Mediterranean World in the Age of Phillip II*, vol. 2 (New York: Harper & Row, 1972).

21. In 1799, Ahmed Pasha al-Jezzar, the Ottoman governor of Acre, turned back the advancing French revolutionary army of Napoleon, enhanced Haifa and its region, and subsequently imposed a lengthy siege on Jaffa, forcing the Ottoman governor to flee. For a brief period, Jezzar became the first master of a part of the territory later known as Palestine. He benefited from the initial stages of the European Industrial Revolution, trading cotton and grain for firearms to equip his soldiers. See Joel S. Migdal and Baruch Kimmerling, "The Shaping of a Nation: Palestinians in the Last Century of Ottoman Rule," *New Perspectives on Turkey* 10 (Spring 1994):

75-94. Other powerful and nearly autonomous governors (*walis*) of the territory were Tahir, Sulayman, and 'Abdallah Pashas.

22. This following the 1864 Provinces (*Wilayat*) Act: The northern district (*sanjaq*) of Acre (including Akka or Acre, Haifa, and Tabarya or Tiberias), Safat, and the mountain region of al-Balq' (including Nablus, Janin, and Tulkarem) were a part of the province (*wilaya*) of Beirut. The country's central areas were included into the province of Damascus, which also held the districts of Hawran and Amman. The district of Jerusalem was the only one that included pure Palestinian subdistricts (*aqdiya*), namely Yafa (Jaffa), Gazza, Hebron, and Beersheba.

23. For a full description and impact of the reforms, see Moshe Ma'oz, *Ottoman Reforms in Syria and Palestine, 1840–1861: The Impact of Tanzimat on Politics and Society* (Oxford: Oxford University Press, 1968).

24. Albert Hourani asserted that the Tanzimat's intention was to strengthen the control of the central government in Istanbul, the consequence of which was to empower the local leadership. Albert Hourani, "Ottoman Reforms and the Politics of Notables," in William R. Polk and Richard L. Chambers, eds., *The Beginnings of Modernization in the Middle East* (Chicago: University of Chicago Press, 1968), 41–60.

25. Other large, wealthy aristocratic families in Mount Nablus were Shak's, Misris, Tuqans, 'Abd al-Hadis, Nimrs, Qasims, and Jarrars. Jaffa was the center for the Dajanis, Qasims, Bitars, Bayydas, Abu Khadras, and Tayyans. Ramla had the Tajis and al-Ghusayns. In Gaza, the Shawwas' and Husaynis' local branches possessed estates of orchards, textiles, pottery, and soap industries. The 'Amrs controlled the Hebron area for a century, manufacturing glass products and breeding sheep and goats, and the Shuqayrs had a base in Acre. Only in Haifa was there a Maronite family such as Bustani and Greek-Orthodox families of Hakim and Nassar. Some intermarriage (*musahara*) eventually took place among the large clans, such as between Nashashibis and Jabris or 'Alamis, or Khalidis and the wealthy Salam clan of Beirut. For a brilliant and detailed description of the Nablusian families and their role in the economic and social development of the territory, see Beshara Doumani, *Rediscovering Palestine: Merchants and Peasants in Jabal Nablus, 1700–1990* (Berkeley: University of California Press, 1995). He also demonstrated the intensive regional trade networks developed by these families, contrary to the initial image that only the coastal region urban families were involved in international trade.

26. From the late nineteenth century until the 1920s, Arab and Palestinian nationalists perceived the lands of Syria, Lebanon, Jordan, and Palestine as a unitary geographical, cultural, political, and economic unit under the umbrella of Greater Syria (*Bilad esh-Sham*). We will see later how, why, and when the Palestinians attached and detached themselves from this identity.

27. For a full description of the rebellion and its suppression, see Baruch Kimmerling and Joel Migdal, *Palestinians*, Chapter 1.

28. Even the poll tax on the non-Muslim minorities (*dhimmis*), the Christians, and Jews was abolished. This had a far-reaching symbolic impact, ending the dominant status of Muslims in the country and creating a universalistic notion of "citizenship" for all subjects of the Egyptian state. This was a major change in the stratified Muslim world order. However, the *dhimmis* also played a central role in the regional economy, as merchants, tax collectors, and financiers of the local strongmen's military and economic enterprises. The Muslim's position was also undermined by the Egyptian emancipation, which included the minorities in the local councils (*majlis idare*). Thomas Philipp, "Jews and Arab Christians: Their Changing Position in Politics and Economy in Eighteenth-Century Syria and Egypt," in Amnon Cohen and Gabriel Baer, eds., *Egypt and Palestine: A Millennium of Association (868–1948)*, (New York: St. Martin's, 1984), 150–166.

29. Shimon Shamir, "Egyptian Rule (1832–1840) and the Beginning of the Modern History of Palestine," in A. Cohen and G. Baer, eds., *Egypt and Palestine: A Millennium of Association (868–1948)* (New York: St. Martin's, 1984), 220–221. Mirian Hoexter draws a different picture of the impact of the short period of Egyptian rule in Palestine, or more precisely on the Jabal Nablus area. Direct rule was not imposed and the Egyptians relied heavily on the local elite families and the 'ulama, especially on the 'Abd al-Hadis. M. Hoexter. "Egyptian Involvements in the Politics of Notables in Palestine: Ibrahim Pasha in Jabal Nablus," in A. Cohen and G. Baer, eds., *Egypt and Palestine: A Millennium of Association (868–1948)* (New York: St. Martin's, 1984), 190–213. For more documents from Cairo archives, see Mohammed Sabry, *L'empire egyptien sous Mohamed-Ali et la question d'orient (1811–1849)* (Paris: Paul Geuthner, 1930), 329–394. Sabry, a great admirer of 'Ali, described the enormous benefits that the Egyptian administration granted to the population of Syria and Palestine, and the great enthusiasm with which Ibrahim was welcomed. He referred to the revolt and to intrigues of the Turks and European powers. Despite this, the short period of Egyptian rule is considered by Tibi (*Arab Nationalism*, 96–105) not only as a first opening to modernization by introducing new educational systems and curricula into Christian schools, but also the first cry of the new Arab nationalism as opposed to older Ottomanism.

30. For detailed documentation, see Asad Jibrail Rustum, *The Royal Archives of Egypt and the Disturbances in Palestine, 1834*, Oriental Series no. 11. (Beirut: American University of Beirut, 1938); Asad Jibrail Rustum, *A Corpus of Arabic Documents Relating to the History of Syria under Mehemet 'Ali Rasha*, vols. 1–5 (Beirut: American University of Beirut, 1929–1934). For an account of some of the events from the perspective of the notable families, such as the Jabel Nablus Nimr family, who supposedly remained loyal to the Ottomans over the entire period of the revolt, see Ihsan al-Nimr, *Ta'rikh Jabal Nablus wa'l-Balqa*, vols. 1–2 (Damascus, 1938). This author argues that the idea of rebellion against the Egyptians was raised during a *hajj* journey of Nimrs and other sheikhs to Mecca, giving the halo to the Nimrs and

a religious meaning to the revolt. A large number of sources are in Mohammed Sabry, *L'empire egyptien.*

31. William Roe Polk, *The Opening of South Lebanon, 1788–1840: A Study of the Impact of The West on the Middle East* (Cambridge, MA: Harvard University Press, 1963), xix.

32. Bernard Lewis, *History: Remembered, Recovered, Invented* (Princeton: Princeton University Press, 1975), 12. Importantly, Lewis warned that there is a danger in the processes of "recovering history," and if it is done for political purposes, it can lead to fabricating or suppressing facts and events, resulting in "invented history." See Eric Robert Wolf, *Europe and the People without History* (Los Angeles: University of California, 1982). In our context, such an invented history is the claim that the ancient Canaanites were in fact Arabs who pre-dated the first Israelite tribes. See Ishaq Musa al-Husayni, *Urubat Bayt al-Maqdis* (Beirut: Palestine Liberation Organization, 1969); or Muhammad Adib al-'Amir, *Urbat Filastin* (Beirut: al-Maktaba al-Asriyya, 1972).

33. Beshara Doumani, *Rediscovering Palestine,* 7.

34. For the economic development of the territory, see Alexander Scholch, "European Penetration and Economic Development of Palestine, 1856–1882," in Roger Owen, ed., *Studies in the Economic and Social History of Palestine in the Nineteenth and Twentieth Centuries* (Carbondale: Southern Illinois University Press, 1982), 10–87; Haim Gerber, *The Social Origins of the Modern Middle East* (Boulder, CO: Lynne Rienner, 1987); Charles Issawi, *An Economic History of the Middle East and North Africa* (New York: Columbia University Press, 1982); Iris Agmon, "Foreign Trade as a Catalyst of Change in the Arab Economy in Palestine 1879–1914," *Cathedra* (October 1986): 107–132 (in Hebrew); Sa'id B. Himadeh, ed., *Economic Organization of Palestine* (Beirut: American University Press, 1939); Roger Owen, *The Middle East in the World Economy* (New York: Metheun, 1981); and Baruch Kimmerling and Joel Migdal, *Palestinians,* 12–14.

35. For an excellent description of the rise of Jaffa as a modern commercial port city, see Ruth Kark, *Jaffa: A City in Evolution,* trans. Gila Brand (Jerusalem: Yad Izhak Ben Zvi, 1990). However, Kark ignores the place of Jaffa as the modern Arab commercial center of the territory, and in general underplays and blurs the basic Arabic character of the city.

36. Von Moltke, then the Germam military envoy in Istanbul, published a plan to establish Palestine as a Jewish autonomous state under German control. See Mordechai Eliav, "German Interests and the Jewish Community in Nineteenth Century Palestine," in *Ottoman Reforms.* 426–427. Guizot wished to internationalize Palestine in the framework of a French Levant, similar to a plan by Palmerston and other British politicians and intellectuals.

37. Shimon Shamir, "The Impact of Western Ideas on Traditional Society in Ottoman Palestine," in *Ottoman Reforms,* 507–516; Hisham Sharabi, *Arab Intellectuals*

and the West: The Formative Years, 1875–1914 (Baltimore: Johns Hopkins University Press, 1968).

38. This assumption goes beyond Edward Carr's assertion that a geographical unit can serve as a source of collective consciousness. See Edward Hallett Carr, *Nationalism and After* (New York: Macmillan, 1945). It also deals with the criticism regarding the invention of an as-yet-nonexistent Palestinian identity by going beyond the general historiographical tendency to consider a territorial unit as corresponding with events that happened long before and after the analyzed period. Here I suggest a methodology that treats a population of a territory as a single analytical unit over a period of about a hundred years. In sociological terms, this is considered a case study.

39. See Baruch Kimmerling, *Zionism and Territory: The Socioterritorial Dimension of Zionist Politics.* (Berkeley: Institute of International Studies, University of California Press, 1983); Gershon Shafir, *Land, Labour, and the Origins of the Israeli-Palestinian Conflict* (Cambridge: Cambridge University Press, 1989). For later developments, see Jacob Coleman Hurewitz, *The Struggle for Palestine* (New York: Norton, 1950). For the most comprehensive and detailed overview, see Mark Tessler, *A History of the Israeli-Palestinian Conflict* (Bloomington: Indiana University Press, 1994).

40. Usually the Balfour Declaration is contrasted with the exchange of a letter between Husayn, the so-called Sherif of Mecca, and the British envoy in Egypt, Sir Henry McMahon, which states that "Great Britain is prepared to recognize and support the independence of Arabs in all the regions within all the limits demanded by the Sherif of Mecca" (October 24, 1915). The Sherif's demands, as well as the British limits, did not included areas of relevance to Palestine. On the British dual obligations, promises, and interpretation of the letters, see Elie Kedourie, *The Anglo-Arab Labyrinth: The McMahon-Husayn Correspondence and Its Interpretations, 1914–1939* (Cambridge: Cambridge University Press, 1976). In 1916, Britain and France divided much of the Middle East among themselves into zones of influence (via the Sykes-Picot agreement). See Elie Kedourie, *England and the Middle East, the Destruction of the Ottoman Empire, 1914–1922* (London: Bowes and Bowes, 1956), 128. Following a meeting in San Remo in April 1920, the Sykes-Picot agreement was implemented, and the allies decided to put Syria and Lebanon under French mandate and Mesopotamia (Iraq) and Palestine under British mandate. In 1921, the Palestine Mandate was cut into in two territories to be granted to another son of Husayn Abdullah, his own emirate; this territory became Transjordan. The League of Nations confirmed these arrangements and granted them international recognition. The boundaries of Palestine were finalized in an Anglo-French convention in March 1923.

41. In many ways, this perception was anachronistic. Since the Young Turks coup of 1908, the whole empire had undergone a Turkification process, accompanied almost from the beginning by the secularization, modernization, and centralization

of the bureaucracy. Thus, in the Nablus area, the government displaced the local Arab notables (of the Tuqan, Abd al-Hadi, and Hammad clans) from their posts with Turkish civil servants. The Nablusites reacted with stormy demonstrations, demanding the return to power of Sultan Abdulhamid and the rules of *sharia*. Zeine Nour-Ud-Din Zeine, *The Emergence of Arab Nationalism: With Background Study of Arab Turkish Relations in the Near East* (New York: Caravan, 1973).

42. See Elie Kedourie, *England and the Middle East,* 76.

43. See Muhammed Y. Muslih, *The Origins of Palestinian Nationalism* (New York: Columbia University Press, 1988), 124.

44. On this exceptional attempt, see A. L. Tibawi, *A Modern History of Syria, Including Lebanon and Palestine* (London: Macmillan, 1969), 305–314. See also George Antonious, *The Arab Awakening: The Story of the Arab National Movement* (London: Capricorn, 1965). Antonious, the young Christian Lebanese nationalist and intellectual, was a member of Faysal's inner circle during the attempt at state building. See also Malcolm B. Russell, *The First Modern Arab State: Syria under Faysal, 1918–1920* (Minneapolis: Bibliotheca Islamica, 1985). Later the British compensated Faysal by nominating him as ruler of Iraq.

45. *Qawm* is used as "people" rather than "nation"; however, both are possible, depending on period and context.

46. On the sudden outbreak of a local proto-nationalist movement, see the next section. As for the description of Palestinian nationalist activity during the Mandatory period, see Yehoshua Porath's three volumes, *The Emergence of the Palestinian Arab National Movement, 1918–1929* (London: Cass, 1974); *The Palestinian National Movement: From Riots to Rebellion, 1929–1939* (London: Cass, 1977); and *In Search of Arab Unity* (London: Cass, 1986). This was a pioneering and comprehensive effort to document and describe the rise of the Palestinian nationalist movement during the British colonial period. However, lacking any analytical framework about nationalism and national movements, or even a working definition of what nationalism is, the author failed to reach any conclusions beyond a detailed chronology of arbitrarily chosen events. See also William B. Quandt, Fuad Jaber, and Ann Mosely Lesch, *The Politics of Palestinian Nationalism* (Berkeley and Los Angeles: University of California Press, 1973); Ann Mosely Lesch, *Arab Politics in Palestine, 1917–1939* (Ithaca: Cornell University Press, 1979).

47. The *al-Karmil* weekly, published in Haifa, was founded in 1908 by Najib Nasser, a Palestinian pharmacist settled in Tiberias, with the major aim of fighting Arab land sales to Jews. *Filastin* (Palestine), founded as a bi-weekly by the al-'Isa cousins in Jaffa in 1911, became the largest-circulating Arab newspaper in the country. The boundaries of the geographical region envisioned by the title are unclear. The paper changed loyalties several times in the course of the local struggle between the Husaynis and the Nashashibis. See Rashid Khalidi, "The Role of the Press

in the Early Arab Reaction to Zionism," *Peules Mediterranees* 20 (July/September 1982): 107–122.

48. Quoted by Mohammad Muslih, *Origins of Palestinian Nationalism*, 181, from Akram Zu'aytir's unpublished manuscript. The Congress included delegates of Muslim-Christian associations from most of the major towns in the country. On these, see the following section of this paper.

49. The origin of the name was coined after the Philistines, a maritime people probably from Phoenician culture who settled the coastal plain of the country in 1190 B.C., at the same time that the mythological Hebrew tribes lead by Jehosuah conquered most of the Land of Canaan and annihilated most of the local inhabitants. King David defeated the Philistines in a series of bitter battles, and they disappeared from history. A long time after these events, following a series of Judean rebellions against their Hellenistic and Roman rulers, the second Jewish Temple was destroyed by the Roman Empire in 70 A.D. In 135 A.D., most of the Jews were exiled, effectively destroying the Jewish polity. The Romans then renamed the territory using the Philistine title. When in 635–7 Arab warriors captured the territory from the Byzantines, they called it *jund* (military district) *Filastin*. These semihistorical and semimythological events, which occurred 2,000 to 3,500 years ago, are still used and abused in the historiography of the present struggle for the land of Palestine.

50. Most of the Jewish population rejected or did not take advantage of most of the goods and services that the colonial state provided, as they attempted to build an independent parallel system, or a state within a state. For this see Baruch Kimmerling, "State Building, State Autonomy and the Identity of Society: The Case of the Israeli State," *Journal of Historical Sociology* 6, no. 4 (1993): 396–430.

51. For the agrarian policy of the colonial state, see Ylana N. Miller, *Government and Society in Rural Palestine: 1920–1948* (Austin: University of Texas Press, 1985). For the general development of Mandatory rule, see Jacob Reuveny, *The Administration of Palestine under the British Mandate, 1920–1948: An Institutional Analysis* (Ramat Gan: Bar Ilan University Press, 1993) (in Hebrew); Baruch Kimmerling, *The Economic Interrelationship between the Arab and Jewish Communities in Mandatory Palestine* (Cambridge, MA: MIT Center for International Studies, 1979).

52. For the impact of Jewish colonization on Palestinian peasants, see Charles Kamen, *Little Common Ground: Arab Agriculture and Jewish Settlement in Palestine* (Pittsburgh: University of Pittsburgh Press, 1991); Kenneth W. Stein, *The Land Question in Palestine, 1917–1939* (Chapel Hill: University of North Carolina Press, 1984); Baruch Kimmerling, *Zionism and Territory*, 1983. Miller also emphasized the impact of land sales on the formation of peasant nationalism. For the formation of a Palestinian semi-urban proletariat, see Rachelle Taqqu, "Peasants into Workmen: Internal Labor Migration and the Arab Village Community under the Mandate," in

Joel S. Migdal, ed., *Palestinian Society and Politics* (Princeton: Princeton University Press, 1980), 261–286, and Sara Graham-Brown, "The Political Economy of the Jabel Nablus, 1920–1948," *Studies in the Economic and Social History of Palestine*, 88–178.

53. Jewish immigration was limited to the so-called absorption capacity of the country, measured by the amount of overall unemployment. Nadav Halevy, "The Political Economy of Absorptive Capacity: Growth and Cycles in Jewish Palestine," *Middle Eastern Studies* 19 (October 1983): 456–469.

54. For the most comprehensive analytical presentation of the development of the Jewish settler-society in colonial Palestine, see Dan Horowitz and Moshe Lissak, *Origins of the Israeli Polity: Palestine under the Mandate* (Chicago and London: University of Chicago Press, 1978). See also Dan Horowitz, "Before the State: Communal Politics in Palestine under the Mandate," in Baruch Kimmerling, ed., *The Israeli State and Society: Boundaries and Frontiers* (Albany: State University of New York Press, 1989). For the presentation of the British economic system in Palestine and its goals and policy, see Nachum T. Gross, "The Economic Policy of the Mandatory Government in Palestine," Discussion Paper No. 81.06, Falk Institute for Economic Research, Jerusalem, 1981 (in Hebrew). For the connection between scarce and high-cost land and the building of the centralized type of Jewish settler-immigrant society, see Baruch Kimmerling, *Zionism and Economy* (Cambridge, MA: Schenkman, 1983). For the best sympathetic analyses of Zionism, see David Vital, *The Origins of Zionism* (Oxford: Oxford University Press, 1975); David Vital, *Zionism: The Formative Years* (Oxford: Oxford University Press, 1982); David Vital, *Zionism: The Crucial Phase* (Oxford: Oxford University Press, 1987). See also Walter Laqueur, *A History of Zionism* (New York: Holt, Reinhart and Winston, 1972). For a history of perceptions of Jewish-Arab relations, see Yosef Gorny, *Zionism and The Arabs: 1882–1948—A Study of Ideology* (Oxford: Clarendon, 1987).

55. The most important report was that of the or the Peel commission: see 1937. Palestine Royal Commission, *Report*, presented by the Secretary of State for the Colonies to Parliament by Command of His Majesty, Cmd. 5479 (London: HMSO, 1937). The commission suggested officially, for the first time, to partition the country, formulating the problem as a struggle between two national movements. The previous reports were the Shaw report, or *Report of the Commission on the Palestine Disturbance of August 1929*, Cmd. 3530 (London: The Jewish Agency, 1930); *Palestine: Report on Immigration, Land Settlement and Development by Sir John Hope Simpson*, Cmd. 3686 (London: His Majesty's Stationary Office, 1930); *Report by Mr. C. F. Strickland of the Indian Civil Service on the Possibility of Introducing a System of Agricultural Cooperation in Palestine* (Jerusalem: Government Printer, 1930); *Report of A Committee on the Economic Conditions of Agriculturalists in Palestine and the Fiscal Measures of Government in Relation Thereto* (Jerusalem: Government Printer, 1930); *Cooperative Societies in Palestine: Report by the Registrar of Cooperative Soci-*

eties on the Development During the Years 1921–1937 (Jerusalem: Government Printer, 1938). For a summary of the development of Palestine, see ESCO Foundation for Palestine, *Palestine; A Study of Jewish, Arab and British Policies* (New Haven: Yale University Press, 1974).

56. Since the 1910s, most of the tenants removed from land purchased by Jews received alternative parcels, compensation, or both. To avoid ethnic or national clashes, the Jews purchased land only when the Arab tenants had been removed by the original Arab owners. Skilled entrepreneurs, specializing in the land market, appeared on both the Arab and Jewish sides. See Baruch Kimmerling, *Zionism and Territory.*

57. For a survey of the development of diverse kinds of Palestinian nationalism and collective identities, see Helena Lindholm, "Official and Popular Palestinian Nationalism: Creations and Transformations of Nationalist Ideologies and National Identities, 1917–1993," licentiate thesis, Peace and Development Research Institute, Goteborg University, Goteborg, 1994.

58. The Christian Arabs were about 15 percent of the Arab population of the country, belonging to various churches and congregations. During the Ottoman period, the Christian Arabs were often threatened with enmity and treated on a formal level as a minority group in a similar manner to the Jews. Several times when there were disturbances in the country, such as during the rebellion against Muhammed 'Ali's regime, the Muslims directed pogroms toward Christian communities. Later, some of the most prominent Palestinian and pan-Arab nationalists were of Christian origin.

59. At the same time and under the influence of developments in Syria and other similar phenomenon in Europe, some semi-clandestine organizations and clubs were established. Here the boundaries between cultural, political, and semi-military activities were highly blurred. If the MCAs were associations of the established notables and elite groups, the clubs were venues for younger and more radical intelligentsia. The most important organizations were the al-Muntada al-Adabi (The Literary Club) and al Nadi al-'Arabi (The Arab Club). Al-Muntada was very active in 1919–1921, mostly dominated by a Nashashibi coalition, but also included some Husaynis, developing a hard core anti-Zionist, pan-Arab ideology. Al-Nadi was an offshoot of the Damascus-based al-Fatat and shared al-Nadi's ideology, but was dominated by a coalition of younger Nablusian and al-Husaynis. The Jamiiyyat al-Ikha wal-Afaf, a grassroots association composed mainly of policemen and other lower officials in the British civil service, prepared to execute Arabs who cooperated or sold land to Jews, but seemed to have been dissolved by British intelligence in 1918–19. Mohammad Muslih asserts that during Faysal's regime in Damascus, some Palestinians formed paramilitary organizations, collecting arms and recruiting members to struggle against the British and Jews in Palestine. See Mohammad Muslih, *The Origins of Palestinian Nationalism,* 171–172.

60. The Jewish Agency for Palestine was the official local branch of the World Zionist Organization, and was recognized by the Mandate as the representative of the Zionist Jewish community. The Arabs demanded the same recognition for the Executive Committee. The British agreed, so long as the Arabs recognized the legitimacy of the Mandate. The Arab leadership refused, anxious not to appear to accept the Balfour Declaration. Thus, de jure, the Arab Executive was never recognized, but for all practical purposes the British referred to it as a fully recognized leadership. See Yehoshua Porath, *The Emergence of Palestinian National Movement*, 1974.

61. The pan-Syrian or pan-Arabic identities and their formulation as a political goal never completely disappeared from the Palestinian public agenda. They were brought up again by several delegates during the Fifth Congress (Nablus 1922), and were a part of the 1930s Istiqlal Party platform. Led mainly by men who had been associated with Faysal, it was also part of one of the slogans used by rebels in 1937–38 and imposed on Palestinian refugees in camps under Egyptian and Syrian rule during the 1950s and early 1960s.

62. Under the Ottoman law and millet system of autonomous religious communities, Christian Arabs were considered to be a minority group like the Jews. However, they were the most educated and wealthy of the mainly urban Arab population. In the Palestinian historiography today, the past and present discrimination of the Christian Palestinians and the occasional tensions among the Muslims and Christians are regarded as taboo subjects, as they contradict the conception of the Palestinians as one unified nation.

63. For more on al-Husayni, see Philip Mattar, *The Mufti of Jerusalem: Al-Hajj Amin Al-Husayni and the Palestinian-Arab National Movement* (New York: Columbia University Press, 1988); Taysir Jbara, *Palestinian Leader Hajj Amin al-Husayni: Mufti of Jerusalem* (Princeton: Kingston, 1985). For a detailed description of the events around the formation of the SMC and British involvement, see Yehoshua Porath, *The Emergence of Palestinian National Movement*, 1974, Chapter 4.

64. Al-Husayni's first Palestinian activity was to exploit Nabi Musa, a local popular religious, mainly folkloric festival, which he tried to convert into a country-wide religious event.

65. A very interesting case is an attempt in the early 1930s to establish a memorial day for Salah al-Din (Saladin) and his Hittin victory (1187) over the Crusaders, which led to the dismantling of the Latin Kingdom of Jerusalem (1099–1187). However, when it became clear that such a commemoration would hurt the Christians, it was canceled. Arab historiosophy has often drawn parallels between the Crusaders and the Zionist settlement as an example of how a technologically superior foreign power conquered the country, but was not able to hold it for a long period of time.

66. See Baruch Kimmerling, "A Model for Analysis of Reciprocal Relations be-

tween the Jewish and Arab Communities in Mandatory Palestine," *Plural Societies* 14, no. 3/4 (1983): 45–68.

67. A version of this perception was preserved in the collective memory of the refugee-camp dwellers as a lost paradise, a memory and social identity of places in Palestine from they were uprooted following the 1948 *nakbah* (catastrophe). See, Rosemary Sayigh, "Source of Palestinian Nationalism," *Journal of Palestine Studies* 6 (1977): 17–40, and Rosemary Sayigh, *Palestinians: From Peasants to Revolutionaries* (London: Zed, 1979). For the formation of the refugee problem, see Benny Morris, *The Birth of the Palestinian Refugee Problem, 1947–1949* (Cambridge: Cambridge University Press, 1987).

68. See Baruch Kimmerling and Joel Migdal, *Palestinians: The Making of a People*, 1994, Chapter 5. For an Arab analysis of the Palestinian disaster, see Constantine K. Zurayk, *The Meaning of Disaster*. trans. R. Bayly Winder (Beirut: Khayat's College, 1956 [1948]).

69. For the history and development of the PLO, see Helena Cobban, *The Palestinian Liberation Organization: People, Power and Politics* (Cambridge: Cambridge University Press, 1984). For a description of the internal ideological struggles, see Alain Gresh, *The PLO—The Struggle Within*, trans. A. M. Berrett (London: Zed, 1988); see also Baruch Kimmerling and Joel Migdal, *Palestinians*, Part 3.

70. Anthony D. Smith, *The Ethnic Origins of Nations* (Oxford: Blackwell, 1986).

71. Benedict Anderson, *Imagined Communities*.

72. See Salim Tamari, "Problems of Social Research in Palestine: An Overview," *Current Sociology* 42, no. 2 (1994): 68–86. Tamari asserted that this was made under the influence the Israeli sociology and historiography that stressed the sui generis character of the Israeli Jewish case study. The view of the incomparable and exceptional nature of the Israeli as well as Palestinian cases was recently broken by Ian Lustick in *Unsettled States/Disputed Lands: Britain in Ireland, France in Algeria, Israel and the West-Bank-Gaza* (Ithaca: Cornell University Press, 1993). Also see Gershon Shafir, *Land, Labour,* and Baruch Kimmerling, "Ideology, Sociology and Nation Building: The Palestinians and Their Meaning in Israeli Sociology," *American Sociological Review* 57, no. 4 (1992): 446–460; Baruch Kimmerling, *Zionism and Territory*, Chapter 1.

Chapter 4. Between Primordial and Civil Definitions of the Collective Identity

1. Shmuel N. Eisenstadt, *Change and Continuity in Israeli Society* (New York: Humanities Press, 1974), 31–37.

2. Virtually all Zionist philosophers have expressed this concept. See, e.g., the comprehensive introductions to Arthur Hertzberg, *The Zionist Idea: A Historical Analysis and Reader* (New York: Doubleday and Herzl, 1959); Shlomo Avineri, *The*

Making of Modern Zionism: The Intellectual Origins of the Jewish State (London: Weidenfeld and Nicolson, 1981); Walter Laqueur, *A History of Zionism* (London: Weidenfeld and Nicolson, 1972); David Vital, *The Origins of Zionism* (Oxford: Oxford University Press, 1975).

3. Royal Institute of International Affairs, "Jewish Nationalism," in *Nationalism* (Oxford: Oxford University Press, 1939), 163–169. *Nationalism* is a report by a study group of members of the Royal Institute of International Affairs.

4. See Elie Kedourie, *Nationalism* (London: Hutchinson, 1960); Anthony Douglas Smith, *Theories of Nationalism* (New York: Harper & Row, 1971); Peter F. Sugar, *Nationality and Society in Habsburg and Ottoman Europe* (Brookfield, VT: Variorium, 1997); Don L. Sturzo, *Nationalism and Internationalism* (New York: Roy, 1946).

5. In certain contexts, religions with particularly universalistic and supernational overtones, such as Catholicism and Islam, may foster and consolidate national movements. The Polish Revolution of the mid-1980s combined social protest with clearly religious intentions. The same is true of nationalism in many Muslim countries, which seek to participate in the pan-Islamic movement through more particularistic nationalist frames of reference. Fazlur Rahman, *Islam* (Chicago and London: University of Chicago Press, 1966), 227.

6. Several Orthodox rabbis took part in the First Zionist Congress, but when their hopes of imbuing Zionism with an exclusively religious character were not realized, they ceased their participation in and support of the movement. The First Zionist Congress, originally due to take place in Munich, was moved to Basel because of severe opposition by the German Rabbinate. On July 6, 1897, the Executive of the Organization of German Rabbis officially condemned Zionism, considering it to be "contradictory to the objectives of Judaism, as expressed in the Bible and subsequent religious sources." The Orthodox Agudat Israel Party, the largest worldwide Jewish political party until the destruction of European Jewry, displayed strong and consistent opposition to the Zionist idea, considering it to be an even greater danger than secularism, perhaps because of Zionism's use of religious symbols. Agudat Israel's approach to Zionism, in both Palestine and the rest of the world, became ambivalent only after the Holocaust and especially after the successful establishment of the state of Israel and its subsequent battles against the surrounding Arab environment. See Menachem Friedman, *Society and Religion: The Non-Zionist Orthodox Community in Palestine* (Jerusalem: Yad Ben Zvi, 1977, pp. 219–226 (in Hebrew).

7. Utter rejection of traditional Jewish life was already inherent in the Jewish Enlightenment (Haskala) revolution and in the processes of secularization that accompanied it. Zionism, which, with some reservations, had inherited this approach from the Haskala and its socialist wing, naturally placed strong emphasis upon productivity and upending the social pyramid.

8. Zionism maintains a very complex attitude toward anti-Semitism. Obviously, anti-Semitism is a pathological and detestable phenomenon, but as such, Zionism cannot define itself as a direct reaction to anti-Semitism. Zionism is prepared to consider anti-Semitism as a factor in emigrating from a country of origin, but not as a pull toward Zion. Nevertheless, the very existence of anti-Semitism constitutes a necessary condition for rejecting all other Jewish alternatives to Zionism, such as assimilation, ethnic-religious integration in democratic and developing societies, or participation in revolutionary movements for a changing world order—a by-product of which will be the disappearance of the Jewish problem.

9. Consider the doctrine of Simon Dubnow concerning the possibility of formulating and maintaining Jewish nationalism, which is not linked to the soil of Eretz Israel. See Simon Dubnow, "The Doctrine of Jewish Nationalism," in Michael Selzer, ed., *Zionism Reconsidered* (London: Macmillan Publishers, 1970), 131–156.

10. See Baruch Kimmerling, *Zionism and Territory: The Socio-territorial Dimensions of Zionist Politics* (Berkeley, CA: University of California, Institute of International Studies, 1983), 204–208.

11. For a discussion of the pioneer image, see Shmuel N. Eisenstadt, *Israeli Society* (New York: Basic Books, 1967).

12. This was essentially a later reaction, resulting largely from the trauma induced by the Sabbetaian and Frankist movements. which attempted to achieve an immediate mass implementation of Judaism's nationalist foundations, disregarding both internal and international political conditions. The relationship between the Sabbetaian and Frankist movements and Zionism—or at least certain components thereof—posed some difficulty for the Zionist movement, as it was both a subject for self-criticism and an attack from the outside, especially regarding Zionism's irrational or messianic dimensions. See Jacob Katz, "Israel and the Messiah," *Commentary* 73, no. 1 (January 1982): 34–41, and Janet O'Dea, "Religious Zionism: Between Messianism and Realism," *Bitefutzot Hagola* 83/84 (1978): 44–49 (in Hebrew).

13. Within the political framework of the pre-state Jewish communities in Palestine, and later in the state of Israel, there were two additional reasons for the rather moderate form of Zionist socialist ideologies. First, as Ben-Gurion declared, the Jews had to change from class to nation, that is, attain predominance within the collectivity by demanding a series of compromises, both with their political rivals for the sake of forming coalitions and within a consociational framework. Second, the Soviet Union's generally hostile attitude toward Zionism did not encourage a positive attitude toward Marxism, even causing Zionists to reject the extremist elements within the system to the point of cooperating with the British (as in the 1920s) in fighting communism and the far left. The reaction was mediated by the Soviet stand regarding the claims of the Arab national movement,

which divided the left within the system. This constituted an additional incentive for the centripetal tendencies of the Zionist left.

14. See Robert J. Brym, *The Jewish Intelligentsia and Russian Marxism: A Sociological Study of Intellectual Radicalism and Ideological Divergence* (London and Basingstoke: Macmillan, 1978).

15. This term is the Hebrew for "citizen," a label referring to the non–labor sector in the Jewish community, roughly similar to the French term "bourgeois."

16. Robert Bellah, "Religion and Legitimation in the American Republic," *Society* 5, no. 4 (1978): 19.

17. John Murray Cuddihy, *The Ordeal of Civility: Freud, Marx, Levi-Strauss, and the Jewish Struggle with Modernity* (New York: Basic, 1974).

18. Due to a combination of economic and political factors, especially regarding local patterns of land ownership, the original Zionist enterprise was constructed in areas peripheral in biblical Jewish history and symbolism, namely, the coastal plain and the Jezreel and Jordan valleys, which were part of Philistia. The core territory in the hilly regions of Judea and Samaria was opened to Jewish settlement only after the 1967 war, except for Jerusalem and other limited regions. See Baruch Kimmerling, *Zionism and Territory*, 147–182, 225–228.

19. Uri Farago, *Stability and Change in the Jewish Identity of Working Youth in Israel: 1965–1974* (Jerusalem: Hebrew University of Jerusalem, Levi Eshkol Institute for Economic, Social, and Political Research, 1977) (in Hebrew); M. Friedman, *Society and Religion: The Non-Zionist Orthodox in Eretz Israel—1918-1936* (Jerusalem: Yad Ben-Zvi, 1977).

20. See S. Aloni, *The Arrangement* (Tel Aviv: Ot Paz, 1971) (in Hebrew).

21. See Zvi Raanan, *Gush Emunim* (Tel Aviv: Sifriyat Poalim, 1980) (in Hebrew).

22. Simon N. Herman, *Israelis and Jews: The Continuity of an Identity* (New York: Random House, 1970); Uri Farago, *Stability and Change.*

23. These statistics are consistent with all other findings in this area. See Gallup Poll, *Maariv*, August 4, 1971; *Gesher* 18 (1972): 108; Pori Poll, *Haaretz*, September 2, 1973; and I. Shelach, *Indications Towards Secular Religion in Israel* (Jerusalem: Hebrew University of Jerusalem, Kaplan School of Economics and Social Science, 1975) (in Hebrew).

24. Kevin Avruch, *American Immigrants in Israel: Social Identities and Change* (Chicago and London: University of Chicago Press, 1981).

25. The concept of Eretz Israel also has a non-primordial, more civic connotation, referring to the small, intimate collectivity that strives for equality among people and within society. The term "Eretz Israel," which is connected with the pre-state, socialistically oriented Jewish community in Palestine, today arouses nostalgia among many veteran settlers who have been largely alienated from the traditional power centers since the 1977 change in government. Eretz Israel is also characterized by a large measure of secular familialism.

26. M. Samet, *Religion and State in Israel* (Jerusalem: Hebrew University of Jerusalem, Kaplan School of Economics and Social Science, 1979) (in Hebrew).

27. Yehuda Ben-Meir and Peri Kedem, "Index of Religiosity of the Jewish Population of Israel," *Megamot* 24, no. 3 (February 1979): 353–362 (in Hebrew).

28. Norman L. Zucker, *The Coming Crisis in Israel: Private Faith and Public Policy* (Cambridge, MA: MIT Press, 1973).

29. See Charles S. Liebman and Eliezer Don-Yehiya, *Civil Religion in Israel* (Berkeley, CA: University of California Press, 1983).

30. Charles S. Liebman and Eliezer Don-Yehiya, *Civil Religion*, 60.

31. Jewish immigration from Yemen commenced as early as 1882 and was purely religious in nature in that it did not confront modern nationalism. Nevertheless, it differed from previous traditional Jewish pilgrimages, in which Jews came to die and be buried in the Holy Land or to participate in a community of scholars. Yemenite immigration had a proto-political character, as it was motivated by rumors that Palestine had passed or was about to pass to Jewish control. See Y. Nini, "Yemenite Immigrants in Eretz Israel (1882–1914)," *Cathedra* 5 (1977): 30–82 (in Hebrew).

32. The key elements of Zionism are immigration to Palestine, readiness to establish a Jewish collectivity, preparedness for immediate implementation, and the personal and collective sacrifice to attain these objectives.

33. Michel Abitbol, "Zionist Activity in the Maghreb," *Jerusalem Quarterly* 21 (Fall 1981): 77.

34. Edward Shils, "Primordial, Personal, Sacred and Civil Ties," *British Journal of Sociology* 8, no. 2 (1957): 130–145; Clifford Geertz, "The Integrative Revolution: Primordial Sentiments and Civil Politics in the New States," in Clifford Geertz, ed., *Old Societies and New States: The Quest for Modernity in Asia and Africa* (London: Free Press, 1963).

35. Edward Shils, "Center and Periphery," in Edward Shils, ed., *Center and Periphery: Essays in Macro-sociology* (Chicago and London: University of Chicago Press, 1975).

36. Israel has no formal constitution; rather, there are regular parliamentary laws and a number of basic laws that, when compiled in a single unit, form a sort of constitution. Basic laws arc distinguished from ordinary laws in that a special majority is required to amend them. One of the reasons for the absence of a constitution is that its enactment would have underscored the dilemma regarding the basic laws upon which the collectivity was to be founded: Would they be those of a modern civil state or those of a Halachic-Jewish state?

37. The more religious members of the population left their social, political, and economic ghettoes and attempted to change the system's basic rules of the game. Simultaneously, they were also running a completely modern society under conditions of conflict with the external environment, especially because the Jewish

religion does not reject modern technology. So long as the religious population lives as a subsociety, it may obtain services from the overall society, such as security, health, public transportation, and communications, without necessarily being bound to the principles of Halacha. Such is not the case, however, if the society is run according to the millennia-old, rigidly interpreted religious codex, which has undergone so little change. Without an official church, degrees of freedom in its interpretation are limited. In Judaism, there is no possibility of adapting Halacha to the demands of modern man beyond its relatively narrow horizons.

The aforementioned restrictions notwithstanding, two institutions have been established to find technological solutions to the economic, social, and security problems demanded by expanding religious Judaism to activities that were previously closed or supplied as services by the external society. Jerusalem's Institute for Science and Halacha seek technological solutions to ad hoc problems, such as medical treatment that does not violate the Sabbath, operating within the essential framework delineated by Halacha alone. The Tzomet Institute, at the new Judean settlement of Alon Shvut, was established with similar objectives, although its basic guidelines are somewhat different: the latter institution will also consider extra-Halachic factors (national objectives, settlement, and the like).

38. John Murray Cuddihy, *The Ordeal of Civility: Freud, Marx, Levi-Strauss, and the Jewish Struggle with Modernity* (New York: Basic, 1974).

39. Clifford Geertz, "The Integrative Revolution," 155.

40. The Jewish religious codex includes an abundance of land-related precepts, such as the Sabbatical year, the calendar, activity cycles, and the ban on sale of land to non-Jews, that significantly affect daily behavior and economic and social transactions in Eretz Israel. The precepts were fixed and reinforced in the Diaspora only through ritualization, and have no significance in the conception of the collectivity of the state of Israel, which, as indicated earlier, is not a Halachic concept. The rise in the permeability of boundaries between the religious sector and other social segments of the collectivity enabled a greater shift toward the Eretz Israel type. See the lecture by Menachem Friedman, "Religion and Politics in Israel," delivered at the annual conference of the Israel Sociological Society, Haifa, February 16–17, 1983.

41. Kevin Avruch, *American Immigrants in Israel: Social Identities and Change* (Chicago and London: University of Chicago Press, 1981).

42. One example of this phenomenon concerns the manner in which the Lebanese war of 1982 was conducted, as well as its societal meanings and consequences. The war stimulated strong protests, compelling the political center to act in a more universalistic manner. One of the salient features of the aftermath of active warfare has been the re-crystallization of a religious-political stream that emphasizes the humanistic and universalistic messages of Judaism.

Chapter 5. State Building, State Autonomy, and the Identity of Society

1. One major limitation of the state-society paradigm is its inability to distinguish clearly between the government and the state, especially when discussing the specific implementation of policy. I propose an analytical distinction between the government and the state by introducing the notions of identity and state's logic.

2. Joel S. Migdal, *Strong Societies and Weak States: State-Society Relations and State Capabilities in the Third World* (Princeton: Princeton University Press, 1988), 142–176.

3. This excludes several enclaves of ultra-Orthodoxy, which traditionally maintained partially separate and parallel institutions toward the state, mainly for ideological and theological reasons. Menachem Friedman, "The State as a Theological Dilemma," in Baruch Kimmerling, ed., *The Israeli State and Society: Boundaries and Frontiers*, (Albany, NY: State University of New York Press, 1989). The Israeli state's relations with different citizen and noncitizen Palestinian populations are discussed later.

4. This statement is conditional because it refers mainly to the income taxes of wage earners, especially in the public and government sectors of the economy. Real taxation of the self-employed is much less impressive. Israel's portions of undeclared incomes were estimated at between 5 and 15 percent of gross national product (GNP), while those of Western Europe are about 10 percent of GNP. Ben-Zion Zilberfarb, "Estimate of the Black Market in Israel and Abroad," *Economic Quarterly* 122 (1984): 319–322 (in Hebrew), and Nachman Ben-Yehuda, "The Social Meanings of Alternative Systems: Some Exploratory Notes," in Baruch Kimmerling, ed., *The Israeli State and Society*, 156–157.

5. Dan Horowitz and Moshe Lissak, *Trouble in Utopia: The Overburdened Polity of Israel* (Albany: State University of New York Press, 1989), 239.

6. Dietrich Rueschemeyer made a similar observation in a private conversation. The same line of argument, presented in a more moralistic manner, appears in Yehoshafat Harkabi, *Israel's Fateful Decisions* (London: LB. Tauris, 1988).

7. Georg Wilhelm Fridrich Hegel, *Grundlinen der Philosophie des Rechts* (Hamburg: F. Meiner, 1955 [1821]), 342.

8. For an example of these approaches, see Shmuel N. Eisenstadt, *Israeli Society* (New York: Basic, 1967); Shmuel N. Eisenstadt, *The Transformation of Israeli Society: An Essay in Interpretation* (London: Weidenfeld and Nicolson, 1985); Dan Horowitz and Moshe Lissak, *Origins of the Israeli Polity: Palestine under the Mandate* (Chicago: University of Chicago Press, 1978); Dan Horowitz and Moshe Lissak, *Trouble in Utopia*; Yonathan Shapira, *Democracy in Israel* (Ramat Gan: Massada, 1977) (in Hebrew); and Yizhak Galnoor, *Steering Politics: Communication and Politics in Israel* (Beverly Hills: Sage, 1992). All of these volumes contain various shades of Judeo-centric perceptions of Israeli society, its boundaries, as well as

strong implicit or explicit perceptions of continuity in the basic rules of the game. For a somewhat simplistic overview of Israeli sociology, schools, and paradigms, see Uri Ram, "Civic Discourse in Israeli Sociological Thought," *International Journal of Politics, Culture and Society* 3, no. 2 (December 1989): 255–272. For a critical analysis, see Baruch Kimmerling, "Sociology, Ideology, and Nation-Building: The Palestinians and their Meaning in Israeli Sociology," *American Sociological Review* 57, no. 4 (August 1992): 446–460.

9. Max Weber is the founding father of this approach; see Max Weber, *The Theory of Social and Economic Organization* (Glencoe: Free Press, 1964). Among major contemporary followers, see J. P. Nettl, "The State as a Conceptual Variable," *World Politics* 20, no. 4 (August 1968): 559–592; Eric Nordlinger, *The Autonomy of the Democratic State* (Cambridge, MA: Harvard University Press, 1981); Robert A. Alford, "Paradigms of Relations Between State and Society," in Leon Lindeberg, Robert Alford, Colin Crouch and Clause Offe, eds., *Stress and Contradiction in Modern Capitalism* (Lexington, Toronto, and London: Lexington, 1975), 145–160; Stephan D. Krasner, *Defending the National Interest: Raw Materials Investments and United States Foreign Policy* (Princeton: Princeton University Press, 1978); Stephan D. Krasner, "Approaches to the State: Alternative Conceptions and Historical Dynamics," *Comparative Politics* 16 (January 1984): 223–246; Peter B. Evans, Dietrich Rueschmeyer, and Theda Skocpol, "On the Road toward a More Adequate Understanding of the State," in Peter B. Evans, Dietrich Rueschmeyer, and Theda Skocpol, eds., *Bringing the State Back In* (London: Cambridge University Press, 1985); Joel S. Migdal, *Strong Societies and Weak States*; and Victor Azarya and Naomi Chazan, "Disengagement from the State in Africa: Reflections on the Experiences of Ghana and Guinea," *Comparative Studies in Society and History* 29, no. 1 (January 1987): 106–131. The European version is well represented by Pierre Birenbaum, *States and Collective Action: The European Experience* (New York: Cambridge University Press, 1988).

10. Anthony Giddens, *The Nation State and Violence: A Contemporary Critique of Historical Materialism* (Berkeley and Los Angeles: University of California Press, 1985).

11. Baruch Kimmerling, ed., *The Israeli State and Society: Boundaries and Frontiers* (Albany, NY: State University of New York Press, 1989).

12. Michael Mann, "The Autonomous Power of State: Its Origins, Mechanisms and Results," in John H. Hall, ed., *States in History* (Oxford: Basil Blackwell, 1987), 109–136.

13. See Peter B. Evans, Dietrich Rueschmeyer, and Theda Skocpol, "On the Road," 347–366. Most of the authors mentioned in Chapter 6, note 1 cannot accept their one-dimensional structural views of the state. For a more critical approach, see Timothy Mitchell, "The Limits of the State: Beyond Statist Approaches and their Critics," *American Political Science Review* 85, no. 1 (March 1991): 77–96.

14. Max Weber, *The Theory of Social and Economic Organization.*

15. If the change in regime is accompanied by changes in the social and political boundaries of the collectivity, which lead to changes in the collective identity, the emerged state may differ substantially from the former state. A transition from an autocratic or totalitarian system to a democratic system is a change in regime but not in identity. The Hungarian identity of postcommunist Hungary is not different from its identity during the communist era. However, in the decomposition of the Soviet Empire, the Russian identity was restructured along with the national-ethnic identities of the other states of the federation. In the decomposition of the former Yugoslavia, ethnic cleansing and boundary redrawing took place. No doubt we are witnessing a rebuilding of old and new primordial identities.

16. Baruch Kimmerling, "Boundaries and Frontiers of the Israeli Control System," in *Israeli State and Society,* 265–284.

17. Robert Bellah, *Beyond Belief* (New York: Harper and Row, 1979).

18. John Keane, *Democracy and Civil Society* (London: Verso, 1988); and Charles Taylor, "Modes of Civil Society," *Public Culture* 3, no.1 (Fall 1990): 95–132.

19. See Shlomo Avineri, *The Making of Modern Zionism: The Intellectual Origins of the Jewish State* (London: Weidenfeld and Nicolson, 1981); Walter Laqueur, *A History of Zionism* (London: Weidenfeld and Nicolson, 1972); and David Vital, *The Origins of Zionism* (New York: Oxford University Press, 1975).

20. The Mandatory boundaries were originally intended to include large areas that are today part of the Hashemite Kingdom of Jordan. In light of the British commitments to Sherif Hussein of Arabia, in 1922 the Emirate of Transjordan was created for Abdullah ibn Hussein, and the areas were excluded from the jurisdiction of the British Palestinian state. See Joel S. Migdal, *Strong Societies and Weak States,* 142–169; and Baruch Kimmerling and Joel S. Migdal, *Palestinians: The Making of a People* (New York: Free Press, 1993).

21. This political concept was rendered obscure deliberately so as not to be highly committed to the final form and scope of the Jewish polity. For the Zionists, in practical terms, the reference was to a future sovereign Jewish state. The reason for the lack of clarity was the desire to overcome opposition, both within Great Britain and among the Arabs of the Middle East and especially in Palestine, and not to contradict Britain's so-called dual obligation expressed in the MacMahon letters to the Sherif of Mecca.

22. Ylana N. Miller, *Government and Society in Rural Palestine: 1948* (Austin: University of Texas Press, 1985); Nachum T. Gross, "The Economic Policy of the Mandatory Government in Palestine," Discussion Paper No. 81.06, Falk Intitute for Economic Research, Jerusalem, 1981 (in Hebrew); Jacob Reuveny, *The Administration of Palestine under the British Mandate, 1920–1948: An Institutional Analysis* (Ramat Gan: Bar Ilan University Press, 1993) (in Hebrew); and Baruch Kimmerling and Joel S. Migdal, *Palestinians.*

23. David Horowitz, *The Palestinian Economy and its Development* (Tel Aviv: Bialik Institute and Dvir, 1948) (in Hebrew); Jacob Metzer, "Fiscal Incidence and Resource Transfer between Jews and Arabs in Mandatory Palestine," *Research in Economic History 7* (1982): 87–132.

24. Baruch Kimmerling and Joel S. Migdal, *Palestinians.*

25. It would appear that both Jewish and Palestinian social historians, for partisan reasons, have tended to deemphasize the part played by the colonial state in this process. For a description of the Mandate's crucial role as a state, in making and implementing rules and functioning with a clear policy and authoritative bureaucracy in rural Arab Palestine, see Ylana N. Miller, *Government and Society,* and in a more subtle way, Jacob Reuveny, *The Administration of Palestine.*

26. Charles Taylor, "Modes of Civil Society," 98.

27. Yehoshua Porath, *The Emergence of the Palestinian National Movement, 1917–1929* (London: Frank Cass, 1974).

28. See Baruch Kimmerling, *Zionism and Territory: The Socio-territorial Dimension of Zionist Politics* (Berkeley: Institute of International Studies, University of California, 1983).

29. I do not find direct historical evidence to confirm these two assumptions, yet without them, the British policy at the stage when a national home was granted to the Zionists, as well as the clear-cut shift in policy in the mid-1920s, cannot be understood.

30. Yehoshua Porath, *The Palestinian National Movement: From Riots to Rebellion* (London: Frank Cass, 1977); and Baruch Kimmerling and Joel S. Migdal, *Palestinians,* 96–123.

31. Prima facie, avoiding transfer of lands from Arabs to Jews does not require the colonial state's legislative intervention. However, in a situation of internal cleavage, internal social control over this kind of deviance is limited. See Baruch Kimmerling, *Zionism and Territory.*

32. Palestine Royal Commission, *Report,* Cmd. 5479 (London: HMSO, 1937). Presented by the secretary of state for the colonies to Parliament by command of His Majesty

33. Dan Horowitz and Moshe Lissak, *Origins of the Israeli Polity: Palestine under the Mandate* (Chicago: University of Chicago Press, 1987).

34. Baruch Kimmerling, ed., *The Israeli State and Society.*

35. Yonathan Shapiro, *Democracy in Israel.*

36. Lev Luis Grinberg, *Split Corporatism in Israel* (Albany: State University of New York Press, 1991); and Michael Shalev, *Labour and the Political Economy of Israel* (New York: Oxford University Press, 1992).

37. The Jewish commonwealth could be established only by the coming of the Messiah, and Zionism was considered as a false messianic movement, which, like previous messianic movements, would end as a great catastrophe for the Jewish

people. See Menachem Friedman, *Society and Religion: The Non-Zionist Orthodox Community in Palestine*. (Jerusalem: Yad Ben Zvi, 1977) (in Hebrew).

38. Baruch Kimmerling, *Zionism and Economy* (Cambridge, MA: Schenkman, 1983).

39. Abraham Zloczover and S.N. Eisenstadt, eds., *The Integration of Immigrants from Different Countries of Origin in Israel* (Jerusalem: Magnes, 1969) (in Hebrew). Symposium held at the Hebrew University on October 25–26, 1966.

40. Menachem Friedman, *Society and Religion: The Non-Zionist Orthodox Community in Palestine* (Jerusalem: Yad Ben Zvi, 1977) (in Hebrew).

41. Shmuel N. Eisenstadt, *The Absorption of Immigrants: A Comparative Study Based Mainly on the Jewish Community in Palestine and the State of Israel* (London: Routledge and Kegan Paul, 1954); Shmuel N. Eisenstadt, *Israeli Society*; Judah Matras, *Social Change in Israel* (Chicago: Aldine, 1965); and B. Kimmerling, ed., *Israeli State and Society*, 97–122.

42. Yair Aharoni, *State-Owned Enterprises in Israel and Abroad* (Tel Aviv: Gomeh, 1979) (in Hebrew).

43. Peter Medding, *Mapai in Israel* (Cambridge: Cambridge University Press, 1972).

44. Yonathan Shapiro, *Democracy in Israel.*

45. Dorothy Willner, *Nation-Building and Community in Israel* (Princeton: Princeton University Press, 1969).

46. Baruch Kimmerling, ed., *Israeli State and Society.*

47. Yagil Levy, "The Roles of the Military in the Construction of the Sociopolitical Order in Israel—The Management of the Arab-Israeli Conflict as a Statist Control Strategy," Ph.D. thesis, Department of Political Science, Tel Aviv University, Tel Aviv, 1993 (in Hebrew).

48. Benjamin Harshev, "Essay on the Re-Birth of the Hebrew Language," *Alphayim* 2 (1990): 9–54 (in Hebrew).

49. Shmuel N. Eisenstadt, *The Absorption of Immigrants.*

50. Dan Horowitz and Moshe Lissak, *Origins of the Israeli Polity.*

51. Ian Lustick, *Arabs in a Jewish State: Israel's Control of a National Minority* (Austin: University of Texas Press, 1980).

52. Charles S. Liebman, "In Search of Status: The Israeli Government and the Zionist Movement," *Forum* 28/29 (Winter 1978): 38–56.

53. See Chapter 6.

54. Lev Luis Grinberg, *Split Corporatism.*

55. Ian Lustick, *Arabs in a Jewish State.*

56. Henry Rosenfeld and Shulamit Carmi, "The Privatization of Public Means, the State-Made Middle Class, and the Realization of Family Values in Israel," in J.G. Peristiany, ed., *Kinship and Modernization in Mediterranean Society* (Rome: American Universities Field Staff, 1976), 131–159.

57. Baruch Kimmerling, ed., *Israeli State and Society.*

58. Some attempts have been made recently, but they have not made much political impact.

59. Amiram Gonen, "Population Spread in the Course of Passing from Yishuv to State," in A. Pilovski, ed., *The Passing from Yishuv to State* (Haifa: Haifa University Press, 1986) (in Hebrew).

60. Shlomo Swirski, *University, State, and Society in Israel* (Jerusalem; Mifras, 1982) (in Hebrew); and Shlomo Swirski, "The Oriental Jews in Israel," *Dissent* 30 (Winter 1984): 77–90.

61. Uri Ben-Eliezer, "Militarism, Status, and Politics: Sabras and Veteran Leadership, 1939–1948," Ph. D thesis, Department of Sociology, Tel Aviv University, Tel Aviv, 1989 (in Hebrew).

62. The Lavon Affair was an internal conflict within the Mapai ruling party that finally led to a split and David Ben-Gurion's departure from the party. The official controversy was around Defense Minister Pinhas Lavon's role in a security mishap in Egypt in 1954, and the way that the investigation should have been handled. In fact, the struggle was between the party's old guard and its young generation, headed by Shimon Peres and Moshe Dayan. Ben-Gurion tried to use the younger generation to regain his personal statist control over the party. After he failed, he formed a new party, Rafi, and later withdrew from politics altogether.

63. Yonathan Shapiro, *Democracy in Israel.*

64. Michael Shalev, *Labour and the Political Economy*; Levy, *op. cit.*

65. Asher Arian, *Politics in Israel: The Second Generation,* revised ed. (London: Chatham House, 1985).

66. Baruch Kimmerling, ed., *Israeli State and Society.*

67. See Chapter 6.

68. Baruch Kimmerling, "Boundaries and Frontiers of the Israeli Control System," in B. Kimmerling, ed., *Israeli State and Society,* 265–284.

69. Alex Mintz, "The Military Industrial Complex—The Israeli Case," *Journal of Strategic Studies* 6, no. 3 (1983): 103–127; Yoram Peri and Amnon Neubach, *Israeli Military Industrial Complex* (Tel Aviv: International Center for Peace in the Middle East, 1984); and Shimshon Bichler, "The Political Economy of Military Spending in Israel," Ph. D. thesis, Department of Political Sciences, The Hebrew University, Jerusalem, 1991 (in Hebrew).

70. Antonio Gramsci, *Selection from the Prison Notebooks* (New York: International Publishers, 1971).

71. Stanley Greenberg, "The Indifferent Hegemony: Israel and Palestinians," unpublished manuscript, 1985.

72. Virginia Dominguez, *People as Subject, People as Object—Selfhood and Peoplehood in Contemporary Israel* (Madison: University of Wisconsin Press, 1989).

73. Don Handelman and Lea Shamgar-Handelman, "Shaping Time: The Choice

of the National Emblem of Israel," in E. Ohnuki-Tierney, ed., *Culture and History: New Directions* (Stanford: Stanford University Press, 1990).

74. Charles S. Liebman and Eliezer Don-Yehiya, *Civil Religion in Israel: Traditional Judaism and Political Culture in the Jewish State* (Berkeley: University of California Press, 1983).

75. Ilan Peleg and Ofira Seliktar, *The Emergence of a Binational Israel: The Second Republic in the Making* (Boulder, CO: Westview, 1989), 202.

76. The autonomy supposed to be granted to peoples and not to lands is along the lines of Moshe Dayan's attempt in the late 1960s to make a functional division of rule between lands ruled by the Israelis and peoples ruled by the Jordanians. In the long run, the envisioned solution probably presumed a confederation or federation of the Palestinian enclaves with Jordan. But it is unlikely that the Bedouin-dominated Hashemite kingdom can change its very identity by including the highly politicized Palestinians into its state. To do so would mean a very quick Palestinization of Jordan, and not the re-Jordanization of the Palestinians. Here we have again a question of state identity.

77. Emanuel Sivan, "The Intifada and Decolonization," *Middle East Review* 22 (Winter 1988/89): 1–12.

78. Paradoxically, Algeria proves this thesis, even though it appears to be a perfect example of a pure settler state-building effort. Algeria was considered to be an indivisible part of the French fatherland, even though apart from the settlers there (the so-called *pieds noirs*) and elements in the right wing and the armed forces, most of the French did not perceive the territory located on the other side of the Mediterranean sea to be an inseparable part of the French state. It was relatively easy for De Gaulle, when he came to power, to destroy this non-obligating consensus and construct a different sociopolitical reality. In France, outside of an extremist minority, there was neither a wide perception that losing Algeria might endanger France's very existence nor a religious sense that the loss would destroy the cosmic order. Most Jewish Israelis understand losing control over the territories of West Bank, Gaza Strip, and even the Syrian [Golan] Heights in both senses.

79. Ian Lustick, *State Building Failure in British Ireland and French Algeria* (Berkeley: Institute of International Studies, University of California, 1985).

80. One of the conspicuous implications or costs of the transformation of the Israeli state into a binational system of control was the reversal of roles played by the Israeli armed forces: The basic character of Israeli forces as preserving the existence of a state that was invaded and besieged from outside changed to an that of an internally-oriented police force, or a community-militia force, guarding the interests and the domination of one community in its contest against its rival. Gideon Aran, "The Beginning of the Road from Religious Zionism to Zionist Religion," *Studies in Contemporary Jewry*, vol. 2 (Bloomington: Indiana University Press, 1985).

81. While the Israeli Arabs or Palestinians are citizens who enjoy many civil rights, they are not really a part of the state, which defines itself as belonging to the entire Jewish people rather than to the citizens who live within the state's boundaries. Yoav Peled, "Ethnic Democracy and the Legal Construction of Citizenship," *American Political Science Review* 86, no. 2 (June 1992): 432–443. See also Chapters One and Eight of this volume.

82. Baruch Kimmerling, *Zionism and Territory.*

83. Yosef Gorny, *The Quest for Collective Identity* (Tel Aviv: Am Oved, 1986), 118–140 (in Hebrew).

84. Charles S. Liebman and Eliezer Don-Yehiya, *Civil Religion in Israel.*

85. Moshe Semyonov and Noah Levin-Epstein, *Hewers of Woods and Drawers of Water: Non-Citizen Arabs in the Israeli Labor Market* (Ithaca: Institute for Labor Relations, Cornell University, 1987); B. Kimmerling, ed., *Israeli State and Society.*

86. Baruch Kimmerling and Joel Migdal, *Palestinians: The Making of a People* (New York: Free Press, 1993).

87. See Ilan Peleg and Ofira Seliktar, *The Emergence of a Binational Israel.* Peleg and Silktar called this new entity The Second Republic, but I prefer to label it the Israeli State in contrast to the state of Israel, established in the territorial and population framework that followed the 1948 war.

88. Ehud Sprinzak, *The Ascendance of Israel's Radical Right* (New York: Oxford University Press, 1991), 38–43.

89. Lev Luis Grinberg, *Split Corporatism*; and Michael Shalev, *Labour and the Political Economy*, 206–207.

90. Ian Lustick, *Unsettled States, Disputed Lands: Britain and Ireland, France and Algeria, Israel and the West Bank–Gaza* (Ithaca: Cornell University Press, 1987).

Chapter 6. Patterns of Militarism in Israel

1. Baruch Kimmerling, "Sociology, Ideology, and Nation-Building: The Palestinians and their Meaning in Israeli Sociology," *American Sociological Review* 57, no. 4 (August 1992): 446–460.

2. Uri Ben-Eliezer, *The Making of Israeli Militarism* (Bloomington, IN: Indiana University Press).

3. See, e.g., Amos Perlmutter, *The Military and Politics in Modern Times: On Professional, Praetorian, and Revolutionary Soldiers* (New Haven: Yale University Press, 1977), 267–280; Edward Luttwak and Dan Horowitz, *The Israeli Army* (London: Allen Lane, 1985), xiii; and Ben Halpern, "The Role of the Military in Israel," in John J. Johnson, ed., *The Role of the Military in Underdeveloped Countries* (Princeton, NJ: Princeton University Press, 1962), 317–358. One notable exception was Al-Qazzaz; see Ayad Al-Qazzaz, "Army and Society in Israel,"

Pacific Sociological Review 16, no. 2 (April 1973): 139–152, who defined Israel as a "garrison state," (144) but his familiarity with Israeli society and its military was highly questionable.

4. Alex Mintz, "Military-Industrial Linkages in Israel," *Armed Forces and Society* 12, no. 1 (1985): 9–27.

5. Ben Halpern, "The Role of the Military."

6. Dan Horowitz, "The Israeli Defence Forces: A Civilianized Military in a Partial Militarized Society," in R. Kolkowitz and A. Korbonski, ed., *Soldiers, Peasants, and Bureaucrats* (London: George Allen and Unwin, 1982), 77–106.

7. Amos Perlmutter, "The Israeli Army in Politics: The Persistence of the Civilian over the Military," *World Politics* 20, no. 4 (1968): 606–643; Dan Horowitz, "Is Israel a Garrison State?" *The Jerusalem Quarterly* 4 (Summer 1977): 58–75; and Dan Horowitz, "The Israeli Defence Forces."

8. Yoram Peri, *Between Battles and Ballots: Israeli Military in Politics* (Cambridge: Cambridge University Press, 1983).

9. Victor Azarya, "The Israeli Armed Forces," in M. Janowitz and S. D. Wesbrook, eds., *The Political Education of Soldiers* (Beverly Hills: Sage, 1983), 99–127; Moshe Lissak, "The Israeli Defence Forces as an Agent of Socialization and Education: A Research in Role Expansion in a Democratic Society," in M. R. van Gils, ed., *The Perceived Role of the Military* (Rotterdam: Rotterdam University Press, 1972), 325–340; and Maurice M. Roumani, *From Immigrants to Citizens: The Contribution of the Army to National Integration in Israe—The Case of Oriental Jews* (The Hague: Foundation for Studies of Plural Societies, 1979).

10. Tom Bowden, *Army in the Service of the State* (Tel Aviv: University Publishing Projects, 1976).

11. Victor Azarya and Baruch Kimmerling, "New Immigrants in the Israeli Armed Forces," *Armed Forces and Society* 6, no. 3 (1983): 455–482.

12. Victor Azarya, "The Israeli Armed Forces."

13. Uri Ben-Eliezer, *Israeli Militarism.*

14. A. R. Luckham, "A Comparative Typology of Civil-Military Relations," *Government and Opposition* 6, no. 1 (Winter 1971): 24–25.

15. Harold D. Laswell, "The Garrison State," *American Journal of Sociology* 46, no. 4 (January 1941): 455–468.

16. Amos Perlmutter, "The Israeli Army in Politics."

17. David C. Rapoport, "A Comparative Theory of Military and Political Types," in S.P. Huntington, ed., *Changing Patterns of Military Politics* (New York: Free Press, 1962), 71–101.

18. Such as Shulamit Carmi and Henry Rosenfeld, "The Emergence of Militaristic Nationalism in Israel," *International Journal of Politics, Culture and Society* 3, no. 1 (1989): 5–49.

19. Uri Ben-Eliezer, "Militarism, Status, and Politics: Sabras and Veteran Leadership (1939–1948)," Ph.D. thesis, Department of Sociology, Tel Aviv University, Tel Aviv, 1988 (in Hebrew).

20. Gad Barzilai, *A Democracy in Wartime: Conflict and Consensus in Israel* (Tel Aviv: Sifriat Poalim, 1992) (in Hebrew).

21. Baruch Kimmerling, *Zionism and Territory: The Socio-territorial Dimensions of Zionist Politics* (Berkeley: University of California, Institute of International Studies, 1983).

22. Baruch Kimmerling and Joel S. Migdal, *Palestinians: The Making of a People* (New York: Free Press, 1993).

23. Martin Shaw, *Post-Military Societies: Militarism, Demilitarism, and War at the End of the Twentieth Century* (London: Polity Press, 1991), 14; see also Stanislav Andreski, *Military Organization and Society,* second ed. (Berkeley: University of California, Press 1968).

24. James S. Coleman and Belmont Brice, "The Role of the Military in Sub-Saharan Africa," in John J. Johnson, ed., *The Role of the Military in Undeveloped Countries*, 359–406.

25. Edy Kaufman, *Uruguay in Transition: From Civilian to Military Rule* (New Brunswick, NJ: Transaction Books, 1979).

26. John J. Johnson, *The Military and Society in Latin America* (Stanford: Stanford University Press, 1964), 13–35.

27. Baruch Kimmerling, "Identity and Nation-Building."

28. The basic situation will not change even if some form of autonomy is granted to the Palestinians in the occupied territories. Even if Israel's armed forces leave populated areas, real power will still remain in Israel's hands. Only the transfer of real authority to another sovereign entity will end the situation of coercive surveillance and control over the Palestinians that has persisted since 1967.

29. Baruch Kimmerling, "Boundaries and Frontiers of the Israeli Control System," in Baruch Kimmerling, ed., *The Israeli State and Society: Boundaries and Frontiers* (Albany: State University of New York Press, 1989), 265–284.

30. Anthony Giddens, *The Nation-State and Violence: A Contemporary Critique of Historical Materialism* (Berkeley: University of California Press, 1985), 192–194.

31. Alfred Vagts, *A History of Militarism: Civilian and Military* (New York: Free Press, 1959 [1937]), 451–498.

32. Oz Almog, "Israeli War Memorials: A Semiological Analysis," *Megamot: Behavioural Sciences Quarterly* 34, no. 2 (1992): 179–210 (in Hebrew).

33. Charles S. Liebman and Eliezer Don-Yehiya, *Civil Religion in Israel: Traditional Judaism and Political Culture in the Jewish State* (Berkeley: University of California Press, 1983).

34. A. R. Luckham, "A Comparative Typology," 17–19.

35. This is an essentially unbalanced and unstable situation, as each social orga-

nization that has repute and access to sources of power is blocked; or, alternatively, each one tries to convert its prestige into political strength.

36. Charles Leibman and Eliezer Don-Yehiya, *Civil Religion in Israel: Traditional Judaism and Political Culture in the Jewish State* (Berkeley: University of California Press, 1983), 93.

37. See Martin Shaw, *Post-Military Societies,* 9: "The war perceptions of the potential adversary are clearly defined as 'militarist.' 'Our own' military activities, however, may not even be counted as war preparations; they are more likely to be seen as a part of 'defence' or 'deterrence' policy, the professed aim of which may be to avoid war rather than to fight it. An ambivalent attitude toward power and toward power being wielded by Jews followed Zionism after its inception (and is reflected in the writings of such figures as Berdichewsky and Max Nordau); a kind of counter-history has developed around this ambiguity—a view that perceives the deployment of power by Jews, who thus act 'like all nations,' has emerged. At its extreme, contemporary Jewish philosophy exercised by apologist writers like Emil Fackenheim utilizes the example of extreme Jewish vulnerability—especially the Holocaust period during which Jews were entirely victimized by the use of coercive power—to accord legitimacy to Israel's deployment of unrestrained violence against 'the gentiles.'" An intriguing review of the ambivalent Jewish response to the responsibilities and vagaries of power and force since the emergence of a modern Jewish national movement, and then later with the establishment of the state of Israel, can be found in David Biale, *Power and Powerlessness in Jewish History* (New York: Schocken Books, 1986), 133–176. This study, however, does not address the issue of militarism directly.

38. Hans Speier, "Militarism in the Eighteenth Century," in Hans Speier, ed., *Social Order and the Risks of War: Papers in Political Sociology* (Cambridge, MA: MIT Press, 1953), 230.

39. The most manifest examples are the development of Israel's nuclear arms potential in the 1950s and 1960s, known as the "delicate matter" in the lexicon of the time, and the clumsy espionage and sabotage affair in Egypt, encoded as "the rotten business," which turned in 1960–61 into the Lavon Affair.

40. Alfred Vagts, *A History of Militarism,* 13.

41. David C. Rapoport, "A Comparative Theory"; also in Samuel E. Finer, *The Man on Horseback: The Role of the Military in Politics,* enlarged ed. (Harmondsworth: Penguin, 1976).

42. See John J. Johnson, *The Military and Society.*

43. Dominant regional or ethnic units that ordinarily bridge religious cleavages, such as Yoruba, Fulani-Hausa, or Ibo, or militarist coalitions that join different units and use their control of armed forces to rule over smaller, weaker elements. The most evident example here is the departure of Ibo Biafra from the Nigerian federation in 1967, a step that caused a bloody civil war won in the end by the so-called Federal Army in January 1977.

44. C. Wright Mills, *The Power Elite* (New York: Oxford University Press, 1956).

45. Anthony Giddens, *The Nation-State and Violence*, 223–237. For basics, see Harold D. Laswell, "The Garrison State."; Arthur Marwick, *War and Social Change in the Twentieth Century* (London: Macmillan, 1977).

46. Steven Lukes, *Power: A Radical View* (London: Macmillan, 1974).

47. This definition bears a resemblance to Michael Mann's judgment, yet it is less sweeping than Mann's conception, which avers that "militarism [is] a set of attitudes and social practices which regards war and preparation for war as a normal and desirable social activity." See Michael Mann, "The Roots and Contradictions of Modern Militarism," *New Left Review* 162 (March/April 1987): 34.

48. The use of the concept of national security is preferable to other terms, as it is widely based and encompasses other spheres. Another advantage of this term, and of the classification of the culture as civilian militarist, is the emphasis on the civilian aspect—that is, civilian experts can also be engaged in national security matters that include political considerations; they might even elevate this realm to the level of science. Such an approach giving high priority to the sphere of national security, and to anything that is or may be connected to security, represents a type of ideology.

49. Bruce Lincoln, *Discourse and the Construction of Society: A Comparative Study of Myth, Ritual, and Classification* (New York: Oxford University Press, 1989).

50. From the state's establishment to the present day, military service has been obligatory. Today, the length of service is three years for men and two years for women. Yet the minister of defense retains the authority to release from service any person or group on his own authority, and release so-called declared (i.e., religious observant) girls, students of traditional Jewish religious academies (*yeshivot*), Muslim Arabs, and all other types of Arabs, except Druze and Circassian. Christian Arabs and Bedouins can volunteer for service. Among large portions of the young Druze generation, military service has come to be perceived as a good career opportunity and source of social mobility. Being included in or excluded from universal and compulsory military service has become, on occasion, a cause of sociopolitical bargaining. See Baruch Kimmerling, "Determinants of the Boundaries and Framework of Conscription: Two Dimensions of Civil-Military Relations in Israel," *Studies in Comparative International Development* 14, no. 1 (1979): 22–41.

51. Andrew Ross, "Dimensions of Militarization in the Third World," *Armed Forces and Society* 13, no. 4 (1987): 562–564.

52. See Dan Horowitz and Baruch Kimmerling, "Some Social Implications of Military Service and Reserve System in Israel," *Archives Européannes de sociologie* 15, no. 2 (1974): 262–276. With the return of the Labor party after the 1992 elections, its leader Yitzhak Rabin wagered a distinction between security settlements that

aim to facilitate outside control of regions of the West Bank and political settlements found within densely populated Palestinian areas. The latter are slated to be
dismantled when autonomy is granted to a Palestinian administration.

53. Charles Tilly, "Reflections on the History of European State Making," in
Charles Tilly, ed., *The Formation of National States in Western Europe* (Princeton,
NJ: Princeton University Press, 1975), 46.

54. Edward Luttwak and Dan Horowitz, *The Israeli Army*, 104–137.

55. Moshe Lissak, "The Israeli Defence Forces."

56. Dan Horowitz, "The Israeli Defence Forces," 77–106.

57. Morris Janowitz, *The Professional Soldier* (New York: Free Press, 1960) vii–x.

58. For descriptions of how society and realities are constructed and restructured, the reader may consult Peter L. Berger and Thomas Luckman, *The Social
Construction of Reality: A Treatise in the Sociology of Knowledge* (New York: Doubleday, 1966);and Bruce Lincoln, *Discourse and the Construction of Society.*

59. Shabtai Teveth, *Moshe Dayan* (London: Weidenfeld and Nicolson, 1972),
240.

60. See the detailed analysis of the institutional and value system in Israel
connected to preparation for war and conduct of war in Baruch Kimmerling, *The
Interrupted System: Israeli Civilians in War and Routine Times* (New Brunswick,
NJ: Transaction, 1985). As for the value system, see Asher Arian, Ilan Talmud, and
Tamar Herman, *National Security and Public Opinion in Israel* (Boulder, CO: Westview, 1988), 83. This research team summarized parts of its findings as follows: "The
'religion of security' is an apt metaphor for considering the phenomenon of security in Israel. Just as a child is born into a certain religion, so too is the Israeli born
into a very difficult geopolitical world with its attendant dilemmas. Just as a child
accepts unquestioningly the religion he was born into and some basic answers he
received . . . so too the Israeli child absorbs at a very early age the basics of the core-
belief of national security." The socialization is so deep that when samples of youngsters were asked if service in the Israeli armed forces was to become completely
voluntary, would they still volunteer for service, around 90 percent expressed their
willingness to serve, about 60 percent being ready to serve for the same customary three years. Moreover, the volunteering for special units or officer courses that
involve high risk and physical and mental stress and hardship—such as paratroopers, reconnaissance, or commandos—always rates higher than the actual needs of
the armed forces. See Reuven Gal, *A Portrait of the Israeli Soldier*, Contribution in
Military Studies, no. 52 (New York: Greenwood, 1986), 61–62; and Ofra Meizels, Reuven Gal, and Eli Fishoff, "World Perceptions and Attitudes of Israeli High School
Students towards Issues of Military and National Security," mimeographed research
report, The Israeli Institute of Military Studies, Zichron Yaacov, 1989, 51–58. For
the military service as a basic factor in shaping individual as well as sociological
generational personalities, attitudes and life cycles, see Amia Lieblich, *Transition to*

Adulthood during Military Service: The Israeli Case (Albany: State University of New York Press, 1989) and Edna Lomsky-Feder, "Youth in the Shadow of War, War in the Light of Youth: Life-Stories of Israeli Veterans," in Wim Meeus, Martinjn de Goede, Willem Kox, and Klaus Hurrelmann, ed., *Adolescence, Careers, and Culture* (Berlin: Walter de Gruyter, 1992), 393–408.

61. Moshe Lissak, "Boundaries and Institutional Linkages between Elites: Some Illustrations from Civil-Military Relations in Israel," *Politics and Society* 1 (1985): 143.

62. Antonio Gramsci, *Letters form Prison* (New York: Harper and Row, 1973).

63. Dan Horowitz and Moshe Lissak, *Trouble in Utopia: The Overburdened Polity of Israel* (Albany, NY: State University of New York Press, 1989), 239.

64. For some reason, in Carmi and Rosenfeld's analysis, socialist or communist regimes cannot be militarist. See Shulamit Carmi and Henry Rosenfeld, "The Emergence of Militaristic Nationalism." In reality, such regimes can, of course, be militarist—see, e.g., the typology that appears in Perlmutter's analysis of military regimes and the party-army regime type. See Amos Perlmutter, *The Military and Politics.*

65. Samuel P. Huntington, *The Soldier and the State: The Theory and Politics of Civil-Military Relations* (Cambridge, MA: Belknap, 1957), 59–79.

66. Morris Janowitz, *The Professional Soldier*, 65–66.

67. The research and development up to the construction of a prototype for a super-advanced combat plane (the Lavi) was carried on, only to be interrupted, after the investment of 1.5 billion dollars, when the United States refused to continue to finance the development and production of the plane.

68. N. Michael Barnett, *Confronting the Costs of War: Military Power, State and Society in Egypt and Israel* (Princeton, NJ: Princeton University Press, 1992), 227–230.

69. See Alex Mintz, "The Military-Industrial Complex: The Israeli Case," in M. Lissak, ed., *Israeli Society and Its Defense Establishment: The Social and Political Impact of a Protracted Violent Conflict* (London: Frank Cass, 1984), 103–127; Alex Mintz, "Military-Industrial Linkages"; and Alex Mintz and M.D. Ward, "The Political Economy of Military Spending in Israel," *American Political Science Review* 83, no. 2 (June 1989): 521–533.

70. Shimshon Bichler, "The Political Economy of Military Spending in Israel," Ph.D. thesis, Department of Political Science, The Hebrew University, Jerusalem, 1991 (in Hebrew).

71. Ariel Halpern and Daniel Tsidon, "The Conversion of the Israeli Defence Industry: The Labor Market," Discussion Paper No. 3–4, Israeli International Institute for Applied Economic Policy Review, Tel Aviv, 1992.

72. Alex Mintz, "The Military-Industrial Complex," 109.

73. Bank of Israel, *Annual Report, 1991* (Jerusalem: Bank of Israel, 1992), 167 (in Hebrew).

74. The first crude manipulation of security-related symbols transpired on July 5, 1961, when a small rocket (Shavit 2) was launched several days before a national election. The missile's purpose was defined as weather research, but the pictures released to the public emphasized the presence of the prime and defense minister (Ben-Gurion) who wore a military uniform, as well as to the chief of staff (Major General Zevi Tzur), and others. The timing of the destruction by Israeli aircraft of the Iraqi nuclear reactor in 1984 was also surely part of the ruling party's electoral campaign. However, for a long time, the most important abuse of security needs was the military censorship of the mass media, deployed many times from the 1950s to the 1970s. See Dina Goren, *Secrecy and the Right to Know* (Ramat Gan: Turtledove, 1979).

75. An apt example of this dynamic is the law that bans political contacts with the Palestine Liberation Organization leadership in exile, on grounds of prevention of terrorism or state security; a small number of people have been judged and imprisoned after they violated this law.

76. Menachem Hofnung, *Israel: Security Needs vs. the Rule of Law* (Jerusalem: Nevo, 1991) (in Hebrew).

77. Alan Dowty, "The Use of Emergency Powers in Israel," *Middle East Review* 21, no. 1 (1988): 34–46.

78. Only much later, in the 1970s, was this demographic policy severely criticized, because it applied mainly to lower-class families of Eastern origin and reinforced their poverty and marginality in Israeli society. But even this criticism was made in security terms, arguing that Israel did not need many low-quality soldiers, lacking instead higher-quality warriors.

79. Deborah Bernstein, "The Plough Women Who Cried into the Pots—The Position of Women in the Labor Force in the Pre-State Israeli Society," *Jewish Social Studies* 45, no. 1 (1983): 43–56; also in Deborah Bernstein, *The Struggle for Equality: Urban Women Workers in Prestate Israeli Society* (New York: Praeger, 1987).

80. Rivka Bar Yosef and Dorit Padan-Eisenstrak, "Role System under Stress: Sex Roles in War," *Social Problems* 25, no. 2 (December 1977): 135–145; also Yael Yishai, "Women and War: The Case of Israel," *Journal of Political, Social and Economic Studies* 10, no. 2 (1985): 196–213.

81. One of the cultural conventions is that girls have to be protected from combat, and especially from captivity. One of the most potent scare rumors of the 1973 war was that some soldier-girls were taken prisoner by Egyptian forces and raped.

82. Anne R. Bloom and Rivka Bar Yosef, "Israeli Women and Military Service: A Socialization Experience," in M. Lissak and B. Kimmerling, eds., *Military and Security: A Reader* (Jerusalem: Akademon, 1984), 616–635 (in English and Hebrew); also in Nira Yuval-Davis, "Sexual Division in Militaries," in W. Chapkis, ed., *Loaded Question* (Amsterdam: Transitional Institute, 1981), 134–152.

83. Eyal Ben-Ari, "Masks and Soldiering: The Israeli Army and the Palestinian

Uprising," *Cultural Anthropology* 4, no. 4 (1989): 372–389; Sara Helman, "Conscientious Objection to Military Service as an Attempt to Redefine the Contents of Citizenship," Ph.D. thesis, Department of Sociology, The Hebrew University, Jerusalem, 1993; A. Ehrlich, "Israel: Conflict, War and Social Change," in C. Crichton and M. Saw, eds., *The Sociology of War and Peace* (London: Macmillan), 121–143.

84. See Naomi Chazan, "Israeli Women and Peace Activism," in B. Swirski and M. Safir, eds., *Calling the Equality Bluff* (New York: Pergamon, 1992), 152–161; Orna Sasson-Levy, "Gender and Protest in Israel," *Israel Studies Bulletin* 8, no. 2 (1992): 12–17. Sasson-Levy observed that in most of the protest movements left of the Peace Now movement against the 1982 war in Lebanon, as well as movements against the Israeli occupation of Palestinian territories, women represent the overwhelming majority, and some protest groups are exclusively female.

85. Menachem Begin, "War of No Choice and War by Choice," *Yedioth Acharonot*, August 20, 1982.

86. Leon Sheleff, *The Voice of Honor: Civil Disobedience and Civic Loyalty* (Tel Aviv: Ramot, 1989) (in Hebrew).

87. Sara Helman, "Conscientious Objection."

88. Eyal Ben-Ari, "Masks and Soldiering."

Chapter 7. The Social Construction of Israel's National Security

1. Peter Berger, *The Social Construction of Reality: A Treatise in Sociology of Knowledge* (Garden City, NY: Doubleday, 1971).

2. For example, many more Israelis were killed and injured in car accidents than in all of the fighting with the Arabs and Palestinians. However, deaths in the latter group are heavily mourned and commemorated by the entire Jewish collectivity; those killed in car accidents are regarded as a private loss.

3. For a very interesting account of this controversy, see Gale Miller and James A. Holstein, eds., *Constructionist Controversies: Issues in Social Problems* (New York: Aldine de Gruyter, 1993).

4. Erich Goode and Nachman Ben Yehuda, *Moral Panics: The Social Construction of Deviance* (Oxford: Blackwell, 1994), 87.

5. Randall Collins, *Weberian Sociological Theory* (Cambridge: Cambridge University Press, 1986), 2.

6. One classic example of this technique and its application was made by Nachman Ben-Yehuda in his analysis of the construction of the Massada myth and its place and role in Israeli culture, collective memory, and identity. Without assuming its absolute historical correctness or truth, Ben-Yehuda took the Yesephus Flavius text about the story of Massada and explained, step-by-step, how and why it was reconstructed and absorbed into the Zionist master narrative. See Nachman Ben-Yehuda, *The Massada Myth: Collective Memory and Mythmaking in Israel* (Madison,

WI: University of Wisconsin Press, 1995); see also Yael Zerubavel, *Recovered Roots: Collective Memory and the Making of Israeli National Tradition* (Chicago: University of Chicago Press, 1995).

7. An interesting example of distinguishing between objective and constructed reality is the relation between academic historiography and collective memory. The academic historiography is supposed to be objective, but is constantly infected by myths and recruited to support national and other claims. The collective memory is by definition highly selective, full of myths and narratives both constructed and invented; however, many times, it contains a factual core around which the memory was built. The opposing views on the roots of nationalism evokes a similar controversy. Anthony D. Smith considers nationalism to have an authentic and ethnic ancient nuclei of nationalism, while Ernest Gellner and Eric J. Hobsbawm see it as a modern invention of interested middle-class intellectuals. See Anthony D. Smith, *The Ethnic Origins of the States* (Oxford: Blackwell, 1986); Ernest Gellner, *Nations and Nationalism* (Oxford and London: Blackwell, 1983); and Eric J. Hobsbawm, *Nations and Nationalism since 1780: Programme, Myth, Reality* (Cambridge: Cambridge University Press, 1990).

8. See also Erich Goode and Nachman Ben Yehuda, *Moral Panics*.

9. This secrecy itself is worthy of a comparative sociological analysis and research.

10. In Israel most of the high-ranked professional officers are obliged to leave the armed forces around the age of forty-five. Promotion of combat officers is rapid, and the technique is up-or-out. This provides to the labor market large numbers of reserve officers looking for second careers. Some are absorbed into the political, economic, and educational spheres, but others go to universities and other research centers, mainly developing so-called strategic studies. The veterans bring with them their recently demobilized buddies, and maintain their connections with their friends and previous subordinates in the military. Thus, a large and elaborate system of "old boys" is established, the field dominated almost exclusively by ex-military officers.

11. The defense establishment in Israel is a complex composed of the "civilian" Ministry of Defense, the general staff, the diverse intelligence services, mostly under the umbrella of the prime minister's office, and the military industry. Two independent bodies are supposed to exercise control over the entire apparatus. The first is the parliamentary committee for foreign and security affairs, but it lacks any long-run planning branch and is occupied only by ongoing issues. The second is the state comptroller, but this body has authority and responsibility only to surveil purely financial and ethical management.

12. Yadin was the head of operations branch of the Israeli unified armed forces, officially established on May 31, 1948. Yaacov Dori was nominally the first chief of staff, but Yadin actually conducted the war due to Dori's illness. On November 9, 1949, Yadin officially replaced Dori as chief of staff.

13. Yehuda Slotzky, *History of the Haganah: From Struggle to War,* vol. 3 (Tel Aviv: Am Oved, 1972), 1955 (in Hebrew).

14. Yehuda Slotzky, *Haganah,* 1957.

15. About 800,000 Arab inhabitants lived in the territories before they fell under Jewish control after the 1948 war. Fewer than 100,000 Arabs remained under Jewish control after the cease fire. An additional 50,000 were included within the Israeli state's territory following the Israel-Jordan armistice agreements that transferred several villages of the so-called triangle to Israeli rule.

16. Plan D was also efficient for the interstate stage of the war because the Arab states' military doctrines were trapped in the outdated conception that advancing military troops must conquer and destroy any settlement or resisting forces on their way, so as not to leave their rear or flanks open to guerrilla warfare. Had the Arabs used an alternative doctrine of quick advances toward the enemy's large centers and concentrations of its main forces, they probably would have achieved a completely different outcome in the 1948 war.

17. Baruch Kimmerling, *Zionism and Territory: The Socio-territorial Dimensions of Zionist Politics* (Berkeley: University of California, Institute of International Studies, 1983).

18. Charles Tilly, "War Making and State Making as Organized Crime," in P. Evans, D. Rueschemeyer, and T. Skocpol, ed., *Bringing the State Back In* (Cambridge: Cambridge University Press, 1988), 169–192.

19. Most of the Muslim and sometime the Christian Arab villages were considered hostile by definition, but even when some were defined as friendly, they were removed, as happened to the Maronite villages of Bir'm and Iqrit and the Muslim downtown quarter of Haifa. See Baruch Kimmerling, "Sovereignty, Ownership and Presence in the Jewish-Arab Territorial Conflict: The Case of Bir'm and Iqrit," *Comparative Political Studies* 10, no. 2 (July 1977): 155–176.

20. This also postponed for many years the dilemma between holding more Arab lands and being a binational entity.

21. Israel Tal, *National Security: The Few Against the Many* (Tel Aviv: Dvir, 1996) (in Hebrew).

22. Baruch Kimmerling and Joel S. Migdal, *Palestinians: The Making of a People* (Cambridge, MA: Harvard University Press, 1994).

23. During the 1960s and 1970s, the words to one of the most popular songs in Israel read, "All the world is against us" (*ha'olam qulo negdenu*), including the subtext that God would save and protect the Israelis.

24. For the perception of settlements in general and *kibbutzim* in particular in the Zionist defense system, territorial expansion, and ideology, see D. Weintraub, M. Lissak, and Y. Azmon, *Moshava, Kibbutz and Moshav: Patterns of Rural Settlement and Development in Palestine* (Ithaca, NY: Cornell University Press, 1969).

25. Except Beit Haarava and Qaliya, which were considered far away from the defense system, it was decided not to abandon any Jewish settlement. Most of the Jewish settlements except those of Etzion Bloc in the Jerusalem area succeeded in defending themselves or were reconquered by Jewish forces during the war.

26. Each settlement prepared to be defended separately.

27. Dan Horowitz, "Flexible Responsiveness and Military Strategy: The Case of the Israeli Army," *Policy Science* 1, no. 1 (March 1970): 191–205.

28. This was the case many times along the Jordan river valley, where Palestinian guerrilla fighters tried to infiltrate from the east to the West Bank.

29. This was the case with officers identified with Hashomer Hatzair, the left wing of the Labor Society, who were suspected of being communists and pro-Soviets, and with Achdut Haavoda, members of which were considered as subversive to Mapai's control over the military and the state. See Edward Luttwak and Dan Horowitz, *The Israeli Army* (London: Allen Lane, 1975), 101. This was also linked to the important political and strategic decision to align with the "Western bloc" as the Cold War started.

30. Edward Luttwak and Dan Horowitz, *The Israeli Army*, 71–103.

31. All the new immigrants had to be "reborn" as new healthy, proud, physically developed, and secular men and women. However, the model that they had to adopt was far closer to the Ashkenazi ideal than to that of the Mizrahim. Thus, the military, by its universal conscription policy, produced and reproduced the inherent inequality within the Israeli society of the 1950s and 1960s. The ethnic division of roles and ranks were very clear: The G.I. Joes were the easterners and the officers were the westerners. See Sammy Smooha, "Ethnicity and Military in Israel: Theses for Discussion and Research," *Medina, Mimshal Ve'Yechasim Benleuiyim* 22, no. 5 (Winter 1984): 5–32 (in Hebrew), and Yagil Levy, *Trial and Error: Israel's Route from War to De-Escalation.* (Albany: State University of New York Press, 1997), 40–42. Only during the 1980s and 1990s was the social mobility of a part of the Mizrahi Jews, as well as religious youth, reflected in the social structure of the military corps up to the top of the chain of command.

32. The solution was found in the dual structure of the military. Separate large regiments, such as the Golani Brigade, were created for the masses, while small and exclusive elite units, such as Unit 101 and later the paratroopers, were composed of loyal veteran soldiers. Sometimes the recruitment to elite units was made based on personal and informal relationship, reinforcing the old boys' system.

33. Dan Horowitz and Baruch Kimmerling, "Some Social Implications of Military Service and the Reserves System in Israel," *European Journal of Sociology* 15, no. 2 (1974): 252–276.

34. See Chapter Six.

35. For a while after the 1973 war, Major General Mordechai Gurr explained it through the doctrinaire needs of creating masses of firepower, expanding the heavy

and medium-size artillery and armor, resembling very much the initial Soviet military doctrine.

36. As Major General Ehud Barak became chief of staff, he made his well-known declaration that he wanted to make the Israeli military small and smart, which implied that it was big and stupid. It does not seem that he was able to fulfill his desire

37. From 1950 to 1954, Israeli retaliations were sporadic, militarily poor in execution, and categorized more as revenge. From February 1955 on, larger and more skilled military units formed for this goal executed the retaliatory raids. The most notable raids were against an Egyptian military base in Gaza and a civilian Jordanian village of Qalqilia on October 11, 1956.

38. Benny Morris, *Israel's Border Wars, 1949–1956: Arab Infiltration, Israeli Retaliation and the Countdown to the Suez War* (Oxford: Clarendon, 1993).

39. Each agreement included in its preamble a declaration that the armistice agreement would be followed by a peace agreement between the belligerent sides. However, the Arab states demanded that Israel withdrawal to the partition borders and allow Palestinian refugees to return. Israelis regarded both conditions as unacceptable.

40. Yigal Allon, *A Curtain of Sand: Israel and the Arabs between War and Peace*, third revised ed. (Tel Aviv: Ha'Kibbutz Ha'Meuchad, 1981) (in Hebrew).

41. David Tal, *Israel's Day-to-Day Security Conception: Its Origin and Development, 1949–1956* (Sdeh Boker: Ben Gurion University of The Negev Press, 1998) (in Hebrew).

42. J. P. Nettl, "The State as a Conceptual Variable," *World Politics* 20, no. 4 (July 1968): 522–559.

43. Maoz Azaryahu, *State Cults: Celebrating Independence and Commemorating the Fallen in Israel, 1948–1956* (Beersheba: Ben Gurion University of The Negev Press, 1995).

44. Uri Ben-Eliezer, *The Making of Israeli Militarism: 1936–1956* (Bloomington, IN: Indiana University Press, 1998); also in Dan Horowitz and Baruch Kimmerling, "Some Social Implications"; and Baruch Kimmerling, "Political Subcultures and Civilian Militarism in a Settler-Immigrant Society," in D. Jacobson Bar-Tal and A. Klieman, eds., *Concerned with Security: Learning from Israel's Experience* (Connecticut: JAY, 1999).

45. Baruch Kimmerling, "Making Conflict a Routine: Cumulative Effects of the Arab-Jewish Conflict upon Israeli Society," in M. Lissak, ed., *Israeli Society and its Defense Establishment: The Social and Political Impact of a Protracted Conflict* (London: Frank Cass, 1984), 13–45.

46. Most states did not recognize the 1949 armistice lines—the Green Line—as a basis for Israel's permanent borders, and Israeli control over so-called West Jerusalem and a part of the Negev desert was considered unacceptable. After Israel's

second withdrawal from the Sinai Peninsula, the first being in 1948, most of the international community de facto recognized the Green Line border. After the 1967 war, the Green Line was almost sanctified.

47. This was the period of the Czech-Egyptian arms deal, which led to a Franco-Israeli pact. Advanced aircraft and armor inundated the region. Moshe Dayan, as chief of staff, transformed the special prestigious Unit 101, built for retaliations, and made it the core of the elite paratrooper corps.

48. Dan Horowitz and Baruch Kimmerling, "Some Social Implications."

49. Michael I. Handel, *Israel's Political Military-Doctrine* (Cambridge, MA: Center for International Affairs, Harvard University, 1973), 37–50.

50. David Ben-Gurion, the premier and defense minister, developed a temporary political-military doctrine that Israel cannot afford to initiate a war itself without the overt or covert support of a superpower. This was one of the reasons for Ben-Gurion's reservations about Israel's adventurous attack on Egypt in June 1967. The other face of this cautious strategy was that Israel identified itself with a colonial war par excellence.

51. Yehoshafat Harkabi, *Arab Strategies and Israel's Response* (New York: Free Press, 1977).

52. Two issues should be added. First, aside from the declared objective of the Suez-Sinai war—the assurance of international free navigation through the Egyptian nationalized canal—the overt objective was to overthrow the Egyptian president, Gamal Abd al-Nasser, and damage the Nasserist pan-Arab ideology. Second, immediately after the spectacular Israeli victory, Ben-Gurion euphorically declared a Third Israeli Commonwealth and intended to annex the Sinai Peninsula and Gaza Strip to the Israeli state. Thus, for a second time, military victory awakened irredentist tendencies that promptly disappeared following international pressures.

53. Usually, Joshua Prawer, the author of two monumental volumes on the history of the Crusades, *The Crusader Kingdom* (1972) and *Crusader Institutions* (1980), denied any analogy or connection between the Latin Kingdom of Jerusalem and the Israeli state. However, in the late 1980s, in some press interviews, he was ready to make these analogies. In 1960, the young poet Daliah Rabikowich published an enigmatic poem titled "The Hittin Battle."

54. See, e.g., Yitzhak Rabin's talk in memory of Yitzhak Sadeh, Tel Aviv, September 21, 1967.

55. Shimon Peres, "Casi Belli," *Bemaarachot* 146 (1964): 3 (in Hebrew).

56. Yigal Allon, *A Curtain of Sand*, 369–375.

57. Ariel Levite, *Offensive and Defense in Israeli Military Doctrine* (Tel Aviv: Jaffee Center of Strategic Studies, Tel Aviv University and Hakibbutz Hameuchad, 1988), 40–44.

58. Baruch Kimmerling, *The Interrupted System: Israeli Civilians in War and Routine Times* (New Brunswick: Transaction, 1985).

59. It was also an election season in Israel, and the government was afraid that the opposition would accuse them of manipulating public opinion and abusing the Jewish Israeli population to be recruited unconditionally under the security banner. The doctrinal concern was also valid: If Israel would adopt total mobilization any time an Arab state concentrated troops, the Israeli society and economy would collapse without shooting a single bullet. Between 1962 and 1967, the Egyptians at least twice concentrated troops near the Israeli border; the Israelis responded by silently and partially mobilizing, and the Egyptians withdrew their troops.

60. The delay was unintentional, caused by hesitations within the political leadership to wage a war without the umbrella of a superpower and disagreements with the general staff, which pushed to open the war. After constituting a so-called national unity government and adding 1956 war hero Moshe Dayan to the government as minister of defense, following popular pressures, the Eshkol government was persuaded to strike.

61. The prominent philosopher Yeshayahu Leibovich, Yitzhak Ben-Aharon, the labor movement elder stateman, and others made such proposals.

62. Only a small fringe of the Israeli ideological domain thought of the peninsula in sentimental and religious terms—Mount Sinai being the mythological place where God granted to his people the Ten Commandments—and considered it as a part of Greater Israel. However, the long territorial strip between Gaza and Sharm-a-Sheikh was sanctified by the civil religion of security and raison d'etat. Thus, Dayan's unforgettable slogan: "Better no peace with Sharm-a-Sheikh than peace without Sharm-a-Sheikh."

63. Some Israeli strategists, such as Colonel Matitiyahu Peled, argued against the static conception of line maintenance or area defense versus flexible and mobile defense strategy by means of combined armor and mechanized infantry, See Ariel Levite, *Offensive and Defense in Israeli Military Doctrine* (Tel Aviv: Jaffee Center of Strategic Studies, Tel Aviv University and Hakibbutz Hameuchad, 1988), 106 (in Hebrew). The majority of military strategists, however, were enchanted by the passive line maintenance doctrine. Similar doctrines were adopted for the Jordan valley, the Jordan River, and the lower part of the eastern hilly region as a security asset.

64. Baruch Kimmerling and Joel S. Migdal, *Palestinians*.

65. See Chapter Nine.

66. See Chapter Four.

67. Stuart A. Cohen, "The Hesder Yishivot in Israel: A Church-State Military Arrangement," *Journal of Church and State* 35, no. 1 (Winter 1993): 114–130.

68. Such as demonstrations, parades, establishing dummy settlements, or random revenge actions against Palestinians.

69. If Israeli Arab citizens could find some room within the secular definition of the state, its citizenship rhetoric, and its Israeliness, despite the legal discrimination

built into the Israeli state, from the primordial Jewish definition of the collectivity, they were still completely excluded and alienated.

70. Meron Benvenisti, *1987 Report: Demographic, Economic, Legal, Social, and Political Developments in the West Bank* (Boulder, CO: Westview Press, 1987).

71. The very definition and construction of the intifada as a war was highly controversial. If the situation was warlike, *la guerre comme a la guerre*, and the military should have been permitted to use any degree of violence to win. However, if the intifada was defined as a popular uprising against oppression, the legitimacy of using the military at all became questionable.

72. A small and cleft entity between West Bank and Gaza Strip and blocs of Jewish settlements cannot be considered as an existential threat to Israel, especially when Israel was supposed to control the airspace, major passages, and water sources.

73. See Chapter Eleven.

74. Rabin tried to distinguish between security-necessary settlements and political or ideological settlements. However, after so many years of Emuni rhetoric, what seemed for Rabin as self-evident was puzzling for a great portion of the Jewish public.

75. The successor of historical Revisionist Zionist and Herut parties, and Etzel and Lehi militant undergrounds.

76. The major reason that it was not done before and will not ever be done is that such an annexation would advance the Israeli state toward becoming a de jure and not just a de facto binational state.

77. There are many indications that, starting in 1971, Sadat made similar or identical proposition to Golda Meir; however, her government preferred territorial assets to abstract peace.

78. Baruch Kimmerling, "The Most Important War," *Haaretz*, August 1, 1982.

79. Baruch Kimmerling, "The Most Important War."

80. Several months before the war, Ariel Sharon tried to prepare the public by accusing the PLO of being one of the major obstacles for implementing the autonomy for the Palestinians of the occupied territories agreed upon in Camp David. See Ariel Sharon, "Ariel Sharon's Perceptions of National Security—A Undelivered Talk," December 19, 1981, in A. Yariv, ed., *War by Choice* (Tel Aviv: Jaffee Center of Strategic Studies, Tel Aviv University and Hakibbutz Hameuchad, 1985), 158 (in Hebrew).

81. In a way, this includes even the 1973 war. Israeli and other intelligence services warned about Egyptian intentions to open a war. Most of the Israeli strategists considered the Sinai Peninsula as a vast trap for the rapidly recovered Egyptian armor, and tended to let them to fall into the trap. The surprise was tactical and not strategic, and spoke to the efficiency of mobile personal antitank and new ground-to-air missles with which the Soviets had equipped the Egyptian forces. The tactical surprise would have been strategic if the Egyptian command

could have exploited the immediate success and advanced their troops faster. Israel did not initiate the 1973 war, but did not avoid it, either, despite the information it possessed.

82. Menachem Begin, "War-of-No-Choice and War-of-Choice," *Yediot Acharonot*, August 20, 1982.

83. Aharon Yariv, "War by Choice—War by No-Choice," in A. Yariv, ed., *War by Choice*, 9–30 (in Hebrew).

84. Sara Helman, "Conscientious Objection to Military Service as an Attempt to Redefine the Contents of Citizenship," Ph.D. thesis, Department of Sociology, The Hebrew University, Jerusalem, 1993 (in Hebrew).

85. The Sabra and Shatilla massacre of Palestinians by the Israeli-allied Maronite militia in September 1982 caught enormous domestic and worldwide public attention, protest, and moral indignation. Following the massacre, a committee of inquiries found indirect Israeli responsibility and recommended removing the minister of security from any security-related roles, which precipitated his resignation.

86. U.S. emissaries periodically inspected the Dimona reactor, but such inspections were probably more symbolic than instrumental.

87. Shai Feldman, *Israeli Nuclear Deterrence: A Strategy for the 1980s* (Tel Aviv: Center for Strategic Studies, Tel Aviv University and Hakkibutz Hameuchad, 1983) (in Hebrew).

88. Shlomo Aronson, *The Politics and Strategy of Nuclear Weapons in the Middle East—Opacity, Theory and Reality, 1960–1991: An Israeli Perspective.* (Albany, NY: State University of New York Press, 1992).

89. All of the Arab countries, and not just Israel, are highly vulnerable in that they have large concentrations of population in narrow strips of land, along either coasts or rivers. Egypt is even more vulnerable to conventional attacks because destroying the Aswan dam could sweep most of Egypt literally out to sea. Meanwhile, an Arab or Islamic nuclear attack on Israel could damage holy sites for Islam and hurt the Palestinian and Jordanian populations.

90. Possessing nuclear weapons, and being technologically capable of building them, also became an issue of national pride and symbol of patriotism. Thus, after Pakistan conducted its nuclear experiments—Pakistan's bomb is considered as "Islamic"—leading its people and those of several other Islamic states to euphorically celebrate its nuclearization.

91. Zeev Schiff, "Old Security Perception in New Reality," *Haaretz*, January 9, 1998.

92. Yehoshafat Harkabi, trans. Lenn Schramm, *Israel's Fateful Decisions* (London: I.B. Tauris, 1988).

93. Recently, several Israeli intellectuals told me about their concern and anxiety about an ultranationalistic, national religious, and irrational government being

formed in the country that would use its nuclear power deliberately (personal communication).

94. On October 5, 1986, the London *Sunday Times* published a large report about Israel's nuclear power and the reactor at Dimona. The material was mainly supplied by a former technical worker of the plant, Mordechai Vanunu. Vanunu was kidnapped from Rome by Israeli agents five days before the article was published and sentenced to eighteen years in prison for treason. According to the *Sunday Times*, Israel possessed in the late 1980s between 100 to 200 atomic, thermonuclear, and neutron warheads. Vanunu became an international cultural hero of peoples and intellectuals who are struggling against nuclear weapon proliferation, but in Israel, less than a handful of persons accepted his motives as ideological and idealistic. Public campaigns to make his prison conditions more humane—to say nothing of being freed after serving two-thirds of the sentence, as is usual—failed.

95. See, e.g., Baruch Kimmerling, *The Interrupted System: Israeli Civilians in War and Routine Times* (New Brunswick, NJ: Transaction Books, 1985).

96. Dan Horowitz, "The Israeli Defense Forces: A Civilianized Military in a Partial Militarized Society," in R. Kolkowitz and A. Korbonski, eds., *Soldier, Peasants, and Bureaucrats* (London: George Allen and Unwin, 1992), 77–106. One of the hottest and most futile debates in the Israeli academy recently was the question of whether Israeli society was militarized or the military was civilized. The amazing part of this debate is that both sides' polemics based their arguments on approximately the same evidence. See Moshe Lissak, "Boundaries and Institutional Linkages Between Elites: Some Illustrations from Civil-Military Relations in Israel," *Politics and Society* 1 (1985): 129–148; see also Yoram Peri, "The Radical Social Scientists and Israeli Militarism," *Israel Studies* 1, no. 2 (September 1996): 230–266.

97. During the last decade, close to one million new immigrants entered the country, mainly from the former Soviet republics. This new wave of immigrants is expected to change the social, cultural, economic, and military fabric of the country.

98. John Keegan, *Fields of Battle* (New York: Knopf, 1996).

99. Shabtai Teveth, *Moshe Dayan* (London: Weidenfeld and Nicolson, 1972), 240.

Chapter 8. Jurisdiction in an Immigrant-Settler Society

1. Adel Qa'adan et al. v. Israel Land Authority et al., HCJ 6698/95.

2. *Brown v. Board of Education* 347 U.S. 483 (1954). See Nomi Levitsky, *Your Honor: Aharon Barak—A Biography* (Jerusalem: Keter, 2001), 319–338 (in Hebrew).

3. About 93 percent of Israel's lands are national or nationalized. Only 6 to 7 percent of total lands are registered with the Land Registry Bureau and titled as private lands. See Baruch Kimmerling, *Zionism and Territory: The Socio-territorial Dimensions of Zionist Politics*. (Berkeley: Institute of International Studies, University of California Press, 1983).

4. In 1952, the State of Israel, the World Zionist Organization, and its local branch, the Jewish Agency, signed a special pact permitting the Jewish Agency to act as an autonomous body in absorbing new immigrants and establishing and developing new settlements, granting the agency control over lands and their allocation. The pact was made part of the body of Israeli legislation by the Status of the Jewish Agency Law of 1952. At the same time, the state transferred 3 million *dunums* of land (one acre is approximately 4.2 *dunums*), mainly abandoned Arab property, to the Jewish Agency. Jewish Agency regulations absolutely ban the leasing of land to non-Jews.

5. Alexander Kedar, "'First Step in a Difficult and Sensitive Road': Preliminary Observations on Qaadan v. Ketzir," *Israel Studies Bulletin* 16, no. 1 (Fall 2000): 7.

6. Moreover, Kedar wrote: "It is worthwhile to contrast the [Israeli] Court's escape from the past with the radical change that taking place in some older settlers' states . . . Thus the Australian Supreme Court, which until the last decade refused to recognize land rights of aborigines, began recently to reframe the legal and political discourse by laying down its famous *Mabo v. Queensland* (1992) and *Wik v. Queeensland* (1996) decisions. In *Mabo* the Court rejected the legal doctrine of 'terra nullius,' which categorized Australia as an empty continent, and instead recognized aboriginal title[s]. Similar moves can be observed in High courts of other settler societies such as New Zealand and Canada. . . . It gives the hope to the prospect of constructing a common and equitable future for these divided societies." See Alexander Kedar, "First Step."

7. Ronen Shamir, "'Landmark Cases' and the Reproduction of Legitimacy: The Case of Israel's High Court of Justice," *Law and Society Review* 24, no. 3 (1990): 781–804.

8. Ronen Shamir, "'Landmark Cases,'" 797.

9. Baruch Kimmerling, *Zionism and Territory: The Socio-territorial Dimensions of Zionist Politics* (Berkeley: University of California, Institute of International Studies, 1983).

10. Baruch Kimmerling, "Religion, Nationalism and Democracy: The Israeli Case," *Constellations* 6, no. 3 (September 1999): 363–391.

11. For a more descriptive and analytical discussion of this, see Baruch Kimmerling, *The Invention and Decline of Israeliness: State, Society and the Military* (Los Angeles and Berkeley: University of California Press, 2001).

12. Frances Raday, "Religion, Multiculturalism and Equality: The Israeli Case," *Israel Yearbook on Human Rights* 25 (1996): 195–241.

13. The frequent equation of the Jewish religion with Judaism may also be explained partially by the legitimacy problem raised by the Jewish-Arab conflict and the impossibility of its resolution. This antagonistic situation has strengthened religiosity and religiously fundamentalist groups that amplify the conflict, thereby creating a vicious cycle of hostilities. See Baruch Kimmerling, "Anomie and Inte-

gration in Israeli Society and the Salience of the Arab-Israeli Conflict," *Studies in Comparative International Development* 9, no. 3 (Fall 1974): 64–89.

14. See also Hassan Gabareen, "Towards a Critical Palestinian Minority Approach: Citizenship, Nationalism and Feminism in Israeli Law," *Plilim: A Multi-Disciplinary Journal of Public Law, Society and Culture* 9 (2000): 53–94 (in Hebrew).

15. The Law of Return—the unconditional right to immigrate to Israel and automatically receive full citizenship and a fixed absorption basket of extra benefits—includes the close non-Jewish kin of every Jewish person, even those three generations apart. Following the recent waves of immigration from the former Soviet republics, 300,000 non-Jews supposedly immigrated to Israel. Because maintaining a demographic balance with the Arabs, mainly the Palestinians, along with controlling land, is considered the core of the conflict, unofficially the Israeli state also welcomes non-Jewish immigrants.

16. Baruch Kimmerling, "Religion, Nationalism and Democracy."

17. During a conference devoted to commemorating the fiftieth anniversary of the Declaration of the Universal Rights of Man, Michael Ben-Yair, the former attorney general of Israel, delivered remarks that focused on Israel's human rights record since 1967. Ben-Yair expressed remorse for a string of state crimes perpetrated against the Palestinians, over and above the expropriation of their lands. His list consisted of occurrences that any reasonable person would have included: mass administrative detentions without trial, destruction of homes, sanctioning of expulsions and torture by the legislature and the courts, and even kidnapping from other states' territories. "We will stand trial before history," shouted Ben-Yair, "for these serious infringements on the human rights of the Palestinians." See Michael Ben-Yair, "Human Rights, since '67," *Haaretz*, December 13, 1998.

18. Even the judicial decisions made regarding the Kfar Qassem massacre were thrown onto judicial history's trash heap of forgotten verdicts. This amnesic inclination extended even to the term "black flag," which Judge Benjamin Halevi originally applied to orders he labeled "unambiguously illegal," and which was never used. The ruling was considered irrelevant to any concrete situation. Apparently, in the eyes of Israeli society, no order given since then has been unambiguously illegal.

19. Emanuel Sivan, "The Intifada and Decolonization," *Middle East Review* 22 (Winter 1989): 1–12.

20. Because the Israeli state wanted to preserve its hegemony over its citizens, a complete constitution was never drafted. Instead, it was decided that a constitution would gradually come into formation through drafting basic laws.

21. The only two institutions that, over the years, have consistently earned the nearly absolute trust of the public are the military and the Supreme Court. An in-depth sociological and cultural analysis of the meaning of this juxtaposition, and whether there is indeed any connection between the two, would be interesting. See, Ephraim Yaar-Yuchtman and Yochanan Peres, *Between Consent and Dissent:*

Democracy and Peace in the Israeli Mind (Jerusalem: The Israel Democracy Institute, 1998) (in Hebrew).

22. Establishing its unofficial role as constitutional court was the Israeli High Court of Justice's own doing, its own interpretation of how it should function. Israeli law assigns the court more limited responsibility for hearing appeals from district courts and calls on it to serve as a high court of justice with jurisdiction over disputes between the state and its different agencies and individual petitioners. Moreover, this basic law gives the court the power to review only statuses that were enacted after Basic Law: Human Dignity came into effect. By doing so, the law perpetuates all of the previously existing discriminatory laws.

23. See Pnina Lahav, *Judgment in Jerusalem: Chief Justice Simon Agranat and the Zionist Century* (Los Angeles and Berkeley: University of California Press, 1997).

24. Nomi Levitsky, *Your Honor.*

25. See the Second Report of the State of Israel concerning the implementation of the United Nations Convention on the Elimination of All Forms of Discrimination against Women (CEDAW), the Ministry of Foreign Affairs and the Ministry of Justice report submitted in 1997 to the UN Committee on the Elimination of Discrimination against Women, and *The Status of Women in Israeli Law: Women in Israel—Information, Statistics and Analysis* (Tel Aviv: The Israel Women's Network Information Bulletin, 1996), 14–15 (in Hebrew).

26. See the highly progressive attitude of the courts toward gay and lesbian rights; Alon Harel, "Gay Rights in Israel: A New Era?" *International Journal of Discrimination and the Law* 1 (1996): 261–278.

27. Ilan Saban, "The Influence of the High Court of Justice on the Status of the Arabs in Israel," *Judgment and Government* 3 (1996): 541–569 (in Hebrew).

28. For more on the complex relations between the Bedouin and the Israeli courts, see Ronen Shamir, "Suspended in Space: Bedouins under the Law of Israel," *Law and Society Review* 30, no. 2 (1996): 231–257.

29. *Hilu et al. v. Government of Israel*, H.C. 302306/72, 1972.

30. See Meir Shamgar, "Legal Concepts and Problems of the Israeli Military Conquest—The Initial Stage," in M. Shamgar, ed., *Military Government in the Territories Administrated by Israel 1967–1980* (Jerusalem: Sacher Institute, The Hebrew University, 1980) (in Hebrew). In fact, Israel never considered the West Bank and Gaza Strip as holding the legal status of occupied territories, preferring instead the term "administered area." The argument was as follows: the UN decision (192) that called to partition Palestine was never implemented because the Palestinians rejected it, the annexation of the West Bank by Transjordan was illegal, and the Gaza Strip was under Egyptian military rule. The result of these circumstances was a "sovereignty vacuum." The Israeli claim was that international law's definition of occupation only applies when one state occupies the sovereign territory of another state. See Yehuda Zvi Blum, *For Zion's Sake* (New York: Cornwall, 1987).

31. So far, no separate branch of sociology devoted to military occupation exists, probably because most contemporary occupations—that is, conquests without annexation—were of short duration. However, this no doubt may be considered a kind of temporary social order. In our case, the entrance of the HCJ into the game was probably instrumental, used as a safety valve and together with the settlement process assisted in making the temporary a nearly permanent-temporary social order.

32. Gad Barzilai, "The Argument of 'National Security' in Politics and Jurisprudence," in D. Bar-Tal, D. Jacobson, and A. Kleiman, ed., *National Security Concerns: Insights from Israeli Experience* (Stamford, CT: JAI, 1998), 243–266.

33. The traditional Palestinian village clerk.

34. *Dawiqat et al. v. Government of Israel et al.,* HCJ 390/79. See also Moshe Negbi, *Chains of Justice* (Jerusalem: Kaneh, 1995), 21–57 (in Hebrew).

35. Menachem Hofnung, *Democracy, Law and National Security in Israel* (Aldershot: Dartmouth, 1996), 234.

36. *Al-Nazar et al. v. Commander of Judea and Samaria,* HCJ 285/81.

37. For example, establishing a Palestinian state with complete and stable peace existing between Israel and Palestine.

38. The state settled Jewish immigrants in old and new areas of settlement in place of the local Arab residents. In 1945, there were 293 Jewish settlements in Palestine/Eretz Israel, among them 27 cities and urban neighborhoods. Following the 1961 census, there were 771 Jewish settlements, among them 63 urban settlements. In contrast, 356 Arab villages, cities, and parts of cities had been uprooted, such as Jaffa, Lydda, and Ramleh. About 3,250,000 *dunums* of land, which had been under Arab ownership, were transferred to the Custodian of Absentee Property. See Baruch Kimmerling, *Zionism and Territory,* 122–123. Some Arab villages were systematically and completely destroyed to prevent their inhabitants from returning. Jews resettled settlements and neighborhoods that were not destroyed. These were not always new immigrants, but often established members of society and army veterans. This was the beginning of an immigration that would change the entire demographic and, later, the cultural and political character of the state.

39. These findings are from among roughly seventy-five villages, of which sixty-five were completely destroyed, such as Iqrit and Bir'm. About twenty-seven villages were abandoned due to expulsions during the war, while the residents of about fifteen villages were expelled after the war, e.g., Majdel. A number of other villages were evacuated fully or partly at the initiative of their residents, who were resettled in other villages.

40. See, e.g., *Ismail v. Chief of Police,* HCJ 197/52, in which it was ruled that "the order that was made by the respondent (the Military Governor) was designed to guarantee the public peace and to establish the public order. It is not for us (the High Court justices) to express an opinion as to whether the goal will indeed be achieved by this. This is given to the final verdict of the respondent '. . . we do not

see any justification to intervene in the matter.'" So too, *46/50 Tal Ayube v. Minister of Defense,* HCJ 126/69 gives the military commander a free hand in handing out expulsion orders, and determines that the court has no say in the matter. In a number of cases (46/50 or 111/53) the judges ruled that secret information that could endanger state security should not be brought before the court.

41. Baruch Kimmerling, "Sovereignty, Ownership and Presence in the Jewish-Arab Territorial Conflict: The Case of Bir'm and Iqrit," *Comparative Political Studies* 10, no. 2 (July 1977): 155–176.

42. *Al-Daf et al. v. Minister of Defense,* HCJ 36/52, 751.

43. According to local tradition, which was recognized by both Ottoman and British colonial law, the lands belonged to God or to the sultan (the representative of God). Individuals, families, and villages had the right only to maintain the land. Private ownership of the land was an unrecognized concept, though starting in 1858, the Ottoman authorities, and later the British, tried without much success to parcel out and register lands, as well as order them in state holdings books. With the end of the British rule in 1948, only about 20 percent of the lands of Palestine–Eretz Israel were ordered, these largely under Jewish ownership or of disputed status.

44. Alexander Kedar, "Time of Majority, Time of Minority: Land, Nationality and Statutes of Limitations in Israel," *Iyunei Mishpat* [Legal Studies] 21 (1998): 665–745 (in Hebrew).

45. Alina Korn, "Crime, Political Status and Law Enforcement: The Arab Minority in Israel in the Period of the Military Government (1948–1966)," Ph.D. thesis, Hebrew University of Jerusalem, Faculty of Law, Jerusalem, 1997 (in Hebrew).

46. Baruch Kimmerling, *Zionism and Territory.*

47. *Ayyub v. Minister of Defense,* HCJ 606/78.

48. For information related to this controversy, see Meir Shamgar, "Legal Concepts and Problems." In comparison, see Allan Gerson, *Israel, the West Bank and International Law* (London: Frank Cass, 1978), and Allan Gerson, "Trustee-Occupant: The Legal Status of Israeli Presence in the West Bank," *Harvard International Law Journal* 14, no. 1 (Winter 1979): 1–49. It must be remembered that Meir Shamgar was the chief military counsel when the rules of military justice in the territories were established, and was then later made a Supreme Court justice who was supposed to critique these rules.

49. This is particularly evident according to clause 78 of the Ottoman Lands Law, which allowed for the acquisition of property rights to land for anyone who could successfully prove that he or she had worked and maintained the land for ten years. British rule adopted these principles, but the Israeli regime made the evidentiary demands to prove maintenance more and more strict, that is, until *State of Israel v. Abdallah Asad Shibli* (HCJ 520/89) in 1992 revoked all maintenance rights that the village of Shibli had to its lands since 1944, which had been awarded according to the principle that "the land shall not be sold forever," making all the unregistered and nonordered lands the property of the Israel Lands Authority.

50. Meron Benvenisti, *1986 Report: Demographic, Economic, Legal, Social and Political Developments in the West Bank* (Jerusalem: The West Bank Data Base Project, 1986), 34.

51. It is unclear from study of international law to which state this refers: the occupying power, Jordan, the British Mandatory government, or the potential state of the local residents.

52. When faced with an activist High Court, which functioned as a quasi-alternative legislature, the legislature enacted a series of laws termed in, political jargon, High Court bypass laws. In addition to the political attacks to which the High Court exposed itself by adopting judicial activism, it also exposed itself to academic criticism and to attacks from the Bar Association. Lately, the High Court has retreat recognizably from this activist position.

53. Aharon Barak, "Fifty Years of Justice in Israel," *Alpayim* 16 (1998): 34 (in Hebrew).

54. Ruth Gavison, *The Constitutional Revolution—Description of Reality or a Self-Fulfilling Prophecy?* (Jerusalem: Israel Democracy Institute, 1998), 101 (in Hebrew).

55. Baruch Kimmerling, *The Invention and Decline of Israeliness.*

56. According to recent developments in Israeli political culture, the concept of a Jewish state is equated with that of a Zionist state, but not with an Israeli state because the latter also includes Arabs. See Ariel Rosen-Zvi, "'Jewish and Democratic State': Spiritual Fatherhood, Alienation and Symbiosis—Is It Possible to Square a Circle?" in Daphne Barak-Erez, ed., *A Jewish and Democratic State* (Tel Aviv: Tel Aviv University Press, 1996), 11–54 (in Hebrew).

57. The leading Israeli jurist Avigdor Feldman stated that democracy and Judaism are two separate bodies of knowledge, orientations with nothing in common. To describe the incommensurability of these two entities, Feldman used the term "differend," coined by Jean F. Lyotard. See Avigdor Feldman, "Jewish and Democratic State: Space without Place, Time Without Duration," in Daphne Barak-Erez, ed., *A Jewish and Democratic State* (Tel Aviv: Tel Aviv University Press, 1996), 261–274 (in Hebrew). See also the symposium on "A Jewish and Democratic State," *Iyunei Mishpat* [Legal Studies] 19, 1995 (in Hebrew).

58. Justice Menachem Elon claims that it was not accidental that the wording of the law places the Jewishness of the state before its democratic character, as any threat of conflict or contradiction would be resolved by preferring Jewishness, though Justice Elon does not elaborate precisely, probably intentionally, to what this Jewishness specifically refers to.

59. Menachem Elon, "Law by Constitution: The Values of a Jewish and Democratic State in the Light of the Basic Law: Human Dignity and Freedom," *Iyunei Mishpat* [Legal Studies] 17 (1993): 654–654 (in Hebrew).

60. Its essence is that Israel is a state of Jews or has a quasi-constitutionally protected Jewish majority. However, no consideration has been made for a situation

in which, by way of natural population growth, non-Jews become the majority and wish to democratically change the name, symbols, and laws of the state.

61. That is, granting Arab citizens equal rights to the common goods of the state.

62. David Kretzmer, *The Legal Status of the Arabs in Israel* (Boulder, CO: Westview, 1990).

63. The rich or the property owner might also be included. See Menachem Mautner's sharp and ironic critique of these two basic laws, which are "clear laws of the 18th century liberalism sort, defending civil rights rather than political or social rights." Mautner lists a series of rights missing from these laws, such as the right to receive health services, the right to housing, the right to support for the disabled, the right to education, the right to a pension, the right to work, the right to unionize, and the right to strike. Menachem Mautner, "The Hidden Law," *Alpayim* 16 (1998): 45–72 (in Hebrew).

Chapter 9. Exchanging Territories for Peace

1. Various sociological conceptions and definitions of anomie exist. In this article, I use Durkheim's original conception as interpreted by Marshall B. Clinard. See Emile Durkheim, *Suicide: A Study in Sociology* (Glencoe: Free Press, 1952); and Marshall B. Clinard, "The Theoretical Implications of Anomie and Deviant Behavior," in Marshall B. Clinard, ed., *Anomie and Deviant Behavior* (Glencoe: Free Press, 1964).

2. In 1948, the Israeli armed forces conquered parts of Northern Sinai, but pressure from the Western powers compelled them to withdraw. In 1956, several hours after Ben-Gurion proclaimed the establishment of the Third Jewish Commonwealth—a kind of declaration of the annexation of conquered territories—American pressure compelled him to admit that he was prepared to withdraw from all conquered areas. In the negotiations following the 1973 war, Israel was forced, primarily by international pressure, to lift its siege of the Egyptian Third Army on the western bank of the Suez Canal and to agree to partially withdraw from the Sinai Peninsula and the Golan Heights, all within the framework of partial arrangements. In general, compensation for these withdrawals came from the United States in the form of intensified economic and military aid. The Arabs, however, also received payment in the form of a temporary de-escalation of the conflict. For the sociological impact of the ward and conflict in generating anomie, see Baruch Kimmerling, "Anomie and Integration in Israeli Society and the Salience of the Arab-Jewish Conflict," *Studies in Comparative International Development* 9, no. 3 (Fall 1974): 64–89.

3. Yehoshafat Harkabi, *Palestinians and Israel* (Jerusalem: Keter, 1974) (in Hebrew).

4. Stephen P. Cohen and Edward E. Azar, "From War to Peace: The Transition between Egypt and Israel," *Journal of Conflict Resolution* 25, no. 1 (March 1981): 87–

114; Stephen P. Cohen and Edward E. Azar, "Peace as a Crisis and War as a Status Quo: The Israeli-Arab Environment," *International Interactions* 6, no. 2 (1979): 159–184; Arnold Lewis, "The Peace Ritual and Israeli Images of Social Order," *Journal of Conflict Resolution* 23, no. 4 (1979): 685–703.

5. Even the nationalistic Herut Party generally tended to play down its aspirations to reopen the issue of Israel's boundaries, at least up to the time of the Six-Day War, especially because it established a parliamentary bloc with the Liberal Party, which maintains a moderate stand in this matter. For a further treatment of Israeli literary content, see Ehud Ben-Ezer, "War and Siege in Israeli Literature after 1967," *Jerusalem Quarterly* 9 (Winter 1978): 20–37.

6. Baruch Kimmerling, *Zionism and Territory: The Socio-territorial Dimensions of Zionist Politics* (Berkeley: Institute of International Studies, University of California Press, 1983), 183–211.

7. Yehoshafat Harkabi, *Israel's Viewpoints in its Conflict with the Arabs* (Tel Aviv: Dvir, 1967), 66–67 (in Hebrew).

8. The possibility of divine intervention in the historical process is a repeated motif of Zionist historiosophy and is not the exclusive province of the more religious elements of the society. See Shlomo Avineri, *The Making of Modern Zionism: The Intellectual Origins of the Jewish State* (London: Weidenfeld and Nicolson, 1981).

9. Dan Horowitz, "Belligerency without Hostilities," *Molad* 2 (1971): 36–55. (in Hebrew); and Dan Horowitz, *The Israeli Conception of National Security: The Constant and the Variable in Israeli Strategic Thinking* (Jerusalem: Eshkol Institute, Hebrew University, 1973) (in Hebrew).

10. Indeed, the reverse was true: Egypt and Syria concluded that they had to reinitiate warfare, even under conditions of strategic inferiority, and not simply change the political status quo. Egypt did, however, enter into negotiations precisely when it considered Israel's military superiority to have been broken following the 1973 war.

11. Michael I. Handel, *Israel's Political-Military Doctrine* (Cambridge, MA: Center for International Affairs, Harvard University Press, 1973).

12. Indeed, the reverse was true: Egypt and Syria concluded that they had to reinitiate warfare, even under conditions of strategic inferiority, and not only to change the political status quo. Egypt did, however, enter into negotiations precisely when it considered Israel's military superiority to have been broken following the 1973 war. See Michael I. Handel, *The Diplomacy of Surprise: Hitler, Nixon, Sadat* (Cambridge, MA: Center for International Affairs, Harvard University, 1981).

13. The concept of the state is emphasized. Palestinian refugees are thus excluded from the overall Israeli political consciousness and ascribed to the countries in which they reside as refugees or, in the case of Jordan, citizens.

14. G. Goldberg and E. Ben-Zadok, "Regionalism and Territorial Cleavage in Formation: Jewish Settlements in the Administered Territories," *State, Government*

and International Relations 21 (1983): 69–94 (in Hebrew); and Baruch Kimmerling, *Zionism and Economy* (Cambridge, MA: Schenkman, 1983).

15. Levy Morab, "Price of the Occupation," *Migvan* (August 1983): 81–82, 22–23 (in Hebrew).

16. Shlomo Aharonson, *Conflict and Bargaining in the Middle East: An Israeli Perspective* (Baltimore and London: Johns Hopkins University Press, 1978); and R.J. Isaac, *Israel Divided: Ideological Politics in Israel* (Baltimore: Johns Hopkins University Press, 1976).

17. Sammy Smooha, *Israel Pluralism and Conflict* (London: Routledge and Kegan Paul, 1978).

18. Eitan Haber, Zeev Schiff, and Ehud Yaari, *The Year of the Dove* (New York: Bantam, 1979).

19. Dov Friedlander and Calvin Goldscheider, *The Population of Israel* (New York: Columbia University Press, 1979).

20. Like Meir Kahane's small but salient Kach Party, which publicly declared that the Arabs of the occupied territories must be evicted. In the 1984 general election, Kahane won one of the 120 seats in the Knesset.

21. Within the bounds of two extreme assumptions—considerable Jewish immigration into Israel, a high Jewish birth rate, and Arab emigration from Israel, versus meager Jewish immigration, little Jewish population increase, and Arab immigration—Jews will constitute 45 to 60 percent of Israel's population in 2010. Certainly, actual developments and processes will likely not be so extreme. Hence, one may assume that by 2010 the Jewish population will constitute 54 percent of all of Israel. See Dov Friedlander and Calvin Goldscheider, *The Population of Israel*, 193–198.

22. Baruch Kimmerling, *Zionism and Territory: The Socio-territorial Dimensions of Zionist Politics* (Berkeley: Institute of International Studies, University of California, 1983), 183–21; Rael Jean Isaac, *Israel Divided: Ideological Politics in Israel* (Baltimore: Johns Hopkins University Press, 1976); Russell A. Stone, *Social Change in Israel: Attitudes and Events, 1967–79* (New York: Praeger, 1982).

23. Interestingly enough, President Sadat himself saw it as a quest for identity for both sides. See Anwar Sadat, *In Search of Identity: An Autobiography* (New York: Harper & Row, 1978).

24. Baruch Kimmerling, *Zionism and Territory.*

25. Robert Neelly Bellah and Phillip E. Hammond, *Varieties of Civil Religion* (San Francisco: Harper & Row, 1980).

26. Dan Horowitz and Moshe Lissak, *Origins of the Israeli Polity: Palestine under the Mandate* (Chicago: University of Chicago Press, 1978).

27. Baruch Kimmerling, "Sovereignty, Ownership and Presence in the Jewish-Arab Territorial Conflict: The Case of Bir'm and Ikrit," *Comparative Political Studies* 10, no. 2 (1977): 155–176.

28. Baruch Kimmerling, "Sovereignty, Ownership and Presence."

29. Shlomo Aharanson, *Conflict and Bargaining in the Middle East: An Israeli Perspective* (Baltimore and London: Johns Hopkins University Press, 1978).

30. Ehud Sprinzak, *The Ascendence of Israel's Radical Right* (New York: Oxford University Press, 1991).

31. Michael Handel, *The Diplomacy of Surprise, Hitler, Nixon, Sadat* (Cambridge, MA: Center for International Affairs, Harvard University, 1981).

32. Elihu Katz and Tamás Szecsko, ed., *Mass Media and Social Change* (London: Sage Publications, 1981).

33. Anwar Sadat, *In Search of Identity: An Autobiography* (New York: Harper & Row, 1978), 302.

34. Russell A. Stone, *Social Change in Israel.*

35. Eitan Haber, Zeev Schiff, and Ehud Yaari, *The Year of the Dove.*

36. Stephen P. Cohen and Edward E. Azar, "From War to Peace."

37. Levy Morab, "Price of the Occupation."

38. Stephen P. Cohen and Edward E. Azar, "From War to Peace."

39. Elihu Katz and Tamás Szecsko, ed., *Mass Media.*

Chapter 10. Nationalism, Identity, and Citizenship

1. Published in 1986 by the mainstream Hebrew-Zionist publishing house Am Oved. Shammas is also well known for his Hebrew translations of Emil Habibi's powerful novels and stories that depict, through satire and irony, the lives of Arabs under Israeli control and the destruction and uprooting of the Arab community during the 1948 war.

2. A. Shammas, "A New Year for the Jews" *Kol Ha'Ir*, September 13, 1985 (in Hebrew).

3. The Arabs are in a continuous dilemma between demanding equal and full (not separate) participation in the common material and cultural goods of Israeli state and society and demanding autonomous spaces within the state. Recently, some Arab intellectuals have suggested a binational state within the entire land of colonial Palestine instead of the two-state solution propagated before. For a historical analysis of the Arab Palestinian identity, its crystallization, and development, see Chapter Three.

4. A. B. Yehoshua, "The Quilt of the Left," *Politika* 4 (1985): 8–9 (in Hebrew). See also A. B. Yehoshua, "An Answer to Anton," *Ha'Ir*, January 31, 1986. For an excellent overview and analysis of the controversy in its wider context, see Chapter 5 of Laurence J. Silberstein, *Postzionism Debates: Knowledge and Power in Israeli Culture* (New York and London: Routledge, 1999). Yehoshua's response was incredibly harsh, resembling the far-right fringe claim of expulsion ("transfer") of all of the Arabs from the so-called Land of Israel.

5. As a matter of fact, Shammas did it: About ten years ago, he left the country

and settled in Ann Arbor, Michigan, where he occupied a permanent post as professor of Arabic and Hebrew cultural studies.

6. Sami Michael, "The Arabesques of Zionism: Footnotes on the Debate between A.B. Yehoshua and Anton Shammas," *Moznayim* 160 (1986): 17 (in Hebrew).

7. A. Shammas, "Your Worst Nightmare," *Jewish Frontier* 56, no. 4 (1989): 10.

8. A. Shammas, "A Stone's Throw," *New York Review of Books*, September 29, 1988, 9.

9. This took place in a private meeting in 1992, when Shammas, who had since moved to the United States, returned to Israel for a visit. He and the writer David Grossman met with Yehoshua at the latter's home in Haifa. D. Grossman reports the debate in *Sleeping on a Wire: Conversations with Palestinians in Israel* (London: Picador, 1994), 250–277. The book was first published in Hebrew in 1992; it edited and adapted the conversation for print.

10. Here Yehoshua adopted the conventional Israeli Zionist belief that Judaism in exile, or Diaspora, can only be a partial identity; the complete fulfillment of Jewishness, whatever it may mean, can be expressed only within the framework of a territorial nation-state, or Zion. Thus, the Israeli is the Jew who has returned to Palestine (Eretz Israel, or the Land of Israel) to constitute the sovereign Jewish nation-state.

11. The armistice border with the Arab states from 1949 to the 1967 wars.

12. A. Shammas, "We? Who is We?" *Politika* 17 (1987): 25–30 (in Hebrew). One can read the debate between Shammas and Yehoshua as one of conflicting interpretations of culture and cultural identity. In contrast to Yehoshua's ethnocentric definition of Israeli identity, Shammas's anti-essentialistic position resembles the recent strongly contested conceptions of identity that have been espoused by thinkers such as Edward Said, Homi Bhabha, Stuart Hall, and the feminist critic Judith Butler. In their writings, cultural identity is perceived as a dynamic process that can best be understood in relation to cultural others, against which a group defines itself. See J.F. Butler, *Gender Trouble: Feminism and Subversion of Identity* (New York: Routledge, 1990).

13. T. H. Marshall, "Citizenship and Social Class," in D. Held et al., eds., *States and Societies* (New York: New York University Press, 1983), 248–260.

14. Charles Tilly, "Reflections on the History of European State Making," in Charles Tilly, ed., *The Formation of National States in Western Europe* (Princeton, NJ: Princeton University Press, 1975), 3–84.

15. R. Brubaker, *Citizenship and Nationhood in France and Germany* (Cambridge: Harvard University Press, 1992), 21–23.

16. Charles Tilly, "Citizenship, Identity and Social History," *International Review of Social History* 40, suppl. 3 (1995): 8.

17. B. S. Turner, "Contemporary Problems in the Theory of Citizenship," in B. S. Turner, ed., *Citizenship and Social Theory* (London: Sage, 1993), 1–18, and B. S.

Turner, "Citizenship Studies: A General Theory," *Citizenship Studies* 1 (February 1997): 5–18.

18. Y. Peled, "Ethnic Democracy and the Legal Construction of Citizenship: Arab Citizens of the Jewish States," *American Political Science Review* 86, no. 2 (1992): 433.

19. M. Roche, "Citizenship, Social Theory and Social Change," *Theory and Society* 16, no. 3 (May 1987): 363–399.

20. See U. Vogel, "Is Citizenship Gender-Specific?" in U. Vogel and M. Moran, eds., *The Frontiers of Citizenship* (New York: St. Martin's Press, 1991), 58–86; S. Walby, "Woman and Nation," *International Journal of Comparative Sociology* 33, no. 1/2 (1993): 81–100; and S. Walby, "Is Citizenship Gendered?" *Sociology* 28, no. 2 (May 1994): 379–395. See also B. Hindess, "Citizenship in the Modern West," in B. S. Turner, ed., *Citizenship and Social Theory* (London: Sage, 1993), 19–21, and N. Yuval-Davis, *Gender and Nation* (London: Sage, 1997).

21. Such as exemption from military service in a system that still exercises a universal and obligatory draft. D. Horowitz and B. Kimmerling, "Some Social Implications of Military Service and the Reserves System in Israel," *European Journal of Sociology* 5, no. 2 (1974): 252–276 (see Chapter Six). The active vs. passive citizenship is Bryan Turner's concept; see B. Turner, "Outline of a Theory on Citizenship," *Sociology* 234, no. 2 (1990):189–218.

22. H. C. White, *Identity and Control: A Structural Theory of Social Action* (Princeton: Princeton University Press, 1992).

23. J. Derrida, "Deconstruction and the Other," in R. Kearney, ed., *Dialogues with Contemporary Thinkers* (Manchester: University of Manchester Press, 1984), 117–118.

24. Y. N. Soysal, *Limits of Citizenship* (Chicago: University of Chicago Press, 1994), 34.

25. J. Habermas, *Legitimation Crisis* (Boston: Beacon, 1975). See also N. Yuval-Davis, *Gender and Nation* (London: Sage, 1997), 16–20.

26. A. Yeatman, "Beyond Natural Right: The Conditions for Universal Citizenship," in A. Yeatman, ed., *Postmodern Revisionings of the Political* (London: Routledge, 1994), 57–79.

27. Or as was stated by Anton Shammas: "My nationality, according to the Israeli Ministry of the Interior, is 'Arab;' and my Israeli passport, doesn't specify my nationality at all. Instead, it states on the front page that I'm an Israeli citizen. . . . If I wrote 'Arab' under *nationalite*, in the French form, I would be telling the truth according to the state that had issued my identity card and my passport, but then it may complicate things with the French authorities. On the other hand, writing 'Israeli' under *nationalite* is worse still, because in that case I would be telling a lie; my passport doesn't say that at all, and neither does my I.D." Shammas continued: "I do not know many people in the Middle East who can differentiate between

'citizenship,' 'nation' (*leom*), 'nationalism' (*leumiut*), 'nationalism' (*leumanut*), 'people' (*am*), and 'nation' (*umah*). In Arabic, as in Hebrew, there is no equivalent for the English word 'nationality.'" A. Shammas, "Palestinians in Israel: You Ain't Seen Nothin' Yet," *Journal of the International Institute* 3, no. 1 (Fall 1995): 25.

28. See Chapter Four of this volume.

29. See, e.g., the appendix of A. Ravitzki, *Messianism, Zionism and Jewish Religious Radicalism* (Chicago: University of Chicago Press, 1996).

30. See, e.g., M. Friedman, "The State of Israel as a Theological Dilemma," in B. Kimmerling, ed., *The Israeli State and Society: Boundaries and Frontiers* (Albany, NY: State University of New York Press, 1989), 163–215.

31. Reines (1839–1915) was an orthodox rabbi of the community of Lida who called for some adaptation of the religious codex (*halakhah*) to the modernizing world to prevent the secularization of the Jews. He first joined the Lovers of Zion movement and later Herzl's political Zionism. His major view was that Zionism should be a genuine religious movement.

32. See Chapter Seven in B. Kimmerling, *Zionism and Territory: The Socio-territorial Dimension of Zionist Politics* (Berkeley: Institute of International Studies, University of California, 1983) and *Zionism and Economy* (Cambridge, MA: Schenkman, 1983).

33. See Basic Law: Knesset, Basic Law: Freedom of Occupation (1992), and Basic Law: Human Dignity and Liberty (1992). The additional regular law is the Parties' Law. A basic law is one passed by a special majority of the Knesset, intended to be incorporated into any future written constitution (Israel lacks a complete written constitution at present).

34. See B. Kimmerling, "Religion, Nationalism and Democracy in Israel," *Constellations* 6, no. 3 (1999): 339–363.

35. Since 1948, the Israeli government has recognized certain established religious groups and granted their leaders special status, even when they are tiny minorities. These communities are entitled to state financial support and tax exemptions. According to Israeli legislation, all residents must belong to religious denominations the rules of which they are obliged to follow regarding marriage, divorce, and burial. British colonial rule recognized ten *millets*, (i.e., Jews and nine Christian denominations). The Israeli state added to these the Druze in 1957, the Evangelical Episcopal Church in 1970, and the Bahai in 1971. Muslims have not been officially recognized, but their religious courts, de facto, have similar authority to a *millet* institution. All other groups from Conservative and Reform Jews to "new religious" groups (i.e., cults) are not recognized.

36. Islamic religious law.

37. One born to a Jewish mother or "converted according to *halakha*"—however, the law does not include this crucial last phrase, thus allowing non-Orthodox converts abroad and even family members who are not converts to enter

and enjoy the privileges granted according to the immigration law known as Law of Return.

38. This proposed law asks that the state recognize only Orthodox conversions to Judaism.

39. M. Daly, *Communitariansim: Belonging and Commitment in a Pluralist Democracy* (London: Watsworth, 1993); A. Oldfield, *Citizenship and Community: Civic Republicanism and the Modern World* (London: Routledge, 1990).

Chapter 11. The Power-Oriented Settlement

1. Various sociological conceptions and definitions of anomie exist. In this article, I use Durkheim's original conception as summarized by B. M. Clinard. See B. M. Clinard, "The Theoretical Implications of Anomie and Deviant Behavior," in B. M. Clinard, ed., *Anomie and Deviant Behavior* (Glencoe: Free Press, 1964).

2. Jews and Arabs drew diametrically opposite political conclusions from this basic approach. The Arabs considered all of the territory of Palestine to be Arab land—in its Islamic version, belonging to God and legally endowed (*waqf*). On this land, Jews have rights as individuals, but have no basis for any collective, political, or nationalistic claims. The Zionists argued that there was no legitimate room for Arab claims on their ancient homeland; rather, the Palestinian Arabs, as a part of the Arab nation, should fulfill and exercise their collective political rights in the framework of the Arab nation and other surrounding Arab states. Those Arabs that remained under sovereign Jewish control would enjoy human and civic rights as individuals. This is one facet of the so-called Arab-Jewish conflict. For a full analysis, see Mark Tessler, *A History of the Israeli-Palestintian Conflict* (Bloomington, IL: Indiana University Press, 1994).

3. For descriptions of the origins of Palestinian nationalism, see Muhammad Y. Muslih, *The Origins of Palestinian Nationalism* (New York: Columbia University Press, 1988). For its development during the British colonial period, see Yehoshua Porath, *The Emergence of the Palestinian National Movement, 1918–1929* (London: Frank Cass, 1974) and *The Palestinian National Movement, 1929–1939: From Riots to Rebellion* (London: Frank Cass, 1977). For a full analysis of its development until 1993, see Baruch Kimmerling and Joel S. Migdal, *Palestinians: The Making of a People* (Cambridge, MA: Harvard University Press, 1994).

4. Baruch Kimmerling and Joel S. Migdal, *Palestinians.*

5. Sammy Smooha, *Arabs and Jews in Israel: Conflicting and Shared Values* (Boulder, CO: Westview, 1989); Ian Lustick, *Arabs in the Jewish State: Israel's Control over a National Minority* (Austin: University of Texas Press, 1980).

6. Fatah is the reversed acronym for Harakat al- Tahrir al-Filastiniyya, or Palestine Liberation Movement. Among the initial founders were Yasir Arafat (under his nom de guerre, Abu Ammar), Khalil al-Wazir (Abu Jihad), Salah Khalaf (Abu

Iyad), Khalid and Hani al-Hasan, Farouq Qaddoumi, Mahmud Abbas (Abu Mazin), Yusuf al-Najjar, and Kamal Adwan. There are varying versions of the precise origins of Fatah founders. Helena Cobban probably has the most accurate inside information on the mainstream group. See Helena Cobban, "Syria and the Peace: A Good Chance Missed," *Middle East Insight* 6, no. 3 (1988): 21–28.

7.   The PLO was established following an inter-Arab rivalry between Abd al-Karim Qasim, the Iraqi president, and Gamal Abd al-Nasir in the late 1950s and early 1960s, when they competed in declaring support for a Palestinian entity (not a state). The PLO was established May 1964, following the first Arab summit in February of the same year. The Arab summit meetings later approved creating the Palestine Liberation Army, ostensibly to recover the rest of Palestine (over and above the West Bank and the Gaza Strip) from the Jews.

8.   Helena Cobban, *The Palestinian Liberation Organization: People, Power, and Politics* (Cambridge: Cambridge University Press, 1984), 33.

9.   Meron Benvenisti (1986) calls this the return of the "communal warfare" situation, in "Israel's Decolonization Crisis," *New Outlook* (December 1989): 16–19; Emanuel Sivan labeled it a "colonial situation."

10.   Ehud Ya'ari, *Strike Terror: The Story of Fatah* (New York: Sabra, 1970).

11.   Baruch Kimmerling and Joel S. Migdal, *Palestinians*, 222.

12.   These passages are taken from Leila S. Kadi, *Political Documents of the Armed Palestinian Resistance Movement* (Beirut: PLO Research Center, 1969).

13.   For many years, the official Israeli position was not to accept the revival of an independent and authentic Palestinian political and military entity; it considered the PLO to be another Arab tool to delegitimize Israel, referring to the population of the West Bank as "Jordanians" and to the inhabitants of the Gaza Strip as "refugees." However, it seems that the Israeli leadership did understand the real meaning of the post-Shuqairi PLO.

14.   Alain Gresh, *The PLO—The Struggle Within* (trans. A.M. Berrett) (London: Zed, 1983).

15.   See Rosemary Sayigh, *Palestinians: From Peasants to Revolutionaries* (London: Zed, 1979); and Laurie A. Brand, *Palestinians in the Arab World: Institution Building and the Search for State* (New York: Columbia University Press, 1988).

16.   Operations such as the attack on a school in Ma'alot (May 15, 1974), Kiryat Shmona (November 1974), attacks on movie theaters, coffeehouses, and hotels (the Hotel Savoy in March 1975) in downtown Jerusalem and Tel Aviv, and a bus on the central coastal highway (March 1978) occupy a salient place in Israeli collective memory. The usual Palestinian response to the accusations that their armed struggle was indiscriminate terror, mostly aimed at civilian targets, was that the entire Israeli Jewish society participates in the military effort, and thus any distinction between civilian and military targets is not valid. This argument is sometimes expanded to include the Diaspora Jewish community as well as the capitalist world

order, due to its support of Israel, or because Israel is seen as its agent in the region. Only since the late 1980s has an effort been made to hit primarily military targets within Israel, or settler targets in the occupied territories.

17. Yehoshafat Harkabi, *Arab Strategies and Israel's Response* (New York: Free Press, 1977).

18. Baruch Kimmerling, "Between the Primordial and the Civil Definitions of the Collective Identity," in Erik Cohen, Moshe Lissak, and Uri Almagor, eds., *Comparative Social Dynamics* (Boulder, CO: Westview, 1985).

19. Baruch Kimmerling, "Patterns of Militarism in Israel," *European Journal of Sociology* 34 (1993): 1–28.

20. In Yiddish, *"der nebech'dicker Shimshoyn."*

21. Mina Zemah, *Attitudes of the Jewish Majority towards the Arab Minority* (Jerusalem: Van Leer Foundation, 1980) (in Hebrew); and Sammy Smooha, *Arabs and Jews,* 132–133.

22. The first planned guerrilla operation was thwarted by the Egyptians, who arrested the entire *fida'i* group in Gaza. In the second operation—apparently against the Israeli national water-carrier project—one guerrilla, Ahmad Musa, was killed by Jordanians and another, Mahmoud Hijazi, was captured by Israelis. During this period, Fatah received some military training and support from Syria. This was probably the reason for attacking the water carrier, which was one of the major sources of conflict between Syria and Israel. However, when in 1966 the Syrians intended to replace Arafat with a pro-Syrian officer, jailing Arafat and Abu Iyad, the cooperation temporarily ceased and Fatah learned how to manipulate inter-Arab rivalries to keep its relative autonomy. See Barry Rubin, *Revolution until Victory: The Politics and History of the PLO* (Cambridge, MA: Harvard University Press, 1994), 11.

23. Joel S. Migdal, *Palestinian Society and Politics* (Princeton: Princeton University Press, 1980); and Baruch Kimmerling and Joel S. Migdal, *Palestinians.*

24. Helena Cobban, "Syria," 30–31. Claims for Jordan as a part of a Palestinian state were considered shortly afterward by the Palestinians as bad politics. First, such claims would turn into a premature total war with the Hashemite Kingdom. Second, establishing a Palestinian state in Jordan could be interpreted as giving up the core lands of Western Palestine. Indeed, the ultranationalist Israeli leader, Major General Ariel Sharon, long asserted that Jordan is Palestine.

25. Israeli experts rushed to explain the meaning of this code to politicians and the public. Between 624 (the battle of Bader) and 630, there were a series of raids between the Meccan Quraysh tribe (Muhammad's original tribe) and the army of Medina (or *Madinat al-nab*—Yathrib, the place where Muhammad received asylum from persecutions, or performed the *hijra,* which included a Jewish community). In 627 the Qurayshs defeated Muhammad and his followers, but in a counterattack, Muhammad assaulted Mecca. The Treaty of Hudaybiyya between the Meccans and

Medinans was supposed to end the rivalries and allowed the Medinans to perform the pilgrimage to Mecca freely. In 630, after Muhammad accumulated enough power, he attacked and took over Mecca, consolidating his power in Arabia, and imposed the new religion on the nomadic Bedouin tribes. With this, his alliance with the Jews of Medina came to an end. Andrew Rippin, *Muslims: Their Religious Belief and Practices, Vol. 1: The Formative Period* (London: Routledge, 1991), 33–34; and Albert Hourani, *A History of the Arab Peoples* (Cambridge, MA: Harvard University Press, 1991), 17–19.

26. Ironically some Israelis titled him the Mayor of Gaza. This poor image was strengthened by a comparison with the portrait of Hussein, the king of Jordan, who was depicted as a smart and strong gentleman and a man of the world, especially after the October 1994 peace accord with Jordan.

27. Yael Yishai, *Land or Peace: Whither Lsrael* (Stanford, CA: Stanford University, Hoover Institution, 1987), 3.

28. Baruch Kimmerling, *Zionism and Territory.*

29. The Allon Plan was never adopted officially, but until 1977, it was a basic guide for the Israeli government. Its basic presumption was that the densely populated territories should be returned to Arab (Jordanian) control, the Jordan River must be regarded as a security border, the Jordan valley should be settled by Jews, and the unified Jerusalem metropolitan area must be considerably enlarged by including the Etzion bloc.

30. Meron Benvenisti, *Report: Demographic, Economic, Legal, Social and Political Developments in the West Bank* (Jerusalem: West Bank Data Project, 1986).

31. Ian Lustick opposed Benvenisti's approach, proposing a highly sophisticated model of thresholds from simple military occupation to hegemonic control. He explored this thesis in a wide comparative perspective. See Ian Lustick, *Unsettled States/Disputed Lands: Britain and Ireland, France in Algeria Israel and the West Bank-Gaza* (Ithaca, NY: Cornell University Press, 1993).

32. Joel S. Migdal, *Palestinian Society and Politics;* and Joost Hilterman, *Behind the Intifadah: Labor and Women's Movements in the Occupied Territories* (Princeton: Princeton University Press, 1991).

33. Salim Tamari, "The Uprising's Dilemma: Limited Rebellion in Civil Society," *Middle East Report* 164/165 Intifada Year Three (May/August 1990): 7–11.

34. Bassam al-Shak'a was elected in Nablus, Fahd Qwasmi in Hebron, Karim Khalaf in Ramallah, and Ibrahim al-Tawil in al-Bireh.

35. It seems that the outside leadership also felt threatened by the new—and in some cases, elected—leadership.

36. Baruch Kimmerling and Joel S. Migdal, *Palestinians,* 211–212.

37. Robert F. Hunter, *The Palestinian Uprising: A War by Other Means* (Berkeley: University of California Press, 1991); and Baruch Kimmerling and Joel S. Migdal, *Palestinians.*

38. Ze'ev Schiff and Ehud Ya'ari, *Intifada: The Palestinian Uprising-Israel's Third Front* (New York: Simon and Schuster, 1990); and Arieh Shalev, *The Intifada: Causes and Effects* (Jerusalem: Jerusalem Post, 1991).

39. Baruch Kimmerling, *State and Society: The Sociology of Politics*, vol. 2 (Tel Aviv: Open University Press, 1995).

40. Ziad Abu 'Ammar, *Islamic Fundamentalism in the West Bank and Gaza: Muslim Brotherhood and Islamic Jihad* (Bloomington, IL: Indiana University Press, 1994); and Anat Kurz and David Tal, "The Hamas: Islamic Zealotry in National Struggle," in A. Kurz, ed., *Islamic Terrorism and Israel* (Tel Aviv: Papyrus and Jaffee Center of Strategic Studies), 157–203 (in Hebrew).

41. Tom Bowden, "The Politics of Arab Rebellion in Palestine," *Middle Eastern Studies* 11, no. 2 (1975): 147–174.

42. The data are based on Majid Al-Haj, Elihu Katz, and Samuel Shye, "Arab and Jewish Attitudes: Toward a Palestinian State," *Journal of Conflict Resolution* 37, no. 4 (December 1993): 619–632 and data provided to the author of this chapter by the Louis Guttman Institute of Applied Social Research. Questions about supporting the establishment of a Palestinian state were not asked before May 1989. Generally, the outcomes of surveys that were done by other institutes showed the same trends. In May 1989, 20 percent of the Israeli Jewish population favored establishing a Palestinian state beyond the present autonomy; in July 1990, 22 percent; in November 1990, the period of the Gulf crisis, 17 percent; in May 1991, 22 percent. A dramatic change occurred following the agreement: in September 1993, 40 percent favored a state; in October 1993, 33 percent; in July 1994, 33 percent. Israeli Arab citizens' support remained very stable at approximately 95 percent. The majority of the Jewish population supported the Oslo agreement, varying between 62 percent and 54 percent (in August 1994, before the major Islamic terrorist activities). Following the agreement, 57 percent of the Jewish population supported stopping the settlement-building process in the occupied territory, but opposed dismantling already existing settlements (only 35 percent supported evacuation). Twenty-five percent of the Jewish population believed that Arafat really wanted peace—a 15 percent increase compared to May 1989. The public's readiness to make further concessions to the Palestinians increased from 54 percent in June 1994 to 60 percent in August, and approval of the government's handling of current affairs increased sharply, from 38 percent in June 1994 to 54 percent following the accord with Jordan. See Eliahu Katz and Hanna Levinson, press releases, Guttman Institute of Applied Social Research, June 14, 1994, and August 7–8, 1994.

43. Yitzhak Rabin was the minister of defense in the National Unity government, under Likud's leadership, when the Palestinian popular uprising erupted in the Gaza Strip and West Bank in December 1987.

44. The first attempt to use this idea was the establishment of the Village Leagues, quasi-military armed groups paid by the Israeli occupation authority and its secret branches and led by Mustapha Doudin. This was the initiative of

Menachem Milson, a professor of Arab literature at Hebrew University, appointed as civilian administrator of the West Bank in early 1982. Milson, equipped with the knowledge of the traditional cleavages between the *fellahin* and the city dwellers, made an attempt at "applied Orientalism," hoping to co-opt a part of the less nationalistic peasantry and use them to oppress the more "Palestinized" urban middle classes and intellectuals. See Mark A. Tessler, *Israeli-Palestinian Conflict,* 549–552. A far more successful move was to establish the Southern Lebanese Army, which operates as a soldier-of-fortune army in the Israeli buffer zone in Southern Lebanon.

45.   Some argue that the Palestinian Authority leaders did not establish the requested institutions to receive financial resources free of donor control. According to this approach, the Palestinian Authority was also playing the chaos and weakness game, in order to save financially without having limits or control imposed on them. This was also done to recruit Israeli influence and maximize received resources

46.   Jordan, with its estimated 60 to 70 percent Palestinian population, is the best-tailored target for expected Palestinian expansion. This knowledge made the Bedouin dynasty rush toward a peace agreement with Israel in 1994 as a kind of alliance and insurance cementing the traditional tacit agreements among the two. Israel is also too powerful at this stage, and in the foreseeable future, to be threatened strategically by a Palestinian state. Paradoxically, the existence of Israel may be the best insurance policy for the continuous existence and sovereignty of the Palestinian state vis-à-vis the power of its Arab neighbors.

47.   See Israel Ministry of Foreign Affairs, "The Washington Declaration," July 25, 1994, available at http://www.mfa.gov.il/mfa (accessed May 29, 2007).

48.   See Bilal al-Hasan in *al-Sharq al-Aswat,* April 26, 1994.

49.   The Israeli interpretation of this historical turn of events was to underplay it as a tactical move, the adoption of a new doctrine with the aim of dismantling Israel in stages; in such a framework, the Palestinians would get their mini-state and be in a better position to conquer the whole of Palestine. See, e.g., Yehoshafat Harkabi, *Arab Strategies.* When accepting the partition plan in 1937, David Ben-Gurion used the same reasoning.

50.   It became clear that the major victims of the settlement from the Jewish side were all or most of the settlers in the occupied territories, including their families. On the other side, millions of Palestinians are called on to give up their hope and right to return to their previous properties, lands, homes, and localities. Peace is an abstract notion that is very difficult to exchange for tangible assets.

51.   This is precisely what raised concern among the educated middle class in the West Bank regarding the formation of a totalitarian and police-state entity.

52.   See Chapter Four.

53.   Baruch Kimmerling, *Zionism and Territory*; and Baruch Kimmerling, "Religion, Nationalism and Democracy in Israel," *Zemanim* 50 (Tel Aviv: School of History, Tel Aviv University, 1994) (in Hebrew). Settlement of the Gaza Strip, Jordan

Valley, the Syrian Heights, and formerly Sinai was a completely different case, as the government initiated and subsidized most of the first settlements.

54. Prima facie, Hamas and the Islamic Jihad are a part of the new worldwide wave of so-called Islamic fundamentalism inspired by its Iranian version, or perhaps a part of a new cosmic clash of civilizations. See Samuel P. Huntington, "A Clash of Civilizations?" *Foreign Affairs* 72, no. 3 (Summer 1993): 22–49. However, both movements, and particularly Hamas, have a very local character, and despite connections with global developments, are a "pure Sunni Palestinian" venture.

55. Tamar Hermann and Robin Twite, eds., *The Arab-Israeli Peace Negotiations: Politics and Concepts* (Tel Aviv: Steinmetz Center for Peace Research, Tel Aviv University, 1993).

Chapter 12. Politicide

1. A. Ben, "Israel's Identity Crisis," *Salon*, May 16, 2005.

2. B'Tselem, "Under the Guise of Security," available at www.btselem.org/english/publications/summaries/200512_under_the_guise_of_security.asp (accessed May 29, 2007).

Epilogue

1. Even the most individualistic identities have political meanings, conclusions, and results. The social profile of Jews who ranked their profession highest seems somewhat alienated. They believe that they can influence national processes, but are not attached to their communities or to the country and consider emigrating from Israel more often than do other groups. Also, they do not trust the ability of the government and the armed forces to keep them safe, and their obedience is conditional, if they believe in obedience at all. Politically, they are mostly left-wingers. Their demographic profile is also different: they tend to be highly educated, upper-income males who are either Israeli-born or of Western origin. They are also the least religious group, with many more holding active anti-religious orientations. It seems that these are the carriers of individualistic orientations, much more so than the other types of agencies (see Chapter Two).

2. Rogers Brubaker and Frederick Cooper, "Beyond Identity," *Theory and Society* 29, no. 1 (February 2000): 1. See also Rogers Brubaker, "Ethnicity without Groups," *Archives européennes de sociologie* 43, no. 2 (2002): 163–189.

3. Rogers Brubaker and Frederick Cooper, "Beyond Identity," 6.

4. Brubaker and Cooper mention, among others who had worked with collective identity, Zygmunt Bauman, Pierre Bourdieu, Fernand Braudel, Craig Calhoun, S.N. Eisenstadt, Anthony Giddens, Bernhard Giesen, Jurgen Habermas, David

Laintin, Claude Levi-Strauss, Paul Ricoeur, Amartya Sen, Margaret Somers, Charles Taylor, Charles Tilly, and Harisson White. Rogers Brubaker and Frederick Cooper, "Beyond Identity," 4.

5. Craig Calhoun, "Belonging in the Cosmopolitan Imaginary," *Ethnicities* 3, no. 4 (2003): 537.

6. Zygmunt Bauman, "Soil, Blood and Identity," *Sociological Review* 40, no. 4 (November 1992): 675–701.

7. Baruch Kimmerling, *Zionism and Territory: The Socioterritorial Dimensions of Zionist Politics* (Berkeley: University of California, Institute of International Studies, 1983).

8. See, Ran HaCohen and Baruch Kimmerling, "A Note on T. Herzl and the Idea of 'Transfer,'" *Israel, Studies in Zionism and the State of Israel, History, Society, Culture* 6 (2004): 163–170 (in Hebrew). Much later, Herzl considered the politically more convenient land of "Uganda," a territory today located in Kenya.

9. For individual salvation, most Jews preferred the United States. Among the sixty-five million Europeans who migrated to the Americas between 1800 and 1850, more than four million were Jews, constituting 6 percent of all immigrants, compared with their 1.5 percent representation in the total population of Europe. During the first quarter of the twentieth century, about 20 percent of European Jews migrated to the Americas. Most of the religious Jews strongly opposed the Zionist idea, arguing that only the Messiah, acting on God's command, could lead the gathering of the Jewish people in Zion; Zionism was viewed as a rebellion against God. Yet the majority of Jews during this period were religious and traditional, still believing in a miraculous messianic return to the Holy Land at the apocalyptic end of days. The strength of messianic belief was evidenced three hundred years earlier, on May 31, 1665, when a self-appointed messiah, named Shabbtai Zvi, made his appearance. Shabbtai Zvi managed to provoke mass hysteria amongst hundreds of thousands of Jews, from the territories of the Ottoman Empire to Poland and Eastern Europe and even in many parts of Western Europe, by proclaiming the Day of Redemption to be June 18, 1666. The Jews, despite the opposition of most prominent rabbis, were ready to march as a mighty army and restore the godly kingdom of David on earth. Eventually, the Ottomans interpreted the millenarian movement as a rebellion and put the so-called messiah in jail, where he converted to Islam. The affair has remained an enormous disaster and a traumatic event in Jewish collective memory. Nonetheless, the hope for the coming of the messiah has never ceased. More recently, a similar phenomenon broke out among the followers of the late Brooklyn Hassidic Rabbi Menachem Mendel Schneerson. The supposed redemption was linked with the miraculous inclusion of Greater Israel—the territories occupied in the 1967 war—into the Israeli state, and the transformation of Jewish Israeli society into a holy, moral community.

10. See Rashid Khalidi, *Palestinian Identity* (New York: Columbia University Press, 1998).

11. See Abraham Zloczover and S.N. Eisenstadt, eds., *The Integration of Immigrants from Different Countries of Origin in Israel* (Jerusalem: Magnes, 1969). Publication following a symposium held at the Hebrew University on October 25–26, 1966. See also Baruch Kimmerling, *Immigrants, Settlers, Natives: The Israeli State between Plurality of Cultures and Cultural Wars* (Tel Aviv: Am Oved, 2001) (in Hebrew).

12. Menachem Friedman, "The State of Israel as a Theological Dilemma," in Baruch Kimmerling, ed., *The Israeli State and Society: Boundaries and Frontiers* (Albany, NY: State University of New York Press, 1989) From the beginning, most streams of Orthodoxy and the religious parties tended to recognize the state at least de facto, and a so-called United Religious Front participated in the first governmental coalition. Coercive secularization of new immigrants, however, provoked a great deal of anxiety and anger that lead to a deeper split between Orthodoxy and the Zionist state.

13. See Baruch Kimmerling, *Zionism and Economy* (Cambridge: Schenkman, 1983), 97–122; J. Matras, *Social Change in Israel* (Chicago: Aldine, 1965).

14. Baruch Kimmerling, *The Invention and Decline of Israeliness: State, Culture and Military in Israel* (Los Angeles and Berkeley: University of California Press), 2001.

15. On November 2, 1917, the British government issued the well-known Balfour Declaration, which stated that "His Majesty's Government views with favor the establishment in Palestine of a national home for the Jewish people and will use their best endeavors to facilitate the achievement of this objective." Later, the Council of the League of Nations put Palestine under British colonial rule in July 1922. The Mandate entitled the British to be responsible for placing the country under such political, administrative, and political conditions "as will secure the establishment of the Jewish national home and the development of self-governing institutions, and also to safeguard the civil and religious rights of all the inhabitants of Palestine, irrespective of race and religion" (article 2 of the charter). The Mandatory charter also granted official representational status of the Jewish community in Palestine to the Zionist organizations and their local branch—the Jewish Agency.

16. The Jewish community was fully aware of the implications of the colonial state-building effort, and made controlling this process their highest priority. The Jews feared the prospect that the natural development of the decolonization process and continuing Jewish demographic inferiority would transfer control of the country to the majority Arab population of Palestine. This forced the Zionists to withdraw from the Mandatory state and establish their own parallel autonomous institutions, including a quasi-underground, paramilitary organization—the Haganah ("defense" in Hebrew). In its first stage, the Haganah was a partisan army, affiliated

with and under the command of the Labor Movement and its highly centralized labor union, the Histadrut. Only following the Arab revolt in 1936 was control over the Haganah passed to the Jewish Agency in response to its need for funding from the entire community. Zionist historiography considers the present Israeli military force a direct continuation of the Haganah militia.

17. Such as the massacre of about 125 villagers at Deir Yassin on April 9, 1948.

18. See B. Morris, *The Birth of the Palestinian Refugee Problem, 1947–1949* (Cambridge: Cambridge University Press), 1988.

19. Self-evidently, there is no symmetry between the two catastrophes. The similarity lies only in the collective trauma experienced by the Jews and Palestinians.

20. On the situation of the Arabs in Israel, see S. Jiryas, *The Arabs in Israel* (Haifa: Al-Itihad, 1966) (in Hebrew); Elia Zureik, *The Palestinians in Israel: A Study in Internal Colonialism* (London: Routledge and Kegan Paul, 1979); D. Kretzmer, *The Legal Status of the Arabs in Israel* (Boulder: Westview, 1990); I. Lustick, *Arabs in a Jewish State: Israel's Control of a National Minority* (Austin: Texas University Press, 1980); D. Grossman, *Present Absentees* (Tel Aviv: Dvir, 1992) (in Hebrew); U. Benziman and A. Mansour, *Subtenants: The Arabs of Israel* (Jerusalem: Keter, 1992) (in Hebrew); S. Smooha, "Minority Status in an Ethnic Democracy: The Status of the Arab Minority in Israel," *Ethnic and Racial Relations* 3 (1990): 389–413; D. Rabinowitz, *Overlooking Nazareth: The Ethnography of Exclusion in a Mixed Town in Galilee* (New York: Cambridge University Press, 1996).

21. S.K. Mar'i, *Arab Education in Israel* (New York: Syracuse University, 1978); Majid Al-Haj, *Education, Empowerment and Control: The Case of the Arabs in Israel* (Albany, NY: State University of New York Press, 1995).

22. The National Committee for the Heads of the Arab Local Authorities in Israel, The Future Vision of the Palestinian Arabs in Israel (Nazareth 2006).

23. In this case, a process of immigration occurs into any designated territory already populated to differing degrees by a local population—or by a population that had previously settled there—with the aim of establishing a permanent community, as in all of the cases of the founding of nations by new immigrants. See, e.g., Louis Hartz, ed., *The Founding of New Societies. Studies in the History of the United States. Latin America, South Africa, Canada and Australia* (New York: Harcourt, Brace amp; World, 1964).

24. See Baruch Kimmerling and Joel S. Migdal, *The Palestinian People: A History* (Cambridge. MA: Harvard University Press, 2003).

25. Moshe Semyonov and Noach Lewin-Epstein, *Hewers of Wood and Drawers of Water: Noncitizen Arabs in the Israeli Labor Market* (Ithaca, NY: Cornell University School of Industrial and Labor Relations, 1987), 63.

26. The researchers explained this by the political weakness of the Arab citizens of Israel, the closure of most public and governmental positions to them, and their inability to convert material resources into cultural capital. See Moshe Semyonov

and Noah Lewin-Epstein, *The Arab Minority in Israel's Economy: Patterns of Ethnic Inequality* (Boulder: Westview Press, 1993).

27. And from there to other Arab countries, such as Jordan, United Arab Emirates, and Saudi Arabia, which officially boycotted Israeli products. The short distances made this movement of goods and lack of customs profitable for both sides.

28. Except the Arabic language, which was declared as one of the state's official languages. In a draft of the constitution issued by the Israeli Institute of Democracy, even this status was erased.

29. Virginia R. Dominguez, *People as Subject, People as Object—Selfhood and Peoplehood in Contemporary Israel* (Madison, WI: University of Wisconsin Press, 1989).

30. Don Handelman and Lea Shamgar-Handelman, "Shaping Time: The Choice of the National Emblem of Israel," in E. Ohnuki-Tierney, ed., *Culture and History: New Directions* (Stanford: Stanford University Press, 1990).

31. Charles S. Liebman and Eliezer Don-Yehiya, *Civil Religion in Israel: Traditional Judaism and Political Culture in the Jewish State* (Berkeley: University of California Press, 1983).

32. Smooha and Peled called it "ethnic democracy" (or "Republicanism"). See S. Smooha, "Minority Status in an Ethnic Democracy: the Status of the Arab Minority in Israel," *Ethnic and Racial Studies* 13, no. 3 (1990): 389–412; Y. Peled, "Ethnic Democracy and the Legal Construction of Citizenship: Arab Citizens of the Jewish State," *American Political Science Review* 86, no. 2 (1992): 432–443. Eliezer Schweid uses the term "Jewish democracy" in *The Idea of Judaism as a Culture* (Tel Aviv: Am Oved, 1986) (in Hebrew). All of them presumed that in Israel, as a Jewish nation-state where the Jews are entitled to collective rights, Arabs would possess only individual citizen rights. The most appropriate terminology used to describe such a political situation—"ethnocracy"—was analyzed by Oren Yiftachel, "Israeli Society and Jewish-Palestinian Reconciliation: 'Ethnocracy' and Its Territorial Contradictions," *Middle East Journal* 51, no. 4 (1997): 505–519.

33. Interestingly, one salient activity of the JNF was planting forests that became a major symbol of Zionist nation-building activity. By locating the JNF in this context, its crucial role in the Zionist-Palestinian conflict as a major actor in land acquisition and control was blurred.

34. A. Arnon, I. Luski, A. Spivak, and J. Weinblatt, *The Palestinian Economy: Between Imposed Integration and Voluntary Separation* (Leiden: Brill, 1997).

35. David Bartram, *International Labor Migration: Foreign Workers and Public Policy* (London: Macmillan, 2005), 54–102.

36. Some 46 percent of Israel's Jewish citizens favor transferring (expelling) Palestinians out of the territories, while 31 percent favor transferring Israeli Arabs out of the country, according to the Jaffee Center for Strategic Studies' annual national security public opinion poll, conducted in September 2005. In 1991, 38 percent of Israel's Jewish population favored transferring the Palestinians out of the territories,

and 24 percent supported transferring Israeli Arabs. "Transfer" (ethnic cleansing) is in fact another face of the recent unilateral disengagement or convergence plan.

37. This despite Article 49 of the Fourth Geneva Convention, which deals with protecting civilians in times of war. It particularly emphasizes protecting civilians, which prohibits an occupying power from transferring "parts of its own civilian population into the territory it occupies." Most international legal experts interpret this as forbidding the establishment of Jewish settlements in the occupied territories, but Israel has insisted that it does not because the territories were not conquered from a sovereign state and did not constitute such a state prior to their occupation; therefore, they are "disputed territories." Israel also wrongly disagrees that its settlement activities violate Article 55 of the 1907 Hague Regulations regarding the use of occupied state lands.

38. Institute for Palestine Studies, *The Palestinian-Israeli Peace Agreement: A Documentary Record*, second ed. (Washington: Institute for Palestine Studies, 1994).

39. For a detailed description of the background, content, and positive and negative results of the Oslo accord, see Baruch Kimmerling and Joel S. Migdal, *The Palestinian People*, Part 4. In the Oslo accords, the Palestinians had recognized Israel's right to exist in 78 percent of historical Palestine in the hope that, following the peace agreements with Egypt and Jordan, and on the basis of the Arab interpretation of UNSC Resolutions 242 and 338, which call for withdrawal from territories occupied in 1967, they might recover the remaining 22 percent, with possible minor border adjustments. The first Israeli negotiators in Oslo were several junior academics, Yair Hirshfield and Ron Pundik, who were later joined by some officials and junior politicians, such as Uri Savir and Vice Foreign Minister Yossi Beilin, who continued the negotiations. See Yair Hirshfield, *A Formula for Peace: Negotiations on the Oslo Agreements, the Strategy, and its Implementation* (Tel Aviv: Am Oved, 2000) (in Hebrew). See also Ron Pundik, *From Oslo to Taba: The Disrupted Process* (Jerusalem: Leonard Davis Institute, 2001) (in Hebrew). Each of the participants in the talks has attempted to make his place in history. A slightly different version is that of Uri Savir. See Uri Savir, *The Process* (New York: Random House, 1998).

40. Talia Sasson, *Unauthorized Outposts: Report Submitted to the Prime Minister*, available at http://www.fmep.org/documents/sassonreport.html (accessed May 31, 2007), 21 identifies 105 settlements but acknowledges that there may be more that she was not able to locate.

41. The intentional ignoring of unauthorized settlements is rooted in sympathy toward them and in the tactical decision to obscure the phenomenon both externally (from the United States) and internally to avoid unnecessary conflicts. Since the start of the colonization project, most of the settlements have been authorized after the fact.

42. In the Wye River Memorandum (October 23, 1998), in which Israel agreed to withdraw in stages from about 13 percent of the territory it occupied in return for the Palestinian Authority's success in suppressing terror and disbanding private militias. A part of the agreement was implemented, including an Israeli withdrawal from some of the territories, a Palestinian crackdown on militants, and the opening of the Palestinian Airport in Gaza. However, the Palestinians did not, or could not, implement the arms reduction clause and other parts of the agreement, and the Israelis did not continue with subsequent stages of withdrawal. Netanyahu's government lost the support of both the Israeli right wing and elements within the coalition, who were dissatisfied either because the government had conceded too much or too little, or because of personal scandals rooted in Netanyahu's personality.

43. Before he was elected, Barak once said that he understood the Palestinians; that if he were one of them, he would join a terrorist organization. This, of course, immediately caused an uproar, and Barak was forced to insist that he had been misconstrued, that his remarks had been taken out of context, and so on. One can believe him: He does not have and has never had any ability to empathize either with his adversaries or with his friends. This is without doubt one of the reasons that his negotiations with both Assad and Arafat failed, and that relations with fellow Israeli politicians, including members of his own party, are poor.

44. In 2006, Hamas tried to regain these bargaining chips by pathetically refusing to recognize Israel's right to exist and the Green Line as a border.

45. Indeed, it was the lowest point of Arafat's political and economic position. He supported Iraq's invasion of Kuwait, mistakenly hoping to improve the position of the 350,000 Palestinians living there under Iraqi rule; he also cheered Iraqi missiles attack on Israel. This political miscalculation made him a pariah among the Arab states and the West. No doubt, this together with pressure from Palestinians inside the territories forced Arafat to offer far-reaching concessions to the Israelis.

46. See descriptions of the Camp David summit in Deborah Sontag, "Quest for Middle East Peace: How and Why It Failed," *New York Times*, July 26, 2001; and Hussein Agha and Robert Malley, "Camp David and After: An Exchange (A Reply to Ehud Barak)," *New York Review of Books*, June 13, 2002. For Barak's version, see, e.g., Benny Morris, "Camp David and After: An Exchange (Interview with Ehud Barak)," *New York Review of Books*, June 13, 2002. See also Shlomo Ben-Ami, *Quel Avenir pour Israe* (Paris: PUF, 2002). For a somewhat apologetic account, see Bill Clinton, *My Life* (New York: Knopf, 2004). "Barak had not been in politics long, and I thought he had gotten some very bad advice," Clinton writes.

47. On another occasion, when the delegations got swept up into an argument over whether the remains of the First Temple were indeed buried beneath the Al-Aqsa Mosque, it was the Protestant Clinton who gave a sermon on Solomon's Holy

Temple according to the Bible. One of the president's Jewish aides intervened to save the embarrassing situation, commenting that this was the President's personal opinion and did not reflect the official position of the United States. Menachem Klein, *The Jerusalem Problem: The Struggle for Permanent Status* (Gainesville: University of Florida Press, 2003).

48. Baruch Kimmerling and Joel S. Migdal, *The Palestinian People*, Part 4.

49. U.S. State Department, "A Performance-Based Roadmap to a Permanent Two-State Solution to the Israeli-Palestinian Conflict," press statement, Washington, DC, April 30, 2003.

50. Yossi Beilin, *Touching Peace: From the Oslo Accord to a Final Agreement* (London: Weidenfeld & Nicolson, 1999); Gilad Sheer, *Just Beyond Reach: A Testimony* (Tel Aviv: Yediot Acharonot, 2001) (in Hebrew).

51. Shaul Mishal and Abraham Sela, *The Palestinian Hamas: Vision, Violence and Coexistence* (New York: Columbia University Press, 2000); Khaled Hroub, *Hamas: Political Thought and Practice* (Washington: Institute for Palestine Studies, 2000).

52. His rival group, the Palestinian Islamic Jihad Movement, is a militant group, far smaller than Hamas, and lacks the wide social network that Hamas has. The Islamic Jihad was founded in the Gaza Strip in 1979 by Fathi Shaqaqi, with the aim of liberating historic Palestine, destroying Israel, and replacing it with an Islamic state. The movement's armed wing, al-Quds (Jerusalem) Brigades, has claimed responsibility for many attacks in Israel, including suicide bombings and Qassam rocket strikes, and is considered more militant then Hamas. Shaqaqi was killed in October 1995 by an unknown assassin. Some people believe the responsible party to be the Israeli government, while others say other Palestinian groups killed him.

53. Sari Hanafi, *Here and There: Towards an Analysis of the Relationship between the Palestinian Diaspora and the Center* (Jerusalem and Ramallah: Muwatin and the Institute of Jerusalem Studies, 2001) (in Arabic).

54. Amal Jamal, *Media Politics and Democracy in Palestine: Political Culture, Pluralism and the Palestinian Authority* (Portland, OR: Sussex Academic), 2005.

55. Baruch Kimmerling, "Religion, Nationalism and Democracy in Israel," *Constellations* 6, no. 3 (September 1999): 339–363.

56. See David Collier and Steven Levitsky, "Democracy with Adjectives. Conceptual Innovation in Comparative Research," *World Politics* 49, no. 3 (April 1997): 430–451; and Karen Dawisha, "Democratization and Political Participation: Research Concepts and Methodologies," in K. Dawisha and B. Parrott, eds., *The Consolidation of Democracy in East-Central Europe*, vol. 1 (Cambridge: Cambridge University Press, 1997).

INDEX

Page locators in italics indicate tables